Activist Pedagogy and Shared Education in Divided Societies

Moral Development and Citizenship Education

Series Editors

Wiel Veugelers (*University of Humanistic Studies, Utrecht, The Netherlands*)
Kirsi Tirri (*University of Helsinki, Finland*)

Founding Editor

Fritz Oser†

Editorial Board

Nimrod Aloni (*Kibbutzim College of Education, Tel Aviv, Israel*)
Marvin Berkowitz (*University of Missouri–St.Louis, USA*)
Horst Biedermann (*St. Gallen University of Teacher Education, Switzerland*)
Maria Rosa Buxarrais (*University of Barcelona, Spain*)
Helen Haste (*University of Bath, UK/Harvard University, USA*)
Dana Moree (*Charles University, Prague, Czech Republic*)
Clark Power (*University of Notre Dame, USA*)
Jasmine Sim (*National Institute of Education, Singapore*)
Joel Westheimer (*University of Ottawa, Canada*)

VOLUME 17

The titles published in this series are listed at *brill.com/mora*

Activist Pedagogy and Shared Education in Divided Societies

International Perspectives and Next Practices

Edited by

Dafna Yitzhaki, Tony Gallagher, Nimrod Aloni and Zehavit Gross

BRILL

LEIDEN | BOSTON

Cover illustration: Artwork and photograph by David Wakstein

All chapters in this book have undergone peer review.

The Library of Congress Cataloging-in-Publication Data is available online at https://catalog.loc.gov

Typeface for the Latin, Greek, and Cyrillic scripts: "Brill". See and download: brill.com/brill-typeface.

ISSN 2352-5770
ISBN 978-90-04-51272-6 (paperback)
ISBN 978-90-04-51273-3 (hardback)
ISBN 978-90-04-51274-0 (e-book)

Copyright 2022 by Koninklijke Brill NV, Leiden, The Netherlands.
Koninklijke Brill NV incorporates the imprints Brill, Brill Nijhoff, Brill Hotei, Brill Schöningh, Brill Fink, Brill mentis, Vandenhoeck & Ruprecht, Böhlau Verlag and V&R Unipress.
All rights reserved. No part of this publication may be reproduced, translated, stored in a retrieval system, or transmitted in any form or by any means, electronic, mechanical, photocopying, recording or otherwise, without prior written permission from the publisher. Requests for re-use and/or translations must be addressed to Koninklijke Brill NV via brill.com or copyright.com.

This book is printed on acid-free paper and produced in a sustainable manner.

To Gavriel Salomon
(12 October 1938–4 January 2016)
academic leader and social activist for peace education and shared life

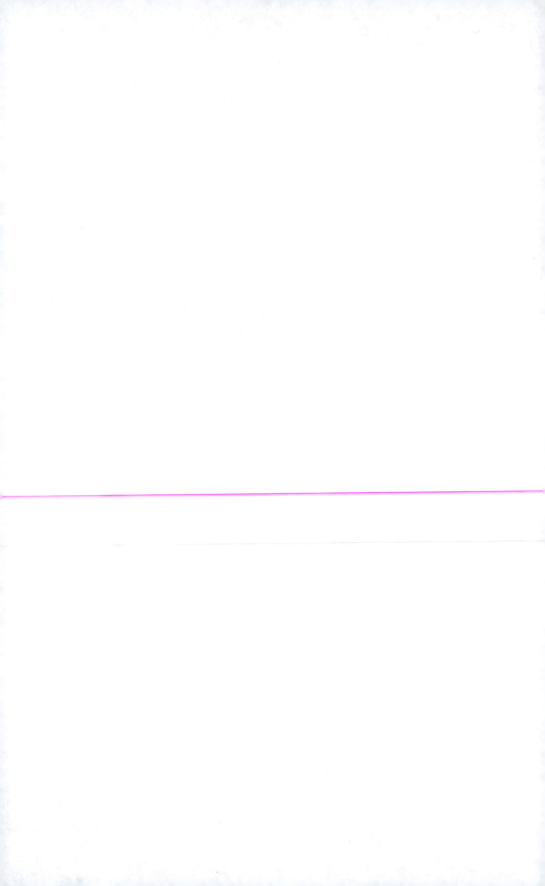

Contents

List of Figures and Tables   XI
Notes on Contributors   XII

Introduction   1
    Dafna Yitzhaki, Tony Gallagher, Nimrod Aloni and Zehavit Gross

PART 1
Educating for a Democratic-Multicultural Citizenship

1   Empowering Agency in the Ethical, Political, and the Teaching/Learning Spheres of Education: An Integrative Model of Activist Pedagogy   15
    Nimrod Aloni

2   Teaching Controversial Issues as Part of Education for Democratic Intercultural Citizenship   32
    Wiel Veugelers and Jaap Schuitema

3   Towards Educating Teachers as Advocators: A Conceptual Discussion and a Historical Example   49
    Jaime Grinberg

4   Democratic Citizenship Education as an Activist Pedagogy: Towards the Cultivation of Democratic Justice on the African Continent   65
    Yusef Waghid

5   Educating for Democratic Citizenship: Arabic in Israeli Higher Education as a Case in Point   77
    Smadar Donitsa-Schmidt, Muhammad Amara and Abd Al-Rahman Mar'i

PART 2
Enhancing Models of Shared Learning

6   Turning Research into Policy: The Experience of Shared Education in Northern Ireland   93
    Tony Gallagher, Gavin Duffy and Gareth Robinson

7   "Moving into Hebrew Is Natural": Jewish and Arab Teachers in a Shared
     Education Project   106
         Dafna Yitzhaki

8   Shared Learning in the Context of Conflict   124
         Shany Payes and Shula Mola

9   Jewish-Arab Bilingual Education in Israel   136
         Assaf Meshulam

10   Minority EFL Teachers on Shared-Life Education in Conflict-Ridden
     Contexts: The Subaltern Speaks Back   154
         Muzna Awayed-Bishara

PART 3
Nurturing Intercultural Competencies

11   Contestation as an Innovative Construct for Conflict Management and
     Activist Pedagogy   171
         Zehavit Gross

12   "Thou Shalt Not Be a Bystander": Holocaust and Genocide Education
     with a Gendered, Universal Lens, as a Path to Empathy and Courage   187
         Lori Weintrob

13   Internationalization for Nurturing Intercultural Communicative
     Competencies in Pre-Service Teachers   203
         Beverley Topaz and Tina Waldman

14   Developing Culturally Proficient Global Peace Education Changemaker
     Educators for Culturally Diverse Schools and Classrooms   216
         Reyes L. Quezada

PART 4
Reconciling Dialogue in the Face of Conflicting Narratives

15   The Holocaust and Its Teaching in Israel in View of the Conflict: General
     and Pedagogical Implications and Lessons   233
         Daniel Bar-Tal and Galiya Bar-Tal

16 Teaching History and Citizenship in Schools in Northern Ireland   253
    Gavin Duffy, Tony Gallagher and Gareth Robinson

17 Successful Failure: A Dual Narrative Approach to History Education: An Israeli Palestinian Project   271
    Eyal Naveh

18 The Narrative Approach to Shared Education: Insights from Jerusalem   286
    Myriam Darmoni-Charbit and Noa Shapira

19 Imagined Communities: Staging Shared Society in Israel   305
    Lee Perlman and Sinai Peter

20 Arts as a Sphere for the Study of History   320
    Philipp Schmidt-Rhaesa, Jürgen Scheffler and Lilach Naishtat-Bornstein

   Concluding Notes: Towards an Activist Pedagogy   335
    Tony Gallagher, Nimrod Aloni, Dafna Yitzhaki and Zehavit Gross

Figures and Tables

Figures

8.1 Shared Education work frame (developed by Mira Monayer and Shany Payes).   127
8.2 Mira Monayer, at the Eitan Frid (Darca) English Center, Ramle, 2017.   130
14.1 Cultural proficiency continuum.   223
19.1 *Return to Haifa*, the Cameri Theatre, 2008. Dov "the soldier" with his biological parents from Ramallah. From left to right: Norman Issa, Erez Kahana and Mira Awad (photo by Moshe Shai).   310
20.1 The Frenkel House memorial.   324
20.2 "The Tree in the Back Yard" 1 (photo by Anna Maria Schneider during the first rehearsal in the courtyard in September 2013, and during the performance in May 2014).   327
20.3 "The Tree in the Back Yard" 2 (photo by Anna Maria Schneider during the first rehearsal in the courtyard in September 2013, and during the performance in May 2014).   328
20.4 "The Tree in the Back Yard" 3 (photo by Anna Maria Schneider during the first rehearsal in the courtyard in September 2013, and during the performance in May 2014).   328
20.5 "The Tree in the Back Yard" 4 (photo by Anna Maria Schneider during the first rehearsal in the courtyard in September 2013, and during the performance in May 2014).   329

Tables

7.1 Challenges and opportunities for teachers in Shared Education in conflictual contexts.   110
9.1 Jewish-Arab bilingual schools in Israel 2019–2020 (updated data were provided by the Jewish-Arab NGOs).   138

Notes on Contributors

Nimrod Aloni
is a professor of Philosophy of Education at Kibbutzim College of Education, Israel. He holds the UNESCO Chair in Humanistic Education and authored ten books and many articles and book chapters in the area of humanistic education. In 2004 he was awarded "Knight of Quality Government" by the Movement for Quality Government in Israel and in 2021 he was awarded the Distinguished Alumni Award from Teachers College – Columbia University.

Muhammad Amara
is a full professor of Linguistics at the Academic College of Beit Berl, Israel. His academic interests include language education, language policy, sociolinguistics, bilingual education, language and politics, linguistic landscape, and collective identities. His recent publications include: *Language, identity and conflict* (Routledge, 2018); *My language is my identity: Towards a comprehensive language policy to meet the challenges of Arabic in Israel* (Dar-Al-Huda and Dar Al-Fiker, 2020).

Muzna Awayed-Bishara
has a PhD in Linguistics from the Department of English Language and Literature at Haifa University. She is a senior faculty member in the Program for Multilingual Education at Tel Aviv University. She studies the intersection between English teacher and intercultural communication in conflict-ridden contexts. She is the author of the book EFL *pedagogy as cultural discourse: Textbooks, practice, and policy for Arabs and Jews in Israel*.

Daniel Bar-Tal
is a professor emeritus at the School of Education, Tel Aviv University. His research interest is in political and social psychology studying socio-psychological foundations of intractable conflicts and peace building, as well as development of political understanding among children and peace education. He has published over twenty-five books and over two hundred and fifty articles and chapters in major social and political psychological journals, books and encyclopaedias. He served as a president of the International Society of Political Psychology and received various awards for his academic achievements.

NOTES ON CONTRIBUTORS   XIII

Galiya Bar-Tal
graduated cum laude from a high school in 2020. She spent a year in the pre-military leadership academy of Givat Haviva and is currently doing her mandatory military service in the Israeli Defense Force.

Myriam Darmoni-Charbit
served as the Director of Civic and Shared Society Education at the Center for Educational technology (2006–2020). With her team, she led the design and implementation efforts of Shared Education in Israel and, in particular, in Jerusalem.

Smadar Donitsa-Schmidt
is an associate professor at the Kibbutzim College of Education in Israel. Her PhD in Educational Linguistics is from the Ontario Institute for Studies in Education (OISE) at Toronto University. At KCE she serves as the Dean of the Faculty of Humanities and Social Sciences. She is also the chief editor of *Dapim*, the main refereed journal of teacher education in Israel. Her publications focus on initial teacher education, teacher professional development, policy in higher education, and learning in multicultural societies.

Gavin Duffy
is a lecturer in Educational Leadership at Queen's University Belfast. His academic interests include education in divided society contexts, shared education, the social and educational impact of school collaboration, educational leadership and the various forms of school exclusion. His recent work has appeared in the *Journal of Educational Change* and *Emotional and Behavioural Difficulties*.

Tony Gallagher
is a professor of Education at Queen's University Belfast, and former Head of the School of Education and Pro Vice Chancellor. His main research interests lie in the role of education in divided societies, collaborative school networks, and the civic and democratic role of higher education. He has authored ten books and over 100 book chapters or academic journal articles and attracted over £10m in external research grants.

Jaime Grinberg
is a full professor of Educational Foundations at Montclair State University. His PhD is from Michigan State University. At Montclair, he served as Chairperson, Director of the Educational Foundations for Elementary Teachers program,

acting Associate Dean for Academic Affairs, and Director of the New Jersey Network for Educational Renewal, a school-university partnership involving 23 school districts. His books and essays focus on philosophical, socio-historical, cultural, and political foundations of education.

Zehavit Gross
is a full professor of Education. She holds the UNESCO Chair in Education for Human Values, Tolerance Democracy and Peace, Faculty of Education, Bar Ilan University, Israel. She is the former president of the Israeli Society for Comparative Education (ICES) and currently participating in four international research projects.

Abed Al-Rahman Mar'i
is a senior lecturer at Beit Berl Academic College, Israel. His academic interests include medieval Hebrew literature, language education, the teaching of Hebrew as a second language among Arab schools in Israel, the linguistic influences between Arabic and Hebrew in Israel. His books include *Walla Bseder: A linguistic profile of Israeli-Arabs* (2013); *A great language: Integration of Arabic into Israeli Hebrew* (2020).

Assaf Meshulam
is a senior lecturer in the Department of Education at Ben-Gurion University. His main research interest is the relation between education and power, focusing on education for democracy and social justice. His recent work has appeared in *British Journal of Sociology of Education*, *Comparative Education Review*, *Discourse: Studies in the Cultural Politics of Education*, and *International Journal of Bilingual Education and Bilingualism*.

Shula Mola
is a postdoctoral fellow at the Schusterman Center for Israel Studies at Brandeis University. She worked at the Centre for Educational Technology (CET) as on-line and off-line content developer, as well as leading teacher training workshops on the topics of racism, human rights, and Shared Learning in Israel.

Lilach Naishtat-Bornstein
is a scholar, artist, and educator. She teaches at the Kibbutzim College of Education and was a visiting scholar in the Department of Comparative Literature, Harvard University (2019–2020). Her recent books are *The song of songs and the poetics of romantic fragment* (Resling, 2019), and *Contemplative*

pedagogy in training teachers (co-edited with N. Bar-Yosef Paz), forthcoming in 2022.

Eyal Naveh

is professor emeritus of history at Tel Aviv University and at the Kibbutzim College of Education. Currently he is the head of the Academic Council at the Kibbutzim College of Education. Naveh is the founder and the chairperson of the Israeli Institute of History Education. He was the coordinator and adviser of the Israeli-Palestinian two narratives history project.

Shany Payes

is co-director of Shared Learning at CET, the Centre for Educational Technology, Israel. Shany is a graduate of St. Antony's College, Oxford, where she received her PhD in Middle Eastern Studies, and a graduate of Mandel School of Educational Leadership. Her book, *Palestinian NGOs in Israel: The politics of civil society*, was published by IB Tauris in 2006.

Lee Perlman

is a Tel Aviv-based associate of Brandeis University's International Center for Ethics, Justice and Public Life. His PhD is from Tel Aviv University. He researches arts, politics and cultural policy and co-leads IMPACT, a global initiative building the Arts, Culture and Conflict Transformation (ACCT) field. He is the author of *But Abu Ibrahim, we're family!* (Tami Steinmetz Center for Peace Research, Tel Aviv University, 2017), a critical study on Jewish and Palestinian theatre cooperation in Israel.

Sinai Peter

graduated from the Theater Department of Tel Aviv University. He acted in several repertory and fringe theaters as well as in films and TV. He directed in some of the main and fringe theaters in Israel and in Theater J and Mosaic Theater in Washington DC. He was the artistic director of Haifa Municipal Theater (2000–2005). He teaches theater in colleges in Tel Aviv and in Acre.

Reyes L. Quezada

is a professor at the University of San Diego in California in the School of Leadership and Education Sciences. His doctorate is from Northern Arizona University in Flagstaff, Arizona. His research focus is on cultural proficiency, family-school and community engagement, and international education. He is the editor for *Teacher Education Quarterly* (TEQ) and serves on the Association for Advancing Quality Educator Programs (AAQEP).

Gareth Robinson

is a research fellow at Queen's University Belfast. His academic interests include transformative potential of education in divided societies; school networks and interschool collaboration; systemic and organizational change; and school improvement. His recent publication appeared in the *Journal of Professional Capital and Community*.

Jürgen Scheffler

studied history and German literature. Until 2019 he was the director of Lemgo museum with three departments: Hexenbürgermeisterhaus (History), Junkerhaus (Art) and Frenkel-Haus (Memorial). In 2019 he curated "The German-Jewish Dilemma: The Story of the Hochfeld Family from the 18th Century until Today", a cooperation with Johannesburg Holocaust & Genocide Centre.

Philipp Schmidt-Rhaesa

is teacher for music, drama and German language and literature at Karla-Raveh-Gesamtschule in Lemgo, Germany. He is the school's manager for cultural education and cooperation.

Jaap Schuitema

is an assistant professor in the Research Institute of Child Development and Education at the University of Amsterdam. His research interests include the moral development of students and citizenship education. He has studied the effectiveness of teaching strategies on students' critical thinking, science skills, and moral reasoning.

Noa Shapira

is a lecturer at the Department of Education and Community at Kinneret College on the Sea of Galilee, Israel. She is also the leader of the Education for Shared Society team at CET, the Centre for Educational Technology, Israel.

Beverley Topaz

is currently a lecturer in the English Department at Kibbutzim College of Education, Tel Aviv, Israel. Her research interests are initial teacher education, intercultural competencies, shared education, professional development, and educational leadership.

Wiel Veugelers

is emeritus professor of education at the University of Humanistic Studies in Utrecht, the Netherlands. He is associate editor of the *Journal of Moral Education*, editor of the book series *Moral Development and Citizenship Education*, and member of the Program Advisory Committee of the International Civic and Citizenship Study (ICCS).

Yusef Waghid

is a distinguished professor of philosophy of education at Stellenbosch University in South Africa. He is the author of *Education, crisis, and philosophy* (Routledge, 2022).

Tina Waldman

is a senior lecturer in the English Teacher Training department at Kibbutzim College of Education, where she teaches courses in language didactics. Her PhD in Applied Linguistics is from Haifa University, Israel. She is the prime compiler of the Israeli learner corpus of written English (ILCoWE), which is an internationally used resource. Her current research interests include social-cultural approaches to foreign language teaching involving intercultural, online collaborative learning.

Lori Weintrob

is the founding director of the Wagner College Holocaust Center and professor of History, in Staten Island, New York. She is co-editor of *Beyond bystanders: Educational leadership for a human culture in a globalizing reality* (2017) and co-chair of the international symposium Heroines of the Holocaust: New Frameworks of Resistance, among other scholarly writing and projects. She received her BA from Princeton University and her MA and PhD from the University of California, Los Angeles (UCLA).

Dafna Yitzhaki

is a lecturer at Kibbutzim College of Education, Tel-Aviv, Israel. She holds a PhD in Sociolinguistics. Her research interests include multilingualism in education and teaching languages in the context of conflict. Her current research focuses on the implementation of the Northern Ireland Shared Education model in the Israeli context. Her recent book is *Education and the Jewish-Palestinian conflict in Israel* (co-edited with A. Yuval), forthcoming in 2022.

Introduction

Dafna Yitzhaki, Tony Gallagher, Nimrod Aloni and Zehavit Gross

This book deals with activist pedagogy, empowering human agency, shared education, and shared life. It conceptualizes the role of educators as agents of change in response to real-world challenging realities of injustice, violent conflict, and lack of commitment to democratic values and genuine cultural diversity. While the book discusses the moral and theoretical justifications for addressing such issues in the educational sphere, it also shows that it is a practical project. Our specific focus in this collection is divided societies – those that struggle with ongoing social conflicts – and the ways in which the education sphere contributes to mitigating tensions, bringing diverse groups together, while working to advance school achievements.

On May 14, 2018, during a visit of a group of researchers from Northern Ireland to Israel, a very conflictual event was taking place – the US embassy in Israel, which had been in Tel Aviv for decades, was relocated to Jerusalem. Despite the move being a declarative act, it created strong reactions among the Palestinians, who saw it as a provocation, signaling US recognition of Jerusalem as the capital of Israel. Demonstrations started throughout the West Bank and Gaza Strip. On the day the embassy officially opened, the protests accelerated, resulting in the deaths of 61 Palestinians, the highest single-day death toll since the 2014 Israel–Gaza conflict. On that afternoon we gathered – researchers, students and educators – for an academic session on Shared Education – an educational initiative developed in Northern Ireland that brings together Catholic and Protestant schools to study, in an attempt to bridge social and political conflicts (Gallagher, 2016). The aim of the session was to assist the Israeli colleagues in their early stages of implanting the model in the Israeli Jewish-Arab context.

The atmosphere in the session was very challenging. Some felt we were engaged in a naïve activity – attempting to bring Jewish and Arab school children together slowly and carefully, while the violence outside was so brutal, that we might be detached from reality. One of the colleagues from Northern Ireland stood up, and in a firm, but empathetic voice, said that even though we could not imagine it at that point in time, the bloodshed would end, and that educational efforts must carry on to build the new days. These words had an immense influence on the participants, creating hope and a feeling of solidarity.

An additional step to deepen the mutual work was taken on March 2019 and an international conference was organized. The idea was to discover what we, as academics, can offer – practically and theoretically – to educators who want to take actions in situations of social and political conflicts. The forum was extended to include researchers from other European countries, the US and South Africa, to explore these issues, not only in deeply divided societies, but also in places which experience tensions, due to the treatment of minorities, the failure to deal positively with cultural diversity, or hostile reactions to immigration. We saw three goals: creating an international perspective; integrating theory and empirical research; and taking a look from within the field by practitioners who are involved in educational projects with an activist aspect. The conference was titled: "Activist Pedagogy for Shared Life and World Betterment."

The fruits of that conference turned into this volume. The ideas and voices heard in the lectures, which were later developed into the chapters of this book, started to create a clearer picture of what is meant by "Activist Pedagogy." This enabled us to outline the following insights:

Activist pedagogy is a form of critical pedagogy, which puts the spotlight on activism, that is, empowering students to develop political agency and political literacy toward a more humane, just, democratic, and multicultural social order.

Activist pedagogy entails social and moral commitment and it is not one specific program. As reflected in this book, it applies to different educational levels (elementary, middle and high schools), as well as higher education. It applies to both teachers and student teachers, in schools characterized by students with common or diverse identities.

Activist pedagogy constantly strives to improve teaching practices in the various fields of study – merging academic interdisciplinary knowledge with the lived reality (merging the tree of knowledge with the tree of life), as well as employing experiential and active modes of learning – mainly in areas of study which are more likely to produce conflictual content, such as civic studies and history, as well as other fields.

Content wise, we suggest that activist pedagogy applies to four main themes, each represented in the four parts of this book: (1) educating for a democratic-multicultural citizenship; (2) models of shared learning; (3) nurturing intercultural competencies; and (4) reconciling dialogue in the face of conflicting narratives.

1   Educating for a Democratic-Multicultural Citizenship

The starting point of the theoretical discussion is Critical Pedagogy, as introduced and developed by Freire (1970) and extended over the years (for a discussion of this topic, see Chapter 1). According to Aloni, activist pedagogy brings together three dimensions: ethical, political and pedagogical. By realizing that the fate of the young is mainly determined in the political domains, rather than in the education system, and by acknowledging the immense influence of social and environmental factors on the development and future of the young, it is the duty of educators to step out from the classrooms into the political arenas. The activist element is phrased as "breaking down the walls," in Dewey's terminology, "between the child and the curriculum, school and society, democracy and education … [to] address and engage with the pressing issues of peace, democracy, social justice, environmental sustainability, gender equality, health, welfare, mass culture and mass communication" (Aloni, this volume, Chapter 1).

In various chapters of the book, the idea of "breaking down the walls" is given concrete form by asking who breaks down the walls, with whom, how such action is initiated and what exactly it will look like. We learn about teachers and school principals who challenge the separation between school systems and practice teaching with the 'other' group: educators, who initiate going beyond what is offered by the standard curriculum, toward more challenging social and political contents. At the same time, questions arise as to the nature of this act and what else needs to be discovered – in theory and in practice – in order to better comprehend it.

In his chapter, Yussef Waghid demonstrates the tension between the wish to phrase general/universal principles and the need to take into consideration local contexts. The chapter adds to our understanding of the specific notions of African activist pedagogy, which is based on what is termed "African philosophy" – a philosophy of education related to human actions on the African continent and about African peoples living on the continent or in the diaspora. The focus of the chapter is on the level of university studies and teaching, claiming that this domain creates an opportunity to cultivate a liberatory pedagogy – one that can emancipate people "from having to endure inhumanity, autocracy, and irrationality." Waghid explains how this is realized in the implementation of education practices, such as "forgiveness," as a pedagogical strategy.

Wiel Veugelers and Jaap Schuitema deal with education for a democratic-multicultural citizenship through the topic of teaching controversial issues in schools in the Netherlands. The school subjects include those known to be more sensitive, such as history, which bring into classroom discussions anti-Islamic and xenophobic contents, reflecting current social dilemmas and public discourse in the country. The writers show how, in other school subjects, which are supposedly neutral, such as biology, teachers are committed to activist pedagogy by dealing with and/or initiating discussions on controversial issues, such as the religious and political aspects of abortion or the bio-industry, which touches upon difficult questions of sustainability.

Jaime Grinberg's chapter provides an historical outlook on activist pedagogy by discussing the Cooperative School for Student Teachers (CST) during the 1930s in New York. This presentation and discussion of this teacher training program illustrate the idea of advocacy and "breaking down the walls" between school and society in very concrete terms. Student teachers, who were trained there, worked in poor neighborhoods, with the children and their families, assisting them to better their lives in areas, such as housing and medical services. The underlying belief was that the role of the teacher is not limited to what goes on at school, but that she also has a responsibility for "the kind of world in which these children are growing up."

Smadar Donitsa-Schmidt, Muhamad Amara and Abed Al-Rahman Mar'i focus their discussion of democratic citizenship on higher education. In this context, going out to the world means viewing university and colleges as arenas for advocating rights for minority students, including rights for their cultures and languages. The chapter reports the findings of a study which examined attitudes and perceptions of Jewish and Arab students and lecturers in higher education institutions in Israel relating to the role of Arabic, shortly before the language lost its official status in Israel. The results show that, contrary to what has been claimed in other places in the world, this potential was not realized in this context: Israeli students and personnel did not show interest in advocating for the status of Arab students and their language on campuses. The writers' analysis of their findings refers to the characteristics of this generation of students and to institutional aspects of higher education of this era. Nevertheless, the writers claim that this potential for social activism can be fulfilled by deepening civic education and social involvement in earlier stages of the students' education, for example, in elementary schools.

2 Models of Shared Learning

The element of activist pedagogy discussed in the second part of the book is models of shared learning. We refer to shared learning in the broad sense and present three models: shared education of schools from different educational streams; integrated or mixed schools, in which students from different groups study together; and the model of minority teachers integrated into the dominant group's schools. Shared education, as mentioned above, is an educational practice which offers an alternative in a reality of separation between school systems. The first three chapters of this part examine different aspects of this model. Tony Gallagher and colleagues present the Northern Ireland case, while Yitzhaki, and Payes and Mola present the Israeli case.

The Northern Ireland approach to shared education, through cooperation between Protestant, Catholic and religiously integrated schools, is now official government policy and is practiced across more than half of all schools. Tony Gallagher, Gavin Duffy and Gareth Robinson describe the key characteristics of this approach which are: its bottom-up character, by empowering teachers to lead the partnerships; tailoring the priorities of school partnerships to deal with local challenges and opportunities; and encouraging innovation in addressing problems, which constrain collaboration. This commitment to innovation has allowed teachers to identify and try out possible solutions, without requiring that every attempt succeed, while affirming a commitment to learn from all successes or failures.

Dafna Yitzhaki puts the spotlight on an element, which is central in Israel, but not in Northern Ireland – the language issue. In Israel, the interaction between the groups is also an interaction between different mother tongues – Hebrew and Arabic – and the language contact reveals many issues of power imbalance (Amara, 2018). Using a case study of a group of Jewish and Arab English teachers, the chapter shows how the teachers negotiate this complex multilingual reality in the shared lessons and within their own group. Shany Payes and Shula Mola summarize the first six years of Shared Education in Israel in mixed cities and homogenous towns, with different age groups and various school subjects. Their insights are phrased using a general scheme which illustrates the role of the four main players in this field: students, teachers, principals and parents.

In a context in which separate schools are institutionalized, such as between Protestants and Catholics in Northern Ireland or Jews and Arabs in Israel, integrated or mixed schools offer a model in which contact is the raison d'etre of education. These are schools in which students from the two groups study together in the same school. In his chapter, Assaf Meshulam describes the creative and progressive tools used by educators in these schools to deal with their emotionally-loaded reality. In Northern Ireland, these schools cater to approximately seven percent of the student population, while in Israel the figures are much smaller, with less than half a percent. These schools provoke some level of opposition, particularly by those whose interests are vested in separate schools. Others argue that there is a more practical challenge – they wonder how long, if ever, it will take until they become the dominant form of schools. They place a mirror in front of the education system and the society as a whole, regarding the gaps that exist between the groups. In Israel these schools are framed in the category of "bilingual schools," since the students come with different mother tongues. However, the reality of Jewish and Arab school children studying together is usually more than what the term "bilingual education" may suggest. In November 2014, the bilingual school in Jerusalem was torched and anti-Arab graffiti was sprayed on the building. Not less shocking was the response of the accused while leaving the court after sentenced to two years in prison, claiming that "it was worth the punishment." Meshulam's analysis in the chapter clarifies that just being a teacher in a Jewish-Arab bilingual school in Israel is an everyday activist action.

Awayed-Bishara presents the third shared model – a Palestinian teacher who teaches English in an Israeli Jewish school. In addition to the Jewish-Arab complexity, the writer places the subject of English as a foreign language (EFL) as a domain with clear and distinct characteristics. The politics of English as a global/international language and the discourses around the notion of the "native speaker" intersect with the minority-majority dichotomies, inspired by Santo's (2014) notion of the "abyssal line" separating the hegemonic and the marginal. Awayed-Bishara's case study shows that marginalized teachers can produce a counterhegemonic model of EFL and create new opportunities for social transformation and educational justice.

These three models – integrated or mixed schools, Shared Education and minority group teachers – enable direct contact with the 'other' group, on different levels and with different degrees of intensity. Not every model can work in every place, but the ability of an education system to offer a variety of such options is an important step in promoting shared life.

3 Nurturing Intercultural Competencies

The world today is characterized by great social and physical mobility, voluntary migration, as well as forced migration. In such a reality, the question of the formation of intercultural competence is not a matter of political correctness, but primarily a question of existential survival. Intercultural competence is the ability to understand, communicate, engage and participate in cross-cultural, social and political settings. One of the main components of intercultural competence is the ability to cope with complexity, and this is connected to an attempt to cope with cultural communication gaps that upset order and create cognitive dissonance (Dervin & Gross, 2016). Intercultural competence is viewed in this book as activism in the sense of breaking away from routine teaching, initiating projects which place students, teachers and future teachers in complex situations in which they need to function, and navigate themselves and their students wisely and sensitively between different cultural norms and new images that challenge common notions.

This part of the book begins with Zehavit Gross's chapter, which looks at intercultural competence from a perspective that does not usually get attention in pedagogic discussions – that of Jewish philosophy and the way it views the concept of contestation. Gross shows that in Judaism a culture of contestation means the acknowledgement of the fact that each of the contesting sides possesses an inherent quality. Gross argues that this approach to disagreements is essential to conflict discourse in Israel and shows how this has been implemented with her work with Jewish and Arab university students for over two decades.

The chapters by Lori Weintrob and by Beverley Topaz and Tina Waldman report on projects that bring students to meet the 'others' – physically and online – and as they are reflected in historical stories. The first is a theatre project that brings the voices of Holocaust survivors by a multi-racial cast. The presenters are mostly non-Jews; the chosen stories are of Jewish survivors, as well as other victims of Nazi violence, such as homosexuals and people with disabilities. The inclusion of non-Jewish voices, particularly of those who risked their lives to save Jews, including Muslims, and the reference to the genocide in Armenia and the genocide in Rwanda shed light on aspects which are not commonly discussed in this historical context. The project brings the students closer to the stories of the 'other' in a very intimate way, not only by using authentic testimonies, but also by presenting them in the students' own voices.

The intercultural aspect in Topaz and Waldman's chapter is internationalization in teacher training and the ways such programs can prepare pre-service teachers to become interculturally effective educators. This is analyzed using two such programs: Virtual Exchange, in which students collaborate synchronously on intercultural online projects with international partners, and a study abroad program, in which students study at an overseas institution for a semester or more. Contrary to what may be expected, the virtual exchange program is shown to create more intercultural awareness in terms of perceptions and stereotypes of the students involved and the writers relate this finding to the explicit mentoring provided by the faculty members.

Reyes Quezada summarizes this part using a six-point theoretical scheme of a cultural proficiency continuum – ranging from cultural destructiveness to cultural proficiency. This scheme is offered as a tool for educators, schools and organizations: they are invited to place themselves on this continuum and to identify their specific obstacles and ways to move forward toward more culturally proficient teaching practices.

4 Reconciling Dialogue in the Face of Conflicting Narratives

One strong theme that emerged across all our considerations is that divided societies not only divide people and communities, but they often provide barriers to transformative dialogue. As a process, dialogue involves the right to speak and the responsibility to listen; however, if both are in a context in which one perspective dominates, then dialogue may become little more than an echo-chamber, reinforcing and embedding already established views and assumptions. In a divided society, this can lead to the promulgation of myths and stereotypes that deepen divides even further and limit our potential to recognize and explore the power relations that underpin the inequalities between communities (Bar-Tal, 2013). Activist pedagogy can and should be about widening opportunities for dialogue – based on mutual trust, attentive openness, empathy, respect, and faith – especially the responsibility to listen, to allow for greater reflection and consideration on options for a better, shared future.

Daniel Bar-Tal, a social psychologist and Galia Bar-Tal, a high school graduate, who recently came back from a journey to Poland, look at the way the Israeli school system deals with teaching of the Holocaust. The claim is that the narrative of the Holocaust has extended beyond the events of the Second World War, and now includes all enemies of Israel – current and historical, including the neighboring Arab states and the Israeli-Palestinian conflict. In the educational context, it is claimed that the "never again" message could have potentially been realized in two ways: the particularistic approach (which avers that Israel needs a strong army) and a universal approach (which avers that human and civil rights must be protected). The writers argue that the Israeli school system chose the particularistic option, which is a "conflict supporting narrative" when teaching about the Holocaust. The journeys to Poland, in which high school students participate, are termed "initiation ceremonies" into Israeli society and the Israeli army. Galia Bar-Tal describes them as "death journeys" that praise the Israeli army and Israel's war victories. Both authors call for a different action, one that uses the memory of the Holocaust to strengthen anti-war, anti-nationalist and human rights messages.

Gavin Duffy, Tony Gallagher and Gareth Robinson examine how conflicting narratives between Catholic and Protestants in Northern Ireland are realized in history and citizenship education, at the curriculum level, and how teachers deal with such issues in an atmosphere they characterize as "a cultural of avoidance." The writers describe areas and domains in which the teachers are successful, seeing them as pioneers of change in the way people examine their past and their sense of identity. In order for this shift to continue, the writers call for both initial and continuous professional development training in these subjects.

The project described by Eyal Naveh is a negotiation between conflicting narratives. The chapter analyzes an initiative to write a dual-narrative history textbooks for schools in divided and post-conflict societies. The project started as a collaboration between Jewish and Palestinian academics and educators at the beginning of the century. The intensive work on the texts, terminology and visuals led to a history textbook summarizing one hundred years of the Israeli-Palestinian conflict from two points of view – the Palestinian and the Israeli one. The textbook has received wide international acknowledgment and has been translated into numerous languages; however, it was firmly rejected in the local school systems. The cooperative process, the existence of an agreed-upon text and the attempts of a small number of teachers to use the book in Israel as extra-curricular content, are viewed as a success, despite the book's failure to become a mainstream text in the system.

In Myriam Darmoni-Charbit and Noa Shapira's chapter, the dialogue occurs at the level of school principals in a series of meetings based on the narrative and the Storytelling approach, proposed by Bar-On (2010). This approach does not look at stories in intergroup dialogue contexts as either true of false, or as independently describing reality, but rather as a way to *construct* the world. The meetings served as a preparation for Jewish-Arab partnerships between the schools and the chapter illustrates the stages the principals underwent, while each group's narrative was contested by the other. The writers describe the transition from a "representative" position, which hides behind general statements, to moments in which a more nuanced view of the other was made possible.

Lee Perlman and Sinai Peter write about theater as a tool to negotiate between conflicting narratives in a somewhat different way. Perlman interviewed Peter – a Jewish Israeli theatre director, activist and an educator in a teacher training college – about theatre productions in which he has been involved for three decades. The narratives are negotiated at the level of the texts of the plays, which challenge the dominant Jewish-Zionist narrative in Israel. Additionally, in all the productions, the actors and staff members come from both groups and add another layer to this artistic and political act.

In the chapter that concludes the fourth part, Philipp Schmidt-Rhaesa, Jürgen Scheffler and Lilach Naishtat-Bornstein describe a unique theater-drama-dance project for school children in Israel and Germany around the story of the Holocaust survivor, Karla Raveh. The project brought together homeroom, drama and music teachers to create a play that was presented several times in Raveh's childhood home in Germany, which was turned into a museum. In an attempt to mediate between the Israeli and German participants, the play used the concepts of "home" to reveal the unusual life story. Furthermore, the educators told the students that "not everything about the Holocaust must be told" and that they are not "to be sad all the time." The chapter brings the voices of the children who participated in the play. Some described it as "the best thing in their whole school time," and others reported that they wish to change their career aspirations to pedagogical professions, based on what they gained from the project.

5 Facing the Future

We found two central issues that arose from the book's chapters, which are worth looking at, when facing the future. The first one relates to the universal question and the wish to create a wide, international perspective. The question is whether a comparison of various contexts deepens our understanding or rather limits it and what kind of categorizations might be helpful in these discussions. One such categorization was offered by Salomon (2002) with regards to peace education: he suggested three categories, based on socio-political context – Intractable Regions, Regions of Inter-Ethnic Tension, and Regions of Experienced Tranquility. Our book focuses on the tension that exists between the specificities of different national settings, for example, the call for a unique African philosophy to examine the educational needs of people living on this continent and Africans living outside it. While many divided societies view their own context to be uniquely difficult, we can also see the potential for real comparative learning across contexts, in regards to actions and measures which have failed, as much as actions and measures which may have helped transformed situations for the better. In her comparative analysis of the separation between Jews and Arabs in Israeli school system and the integration of black and white students in the United States in the 1950s, Ruth Gavison, a distinguished Israeli legal expert, claimed that, at the end of the day, there is a relatively limited set of options to deal with such dilemmas, due to "human nature and the boundaries of social organizations" (Gavison, 2000, p. 71). We can say that the book attempted to navigate carefully between these two poles.

The second question, which is probably always beneath the surface, is whether activist pedagogy is a successful project. This, of course, depends on what one defines as "successful" in this context. It is apparent that this book is not based only on success stories, in the straightforward sense. Naveh, for example, considers the dual-narrative textbook that failed to integrate into the school systems a success, or a "successful failure," using his term, taking into consideration its impact in other aspects. If we consider success in the sense of "changing society" (Apple, 2013), we are reminded that schools are not separate from society: "[t]hey are *central* elements of that society – as work places, as sites of identity formation, as places that make particular knowledge and culture legitimate, as arenas of mobilization and learning of tactics, and so much more" (p. 158).

Following the words of the educator, James Banks:

> ... educational equality, like liberty and justice, is an ideal toward which human beings work but which they never fully attain [and thus] ... education must be viewed as an ongoing process, not as something that we "do" and thereby solve the problems. (Banks, 2013, p. 4)

This should be seen not as a discouraging message to educators, but as one that looks squarely at reality.

References

Amara, M. (2018). *Language, identity and conflict: Arabic in Israel*. Routledge.

Apple, M. W. (2013). *Can education change society?* Routledge.

Banks, J. A. (2013). Multicultural education: Characteristics and goals. In J. A. Banks & C. A. M. Banks (Eds.), *Multicultural education – Issues and perspectives* (8th ed., pp. 3–24). Wiley.

Bar-Tal, D. (2013). *Intractable conflicts: Socio-psychological foundations and dynamics*. Cambridge University Press.

Dervin, F., & Gross, Z. (2016). Towards the simultaneity of intercultural competence. In F. Dervin & Z. Gross (Eds.), *Intercultural competence in education – Alternative approaches for different times* (pp. 1–10). Palgrave Macmillan.

Freire, P. (1970). *Pedagogy of the oppressed* (M. Bergman Ramos, Trans.). Seabury Press.

Gallagher, T. (2016). Shared education in Northern Ireland: School collaboration in divided societies. *Oxford Review of Education, 42*(3), 362–375.

Gavison, R. (2000). Does equality require integration? *Democratic Culture, 3*, 37–87.

Santos, B. (2014). *The epistemologies of the south*. Paradigm.

Salomon, G. (2002). The nature of peace education: Not all programs are created equal. In G. Salomon & B. Nevo (Eds.), *Peace education: The concept, principles, and practices around the world* (pp. 2–14). Lawrence Erlbaum Associates.

PART 1

Educating for a Democratic-Multicultural Citizenship

∴

CHAPTER 1

Empowering Agency in the Ethical, Political, and the Teaching/Learning Spheres of Education

An Integrative Model of Activist Pedagogy

Nimrod Aloni

> He who is not busy being born is busy dying.
> BOB DYLAN

∙∙∙

> I hate everything which merely instructs me without increasing my activity.
> GOETHE

∙∙∙

> He who cannot obey himself will be commanded.
> NIETZSCHE

∙∙∙

> If you are lacking self-agency you become an instrument in the agency of others.
> HENRY GIROUX

∙∙∙

> To make people livelier, to increase in them the concentration and force of the vital spirit.
> JACQUES BARZUN

∙∙

There are manifold forms of crippling and disempowering personal autonomy and human agency. Most notable in human history are the phenomena of enslavement, tyranny, racism, male chauvinism, castes, religious fundamentalism, authoritarian hierarchies, social exclusion, impoverishment, and political populism. In the 20th century, humanity witnessed novel means and new peaks of injuring human agency, by means of totalitarian regimes, concentration and reeducation camps, workaholism, bureaucratization, technocratic thinking, and the commercialization of everyday life. There is wide agreement among cultural critics concerning the dominant factors that endanger personal autonomy and obstruct human agency in our 21st century's global reality. These include the colonization of the mind by digital technology, artificial intelligence, obsessive consumerism, and the growing alienation from one's own authentic self, from social relations, from the riches of culture, as well as from the natural environment.

Such processes of diluting human agency were not left unnoticed by humanist philosophers – from various perspectives and ethical commitments – who raised harsh criticism. Among the most significant in the realm of education are: Montaigne's complaint about treating students as prisoners and obstructing their vitality; Spinoza's criticism on extinguishing the spark of reason and degrading humans to beasts; and Rousseau's attacks on bourgeois culture that puts humans in chains and forges them into artificial creatures. Furthermore, Kant argued that most humans are raised to become heteronomous infants; Mill mocked the ape-like imitation of others in the process of socialization; and Marx provided insights regarding dehumanization by impoverishment and religious stupefaction. Thoreau asserted that most humans serve the state as thoughtless machines; Virginia Wolf attacked the male-chauvinist view that women are inferior to man in body, mind and morality; and Nietzsche criticized the diminution of humans into herd-animals.

Some recent critiques include Hanna Arendt's warning, in *The Human Condition* (1958), that the predominance of calculative thinking and glorification of technology erode our human agency in two major ways. First, it makes us "slaves of our know-how, thoughtless creatures at the mercy of every gadget which is technically possible, no matter how murderous it is" (p. 3). Second, "it makes us forget the higher, nobler and more meaningful human activities 'for the sake of which freedom would deserve to be won'" (p. 5). Herbert Marcuse, to give another example, forcefully made the point in *One Dimensional Man* (1966) that the social organization of life in advanced capitalist societies – which identifies the good and worthy life solely with making money – is completely irrational concerning the hindrances and obstacles it erects for full actualization of human potentiality. Since the 1960s, we have seen responses to these former crippling actions. There have been major emancipatory and humanizing struggles regarding gender equality, anti-racist and decolonizing social struggles. Moreover, postmodern thinking introduced multiculturalism into the core of moral and political considerations.

Instead of listing more examples, it feels safe to say that it was Paulo Freire, in his *Pedagogy of the Oppressed*, who encapsulated the manifold critiques of maiming and obstructing human agency. He asserted that *dehumanization has been the central problem of humanity* and that the principal challenge of critical pedagogy is to lead the struggle, by various forms of liberating and empowering education, toward a more humane and just society.

Having in the background the above-noted critiques regarding human agency and its enemies, it is my aim in this chapter to introduce activist pedagogy as an educational strategy to prevent, counter and combat such mechanisms of dehumanization, as well as to offer ways for regenerating and empowering aspects of human agency that are crucial for humanizing pedagogy. By no means would I be able to cover here all the aspects of human agency or the manifold educational forms for its empowerment. However, drawing on diverse philosophers and educationists, in my integrative model of activist pedagogy for empowering agency, I shall relate to three main dimensions. The first is the *ethical-existential dimension* of personal autonomy and authenticity that includes a greater sense of subjectivity and individuality. The second is *the political dimension*, which consists of engaging teachers and students with pressing human predicaments, and developing their political literacy in matters that have crucial effects on both individuals and the common good. The third dimension is *the pedagogical or didactic dimension*, which is comprised of the kind of curriculum and teaching learning methods most profitable for experiential, meaningful, explorative, constructivist, inspiring and agency-promoting schooling.

Let us begin then with a short exploration of the terrain of human agency. In line with my integrative theory of humanistic education (2007, 2011, 2016), in my discussion of human agency, I shall draw on diverse and even conflicting theoretical traditions. Hence, I shall employ various conceptions of human flourishing and a worthwhile life, which were introduced by classical neo-humanist thinkers, such as Jacque Maritain, Mortimer Adler and Martha Nussbaum. I shall further relate to visions of naturalistic authenticity and full humanity held by humanist psychologists, such as Maslow and Rogers. Similarly, I will employ existentialist insights regarding creative authenticity proposed by Nietzsche, Martin Buber and Maxine Greene, combining these with notions of humanization, equity and participatory democracy, introduced by Freire, Giroux, Simon and other endorsers of critical pedagogy. From our most recent educational discourse, it is indeed reassuring to have the OECD's recent position paper, *The Future of Education and Skills: Education 2030*, as a resource upon which to draw for empowering the self-agency of students. As stated there, "future-ready students need to exercise agency," enabling them to "frame guiding purposes," to develop competencies for "navigating through a complex and uncertain world" and be able "to shape their own lives and contribute to the lives of others" (2018, p. 4).

I believe that in the context of an ethical-political-pedagogical discourse, the most fundamental denotation of human agency consists in "exercising our humanity." It assumes some set of distinctly human powers by which humans affirm and assert themselves in the world and to which we relate our ethical notion of human dignity.

There are many ways to look into the nature of this notion of "exercising our humanity." Some famous examples of this undertaking include Socrates' notion of "the examined life," della Mirandola's identification of human dignity with the capacity to fashion one's own identity, and the mark one makes in the world. There is also the German conception of Bildung, denoting humanizing self-formation by means of proper development of one's talents and natural capacities and educative engagement with the best and highest in human culture.

However, since the word, "activity," is most often employed to characterize agency – including the elements of intention, initiation, exploration, and execution – I wish to focus on the famous distinction made by the Spanish philosopher Ortega y Gasset between regular life of inertia and noble life of activity. In his *Revolt of the Masses,* he argues that:

> the most radical division that is possible to make of humanity is between … a life of effort [noble life], ever set on excelling oneself, in passing beyond what one is to what one sets up as a duty and an obligation … and [the inert life] of those who demand nothing special of themselves, but for whom to live is to be every moment what they already are, without imposing on themselves any effort towards perfection; mere buoys that float on the waves. (p. 5)

Ortega's notion of noble life has two meanings: on the one hand, it addresses the dichotomy between inner-directed and other-directed activity – focusing on the virtue of generating or originating the direction and content of one's life from one's inner being. On the other hand, it emphasizes the pursuit of perfection in the art of living. As stressed by his precursor, Nietzsche, it seems that the most common characteristic of people is that they "tend to be inert …

hiding behind customs and opinions" (1965, p. 1). "There is no more detestable and empty creature in nature than the man who runs away from his *daimon*" (soul or personal destiny) (p. 2). Under this harsh criticism lies an ethical ideal of creative or artistic authenticity, which holds artists in high esteem as the model of people who "hate this idle drifting along in borrowed manners and superimposed opinions" (p. 2); individuals who are hard with themselves in their existential project of self-formation, and "do not permit [their] existence to resemble an unthinking product of chance" (p. 4).

The metaphor Nietzsche chose for portraying the special inner power of self-efficacy and perfectionist self-formation is the one of the "self-propelled wheel":

> Do you want to go the way of your affliction, which is the way to yourself? Then show me your right and your strength to do so. Are you a new strength and a new right? A first movement? A self-propelled wheel? ... You call yourself free? Your dominant thought I want to hear, and not that you have escaped from a yoke. Free from what? As if that mattered to Zarathustra! But your eyes should tell me brightly: *free for what?* Can you give yourself your own evil and your own good and hang your own will over yourself as a law? Can you be your own judge and avenger of your law? (1968, pp. 174–175)

A different angle for investigating human agency is found in the ethical ideal of rational autonomy. A good anchoring point for this perspective is presented in Aristotle's teleological and Eudemonistic conception of human flourishing. It is the very idea that the mission of a good liberal education is to guide the young toward successful actualization of their human nature – i.e. to do all that there is in their power to lead their lives by the faculty of reason in both its contemplative and practical aspects (1980, Book X). The justification for this imperative lies in the view that reason, or rational inquiry and deliberation, is the highest and most distinct element in human nature. Here, Aristotle followed the understanding of his teacher, Plato, who identified the good life with the rule of the reasonable soul over the appetitive soul. It is the conviction that the "unexamined life is not worth living for man" (Plato, 1969, p. 72). It is only by the sound exercise of reason that one becomes one's own person: liberating oneself from the fetters of bestial drives, ignorance, prejudice, negative emotions, and public opinion and moving forward to achieve a sense of sovereignty, and rational autonomy, as well as moral and civic responsibility.

This classical conception of rational autonomy, as the foundation of human agency, has many modern versions. Here, I wish to explore two famous one's –

Spinoza's and Kant's. In the naturalistic world view developed by Spinoza, existence is a perpetual struggle for self-preservation and self-affirmation (Nadler, 2006, p. 221). Each person endeavors to remain in his own being and to act in accordance with his/her true and essential nature. Spinoza designates this inner drive or endeavor, *conatus,* and it functions in the life of every individual. The person seeks the required vitality for generating the activity from one's inner nature, rather than being forced by external sources – social pressures, traditions, public opinion, sensual temptations, etc. Spinoza avers that reason is the most essential nature of humans: it is the path for enhancing human agency, increasing one's power and liberty in relation to other things and acting from one's inner nature. It consists of drawing on one's own cognitive resources, and reaching higher levels of thought and knowledge. Therefore, people lead a rational life that is generated and governed by reason (Hampshire, 1971).

While being very different in its metaphysical premises, Kant's conception of human agency is quite similar. Following his distinction between the realm of natural phenomena and the realm of rational deliberation, Kant (1966, 1973) views human growth, from infancy into maturity, and from inertial servility to external authority into enlightenment, only by means of people exercising their rational, reflective and critical autonomy.

Perhaps the most famous modern text articulating the ideal of acute human agency in the form of rational autonomy was written by Isaiah Berlin regarding "positive liberty" (1969):

> I wish my life and decisions to depend on myself, not on external forces of whatever kind, I wish to be the instrument of my own, not of other men's acts of will. I wish to be a subject, not an object; to be moved by reasons, by conscious purposes which are my own, not by causes which affect me, as it were, from outside. I wish to be somebody, not nobody; a doer – deciding, not being decided for, self-directed and not acted upon by external nature or by other men as if I were a thing, or an animal, or a slave incapable of playing a human role, that is, of conceiving goals and policies of my own and realizing them ... I wish above all to be conscious of myself as a thinking, willing, active being, bearing responsibility for his choices and able to explain them by reference to my own ideas and purposes.

The third aspect of human agency, in the sense I employ here of "exercising our humanity," is also linked to Aristotle's Eudemonistic ethics. This consists of the sphere of personality traits and the sound exercising of character dispositions. I do not wish to delineate any mechanistic or cause and effect relations in these matters, but rather to argue that certain qualities of personality and character are instrumental for exercising and executing human agency. From the psychological perspective, Maslow focuses on the quality of "being in touch with their own inner signals," and "having clear impulse voices about matters of ethics and values" (1971, p. 184) – a quality which enables people to move, due to intrinsic motivation and grow into healthy, self-actualizing individuals.

From the philosophical vantage point, John Rawls referred to "the most important primary good," without which "nothing may seem worth doing" (1971, p. 440). In his view, self-respect or self-esteem emphasizes its twofold value. The first is the person's sense of his/her own value, "his conviction that his plan of life is worth carrying out" (1971, p. 440). The second is his or her "confidence in one's ability to fulfill one's intentions" (1971, p. 440). Other qualities, traits or dispositions of great value, regarding one's ability to act meaningfully in the world as a unique individual and in collaboration with others, include courage and creativity, empathy and compassion, perseverance and resilience, self-efficacy, inner motivation, and moral passions, as well as narrative and social imagination.

Let us now shift to a short explication of the concept of activist pedagogy. As I employ it here, activist pedagogy, first and foremost, breaks free from the orthodoxies and technocratic features of conventional education and substitutes the vocational mission of socialization and normalization with the mission of humanization and social transformation. It further implies moving beyond the advancements made by progressive education – breaking the walls, in Dewey's terminology, between the child and the curriculum, school and society, democracy and education – and stepping into the new arena of social and political activism. Its starting point is the realization that the fate of the young – for life or death, development or stagnation, happiness or misery, liberty or bondage, impoverishment or well-being – is mainly determined not in the education system, but rather in the political arena. It is determined in the policies that decide the extent to which all humans have an equal opportunity to achieve a worthwhile and flourishing life. Hence, acknowledging the immense influence of social and environmental factors on the development and future of the young, activist educators undertake their professional mission, not only in the academic sphere, but also in the political one. They address and engage with the pressing issues of peace, democracy, social justice, environmental sustainability, gender equality, health, welfare, mass culture and mass communication.

The unavoidable conclusion, as expressed by Henry Giroux, is "to struggle for ways in which the pedagogical can be made more political and the political made more pedagogical" (1988, pp. 63–64; also in Aronowitz & Giroux, 1985, dedication). Activist pedagogy, in other words, must also be radical and critical. It adheres to the original meaning of radical, in the sense of going directly to the roots of things, and is impatient with slow reforms and policies of gradualism, which most often offend intellectual and moral integrity. Moreover, it is driven by a passionate commitment to examine, inquire, unmask and disclose the power relations that are part of every social relation and organization.

As noted in the opening paragraphs, throughout human history, there have been manifold forms and mechanisms of dehumanization, many of which have been analyzed and criticized by thinkers, such as Spinoza, Rousseaux, Marx, Mill, Thoreau, Wolf, and Nietzsche. We have also noted, with respect to the 20th century, that it appears impossible to exaggerate criticizing the political and social structures that have mutilated human agency and robbed humans of the very fundamental possibilities to lead lives of dignity and personal fulfillment. In light of this, one cannot repudiate the truth in George Bernard Shaw's assertion that "man measures his strength by his destructiveness" (Shaw, 1951, p. 152) and that, in most cases, as also demonstrated in Orwell's *Animal Farm* and *1984*, the members of the political elite are "liars ... to the very backbone of their souls" (Shaw, 1951, p. 176).

Moreover, as Neil Postman, one of the most notable educational critics, pointed out, manipulative language has become predominant in our lives. "America in no longer a culture but just an economy" (2005, p. 470). Furthermore, most of us are devoting our lives to "amusing ourselves to death" (1985). This cultural ill, as Krishnamurti put it, has horrible implications for the upbringing of our children: "Our present education is geared to industrialization and war, its principal aim being to develop efficiency; and we are caught in this machine of ruthless competition and mutual destruction" (1955, p. 6).

Let us now shift from criticism to construction. As stated in the beginning of the chapter, I aim to portray a theoretical outline or pedagogical narrative for educational empowerment of human agency. A good point of departure is Freire's notion of liberating and empowering dialogue. In his view, dialogical relations, rather than authoritarian, hierarchical or instrumental ones, are essential for enhancing human agency. More specifically, he notes the attributes that are necessary for such dialogues to be successful. One attribute is love of humanity, which includes attentive, empathetic and respectful caring for the well-being of the other as a human being and as a unique individual. Another attribute is trust in the potentiality and ability of the other, for leading a fulfilling life and making a difference in the world. Thirdly, there is a need for a combination of cultural, critical and political literacies that form sound foundations for action that promotes human solidarity, social justice and participatory egalitarian democracy.

As I elaborated elsewhere (2007, 2008), in the various traditions and approaches in education, there are manifold forms of dialogue, some of which are vital for empowering human agency that differ from the aspects emphasized by Freire. One such empowering dialogue is the Socratic one. This seeks intellectual and moral empowerment to promote a life of moral rigor and self-reflection. There is a rationalist attentiveness to "truth and understanding and the perfection of the soul" (Plato, 1969, p. 61). This begins with the dictum to "know thyself," the educator's revelation that his/her wisdom consists in knowing the limits of her/his knowledge, and in inviting her/his students to participate in the most essential mode of exercising one's humanity – reflective and critical examination of one's own life and of her/his natural and social surroundings. The overarching goal of such undertaking is the good (virtuous and happy) life and the central avenue for this, as stressed later by both Aristotle and Isocrates, is by achieving proficiency in the employment of conceptual language – the true distinguishing mark of humans – and mastering, along with others, a dialectics toward wisdom in the art of living.

As I noted above, in more practical terms, Spinoza's ethical recommendation was that the path for enhancing human agency consists of drawing upon one's cognitive resources, which is governed by reason. The more one achieves such inner-directed generation of one's own conduct, the less one is susceptible to influence and manipulation by external factors.

A form of agency empowering dialogue that is completely different from both the Freirean and the Socratic one – neither political nor rationalist – was introduce by Nietzsche. This dialogue emanates from the rich personality, creative drives, and generous spirit of the educator, who seeks out "fellow creators," "those who "write new values on new tablets" (1968, p. 136). Nietzsche wrote about those that add meaning and value to life through their creative self-perfection and self-affirmation.

Such educational dialogues aim to develop a powerful human being, who is understood to be an individual who breaks free from the herd, and seeks to be demanding of her/himself for the sake of perfectionistic self-overcoming. Such individuals authentically forge and fashion their modes of living and contributions to humanity. As introduced in the "gift-giving virtue" chapter of *Thus Spoke Zarathustra*, such generosity, on the part of the educator, is very rare. In this paradigm of empowering education, "One repays a teacher badly if one always remains nothing but a pupil" (1968, p. 190). For humans to be truthful to themselves, Nietzsche argues, people imagine themselves as "unique, incomparable, who give themselves laws, who create themselves" (1974, sec. 335). Hence, the challenge such educator sets for his students is:

> You had not yet sought yourselves: and you found me. Thus do all believers; therefore all faith amounts to so little. Now I bid you to lose me and

find yourselves; and only when you have all denied me will I return to you ... with a different love shall I then love you. (1968, p. 190)

The next form of empowering educational dialogue has much in common with both Freire and Nietzsche. It is the Buberian conception of "I and Thou" – dialogue which challenges the interlocutors to be present for the other and to attend to the other in her/his full humanity and individuality. Such dialogue refuses to engage in any form of instrumental reductionism and to relate to people as objects, but rather as subjects. Being a witness to the horrors of the first half of the 20th century, and to the totalitarian regimes that sought to destroy any sense of autonomous human agency, Buber ascribed educators a special humanist rescuing task:

> Today host upon host of men have everywhere sunk into the slavery of collectives, and each collective is the supreme authority for its own slaves ... This is true, not only for the totalitarian countries, but also for the parties and party-like groups in the so-called democracies. Men who have so lost themselves to the collective Moloch cannot be rescued from it by any reference, however eloquent, to the absolute whose kingdom the Moloch has usurped. One has to begin by pointing to that sphere where man himself, in the hours of utter solitude, occasionally becomes aware of the disease through sudden pain: by pointing the relations of the individual to his own self. (1971, pp. 491–492)

In order to achieve successful "I and Thou" agency, which promotes dialogical relations, Buber lists three major pedagogical principles. The first one is the teacher's ability to earn the trust of the students, as an educator who is not a mere functionary in the service of social apparatuses, but is fully and primarily dedicated to the student. Secondly, it is the ability to awaken trust in the human spirit in the students – in the arts and sciences, morality and solidarity, friendship and community, creative imagination, social engagement, philosophizing and all else that makes life worth living. The third principle is "personality," namely education by means of pedagogic Eros, example and inspiration. "A teacher can only be present to his students," as Maxine Greene puts it, "if he appeals to their freedom ... if he himself is engaged in searching and choosing" (1974, p. 84); "if he is no longer content to be a mere cipher, a functionary, a clerk [...] breaking with fixed, customary modes of seeing, removing the blinders of complacency, [...] taking responsibility for his pursuit of norms and meanings" (1973, pp. 7–8).

More recently, Chris Higgins wrote:

> In order to cultivate selfhood in students, teachers must bring to the table their own achieved self-cultivation, their commitment to ongoing growth, and their various practices, styles, and tricks for combating the many forces that deaden the self and distract us from our task of becoming. (2011, p. 190)

Finally, returning to the original words of Buber:

> Only in his whole being, in all his spontaneity can the educator truly affect the whole being of his pupil. For educating characters you do not need a moral genius, but you do need a man who is wholly alive and able to communicate himself directly to this fellow being. His aliveness streams out to them and affects them most strongly and purely when he has no thought of affecting them. (1971, p. 488)

Participatory democracy, very much like dialogue, is another form of social interaction that is marked by the quality of eliciting and empowering human agency. By this I do not mean the formal sense of a political regime, but rather a culture or ethos – from kindergarten onward – in which the cultivation of traits and the norms of conduct are anchored in the values of dignity, equity, diversity, community and pluralism, as well as in the practices of open discussion and shared deliberation. It is a space that enables the full expression of multiple voices to engage in dialogic encounter (Simon, 1987, p. 375). It adheres to the principle of "nothing about me without me" – being respectful and attentive to the "other" – and the common pursuit for the general good.

Regarding intentional cultivation and enhancement of human agency in an ethos of participatory democracy, I wish to draw here on two different, yet complementing educational paradigms. Wiel Veugelers introduced the first one: he favored the critical-democratic type of citizenship education over the adaptive and individualized ones. His reasons for this preference were that this type "finds social involvement and autonomy very important" and stresses the dispositions of "critical engagement with the common good … individual autonomy, and personal articulation" (2020, p. 5). This is the kind of education that gives much attention to "active student participation in dialogue," as well as to "cooperative and inquiry-oriented learning" (2020, p. 5).

The second educational paradigm for agency enhancing in democratic citizenship was offered by Martha Nussbaum and includes both the cognitive and the affective engagement with others. The first is "the capacity for critical examination of oneself and one's traditions – for living what, following Socrates, we may call 'the examined life'" (2002, p. 293). This mode of living "questions all beliefs and accepts only those that survive reason's demand for consistency and for justification" (p. 293). The second element is what Nussbaum calls the ability for narrative imagination. It is the:

> ability to think what it might be like to be in the shoes of a person different from oneself, to be an intelligent reader of that person's story, and to understand the emotions and wishes and that someone so placed might have. (2002, p. 299)

So far, in this essay, we have touched on many elements of human agency, explored their nature and ways for their empowerment, by presenting the understandings of some distinguished philosophers and educationalists and by focusing on the ethical, political and the pedagogical dimensions. Overall, however, and beyond the different approaches, the common cause amounts to adhering to a humanist stance. The diverse conservative neo-humanists philosophers, humanist psychologists, existentialist thinkers or critical pedagogues presented here all share a commitment to developing human agency and facilitating their students flourishing life, while seeking and promoting this same blessing for all humans. This commitment is presented concisely and directly in these three following statements:

> Humanism ... essentially tends to render man more truly human and to make his original greatness manifest by causing him to participate in all that can enrich him in nature and in history .... It at once demands that man make use of all the potentialities he holds within him, his creative powers and the life of reason, and labor to make the powers of the physical world the instruments of his freedom. (Maritain, 1954, p. XII)

> There is only one subject matter for education, and that is Life in all its manifestations .... Education is the guidance of the individual towards a comprehension of the art of life; and by the art of life, I mean the most complete achievement of varied activity expressing the potentialities of that living creature in the face of its actual environment. (Whitehead, 1967, pp. 6–7, 39)

> Every child should be able to look forward not only to growing up but to continued growth in all human dimensions throughout life. All should

aspire to make as much of their powers as they can ... to enjoy as fully as possible all the goods that make a human life as good as it can be. (Adler, 1982, pp. 17–18)

These beautiful and promising humanist declarations are truly concerned with humanization and empowering human agency – but only as foundations. They represent the culmination of the school of neo-humanism and the "Great Books" tradition. However, as we noted in the examples and discussions above, from Montaigne onward, true empowerment of human agency requires active engagement with the more modern and post-modern educational approaches associated with progressive, existentialist and critical educational practices. Modernity brought dramatic changes in the set of values that education needs to address, especially those of individuation, authenticity, equity, critical autonomy, diversity, democratization, and educational personalization – ethical, political, and pedagogical aspects that have emerged as crucial for present day human agency.

As stressed in many texts quoted above, and experienced in our daily life, very little of the great moral and political ideals that are taught in schools are learned beyond "inert ideas" and put into practice by people. Instead of awakening in students concerns for moral, political, aesthetic, and environmental issues, the content of the curriculum is sterile, and the teaching methods only make the students more numb, indifferent and cynical. With a spirit of social criticism and moral rage, the American philosopher, Maxine Greene, writes about schools that are totally devoid of any social engagement and moral consideration:

> Little, if anything, is done to render problematic a reality that includes homelessness, hunger, pollution, crime, censorship, arms build-ups, and threats of war, even as it includes the amassing of fortunes, consumer goods of unprecedented appeal, a world travel opportunities, and the flickering faces of the "rich and famous" on all sides. Little is done to counter media manipulation of the young into credulous and ardent consumers – of sensation, violence, criminality, things. They are instructed daily, and with few exceptions, that human worth depends on the possession of commodities, community status, a flippant way of talking, good looks. What they are made to believe to be the "news" is half entertainment, half pretenses at being "windows to the world" .... In the midst of the marketing and the sounds of sitcom shotguns, there are opportunities to become voyeurs of starvation, massacres, torture, and the beat of MTV goes on and on. (1988, pp. 12–13)

Hence, upon reaching the end of this chapter, we return to one of the statements with which it opened: that "it is necessary to struggle for ways in which the pedagogical can be made more political and the political made more pedagogical" (1988, pp. 63–64; also in Aronowitz & Giroux, 1985, dedication). Teachers who truly seek to empower the agency of their students must change the professional image from agents of socialization to agents of social transformation. They need no longer view themselves as passive conduits, whose purpose is to convey the messages of the political establishment, or as agents who replicate social gaps and an alienated experience. As Giroux argues, they should be able: "to participate fully in the ongoing struggle to make democracy the medium through which they extend the potential and possibilities of what it means to be human and to live in a just society (1989, p. 186).

To empower students, as Roger Simon writes, is not only to "encourage and make possible the realization of a variety of differentiated human capacities" (1987, p. 372); it also often involves the political aspect of:

> ... enabling those who have been silenced to speak. It is to enable the self-affirming expression of experiences mediated by one's history, language, and traditions. It is to enable those who have been marginalized economically and culturally to claim in both respects a status as full participating members of a community. (1987, p. 374)

Moreover, it requires a "pedagogy of possibility" that "gives credence to alternative realities" (Greene, 2013, p. 3): empowering teachers and students to "define themselves as active authors of their own world" (Simon, 1987, p. 377) and reconstructing together "social imagination in the service of human freedom" (Simon, 1987, p. 377).

Furthermore, there is, of course, the issue of content and the curriculum. In Montaigne's *Essays*, Whitehead's *The Aims of Education*, and Maxwell's book, *Global Philosophy*, it is not knowledge, but rather wisdom, that should lie at the core of the teaching-learning activities at schools. This involves shifting our orientation and dedication from the acquisition and inculcation of disciplinary knowledge to the exploration of the ways by which rational inquiry and education can empower us to deal constructively and successfully with our pressing real life predicaments and challenges. These challenges range from peace building, racism, climate crisis and social gaps, to obesity, drug abuse, obsessive consumerism and the manifold forms of addictions. It requires attending to the lived reality of the teachers and the students, as well as to the pressing social and cultural public issues, so that we can integrate these human narratives and social predicaments into the knowledge and cultural assets offered by the academic disciplines. In other words, it amounts to merging the tree of life with the tree of knowledge, for the sake of developing wisdom in the art of living.

Finally, empowering human agency in schools should be based on personal example, on the part of the teachers. It consists of generating the intellectual vitality of the students, exciting them emotionally, inspiring their creative abilities, opening their hearts for empathy and solidarity, activating their social imagination, awakening their moral sensitivity, refining their tastes and igniting in them motivation for the demanding and creative life of self-education and self-determination. In words and deeds, teachers should awaken their students to "recognize lack or deficiency and learn how to repair and transcend" (Greene, 1978, p. 19). They should inspire their imagination "to look at things as if they could be otherwise" (Greene, 2013, p. 19). They should aim to challenge them "to make cognitive sense of their experience, to engage with their environments as perceptual and imaginative and feeling beings" (Greene, 1981, p. 32).

Activist teachers, who seek to empower human agency, should begin by awakening their students' sense of being the authors of their own lives. They should help them realize that human beings are largely the thinkers, scriptwriters, directors, actors and audience of the reality of their lives. Hence, there is a great responsibility for enhancing the quality of this drama, which is their – and our – lives. It should then involve motivating their students to go beyond what is taken for granted, to break free from the "sacred cows" and cultural myths, from the lies of life and politicians' deceits, and from the penetration of technology and bureaucracy into all of life's strata. By addressing the student's freedom and stimulating his/her, consciousness with alternative perceptions and facts – about what is not, but can still be – the educator seeks to assist the pupil in breaching the banality of quotidian life. By helping students identify the cracks and fissures, teachers can enable students to see reality in a new light, to continuously re-define themselves within it, by according reality their own interpretations, meanings and values.

References

Adler, M. (1982). *The Paideia proposal: An educational manifesto*. Macmillan.
Aloni, N. (2007). *Enhancing humanity: The philosophical foundations of humanistic education*. Springer.
Aloni, N. (Ed.). (2008). *Empowering dialogues in humanistic education*. HaKibbutz HaMeuhad. [in Hebrew]

Aloni, N. (2011). Humanistic education: From theory to practice. In W. Veugelers (Ed.), *Education and humanism: Linking autonomy and humanity* (pp. 35–46). Sense Publishers.

Aloni, N. (2016). Humanist schools in the face of conflicting narratives and social upheaval – The case of Israel. In H. E. Lees & N. Noddings (Eds.), *The Palgrave international handbook of alternative education* (pp. 369–383). Palgrave-Macmillan.

Aloni, N. (2017). Educators worthy of the name: Intellectuals, generous, master dialogicians. In N. Aloni & L. Weintrob (Eds.), *Beyond bystanders: Educational leadership for a humane culture in a globalizing reality* (pp. 61–74). Sense Publishers.

Aloni, N., & Weintrob, L. (2017). Introduction. In N. Aloni & L. Weintrob (Eds.), *Beyond bystanders: Educational leadership for a humane culture in a globalizing reality* (pp. 1–15). Sense Publishers.

Arendt, H. (1958). *The human condition*. University of Chicago Press.

Aristotle. (1980). *The Nicomachean ethics* (D. Ross, Trans.). Oxford University Press.

Aronowitz, S., & Giroux, H. (1985). *Education under siege: The conservative, liberal, and radical debate over schooling*. Bergin & Garvey.

Berlin, I. (1969). *Four essays on liberty*. Oxford University Press.

Buber, M. (1971). The education of character. In J. P. Strain (Ed.), *Modern philosophies of education*. Random House.

Dewey, J. (1966). *Democracy and education*. Macmillan Co.

Freire, P. (1970). *Pedagogy of the oppressed* (M. Bergman Ramos, Trans.). Seabury Press.

Giroux, H. A. (1988). Literacy and the pedagogy of voice and political empowerment. *Educational Theory, 38*(1), 61–75.

Giroux, H. A. (1989). Educational reform and teacher empowerment. In H. Holtz (Ed.), *Education and the American dream: Conservatives, liberals, and radicals debate the future of education* (pp. 173–186). Bergin & Garvey.

Greene, M. (1973). *Teacher as stranger: Educational philosophy for the modern age*. Wadsworth.

Greene, M. (1974). Literature, existentialism, and education. In D. Denton (Ed.), *Existentialism and phenomenology in education* (pp. 63–87). Teachers College Press.

Greene, M. (1978). *Landscapes of learning*. Teachers College Press.

Greene, M. (1981). Contexts, connections, and consequences: The matter of philosophical and psychological foundations. *Journal of Teacher Education, 32*(4), 31–37.

Greene, M. (1988). *The dialectic of freedom*. Teachers College Press.

Greene, M. (2013). *Releasing the imagination: Essays on education, the arts, and social change*. Jossey-Bass

Hampshire, S. (1971). Spinoza's theory of human freedom. In E. Freeman & M. Mandelbaum (Eds.), *Spinoza: Essays in interpretation*. Open Court Publishing.

Higgins, C. (2011). *The good life of teaching: An ethics of professional practice*. Wiley-Blackwell.

Kant, I. (1966). *Education* (A. Churton, Trans.). University of Michigan Press.
Kant, I. (1973). What is enlightenment? In P. Gay (Ed.), *The enlightenment: A comprehensive anthology*. Simon & Schuster.
Krishnamurti, J. (1955). *Education and the significance of life*. Harper.
Marcuse, H. (1966). *One dimensional man*. Beacon Press.
Maritain, J. (1954). *True Humanism*. Charles Scribner's Sons.
Maslow, A. H. (1971). *The farther reaches of human nature*. Viking.
Maxwell, N. (2014). *Global philosophy: What philosophy ought to be*. Imprint Academics.
Montaigne, M. de. (1976). *Essays* (J. M. Cohen, Trans.). Penguin.
Nadler, S. (2006) *Spinoza's ethics—An introduction*. Cambridge University Press.
Nadler, S. (2011). *A book forged in Hell: Spinoza's scandalous treatise and the birth of the secular age*. Princeton University Press.
Nietzsche, F. (1965). *Schopenhauer as educator*. Regency-Gateway.
Nietzsche, F. (1968). Thus spoke Zarathustra. In W. Kaufmann (Ed.), *The portable Nietzsche*. Viking Press.
Nietzsche, F. (1974). *The gay science* (W. Kaufmann, Trans.). Vintage Books.
Nussbaum, M. (2002). Education for citizenship in an era of global connection. *Studies in Philosophy of Education, 21*(4–5), 289–303.
OECD. (2018). *The future of education and skills: Education 2030*. https://www.oecd.org/education/2030/E2030%20Position%20Paper%20(05.04.2018).pdf
Ortega y Gasset, J. (1957). *The revolt of the masses*. W. W. Norton and Co.
Orwell, G. (1949). *Nineteen eighty-four*. Secker and Warburg.
Plato. (1969). *The last days of Socrates*. Penguin.
Postman, N. (1995). *The end of education*. Knopf.
Postman, N. (2005). Education needs a vision, not a machine. In N. Aloni (Ed.), *On becoming human – Anthology in philosophy of education* (pp. 470–471). Hakibbutz HaMeuhad and Mofet. [in Hebrew]
Rousseau, J. J. (1979). *Emil or on education* (A. Bloom, Trans.). Basic Books.
Shaw, B. (1951). *Man and superman*. Penguin.
Simon, R. (1987). Empowerment as a pedagogy of possibility. *Language Arts, 64*(4), 370–382.
Spinoza, B. (1974). *The rationalists*. Doubleday.
Thoreau, D. H. (1962). *On the duty of civil disobedience and Walden*. Collier Books.
Veugelers, W. (2020). How globalization influences perspectives on citizenship education: From the social and political to the cultural and moral. *Compare: A Journal of Comparative and International Education*. doi:10.1080/03057925.2020.1716307
Whitehead, A. N. (1967). *The aims of education and other essays*. Free Press.

CHAPTER 2

Teaching Controversial Issues as Part of Education for Democratic Intercultural Citizenship

Wiel Veugelers and Jaap Schuitema

Democracy implies that students have to learn to deal with controversial issues. For teachers, it is difficult to teach issues that are considered controversial in society, or by some participants in schools, like students, parents, other teachers and principals. It is particularly difficult when there are opposing groups and perspectives in the classroom itself. Controversial issues are at stake in many subjects, but especially in subjects, like history, social studies and religious studies. However, more technical subjects, like biology, are also full of controversial issues.

Addressing controversial issues, in a pedagogical setting, requires paying attention to different perspectives and their social, cultural and political foundations. Learning from different perspectives can be best developed if teachers use multiple perspectives with all kind of topics, as a regular way of learning and teaching. Such a pedagogical mode can train students to have open dialogues, before issues really become controversial, and are also useful in the midst of heated controversial debates.

1   Introduction

Nations use education to build a national identity and social cohesion. Each nation tries to socialize its students to integrate in society. According to Spring (2004), such policy tries to create one nation by enforcing a dominant language, a common culture and a common view of history. Integrating and harmonizing are important social, political and educational processes. However, many nations do not have a common language, culture and history. They have controversies about their identity and how much diversity they accept. They also have controversies over what the dominant culture is, how to treat minority cultures, and how they interpret their history. Mouffe (2005, 2018) argues that such controversies are normal parts of a modern democratic society, and such controversies should not be avoided, but rather should be part of societal dialogues. Mouffe (2005) uses the concept, agonistic democracy, to show that controversies should be valued in a democracy. Too much focus on consensus and deliberation mystifies contradictions in society and does not help build a stronger and more social justice-oriented democracy that tries to treat contradictions and inequalities in society in a more just way (Veugelers, 2019, 2020a).

We argue for a dialogical and multiperspective educational methodology, as part of a critical-democratic approach of moral and citizenship education. Such approach supports the development of autonomy, social concern and justice, and values diversity (Veugelers, 2007, 2020b). Critical-democratic citizenship tries to balance autonomy with a social orientation. It is an engagement in critical dealing with controversies that take other perspectives seriously. Such a critical and democratic approach is relevant in all societies, but in particular in diverse societies (Veugelers, De Groot & Stolk, 2017).

Education always involves moral values (Hansen, 2017). Moral values are embedded in teachers' work with students, colleagues and parents. Much attention has been given in research to teachers' roles in the school culture and in the interpersonal relationship with students. Of course, these interactions, between students and teachers, are part of teachers' ethos. However, there is a lack of attention in research on moral education and teachers' pedagogical action on the content of the curriculum, on how the content of education influences teachers' ethical role and shapes the pedagogical relationship between teachers and students. In this chapter, we will focus on teachers and the curriculum content, in particular, when addressing and dealing with controversial issues.

Controversial issues are topics over which people can disagree, and this disagreement is because of different articulations of moral values (Hess, 2009) – articulations that are often expressions of different political, cultural or religious frameworks. These controversial issues arise in the classroom because they are part of the curriculum; for this reason, teachers have to work with these topics, or because students bring in these controversial issues in their contribution to the dialogue in the classroom.

1.1   *Critical-Democratic Citizenship Education*

Education tries to prepare students for their participation in society. Nowadays, the concept of citizenship is used in policy, research and practice to speak about this socializing role of education. It is about the kind of person education is trying to develop. Over time, the concept of citizenship has changed. The concept of citizenship, in its deeper sense, is now on the political, cultural and social levels of society. In its broader sense, the concept is enlarged from the national to regional and global education. People can have different ideas about citizenship, and different ideological orientations can be distinguished in citizenship.

In our research in the Netherlands, we found three types of citizenship: an adapted orientation, an individualized orientation and a critical-democratic orientation (Veugelers, 2007). A critical-democratic citizenship addresses autonomy and social concern and social justice. It tries to balance autonomy and the social, and it respects diversity. It supports democracy and the active critical and engagement participation of all involved. Its focus is on intensifying democracy in its formal and informal ways.

It is important to note that the concept of democracy is not viewed as being a smooth way of consensus-building, in which all contradictions disappear, or, at least, stay hidden. A lively democracy recognizes differences, values the struggle about different ideas, and respects minorities. It values open dialogue, about controversial issues, as well, of all involved. These are characteristics of a strong democracy (Veugelers, 2019b).

In this chapter, we analyze how teachers work, and can work, with controversial issues so they can support critical-democratic citizenship development. We use the results of a qualitative study on how teachers deal with controversial issues. Our questions were: What topics do teachers find controversial? How do teachers work with these controversial issues? And, how do teachers react when students bring in these controversial issues into the classroom? We undertook a qualitative research study, in which we interviewed 10 teachers of history and biology in Dutch secondary education.

2   The Context of the Curriculum: Teachers Navigating in Power-Relations

People can have different ideas about all kind of things. These ideas and perspectives enter schools. In the curricula of many educational courses, there are themes that can be thought about differently, and these differences are often linked to ideological, cultural and political orientations. These differences in content may already be included in the subject matter itself (in the formal curriculum), relate to the specific vision of the teacher concerned (teachers' beliefs and values), or the students can bring these differences into the classroom (students' experiences). Teacher's work is very complex: they navigate within the context of the policies and practices of their schools, the demands that the government imposes on education, and the direct relationship they have with the students and their parents, in and out of the classroom.

We have selected the subjects of biology and history, because these subjects involve philosophical and political themes that can be controversial, and because both courses have a prominent place in the curriculum of Dutch secondary education. We interviewed teachers in public education and in religious schools. In the Netherlands, two-thirds of the schools are religious, but they are fully financed by the government and they are required to follow the national curriculum, except concerning religious studies. However, the religious oriented curriculum debates transcend the subject of religious studies. At times, in the Netherlands, there is debate about the topics in other subjects that are 'religious related,' like evolutionary theory in biology and about the role of religions in teaching history. Because of the strong influence of Christian political parties and school boards, the Dutch government is careful when it comes to creating curriculum policy, in which religious aspects can be involved. They try to carefully avoid controversial issues.

2.1 Different Levels of the Curriculum and Controversial Issues

Controversial issues can be found at different levels of the curriculum: in educational policy, in school politics, in the classroom, in contacts with parents, etc. When constructing a curriculum, many choices have to be made. For example, decisions have to be made about having a united, inclusive school system or different types of schools (academic versus vocational); deciding what are relevant school subjects and what is their position in the curriculum; what is the content of each school subject, who develops teaching materials, what is the autonomy of the teacher, etc. At each level, choices can be made.

The choices made are according to curriculum sociology an expression of power relations (Apple, 1979; Bourdieu & Passeron, 1977). A central question is: who decides what is learned. Debates about the curriculum should be considered as a normal part of a democracy. The balance of power between various political, social and cultural groups, and the hegemony in it determines what is in the curriculum. It shows what is considered 'legitimate knowledge' and 'useful knowledge.' Different social, cultural and political groups can relate differently to this 'legitimate educational knowledge.' Dominant groups consider the curriculum to be a recognition and reaffirmation of their knowledge. Non-privileged groups, however, realize that their knowledge is not recognized, as 'legitimate knowledge' (Freire, 1972). They understand that their voice is not heard; that they are marginalized. The knowledge that is taught influences the socialization of the students.

2.2 Controversial Issues in Dutch Society and Education

Controversies over the curriculum can cover a variety of topics (Hess, 2009; Parker, 2003). We cite a few recent examples of controversies in Dutch education that became part of public debates. These are: evolution versus creationism in biology; sexuality in biology; the 'Dutch canon' in history; the colonial past of the Netherlands in history; what kind of culture is the focus in cultural education; what literature is discussed in language classes; what picture of different religions is given, etc. All these topics are controversial in Dutch society and, therefore, also in Dutch education. In Dutch education, partly because of the strong position of religious schools, there are not many regulations for teaching such culturally sensitive subjects. Schools are called upon to arrive at concrete interpretations of the curriculum.

2.3   Research on Controversial Issues in Education

Research on controversial issues has been undertaken, in particular, from a curricular perspective. Studies have explored how controversial issues are treated in curriculum material, for example, in science education, in social studies (Hess, 2009; Hess & McAvoy, 2015; Parker, 2003) and in multicultural studies (Radstake & Leeman, 2010). In research on moral education, researchers speak not of controversial issues, but rather of moral dilemmas (Oser, 1994; Tirri, 1999). We focus here on the teachers' task: on how teachers, as part of their pedagogical and professional ethos, deal with moral values when controversial issues are involved. In this research, we build on earlier research about different ways of teaching values (Veugelers, 2000), education and 9/11 (Veugelers, Derriks & De Kat, 2006), multicultural contacts of students (Schuitema & Veugelers, 2011), and dialogues in classrooms (Schuitema, Radstake, Van de Pol & Veugelers, 2018).

2.4   Active Participation of Teachers and Students at the Micro (Classroom) Level

Supported by the curricula frameworks (formal curricula, guidelines and textbooks), the teacher enters the classroom and considers pedagogical and didactic actions. The teacher interprets the curriculum frameworks. How a teacher, in the classroom, deals with controversial issues depends greatly on her/his pedagogical, ethical and political views, and teaching style.

Traditionally, students have been exposed to a transfer-oriented mode of education: passive learners absorb knowledge, in an unfiltered manner. The teacher 'imposes' his/her vision. From a more constructivist learning perspective, students reconstruct the curriculum offered; the learning is connected to prior knowledge, and personal interests and beliefs (Veugelers, 2019). When a teacher provides space for students to be active in the learning process, learning becomes more dialogical. In real dialogical learning, there should be a common search for answers, and, thus, outcomes are not fixed (Aloni, 2011; Freire, 1972; Veugelers, 2017). Such an open dialogue, however, is idealistic. In regular education, teachers work from curricular frameworks and different knowledge is judged differently. Formal education is not without power relations. Certain knowledge is considered more legitimate than others. There is no power-free dialogue; the teacher must navigate in this power-related field.

Political, social, cultural and ideological viewpoints can lead to different perspectives on many themes. The formal curriculum usually includes the dominant viewpoint. Teachers may have a different view on the topic. Teachers can also be faced with students putting forward different views in the classroom. Teachers have to relate both to the formal curriculum and to the input of students.

3 Findings from Our Research Studies

3.1 *What Issues Do Biology and History Teachers Perceive as Controversial?*

The issues biology teachers call controversial can be classified into four categories. Most biology teachers cite sexuality as a topic that contains many controversial issues, for instance, having sex outside marriage, the use of contraception and homosexuality. A second category in biology includes topics about the natural environment. This involves topics such as sustainability, climate change, animal welfare and genetic engineering. A third category consists of decisions about life and death, such as abortion and euthanasia. Fourth, life itself, and the theory of evolution, are considered by some teachers to be controversial topics. Altogether, this broad area of controversial topics shows that biology is not only a natural science, but is embedded in social, cultural and moral contexts and practices. There are ideas and practices that some people consider controversial, that enter the classroom.

The second subject, we studied a few years ago, was history. Many of the topics that were mentioned as controversial in history, at that time, were, to some degree, related to Islam. When the policy of the Dutch right wing PVV party – and, in particular their negative attitudes about immigrants – was discussed, this led to different student responses. Some, mostly native Dutch students, supported such ideas. Muslim students often reacted negatively to these opinions. Another controversial issue that was often mentioned by the teachers was the Israeli-Palestinian conflict. This provoked many reactions, especially from students with a Muslim background. This came to the fore, for example, when the students discussed the Gulf War and the Second World War. Some students sometimes reacted with strong anti-Jewish remarks, especially when this related to the Holocaust. The teachers experienced these conversations as being very intense.

Other controversial topics mentioned by the teachers connected to faith itself. Christian and Muslim students were often sensitive to opinions that were critical about religions and their relevance in society. Furthermore, some history teachers noted that discussions on abortion and homosexuality could become controversial, when these topics were discussed, for example, in history lessons on the period of "the sixties."

A topic that is now controversial in Dutch public debate is slavery. This was not a topic that was indicated as being controversial in the classroom, a few years ago, by the teachers we interviewed. We do not know if they avoided the topic of slavery or that slavery was not considered controversial in their classrooms. When we would undertake research now, probably due to 'Black Lives Matter,' and the Dutch discussion on 'Black Peter,' an assistant of Saint Nicolas, slavery is mentioned as a controversial issue. This clearly shows how controversial issues in education are determined by societal developments and current discussions in society. While controversial issues change, the fact that there are controversial issues, does not change. This contextual influence makes it even more important to develop a more general educational approach to dealing with controversial issues.

3.2 What Makes Topics Controversial Issues?

Teachers indicated that an issue is controversial when there are different views about the topic being discussed and when the issue is very sensitive for the students. The paradox is that students are often more interested in these controversial topics than in 'normal' topics. For example, teacher Frans, said this about the Israeli-Palestinian conflict:

> You see people sitting on the edge of their seats and make remarks. Then you see, of course, that there is a difference between Muslim and non-Muslim students that could even lead to a clash. This shows that the topic is simply controversial.

Controversial issues affect the identity of students. These are issues that are important for their personality and for who they are. It can appear that what they hear at school collides with what they hear at home or how they talk about it with their friends.

Teachers found it generally difficult to identify whether the controversy surrounding a topic is religious, philosophical, political, cultural or social. In some cases, it was clear that it derived from religious beliefs, for example, the theory of evolution. Students hear a different view of the origin of life at home than they hear at school. Some teachers think that attitudes, for example, about abortion or homosexuality, are determined more by culture than by religion. According to those teachers, political and cultural backgrounds play a more important role than religious or philosophical beliefs do.

The composition of the class is an important factor in the prominence of the controversy surrounding a topic. Certain topics are more important in certain social and cultural groups of students than in others, and are only controversial in classes in which there are a number of students from such a group. For example, evolutionary theory in biology is controversial in a school with many traditional Christian students.

3.3 *Teaching Strategies When Dealing with Controversial Issues*

None of the teachers indicated that they completely avoid topics because they are controversial. However, there was a difference, in the degree, to which teachers really focus on the controversy. Teachers can deliberately provide space for the controversy, by including different perspectives, including those of the students, so that students can share their views and feelings with other students. However, teachers can also choose to avoid the controversy. For example, the teacher might treat the subject without including other perspectives, even those of the students. Alternatively, a teacher can choose only to discuss 'the facts,' without going into students' opinions. When the teacher provides no space for the perspectives of students, students are given no chance to make their own views heard in the classroom and to discuss them.

An important reason that biology teachers do not make a topic too controversial is that they believe that certain ideas should not be part of the biology curriculum. They consider biology as science, without social and normative influences. For example, these teachers feel that they have to teach the theory of evolution, as reflected in the material. At times, a student makes a remark that expresses a different view. Teachers, then, try to explain to the students that they may have a different view, but that it is important that the students learn the theory of evolution at school. This means that teachers teach only the cognitive elements of such a topic, without addressing the underlying moral values.

In other cases, teachers provide no space for the perspectives of students, because they find that some opinions of students are morally and socially unacceptable and, therefore, not admissible in class. This is the case, for example, with negative beliefs about homosexuality. Some of the teachers, who participated in the research, believe that homosexuality is something that should be respected and accepted and should not be up for discussion.

The history teachers appeared to be more willing to argue about all topics. Some teachers felt it was important to go into discussion that include comments that they find unacceptable, such as discriminatory remarks about homosexuality, Muslims or Jews. According to these teachers, different opinions and perspectives are an integral part of the teaching of history. Nonetheless, sometimes, history teachers may not want to incorporate the perspectives of students in the classroom discussions, when dealing with a controversial subject. When teachers find comments from students to be strongly offensive or discriminatory against certain groups, such as gay or Jews, they sometimes choose to cut off a discussion and provide little room for students to express their views.

3.4   Responding to the Controversy Introduced by Students

In many cases, a discussion on a controversial topic is not planned by the teacher, but arises spontaneously, by the students' responses. Sometimes, such a remark can be totally unrelated to the subject matter at that time – for example, when a student calls another student 'gay' or 'fucking Moroccan.' A history teacher indicates that punishment, in such situations, is often not the best response, and that students need to learn where the boundary lies. They do this by entering into conversation with a student.

Lessons about controversial issues are different from ordinary lessons, because they are unpredictable. A teacher does not always know how students will respond, and this can vary by class. In order to discuss a controversial issue, in which students can express their opinions, at times, it is very important to create a safe classroom climate. Students must feel safe with the teacher and with their peers. Teachers sometimes find it difficult to judge whether students feel safe enough. However, they note that students sometimes do not openly express their views. A history teacher said he noted that the discussions were much livelier outside the classroom, than in the classroom. One teacher, Cindy, said: "Yes, there are quite a lot of conflicting ideas, but that does not mean that they share them in class. They still often give more socially desirable answers to avoid discussions of it."

3.5   Teacher's Personal Opinion

We asked the teachers if, when dealing with controversial issues, they express their own opinions or try to remain neutral. In general, teachers indicated that they try to keep their own opinions private, as much as possible, when it comes to controversial issues. A number of teachers indicated that they themselves have no problem sharing their opinion, but that it is more important to allow different perspectives to emerge. When a teacher clearly expresses her/his opinion, this can hamper the goal to advance as many perspectives as possible. During a discussion on a controversial topic, teachers generally take a different role than in other lessons. The teachers try to give students a voice, and keep themselves more in the background. They take the role of moderator and ask critical questions. Yvonne said:

> I always try, if such an issue is discussed, to keep my own ideas in the background and ask as many questions as possible to students. It is my main concern that students learn to form an opinion and to dare to tell their own opinion.

Teachers are aware that students are easily influenced and that their opinion, as the teacher, is sometimes weighed differently than the opinion of the students' peers. To allow students the chance to form their own opinion, some teachers find that it is better not to share their opinion. One teacher, Cindy, said that, as a teacher, you can give your own opinion as long as you do not try to impose your view on the students. She emphasized how important it is to listen carefully to the views of students on controversial topics.

> The biggest mistake people make is when they are just in front of the class and tell how it is with these kinds of issues. Then all hell breaks loose, and you need 50 minutes to get quiet again and no one has learned anything. [...] If you listen carefully to students and not just say, 'You have a wrong opinion.' If you listen to what's under there, what motivations, why they cry or parrot those things, then you get much further.

3.6 Learning Goals When Teaching Controversial Topics

What are teachers' learning objectives when they deal with a controversial issue? Are these objectives different when engaging with other topics? In particular, teachers mentioned learning to think critically and learning to substantiate an opinion. When controversial issues arise, teachers often focus on the formation and support of a personal opinion. Ilse said:

> I want them to write down their own position, but also two other points of view. That they are really aware, that this is controversial. That is also the reason I first give some theoretical explanation before they get started with the discussion.

In general, teachers do not have the goal that students radically change their opinions, but they hope for more nuanced thinking on the topic. They hope that students will see that other opinions may be justifiable. In some cases, teachers want to address a controversial topic in order to foster a more engaged attitude and an open attitude toward others: they want their students to learn to be respectful of dissenters. Teachers hope that students can form an opinion, which is based on knowledge and good arguments, and that they learn to better support their opinions. Cindy said:

> I personally find it very important that when students leave school, they are ready for society and, in my experience, they are better prepared for life in society if they can deal with controversies. If they were able to form an opinion, whatever they may be. If they can make informed choices, can listen to another, but also stand up for themselves.

Teachers found it difficult to say whether the intended learning objectives are realized. Knowledge can be tested, in general, but teachers find it more difficult to test critical thinking. It is even more difficult to evaluate the opinions and attitudes of students. When it comes to critical thinking and reasoning skills, teachers are reasonably optimistic about what students learn. Teachers generally think that they cannot bring about major changes in the minds and attitudes of students. According to the teachers, many factors influence the development of students. Teachers feel that they contribute only a small piece to this development. Moreover, it is difficult to see the change. Teachers assess their pupils' knowledge, not their opinions on controversial topics. Cindy noted:

> I have the impression that students make contact with me. The openness with which I deal with the issues, but whether they will really make conscious choices [...] A few people I know, for sure, but the majority I do not know, I hope so.

Teachers find it difficult to determine exactly what students learn when dealing with controversial subjects. However, they did find that students talk very much about these kinds of issues. When a controversial issue is covered in the lesson, students are often more motivated and more interested than they usually are.

3.7 Controversial Issues in Teaching Methods

The textbooks and other teaching materials that teachers use do not pay much attention to controversial issues. These issues cannot be avoided in the methods, but they do not receive more attention than other issues. Teachers should decide for themselves what issues they discuss further. They also find that the textbook should remain neutral, as much as possible. Some teachers would find it useful if the textbooks would provide a little more attention than they currently provide. It is important that there be good material about a controversial issue, and it takes teachers a lot of time to develop it by themselves.

Teachers argue that they have limited time and resources – both with respect to the space in the curriculum and the time it takes to prepare lessons on controversial topics. Moreover, dealing with a controversial issue requires teachers' expertise. Yvonne said:

> In many topics, there are hidden controversies, but certainly in pre-university schools, the pressure is quite high to rapidly go through the curriculum and you do not always have time to reflect on the topic.

4   Conclusions

Teachers characterized controversial issues as those issues which touch the identity of the students and about which there are different views. The controversial aspect becomes apparent in classrooms, when some students have very different feelings about a topic than the teacher holds, or what is in the curriculum material. The teachers called various topics controversial. The topics mentioned most in biology were the theory of evolution, sexuality, topics related to life, like abortion and euthanasia, and issues related to sustainability and modification of food, like the bio-industry. In history, the controversial topics were the Israeli-Palestinian conflict, Geert Wilders and the PVV, and their anti-Islam expressions. Slavery and colonialism were not noted as controversial issues in the classroom. However, none of these topics were covered much in the formal curriculum.

The teachers stated that the composition of the class could turn a topic into a controversial one. Certain topics are more important to certain groups of students than to others. Controversies surrounding the theory of evolution, for example, are more evident in a Christian school comprised of many religious students than in non-religious schools. In schools with many Muslim students, topics involving Israel, America or Judaism are more likely to become controversial.

If teachers want to pay attention to a controversial topic, they usually provide space for discussion in class. The teachers indicated that it is important that the students are allowed to share their opinions. It is also important that students hear the opinions of their peers. Addressing a controversial topic takes time, and it is not always easy to plan or include such discussions in the classroom. It is important to create an open environment, in which students feel safe to freely give their opinions.

To let students deepen their views and become acquainted with other perspectives, it is important that students have the time to empathize with other perspectives. This requires much time and teacher expertise. There is generally no clear vision from the school leadership about how to deal with controversial issues. Moreover, the subject departments do not engage in dialogues about dealing with controversial subjects. The general picture is that if in the classroom a teacher deals with controversial issues, it is the responsibility of the individual teacher to handle the issue. The teacher decides for her/himself to what extent and in what way s/he pays attention to this.

5   Discussion and Recommendations

5.1   *The Societal Role of Education in Controversial Issues*

Education prepares students to be able to participate in current and future society. This means that students should acquire knowledge about how people in society think about various issues, including controversial issues. For the future societal orientation of the students, it is important that they become acquainted with different views and acquire the skills needed to substantiate their own opinions on such issues and develop a view on the future.

Educational policy should encourage more learning about controversial topics, and not only focus on the dominant view, but also focus on other perspectives. This is not to suggest that all knowledge and all perspectives are scientific to the same degree or equally accepted. The different perspectives should be presented in their societal relationship. This means, for example, that all Christian schools treat evolution as the most recognized scientific vision, and public schools should point out that, in strict Christian circles, "creationism" is seen as an explanation for the origin of life. The education policy should clearly convey that society would benefit from critical, informed and engaged citizens.

5.2   *Methods, Subjects and Controversial Topics*

Addressing controversial issues requires much preparation and expertise. Therefore, methods can support teachers in this endeavor. In biology, there is often a presentation of scientific knowledge, but a neglect of its cultural influences. In history, there is more attention for interpretation. Interpretations can differ, even if the 'official knowledge' neglects other interpretations. We believe that all subjects should pay attention to controversial issues.

An interesting question is whether it would be better to have multiple methods, each with its own 'color,' with its own perspective on a controversial topic. This would indicate the possibility of achieving greater diversity in education.

Education would then however, even more than now, support differences, rather than focusing on knowledge of the diversity in society and support appreciation of this diversity. We prefer education that shows the different perspectives and substantiates the social embedding of these perspectives. We are in favor of education that supports students becoming capable of making informed choices and, moreover, focuses on commonalities, and on contributing to the common good.

5.3 The School and Controversial Issues

In most schools, there is no clear policy regarding controversial issues and the teachers talked little about them. We would like to see more reflection on the practice in schools, and that the practice is based on the analysis of underlying moral and political frames. In particular, we would like to see diversity in perspectives offered and training of students in formulating and substantiating their own opinions. This reflection should lead to a more detailed and balanced support for the development of critical thinking of students. From our perspective, school, like society, is a diverse community of values, in which differences are visible, valued and seen as challenges for innovation. Many educational change initiatives are designed to hide differences, instead of learning how to deal with differences. Controversial issues are part of a vibrant and open society and education. 'Official knowledge' should be challenged.

5.4 The Teacher in the Classroom and Controversial Issues

The teacher must decide, often in a split second, whether and how the subject is handled. Many teachers find it important to involve controversial issues and perspectives of students in the classroom. Nevertheless, the teachers often reported in the interviews that they did not treat certain controversial topics as controversial. They only present the dominant view, or they go over the topic quickly and avoid the controversies. Handling a controversial topic is time-consuming and comes at the expense of addressing other topics. Some teachers do not find the conditions good enough to expose the controversy: they do not feel knowledgeable enough, or the composition of the student population does not support a safe learning environment. A good classroom climate is an important condition for discussing controversial issues. However, this is a paradox: classes that may need dialogues on controversial issues the most often have the most difficult conditions.

We would like to see more proactive behavior on the part of the teachers. Reactively responding to spontaneous utterances by students is difficult when students give unexpected reactions and when the teacher has not actually planned to pay attention to controversial issues. A proactive attitude can help address controversial issues in a sensible and thoughtful way. Both a proactive and a reactive approach to controversial issues require high teacher professionalism. Support from the department and school leadership and access to good examples and teaching materials can contribute to teachers' competence for dealing with controversial issues.

Many teachers place emphasis on studying different perspectives, and on forming reasoned judgment. This requires space for an inquiry-based approach and dialogue. Small classes and longer teaching periods could contribute to this. Moreover, a safe classroom environment is essential. The teachers are aware that they cannot entirely avoid controversial issues. Ignoring them completely would seriously hinder the students in their preparation for meaningful critical and social participation in democracy.

An interesting question is how do teachers handle their own values and their own views on controversial issues? Like any other citizen, the teacher expresses values and a vision. The educational role, of a teacher in a democracy, asks for the presentation of different perspectives, shows the societal context of these perspectives, and supports the students in arriving at their own judgments. However, the teacher is also an active participant in the process of signification. Moreover, the teacher is an expert in the substantive problem and in developing critical thinkers. The teacher should provide students with the space and opportunities for their own process of signification.

5.5   Students and Controversial Issues

The controversial issues enter the classroom through the methods of the teacher or through the students. The perspective of the learner must do justice to the voice of the learner and contribute to connecting the personal experience with the topic presented. The perspective of the learner must also contribute to the experience of being part of a vibrant community of values that are explored in dialogue with each other. Taking seriously the input of students also means that multiple perspectives are taken into consideration and that the teacher does not quickly present the dominant perspective, which obscures viewing other perspectives. Students should be given the space for reaching personal meaning and for having voice.

5.6   Controversies as Educational Conditions

Whether topics are considered crucial or not depends partly on the identity of the school and of the student population. The school's identity is particularly relevant in traditional Christian schools. The student population becomes relevant when there are students, in the classrooms, who hold religious fundamentalist ideas (mostly Christian or Muslim), or come from non-Western countries that were either former Dutch colonies or from the Middle East. However, in order to become a critical-democratic citizen, all students should learn to work with controversial issues.

The study clearly shows that discussing controversial issues, from different perspectives and with respect for diversity and pluralism, should be the normal practice in school. In line with Mouffe (2018), we argue for an agonistic classroom that takes controversies seriously and helps students work with them. In such a dynamic value community, there is a better chance that when topics become highly controversial, the dialogue can continue. The learning processes should not only be more dialogical, but also more reflective. This implies not only analyzing logical reasoning, but also analyzing the moral values that are at stake. Engaging in true critical thinking and moral reasoning means that there is reflection on the moral values that are used as criteria for reaching decisions on perspectives. Education for democratic intercultural citizenship should be reflective, dialogical and democratic.

References

Aloni, N. (2011). Humanistic education from theory to practice. In W. Veugelers (Ed.), *Education and humanism* (pp. 35–46). Sense Publishers.
Apple, M. (1979). *Ideology and curriculum*. Routledge.
Bourdieu, P., & Passeron, J. C. (1977). *La reproduction*. Les Editions de Minuit.
Freire, P. (1972). *Pedagogy of the oppressed*. Penguin.
Hansen, D. (2017). *Education and leadership in schools today*. In N. Aloni & L. Weintrob (Eds.), *Beyond bystanders* (pp. 19–32). Sense Publishers.
Hess, D. (2009). *Controversy in the classroom*. Routledge.
Hess, D., & McAvoy, P. (2015). *The political classroom*. Routledge.
Mouffe, C. (2005). *On the political*. Routledge.
Mouffe, C. (2018). *For a left populism*. Verso.
Oser, F. K. (1994). Moral perspectives on teaching. *Review of Research in Education, 20*, 57–127.
Parker, W. (2003). *Teaching democracy*. Teachers College.
Radstake, H., & Leeman, Y. (2010). Guiding discussions in the class about ethnic diversity. *Intercultural Education, 21*(6), 429–442.
Schuitema, J., Radstake, H., Van de Pol, J., & Veugelers, W. (2018). Guiding classroom discussions for democratic citizenship. *Educational Studies, 44*(4), 377–407.
Schuitema, J., & Veugelers, W. (2011). Multicultural contacts in education. *Educational Studies, 37*(1), 101–114.
Spring, J. (2004). *How educational ideologies are shaping global society*. Erlbaum.

Tirri, K. (1999). Teachers' perceptions of moral dilemmas at school. *Journal of Moral Education, 28*(1), 31–47.

Veugelers, W. (2000). Different ways of teaching values. *Educational Review, 5*(1), 37–46.

Veugelers, W. (2007). Creating critical democratic citizenship. *Compare, 37*(1), 361–373.

Veugelers, W. (2017). The moral in Paulo Freire's work: What moral education can learn from Paulo Freire. *Journal of Moral Education, 46*(4), 412–421.

Veugelers, W. (Ed.). (2019). *Education for democratic intercultural citizenship*. Brill Sense.

Veugelers, W. (2020a). How globalisation influences perspectives on citizenship education: From the social to the cultural and moral. *Compare*. doi:10.1080/03057925.2020.1716307

Veugelers, W. (2020b). Different views on global citizenship education. In D. Schugurensky & C. Wolhuter (Eds.), *Global citizenship education and teacher education* (pp. 20–39). Routledge.

Veugelers, W., de Groot, I., & Stolk, V. (2017). *Teaching common values in Europe*. European Parliament, Policy Department for Structural and Cohesion Politics.

Veugelers, W., Derriks, M., & de Kat, E. (2006). Education and major cultural incidents: 11 September and Dutch education. *Journal of Peace Education, 3*(2), 235–249.

CHAPTER 3

Towards Educating Teachers as Advocators

A Conceptual Discussion and a Historical Example

Jaime Grinberg

1   Introduction

This chapter argues that the cultural and political engagement of teachers, vis-à-vis the understanding that education is a human right and an act of socio-cultural and political transformation, is pertinent and needed. Teachers practice advocacy to favor their students' learning and well-being. As an advocator, a teacher acts and engages actively in altering dimensions of the communal and social structures that influence the lives of the students, teachers, and schools. These social, institutional, and organizational structures affect their own work and the lives of their students, inside and outside of the schools. Furthermore, if a teacher embraces such advocacy to advance social justice, then potentially s/he can contribute to altering the contextual arrangements that historically, socially, culturally, and, in particular, economically have operated in detriment of the living conditions and educational opportunities presented to disenfranchised groups.

In this discussion, a teacher advocator is one, who beyond their commitment to do a good job teaching, also has dispositions and critical propensities to articulate, conceptualize, create, and promote spaces and practices to change the conditions that have functioned to benefit some at the expense of others. The teacher does this by reclaiming, appropriating, sustaining, and advancing inherent human rights of equity, equality, and fairness through personal and educational relationships. This chapter proposes that teacher preparation is a place where dispositions, knowledge, and scrutinized experiences could help develop the practice of advocacy, which could be fostered and sustained by broad coalitions within and outside educational contexts.[1]

In this chapter, I first discuss conceptual constructions, as they are relevant for explaining the meaning of "teachers engaged in advocacy," or teachers as advocators. Then, I will use a historical example to provide a context that better portrays the roles and challenges in the preparation of teachers as advocates, from the particular progressive perspective and context of the US in the 1930s. This example represents a different historical moment and a particular form of engaging in advocacy that transforms the given social structures. The example is that of the Cooperative School for Student Teachers. I chose to present this historical case, since others in this volume present contemporary cases and examples. Furthermore, I suggest that this example is still relevant for contemporary teacher preparation programs that embrace, design, and structure experiences relevant for teachers to be advocators.

2 Towards Teachers as Advocators

When I started writing this chapter, we were not yet exposed to the global pandemic that affected our lives in ways we weren't expecting. I pondered, under these new circumstances, how to approach this writing, given that a new reality of how, at a global, as well as at a local level, we started to do "schooling," in general and, in particular, teaching. While reinventing oneself is not easy, most teachers have managed, somehow, to continue cultivating a love for learning: they have been investing themselves in doing good work, and caring about and advocating for their students and their families, all while having to adapt and adjust the ways they educate.

Perhaps one of the biggest challenges, besides that of personal tragedies, has been how to address significant inequities among the student populations, as well as among communities and their available allocated resources. Many students do not have high-speed internet, equipment necessary for online learning, or the space in their living quarters where they can focus and maintain some level of privacy. Furthermore, the students of parents with higher levels of formal education and with more social and cultural capital have been at an advantage, given the support to which they have access, while others do not.[2] Returning to school is exceptionally uneven and erratic, since health concerns are not only relevant to the students and their families, but also preponderant among teachers.

Nevertheless, teachers have been managing to stand up for what is right. Teachers organize and advocate for their students' needs, for their schools' needs, and for the type of policies that are reasonable under the extreme present circumstances. Teachers also advocate for themselves, for their instructional needs, for the materials, equipment, and resources required to do the best they can. They also advocate for their own safety and their rights as workers and as members of families and communities, to whom they have responsibilities and binding commitments.

While I have been generalizing in the above paragraphs, I am very aware that these divides existed before the pandemic and that these have been exacerbated by the present conditions. I am also very aware that in many parts of the world the conditions are so extreme that the divisions between public and private spheres have been further exacerbated by lack of access and the extreme differences between the haves and have nots, the affluent and the disenfranchised, the educated and the marginalized. In many cases, basic human needs must be satisfied before starting to think about online access, teaching strategies, or safe spaces and healthy habits in schools returning to some form of physical presence.

Given these conditions outlined above, and what I observed among teachers engaged in individual and collective strategies of resistance, advocacy, and service, I am convinced that teachers, who are advocators, are crucially important, now more than ever before. It is also the case because of what teachers, together with their organizations, unions, and partnerships with communities, universities, and other civil society institutions, have been doing as part of a tradition and ethos of the role of the teacher, in exercising agency to alter, and to transform injustices.[3] Such advocacy has to be named/identified by many, and discussed by many more. This will enable a polyphony and multiplicity of standpoints that include problematizing what has been taken-for-granted. We will ultimately ask: in favor of whom are we doing what we are doing? I may also ask: for what purposes? Under which conditions? Who benefits, and who does not? I contend that the preparation of teachers is a privileged space to start asking and answering these questions.

Therefore, agency, engagement, activism, and advocacy, within this particular standpoint, are in favor of creating inclusive, equitable, embracing, accepting, respectful, trustful, intellectually stimulating and demanding, curiosity nurturing, imaginative, hopeful, liberatory, celebratory, challenging, interrogating arguments, facts, evidence, and methods, in exploratory, student-centered, inquiry-oriented learning communities. These are also environments in which no form of discrimination is tolerated and in which there is an agenda to eradicate malicious, violent, and pernicious systems of beliefs and behaviors. These environments understand that legitimizing who the students are is crucial for the purposes of accepting, inviting, and embracing them, seeing their characteristics not as challenging factors, but rather as resources.

Advocators care about where they come from, who their families or caregivers are, who they worship, or if they do not worship, who they love, what they look like, what they can or cannot do, what they have or do not have, or what the pigmentation of their skins are. These differences, once again, are viewed as a resource and not as a disadvantage or a risk. Moreover, for inclusion and acceptance purposes, we acknowledge and validate who they are. Advocators do not label people based on what languages they speak, what their cultural backgrounds are, and/or how they do learning, because the purpose is to advance justice and opportunities, collective and individual, for all, in classrooms, in schools, as well as outside classrooms, in informal environments, in the community, and in the larger social, cultural, and political contexts. Designing learning environments and advocating inside and outside of the schools comprise cultural awareness and purposeful curricula that incorporates, understands, and celebrates such diversity. It means that everyone is welcome and accepted before setting any other conditions, and then it is about validating and building upon what is it that students bring to the experience.

Teachers can open or close possibilities; they can also reinforce and exacerbate conflicts. However, the type of teacher advocacy discussed here is one that can help to bridge and integrate differences, such as those that are derived from assumptions and misconceptions. Teachers can shape learning experiences, and make them meaningful, exciting, relevant, and inclusive. However, if they are not aware and reflective about the implications of the curriculum they implement, and the pedagogies they foster, they can teach that who the students are and what they bring with them, as cultural beings, are of no value. Hence, there are at least two tasks to address: (1) how teachers are prepared to advocate, including pedagogical and curricular dimensions, and (2) what curricula and programmatic intentionality can contribute to such advocacy.

In the above paragraphs, I have also utilized rhetorical signifiers, because they convey shared meanings within the cultural boundaries of located language and contingent knowledge. Nonetheless, the risk is that these signifiers, what marketing experts would often call "slogans," may become just that, "for the relevance is to be taken not merely as a fashionable slogan but as a serious educational doctrine," as the philosopher, Israel Scheffler, pondered (1969, p. 764). Fashionable slogans are also devoid of a deeper systematic and careful unpacking of their enactments in practice, as well as lacking a discursive critique. This is also so because, as Tom Popkewitz (1980) has warned, "a slogan can have different purposes, and that educators must consider the values that underlie the slogans and noble words that are used to describe pedagogical purpose" (p. 306). Furthermore, in a more contemporary commentary discussing campus policies and students' demands vis-a-vis controversial or unpopular political views, the author sends out alerts and warns about the danger of accepting slogans as complete truths, at the expense of developing the habits of argumentation (McWhorter, 2016).

Hence, teaching for social justice, teacher activism, teacher advocacy, and other common liberal and progressive slogans, risk remaining fashionable and superficial. I prefer to appropriate such statements/slogans and (1) conceptualize their meaning, and (2) problematize their enactments, not in order to dismiss or belittle their potential value, but rather to enable inquiry. As Maxine

Greene (1986, p. 68) has argued: "Because of the persistence of reassuring slogans ... the intentional dimension is overlooked, along with many possible ways of thinking about the teaching act." Thus, there is the demand to maintain vigilance over how a discourse-practice might undermine the very same assumed nobility of the purpose, since many readings of the same practice and/or of the same statements are possible (Cherryholmes, 1992).

2.1   What Is Teacher Advocacy?

As the primary institution with the opportunity and ability to reach a significant sector of the population at a formative stage of life, public schools, in general, and particularly in the case of the US, have been in a unique position to play a central role in educating to value living in a democracy. Furthermore, schools have the opportunity to advance collective civil rights and social justice. An enduring pattern has been the role of the public school teacher as an advocator, having the responsibility not only to teach content to students, but also to teach the development of community and character, regardless of the subject matter or grade level they teach. While not all teachers engage in actively advancing agendas that embrace democracy and social justice at the core, often, the very same role of teaching potentially provides for social justice practices. For example, teachers engage in providing opportunities to students, who have not had them before. Teachers investigate, and can eradicate in their classrooms, practices that have perpetuated discrimination, such as tracking and ability grouping, ableism, sexism, or racism to name a few. They can unmask the hidden curriculum of school norms and routines that tend to docilize minds and bodies, and they can provide space for multiple voices and experiences of students to become legitimate and valid. Furthermore, teachers can present alternative perspectives, including historical accounts or literary and artistic work, while nurturing curiosity and fostering dialogical and inquiry-based practices that can enable students to problematize and imagine alternative conditions and solutions, including the specific subject matter they are teaching. The historical example provided in this chapter also helps to illustrate how such advocacy, inside and outside of the classroom, could take place.

I conceptualize such engagement as "advocacy"; hence in this chapter, I focus on teachers as advocators and teaching as a form of advocacy, because teachers can open or close possibilities, can reinforce and exacerbate conflicts, or can bridge and integrate differences. Teachers can shape the learning experiences, and make them meaningful and exciting, liberatory, and mighty in defiance of institutional hegemonies.[4]

Because schools are in the position of reaching the population during formative years, as mentioned above, teachers' work, and the curricula they create, could serve as hegemonizing factors. Furthermore, teachers could serve as instruments of such agendas without realizing it, which would change their advocacy from having a transformative role to a reproductive role. However, as many scholars have argued (Freire, Greene, and Giroux, among others), common practices of reproduction that foster otherness, that construct who the students are and what they bring to the classroom, from the personal dimensions of their lives, is irrelevant and valueless to school.[5] Hence, a problematic paradox emerges in which success depends on students abandoning who they are. They must abandon their heritages, languages, behaviors, values, cultural norms, and ways of knowing, in order to conform to the "normal," or at least to "pass" as normal. This is what Joel Spring (1998) called deculturalization.[6]

In this context, I appropriate the practice of teacher advocators as one that advances social justice. Social justice is an elusive concept and practice, which could mean multiple things to multiple people. However, grounded in the perspective of teacher advocator presented here, social justice means the exercise of teachers engaged in altering the contextual arrangements that historically, socially, culturally, and economically have operated to limit living conditions and educational opportunities for disenfranchised students. This is accomplished by actively reclaiming, sustaining and advancing equity, equality, and fairness through personal and educational relationships, and particularly through progressive teaching (Grinberg & Goldfarb, 2015).

Such advocacy can promote a different curriculum and a different set of pedagogical practices, in which diverse voices are validated and legitimized. It has to be dialogical and critical.[7] This is dialogical and critical engagement that reflects what Bakhtin (1984) called "polyphony," the notion of many simultaneous independent voices, many truths. This is necessary, because if we do not consider the possibilities that Maxine Greene invited us to explore, the potential multiplicity of standpoints, we would preserve the superficiality of the politically correct practice, risking that the advocacy teaching would become dogmatic, thus replacing one regime of truth of hegemony, in a Gramscian sense, by another regime of truth. Such replacement could constitute the illusion of a liberatory pedagogy that, too, becomes a totalizing and restrictive oppressive alternative.[8]

In what follows, I provide a historical example to illustrate the conceptual approach to what a teacher could be vis-à-vis a progressive, student-centered, and social justice-oriented practice, in and out of schools.[9] This example is not a comprehensive explanation of what the institution was, or of the whole range of activities and curricular approaches they used in the preparation of teachers. It is rather a snapshot aiming to illustrate and to awake the imagination.[10] I selected this historical example not only because I have researched it extensively, but also because of the relevancy for contemporary possibilities.

3. A Historical Example: The Cooperative School for Student Teachers

The Cooperative School for Student Teachers (CST) was a teacher education program developed in partnership with progressive schools of the time (1930s). This institution evolved into what nowadays is known as Bank Street College of Education, one of the premier and most influential educational places in the United States. The need for progressive teachers was the result of dissatisfaction with how teachers were prepared by the normal schools of the time. The first years of the program focused on preparing teachers of young children, including elementary school years. They were located in New York City, in what was, at the time, a mixed neighborhood, populated by many tenements with immigrants and poor working-class families, as well as many artists and others who could not afford better, sanitized and more resourceful accommodations (Grinberg, 2002, 2005).

The partnership wanted to educate teachers who would be transformative, student-centered, committed to the communities, where the schools in which they would teach were located, and who would understand education as more than provision of opportunities to learn the subject matter (Grinberg & Goldfarb, 2015). As one of the most influential leaders, Barbara Biber, summarized advocacy, "We were in education because we thought there was a way to make a better world" (Grinberg & Goldfarb, 2015, p. 51). In a more punctual statement, another faculty member wrote:

> How much of an influence we can be unless we ourselves feel strongly enough about a new society to be willing to take part in building it. Isn't this influence an important factor in the learning process? Will we develop social attitudes in students unless we ourselves have a philosophy strong enough to be doing something about the condition of the world? (Eleanor Bowman, cited in Grinberg & Goldfarb, 2015, p. 53)

Such a call for action denotes a disposition in which the teachers of teachers are to model engagement and advocacy. Students also believed in such commitments, as expressed in the following quote:

> We believe that a teachers' job is not only in the classroom. That while a teacher's primary responsibility is to help children grow and develop to the best of their potentialities, she (sic) has a responsibility also for the kind of world these children are growing up in. She (sic) cannot ignore the influences outside the classroom that are shaping children's lives. ... This year we are continuing our effort for a low-income housing project.

> We are working with Greenwich House on their health program. We are cooperating with a public school in their after-school recreation activities and we are running a Saturday Playgroup for neighborhood children. (cited in Grinberg, 2005, p. 33)

This note provides an illustration of how the system of dispositions and the system of action were amalgamated. These future teachers committed to influence the social and physical environment of the children in the neighborhood, where they were studying and who eventually could be their own students. It is a disposition to actively engage and not to be passive or accepting of objective realities. In other words, they believed in advocating by doing something about what they understood to be incorrect or about what they perceived was a need.

The curriculum also involved dimensions of learning to teach, related to an exploration of the self, as well as the world (the context). Learning to teach incorporated self-exploration and introspection, hence providing rich personal experiences.

> You hoped that you could help the students see how they as people were relating to this profession. What in their background really led them to it, what in their background supported it, where their greatest satisfactions were, where there were problems that could be worked out? (Biber, cited in Grinberg & Goldfarb, 2015, p. 56)

Furthermore, the students in the program attended a weekly meeting, called the "advisory" class. Here they reflected about their experiences practicing in schools, how they felt about these experiences, their own social perceptions, and how they were constructing themselves, as teachers, who were concerned with social justice.

Learning about the world meant that prospective teachers engage in social, community, and political activities outside the school for the improvement of social conditions that affect the lives of the children. This learning included educating themselves about events in the city, country, and world. This was important since the decade of the 1930s not only exacerbated poverty and savage differences between poor and rich, anchored in the economic crash in the United States, but was also characterized by the frightening growth of totalitarianism and fascism, particularly in Europe, but also, to some extent, in the US. This context provided a deep concern with democracy and social justice among Progressives, in general, and, in particular, for educational purposes, as these cannot be divorced from their context, since teaching, alone, might not be enough to address these conditions.[11] Hence, learning about the world was related to all other aspects of learning to teach. As the brief description of the class on Environment below presents, the teachers were also engaged in advocacy.

Dewey's conceptual proposals about teaching were adapted to the particular contexts of the student teachers' own classrooms, during their student-teaching activities. Furthermore, they also embraced Dewey's conception of the relationship between classroom experience and learning – to live in a democratic community, by looking at the classroom as a primary source of such learning through experiencing it.

> When the school introduces and trains each child of society into membership within such a little community, saturating him with the spirit of service, and providing him with the instruments of effective self-direction, we shall have the deepest and best guarantee of a larger society which is worthy, lovely, and harmonious. (Dewey, 1915, p. 29)

The service aspect that Dewey mentions also hints at the commitment for advocacy, which is not only to be modeled by the teacher, but also to be experienced by the student. In what follows, I will briefly describe one influential class taught by the main person behind this whole idea, Lucy Sprague Mitchell.

3.1   The Example of the Class on Environment

The "Environment," served as a course that did much to promote learning to teach the social context (Grinberg, 2002). The course focused on learning the local and larger systems, in which communities were immersed, vis-à-vis social, geographical, and economic characteristics. It was used also for learning to teach social studies, and for learning first-hand about social issues and ways of advocating in favor of these who were voiceless and dispossessed (Grinberg, 2002).

During the first part of the course, each student investigated, observed, conducted interviews, and used other sources of information, like statistics, articles and magazines, to study the local context. They collected data about food, housing, everyday routines of people, businesses, institutions, and life conditions. These experiences enabled the making of conceptual connections about social and material relationships in the community and the influences on the school setting. By the end of this fieldwork, students organized into study groups and concentrated on a contemporary social issue for the community. Study groups analyzed the data collected about the historical, geographical, cultural-ethnic, and economic backgrounds of a local community (Grinberg, 2002). Then, they focused on how to use this knowledge for teaching children: "On the trips around New York, apparently, we were also thinking about children's trips; what they would see" (Tarnay, cited in Grinberg & Goldfarb, 2015, p. 54).

Toward the end of the year, there was a field trip to the "coal areas" of Pennsylvania and West Virginia, and to Washington DC. Students learned about geology and animal life, about social conditions, workers' unionization, government, and about teaching implications. After exploring the mining and rural areas, they went to the nations' capital to understand better the social policy and its implications for education. Because of the personal relationship between Sprague Mitchell and Eleanor Roosevelt, it was possible to have Roosevelt as a guide (Antler, 1987).

Becoming aware, evaluating, analyzing, and thinking about how to build the connection for teaching is what made this a learning experience:

> Our final was a question which we had to answer ... "Can human nature be changed?" ... committees had to look at different aspects of this; for example, some were looking at the biological and some were looking at it from the point of view of psychology, some politically, and some sociologically ... each committee reported on what it had uncovered. And at the end of the whole thing there was a resounding "yes!" – complete agreement. (Cohen, cited in Grinberg & Goldfarb, 2015, p. 55)

Their conceptualization was that teachers should be grounded in the understanding of social contexts and that they engage in social advocacy, as part of their roles as future teachers. They not only would advocate through a curriculum that would be relevant and connected to the diverse and different students they would teach, but also they learned how to advocate for what they thought was needed and right, using their own cultural and social capital, vis-a-vis the political institutions that had the structural power to address such needs. This was applied once they were back in the city: "We got all involved in the whole issue of unions and unionization and social justice and we went around with social workers to see what it was like to live in tenements" (Kerlin, cited in Grinberg & Goldfarb, 2015, p. 55).

3.2 What Can We Learn from This Historical Example?

The CST program was designed so that these future teachers would be advocators for social justice in their teaching and would advance social justice agendas outside of the classroom.

> For this to happen they had to have knowledge and understanding of the influences of the immediate contexts, the interconnection of those primary social institutions and the influences generated by such relationships, and the impact of larger socially constructed structures, such as

workplace and values in understanding and teaching the whole child. (Grinberg & Goldfarb, 2015, p. 58)

Classes such as "Advisory" or the "Environment" are examples of learning experiences that could serve as blueprints for contemporary programs committed to address the understanding of contexts – be they local, societal, personal, and/or public. This pioneering program presented a model of preparing teacher advocators for contexts that were different from their own personal experiences and provided them with skills to bridge the micro context of the classroom to broader social inequities and challenges. This was done through personal and educational relationships, including learning to develop student and community centered practices, hands-on and minds-on, inquiry-oriented pedagogies, dialogical and intellectually challenging activities, such as in the experiences they had in their coursework. Such experiences fostered acceptance of differences (cultural, linguistic, social, and ideological). Furthermore, as exemplified in their trip experiences, the student teachers also engaged in building coalitions with leadership, community activists, and local and national organizations to advocate and bring about change of unjust conditions.

Given these experiences, I maintain that CST students applied their learning in terms of practicing social justice by fostering advocacy that facilitated and created sanctuaries by working "with" the learning communities and not "on" the communities, as well as creating a safe (trusting) environment engaged in active participation in the particular place and space where the educator practiced. Furthermore, students of teaching, in this framework of advocacy, experienced and practiced how to investigate and how to problematize[12] what to teach, how to teach, who should be taught what, by whom, where, when, how, under which conditions, and for what purposes. They learned and practiced how to be advocators that affect change, how and with whom to build solidarity and coalitions, and, ultimately, they repeatedly reflected on whom they were educating. Perhaps equally relevant is the experience of self-interrogation/exploration, which could be a highly relevant dimension of learning to teach, to advocate effectively, by engaging in transformative practices, from a pedagogical and social standpoint. Moreover, they investigated their own purposes and their relationships with students and others, as well as their own pedagogical practices and the relevancy of what and how they were learning to teach.

4   Conclusions

I have argued that teachers can and should be advocators. An advocator not only engages in advocacy and activism, but also engages in affecting change through a number of practices inside and outside of the classroom and the school. I have also argued that to be an advocator, a teacher needs to be prepared to adopt this role. This means that the lived experiences of a future teacher during her/his teacher education time, incorporate practices in which the teachers unpack, analyze, investigate, problematize, relate, and reflect about their own learning and participation, including their propensities and dispositions. These experiences are also crafted to engage the future teachers in understanding what and how students make sense and learn, particularly because many of these future teachers never experienced this type of learning themselves, when they were school pupils.

Furthermore, by providing the historical example of the CST, I contended that this was a relevant approach for educating advocators and an invitation to think and adapt how teacher advocators can be prepared nowadays. Such preparation should be purposeful, designed to provide experiences, skills, and strategies to become advocators in favor of their students, their schools, the community at large, as well as larger social issues. They should also certainly become advocators for themselves. Such an approach not only enables deeper and meaningful learning by fostering student-centered, inquiry-oriented, intellectually and socially engaging pedagogies, in a learning community that celebrates its own diversity, as well as includes and accepts all students, regardless of their differences, but also advances and implements social justice.

In this chapter, I proposed conceptualizing teachers as advocators, who are knowledgeable about content knowledge, who foster integrated learning communities, who foster and experience democracy, as a relational culture, and who relate, in meaningful, respectful and trustworthy ways, to others. I also suggested that teacher are advocators, who know how to participate and exercise individual and collective agency, who are willing to resolve conflict, to negotiate, to build consensus when relevant, and to listen and communicate eloquently. Such practices aim to advance individual and collective civil rights, to eradicate agendas that favor sectarian interests that deny the public good, and to encourage the solidification of shared set values, norms, rules, and rights, considering the contingency of place, time, and ideologies. Hence, investigation and problematization of the teachers-advocators' own contexts, practices and discourses are necessary, as well, for advocators risk promoting fashionable slogans, leaving empty the deeper analysis of their meaning, some of which could work against the very purpose of their positionalities and advocacy. I also conclude by proposing that the pedagogy enacted by teacher advocators is neither liberatory nor oppressive by virtue of declaration, it is contingent on the enactment of such practice in a particular context that determines its value.

Notes

1 For instance, Picower (2012) and Valdez et al. (2018) report that activist teachers, whom I see as advocators, focus on coalition building with other social movements. They create support systems for educators in order to develop solidarity, strategies and engage in a healing process vis-à-vis national policies and educational reform efforts that are detrimental to students, teachers, and communities, from a progressive standpoint. For example, Teacher Activist Groups (TAG) is a national coalition of grassroots organizing groups that engage in shared political education and action, while Social Justice Educators of Color aims at advancing healing, empowerment, love, liberation, and action. Other organizations include: the Institute for Teachers of Color Committed to Racial Justice (ITOC), The Newark Teachers Project, or The Education for Liberation Network, which is a coalition that includes community activists, youth, parents, researchers, and teachers, who believe a good education should teach people – particularly low-income youth and youth of color – how to understand and challenge the injustices their communities face. However, "Although more educators are turning to teacher activist groups as a strategy to create liberatory educational environments and to fight increased inequality and oppression, how teacher activism advances work in these two areas remains unclear" (Picower, 2012, p. 561).

2 "Cultural capital" refers to cultural "instruments for the appropriation of symbolic wealth socially designated as worthy of being sought and possessed" (Bourdieu, 1977, p. 488). "Social capital" refers to the intangible resources embedded within interpersonal relationships or social institutions. Coleman (1988) argued that the educational expectation, norms, and obligations that exist within a family or a community are important social capital that can influence the level of parental involvement and investment, which, in turn, affect academic success.

3 In social settings, such as schools, agency is defined as the "person's ability to shape and control their own lives, freeing self from the oppression of power" (Kincheloe, 2004, p. 42).

4 I explain hegemony here as grounded in the classic work of Italian thinker, Antonio Gramsci (1971). This is the process of using dominant power to maintain privilege. It is important to note that, in modern times, in general, "power" is not always imposed by physical means, but by complex psychological processes (developing "common sense" and "normality"). It influences public opinion to gain consensus about taken-for-granted routines, habits, norms, and common sense, through cultural institutions, including media and schools. Gramsci further argues that the point of view of those in power becomes common sense and, thus, dominated groups and social classes accept their economic conditions and social positions as natural and unchangeable.

5 The dominant language of schooling that most leaders adopted in the 19th and early 20th Centuries in the USA has described minorities, working class, poor families, and also immigrants, with labels that indicate inferiority, savagery, deprivation, and difference. Presently, we are experiencing similar patterns. This is a common way of constructing the "other," that is, as different from what is established as normal, desired, and dominant, something that challenges homogeneity and that is undesired, unwanted. In turn, in a circular way, it redefines "normal" as different from the "other." The struggle and challenge have been about inclusion and access of the "other" to the same opportunities, and expectations for high quality of education as the rest of the population – not different, not less (Grinberg, 2009a).

6 It is the destruction of the culture of a dominated group and its replacement by the culture of the dominating group. Methods of deculturalization in education include forceful replacing of language, implementation of the superior culture's curriculum in schools, instructors are

from the dominant group, avoidance of the dominated group's culture in curriculum, and oftentimes includes geographical segregation. In short, it is the process by which an ethnic group is forced to abandon its language and culture.
7   Dialogical in this context means a purposeful interaction that involves empathy, caring, and active listening among all participants of a conversation. Critical means the process of unpacking how institutional and organizational power arrangements, also manifested through practices in their daily routines, operate often in favor of few and in detriment of many –hence developing hegemony as discussed above.
8   A regime of truth, according to Foucault (1980), is as a system of ordered procedures for the production, regulation, distribution, circulation, and operation of statements. Truth is linked in a circular relation with systems of power, which produce and sustain it, and to effects of power which it induces, and which extend it (Anderson & Grinberg, 1998, p. 133).
9   Progressive teaching in this particular context refers to what Antler (1987) explained: "During the Depression, the search for a redefinition of the relationship between individuals and society brought fresh support to progressive educators who believed that the classroom could become the model for a new collectivism, integrating self-expression with larger social goals" (p. 307).
10 For a more comprehensive understanding of the relevancy and influence of this program, including dimensions of practice and curricula, see Grinberg (2002, 2005); and Grinberg and Goldfarb (2015).
11 Westbrook (1991) explains that John Dewey, the prominent progressive philosopher and educator of the time, viewed a community centered social agenda as a crucial element for sustaining democratic life since formal education alone might not be enough: "By the eve of World Word I, Dewey was more fully aware that the democratic reconstruction of American society he envisioned could not take place simply by a revolution in the classroom, that, indeed, the revolution in the classroom could not take place until the society's adults had been won over to radical democracy" (p. 192).
12 "Problematization" serves as an intellectual tool that enables ways of looking at situations, experiences, information, and arguments by unveiling and by challenging underlying assumptions, revising ideas and thinking of different possible ways of analyzing, explaining, and interpreting. It incorporates developing the habit of interrogating what has been taken for granted, to ask questions that were or were not asked before. Furthermore, there has to be a dimension of discomfort, of confusion, of uncertainty about what is known and the unknown. There needs to be a daring to ask and a daring to search for more than common sense, in order to understand the limitations of our own knowledge and the hidden ways by which power operates and in service of whom, under which conditions and for what purposes (Grinberg, 2009b). Interrogation can be summarized by the following statement: "to question over and over again what is postulated as self-evident, to disturb people's mental habits, the way they do and think things, to dissipate what is familiar and accepted, to reexamine rules and institutions" (Foucault, 1980, p. 26).

References

Anderson, G., & Grinberg, J. (1998). Educational administration as disciplinary practice: Appropriating Foucault's view of power, discourse, and method. *Educational Administration Quarterly, 34*, 329–353.

Bakhtin, M. M. (1984). *Problems of Dostoevsky's poetics* (Vol. 8). University of Minnesota Press.

Bourdieu, P. (1977). Cultural reproduction and social reproduction. In J. Karabel & A. Halsey (Eds.), *Power and ideology in education* (pp. 487–511). Oxford University Press.

Cherryholmes, C. (1988). *Power and criticism: Post-structural investigations in education.* Teachers College Press.

Coleman, J. (1988). Social capital in the creation of human capital. *American Journal of Sociology, 94,* 95–120.

Dewey, J. (1915). *The school and society* (2nd ed.). University of Chicago Press.

Foucault, M. (1980). *Power/knowledge: Selected interviews and other writings by Michel Foucault, 1972–1977.* Pantheon.

Goldfarb, K., & Grinberg, J. (2002). Leadership for social justice: Authentic participation in the case of a community center in Caracas, Venezuela. *Journal of School Leadership, 12,* 157–173.

Gramsci, A. (1971). *Selections from the prison notebooks.* International Publishers.

Greene, M. (1986). Reflection and passion in teaching. *Journal of Curriculum and Supervision, 2*(1), 68–81.

Grinberg, J. (2002). "I had never been exposed to teaching like that": Progressive teacher education at Bank Street during the 1930's. *Teachers College Record, 104*(7), 1422–1460.

Grinberg, J. (2005). *Teaching like that: The beginnings of teacher education at Bank Street.* Peter Lang Publishing.

Grinberg, J. (2009a). The foundations of a public-school system. In J. Price & J. Grinberg (Eds.), *A brief history of American schools: Selected documents* (p. 9). Kendall-Hunt.

Grinberg, J. (2009b). Critical pedagogy and teacher education: Some notes on problematization. In T. Lewis, J. Grinberg, & M. Laverty (Eds.), *Philosophy of education: Modern and contemporary ideas at play* (pp. 818–821). Kendall & Hunt.

Grinberg, J., & Goldfarb, K. (2015). Learning to teach for social justice: Context and progressivism at Bank Street in the 1930s. *Journal of Education and Human Development, 4*(2), 50–59.

Kincheloe, J. (2004). *Critical pedagogy: A premier.* Peter Lang Publishing.

McWhorter, J. (2016). When slogans replace arguments. *Chronicle of Higher Education, 62*(32), 10–12.

Picower, B. (2012). Teacher activism: Enacting a vision for social justice. *Equity & Excellence in Education, 45*(4), 561–574.

Popkewitz, T. (1980). Global education as a slogan system. *Curriculum Inquiry, 10*(3), 303–316.

Scheffler, I. (1969). Reflections on educational relevance. *The Journal of Philosophy, 66*(21), 764–733.

Spring, J. (1994). *Deculturalization and the struggle for equality: A brief history of the education of dominated cultures in the United States.* McGraw-Hill.

Valdez, C., Curammeng, E., Pour-Khordish, F., Kholi, R., Nikundiwe, T., Picower, B., Shallabi, C., & Stovall, D. (2018). We are victorious: Educator activism as shared struggle for human being. *The Educational Forum, 82,* 244–258.

Westbrook, R. B. (1991). *John Dewey and American democracy.* Cornell University Press.

CHAPTER 4

Democratic Citizenship Education as an Activist Pedagogy

Towards the Cultivation of Democratic Justice on the African Continent

Yusef Waghid

1   Introduction

Literature on democratic citizenship education abounds. Any humanely and democratically inspired form of activist pedagogical action has to involve two interrelated processes. Firstly, there is the cultivation of democratic citizenship education and secondly, there is attuning one's pedagogical actions toward the enhancement of democratic justice. In this chapter, I identify pertinent meanings that underscore the cultivation of democratic citizenship education and then argue as to why and how such meanings can engender an activist pedagogy. In my view, autonomous action, deliberative iterations, and a reflexive openness toward that which is in becoming can most appropriately be considered important pedagogical actions that can enhance pedagogical activism.

In relation to my work on African philosophy of education, I make a case for activist pedagogy vis-à-vis the aforementioned meanings of democratic citizenship education and show how democratic justice can be enacted on the African continent. If one considers that societal malaises are very prevalent on the continent, in particular, dystopias, such as human rights violations and injustices, more specifically human trafficking, pseudo-political hegemonies, and ongoing ethnic conflicts, it makes sense to argue for a defensible form of democratic citizenship education as a way in which activist pedagogy can be developed. In this way, hopefully, one can make a claim to justify an African philosophy of education underscored by the enactment of democratic citizenship education.

Much has been written about democratic citizenship education concerning the seminal thoughts of Eamonn Callan (1997), Nancy Sherman (1997), Iris Marion Young (2000), Martha Nussbaum (2001), Amy Gutmann (2003), and Seyla Benhabib (2006). I have engaged with most of the theoretical ideas of the aforementioned scholars, in particular how one can educate for democratic citizenship. This chapter builds on some of the seminal thoughts of these scholars and offers an understanding of African philosophy of education as a way to enact an activist pedagogy in online university classrooms. My previous work on democratic citizenship education connects with notions of autonomy (freedom), dialogical action, and responsibility (Waghid, 2010). This chapter extends the arguments proffered in and about democratic citizenship education vis-à-vis an African philosophy of education, while specifically focusing on activist pedagogy in university education in South Africa. This brings me to an analysis of meanings pertaining to democratic citizenship education.

2   Re-examining Meanings of Democratic Citizenship Education

In this chapter, I envisage education to be constituted by human encounters. Put differently, education is the basis upon which people engage with themselves, one another, and with their environments. As a result, what is formed is an encounter in which human beings play a significant role.

Such a view of education, in which people engage in encounters, emanates from the Aristotelian perspective that educated citizens participate in civic life (Aristotle, 1995). The emphasis that Aristotle places on participation in civic life relates to what connects human encounters with democracy and citizenship. Both democracy and citizenship involve practices that relate to the public or civic sphere. In liberal communities, human beings cannot be said to engage in public or civic life if their actions are not attuned to democracy and citizenship.

Seyla Benhabib (1996, p. 68) offers a view of democratic participation in civic life based on "free and unconstrained public deliberation." According to such a view of democratic participation, people engage with one another through free and reasoned deliberation as moral and political equals (Benhabib, 1996, p. 68). In other words, when people engage in deliberative action, their participation is governed by norms of equality and symmetry. In this way:

> all have the same chances to initiate speech acts, to question, to interrogate, and to open debate ... [and] all have the right to question the assigned topics of conversation; and ... all the right to initiate reflexive arguments about the rules of the discourse .... (Benhabib, 1996, p. 70)

My emphasis on such a view of democratic deliberation is that when human beings engage in encounters, they articulate views that they can justify to others. Moreover, when they are challenged, or provoked, to think differently, they reconsider and reflexively re-examine their views to come up with more plausible perspectives.

In this way, Benhabib (1996, p. 76) posits that participant in a deliberative discourse focus on "noncoercive and nonfinal processes of opinion formation in an unrestricted public sphere." Put differently, their deliberative democratic education is based on engagement and critical reflection without silencing dissent and curtailing minority viewpoints (Benhabib, 1996, p. 77). Similarly, when people engage in deliberative encounters, their actions are not subjected to the tyranny of the majority. This suggests that, in such encounters, the basic rights and liberties of participants are protected, since all who participate in such encounters are deserving of autonomy (Benhabib, 1996, p. 78). That is, people's citizenship is secured, since as individuals, they are entitled to certain moral rights (Benhabib, 1996, p. 78).

Therefore, any form of discursive democratic citizenship education practice ought to be premised on two assumptions. Firstly, when individuals, who are engaged in such an educational encounter, articulate their claims and, perhaps experience controversy in this encounter, they (individuals) exercise their right to respond to criticisms and dissenting claims. Secondly, all individuals engaged in such encounters have the moral responsibility to protect one another's autonomy, so that the expression of arguments can remain subjected to reflexive judgements and free public deliberation, without unduly dismissing the claims of one another. The point I am making is that democratic citizenship education aims to ensure public deliberation and the enactment of human beings' moral autonomy, whereby their basic rights and civil liberties are sufficiently protected.

I now turn to an examination of how such a deliberative democratic citizenship education discourse is commensurate with the notion of an African philosophy of education.

3 Cultivating African Philosophy of Education in Relation to Democratic Citizenship Education: A Move toward Educational Activism

African philosophy of education, like Anglo-Saxon, Muslim and Jewish philosophies of education, is a particular philosophy of education related to human actions on the African continent and about African peoples both living on the continent or in the diaspora. Simply put, African philosophy of education is uniquely African because of the African-relatedness of the philosophy of education. Therefore, the question is, what constitutes African philosophy of education? Elsewhere, I have argued that the philosophy of education elucidates what the nature of education is pertaining to Africa (Waghid, Waghid, & Waghid, 2018, p. 86). More specifically,

> [c]onsidering that African philosophy of education aims to examine and resolve problems on the continent on the basis of an unconstrained deliberation among a community of thinkers, a philosophy of education envisages to identify and respond to problems on the continent with the aim of liberating societies from inhumanity, autocracy and irrational belief systems.

Firstly, identifying problems pertaining to the African continent is what makes such a philosophy of education a human activity aimed at doing something transformative. Secondly, problems are identified and a community of thinkers embarks on unconstrained deliberative action to find ways to respond to the problems. Thirdly, and most poignantly, doing African philosophy of education involves getting to know how to liberate human practices from what is inhumane, autocratic and irrational. Conceiving of African philosophy of education as geared toward liberating human practices from inhumanity, autocracy, and irrationality, one can argue that such a philosophy of education has an emancipatory potential to free African societies from inhumanity, autocracy and irrationality.

If an African philosophy of education were to undermine inhumanity, it would draw our attention to what is humane, and this is what African philosophy of education seemingly does. Human beings use their collective humanity to take decisions that are of interest to the broader community of Africans. The basis of anything African, philosophical and educational, is that people recognize one another as fellow humans, whose humanity should be enhanced by strengthening mutuality and respect for one another, as persons. Any attempt to relate to others as less than human invariably gives rise to attitudes of intolerance and dismissiveness – human actions that work against any form of humanity.

It is in this regard that we agree with Stanley Cavell (1979), who averred that a person first acknowledges herself as a person, based on whether she recognizes others, from their points of view (Cavell, 1979, p. 441). In other words, human beings bear an internal relation to all other human beings, based on their common humanity. Thus, doing African philosophy of education is inextricably linked to the notion that all others, as human beings, deserve to be honored and respected morally, as persons.

Furthermore, by holding such a perspective, one becomes responsible for what happens to them (Cavell, 1979, p. 438). If one acts inhumanely toward others, then one has failed to enact one's role as a human being toward another human being (Cavell, 1979, p. 438). Therefore, the first aspect of doing African philosophy of education is to treat and consider all other human beings as human beings, who deserve to be respected morally.

An African philosophy of education that opposes autocracy does so because it sees the point of resolving matters communally, and by implication, deliberatively. The African practice of engaging in a "Bantaba" – a Gambian word that means sitting under a tree and deliberating with others – refers to deliberations that occur among Africa's people in the confines of a hut or sheltered space. The height of the actual sheltered space, in which the "Bantaba" happens, is relatively low in the sense that it deters people from abruptly standing up, for fear of knocking their heads against the ceiling. This serves as a reminder to participants in the "Bantaba" to constrain their anger and continue with deliberations, irrespective of how unsettling such deliberations might be. As long as deliberations occur, there is always the possibility for participants to find some sort of compromise, regardless of how provocative the deliberative encounters might turn out to be.

Considering that collective decision-making and political agreement constituted the political-social activities of traditional African societies, it can only be concluded that the notion of a "Bantaba" symbolizes a physical and metaphoric space, in which communal and deliberative human practices were already very pervasive in African communities. Moreover, it can be inferred that for traditional African communities, engaging in a "Bantaba" implies that communal and deliberative engagement ought to guide their human encounters. When Africans engage communally, they recognize one another's presence and, thus, alter the conversations. Moreover, when they do so deliberatively, they are persuaded by one another's justifications, without resorting to antagonism and unwelcomed hostility.

What is significant about the African "Bantaba" is the premise that deliberative human encounters ought to be enacted through the virtues of respect, caring and trust among people, without dismissing and excluding participants from the encounters (Waghid, 2014). The point is that for Africans, relations of respect, care and trust are exercised as they endeavor, both communally and deliberatively, to resolve societal matters. Africans, who are engaged in "Bantaba," trust one another because they do not hesitate to make mistakes in proffering their judgements about societal matters. When people endeavor to proffer judgements, without being constrained by the possibility that they can make mistakes, they are more inclined to take risks because the possibility of error of judgment does not deter them. In this way, their communal and deliberative encounters are enhanced by the willingness to take risks when pursuing matters of public concern. In other words, people engaged in "Bantaba" do so cordially and communally, as well as provocatively and belligerently. They do not hesitate to scrutinize one another's claims critically and eloquently. In this way, a "Bantaba" is recognized by the capacity of people to evoke one another's potentialities so that their communal deliberations remain legitimized as non-autocratic human actions.

Moreover, counteracting irrational speech is central to what it means to practice African philosophy of education. Nowadays, African philosophy of education often focuses on decolonizing practices and institutions on the African continent. In other words, decoloniality, as I argue elsewhere (Manthalu & Waghid, 2019), offers a viable response to transforming practices that are in line with tenets of democratic change. I argue that decoloniality is a form of democratization, according to which iterations, recognition of otherness, and the critical and rational pursuit of claims and counterclaims are proffered in order to take risks and unveil differences among those engaged in decolonizing practices. Put differently, we aver that democratization, as decoloniality, is a matter of opening up educational practices to marginalized epistemologies, in an atmosphere characterized by deliberative inquiry and the (re)construction of human thought, alongside notions concerning what is rational and just for all humans.

This brings me to a discussion of one of the aims of an activist African philosophy of education, namely democratic justice.

4   On Democratic Justice in Becoming

As alluded to earlier, central to pursuing an African philosophy of education is the understanding that people ought to be liberated from inhumanity, autocracy, and irrationality. My argument in this section is that promoting the liberation and empowerment of people, by counteracting inhumanity, autocracy and irrationality, is tantamount to advocating a defense of democratic justice. Firstly, democratic justice is about recognizing the ethical agency of ensuring that all human beings live decent lives and are respected by all others (Gutmann, 2003, p. 26). It is inconceivable to say that many Africans are living decent lives and being respected by others, if human suffering, poverty and hunger seem to permeate so many societies on the continent. If people continue to suffer deprivation of food, shelter and protection in some parts of the continent, democratic justice has not yet entered their lives. Here, I am reminded specifically of post-colonial Zimbabwe that is currently experiencing high levels of food shortages. Furthermore, many citizens are being deprived of access to basic liberties and amenities. The point is that some people on the continent have not yet been liberated from experiences of inhumanity.

Secondly, democratic justice demands that all human beings be treated equally as citizens of a democratic polity. The problem in many parts of the continent is that autocratic regimes continue to rule with impunity and dissenting citizens are either incarcerated without trial or excommunicated. The equal agency of citizens is undermined because autocratic regimes have continued to disrespect the equal liberties of all citizens. For instance, in some countries, such as Congo-Brazzaville, Democratic Republic of Congo, Burundi, Rwanda and Burkina Faso, current presidents have tried to amend the constitution to extend their terms in office.

Thirdly, democratic justice involves citizens having basic opportunities to access education, health and welfare, and security and protection (Gutmann, 2003, p. 27). Just thinking about so many women on the continent who continue to be subjected to domestic abuse and violence corroborates the claim that democratic justice has not been realized on the continent. For example, in the Democratic Republic of Congo, there are female ex-combatants, wives of ex-combatants and women, who have experienced trauma at the hands of militia groups. In Zimbabwe, women have been victims of sexual violence or domestic abuse, and work with traditional leaders to prevent violence against women. In other parts of Africa, such as Burundi and Burkina Faso, women are often the worst affected by conflict and often become targets of sexual violence. Clearly absent from many of the practices of some people on the continent is a willing and rational recognition that women need to be protected against abuse and violence.

Pursuant to the above discussion, we infer that African philosophy of education is not yet manifest in some practices on the continent and that democratic justice remains evasive. Of course, the African philosophy of education can assist with identifying the aforementioned societal malaises as problems that ought to be remedied. Here, the African Union and its many organizational structures can, and should, play a more significant role in cultivating unconstrained deliberations among Africa's peoples to act more decisively concerning eradicating the continent's problems.

I now turn to university pedagogy (teaching and learning), as an opportunity to cultivate a liberatory pedagogy – one that can emancipate people on the continent from having to endure inhumanity, autocracy, and irrationality.

5   Activist University Pedagogy (Teaching and Learning) Enhanced through Democratic Justice

Over the past two decades, I have been responsible for the teaching of democratic education in my institution. One of the modules for the B.Ed Honors students is called "Education and Democracy." This module is divided into nine sections that deal with the following themes: democratic citizenship education in the making – belligerence, deliberation and belonging; democratic citizenship education, through compassionate imagining; democratic citizenship education, through friendship; democratic citizenship education, through respect and forgiveness; cosmopolitanism, through democratic citizenship education; democratic citizenship education without violence and extremism; democratic citizenship education, through *ubuntu*; democratic citizenship education and educational transformation in South Africa; and, democratic citizenship education as a skeptical encounter with the other.

The rationale for the module, Education and Democracy, is three-fold. First, we wish to engage postgraduate students in deliberative action about knowledge interests that advance the cultivation of democratic citizenship education in educational institutions. Second, students are provoked to think about engaging in iterations, compassionate imagining, and cosmo-*ubuntu*, so that they can recognize the vulnerabilities of marginalized others and work to change others' impoverished conditions. Third, to evoke the potentialities of students to connect with one another in skeptical encounters so that they can become attuned to dissent, disagreement and dissonance. In a way, this module aims at enhancing the democratic citizenry potentials of students and summoning them to engage in iterations, criticism, and dissonance – all the human capacities that can contribute to students' abilities to become active democratic citizens.

Whereas learning to iterate would enhance students' capacities to engage deliberatively with others, learning to imagine and to act on their compassion would arouse in them an emotive sensitivity toward vulnerable others in their communities. More poignantly, the idea of learning to enact cosmo-*ubuntu* involves looking openly and reflexively at their self-understandings and then to be responsive to what is still to become. This is a matter of preparing themselves for what is not yet, and by implication, which remains a potentiality. *Ubuntu* involves being in association with others, whereas cosmos refers to the pedagogical spaces in which all others are situated. By implication, cosmo-*ubuntu* aims at cultivating human selves that connect through difference and (dis)agreements.

My pedagogical stance through online education is to be provocative. Through continuous engagement in online messaging, my task as a teacher is to provoke students to speak. That is, they are encouraged to speak their minds without always being told to do so. Put differently, teaching is provocative in the sense that students are aroused to see the point of the themes with which they are engaging and to offer arguments, in a deliberative fashion, either to challenge what has been taught or to make sense of our teaching in their contexts. At times, our deliberative online encounters are belligerent, not because we want to dismiss the relevance of students' claims, but rather to encourage them to look at things as if they could be otherwise (Greene, 1995). Inasmuch as my teaching is provocative, so students' learning becomes evocative. In other words, the potentialities of students are evoked so that they can imagine a better social world in which democratic encounters and respect for others based on reconciliation and forgiveness are accentuated.

My emphasis on reconciliation stems from our historical legacy as South Africans deeply scarred by racist apartheid and from the need to rebuild our society, based on articulation and listening to what others have to say. I use forgiveness as a pedagogical strategy in the sense that people (teachers and students) should be prepared to acknowledge their mistakes and that there is more to learn if one remains open to the unexpected. That is, teaching and learning remain inconclusive in the sense that there is always more to know, and ideas remain in the making, as Maxine Greene (1995) averred.

Considering that our teaching-learning encounters are provocative and evocative, we remain open to what is humane and just. Our pedagogical encounters are underscored by a notion of skepticism in which our connection with one another is centred on an acknowledgement of humanity within ourselves and others. As Stanley Cavell (1979, p. 433) posited, "I have to acknowledge humanity in the other, and the basis of it seems to lie in me." After years of conflict among different racial groups in South Africa, it is paramount that people proceed from the point of acknowledging their own humanity – that is, their emotions, feelings, beliefs, and values – before they can begin to recognize the vulnerabilities of others. Therefore, what we think Cavell (1979, p. 434) purports is that hedging one's acknowledgement of humanity in others is hedging one's own humanity.

What follows from the above, is that democratic citizenship education aims at cultivating persons that treat others with hospitality without undermining the personhood of the other. Likewise, democratic citizenship education also expects one to become responsible in promoting the creation of opportunities for both attachment and detachment. This means that responsible action involves people acting forgivingly towards others, while not hesitating to reproach someone if she errs. In this way, it becomes possible to confront wrongs with the possibility that ills, like oppression and racism, can be avoided (Waghid, 2010, p. 142).

The question is, what makes our (the students' and my) pedagogical encounters activist encounters? Firstly, our emphasis on analyzing violence, in particular how people impose their will on others through coercion (Arendt, 1969, p. 56), is contested. Our understanding of violence is that it only results in more violence and can never be a way to resolve disputes among people. Apartheid could only be undermined through deliberative encounters. Violence, in itself, remains "incapable of speech" (Arendt, 1969, p. 19). As a result, our pedagogical activism is one of non-violence that draws on deliberative and authoritative speech through belligerent human encounters.

Secondly, pedagogical activism requires teachers and students to act respectfully and humanely. In other words, when teachers and students engage iteratively, they do so by confronting and engaging with those acts of inhumanity that are often associated with the "unforgiveable" (Derrida, 1997, p. 45). When we talk and deliberate about what seems to be "impardonable" (Derrida, 1997, p. 47), then we are prepared to bring the "unforgiveable" into our encounters. Thus, when we (teachers and students) are prepared to deliberate about what seems to be "unforgivable" and "impardonable," then the possibility will be there to consider new beginnings, such as we have witnessed from apartheid to the current democratic South African society. The point is, pedagogical activism is possible when teachers and students are prepared to engage iteratively what that which seems impossible.

Thirdly, pedagogical activism involves treating one another hospitably; that is, teachers and students consider one another as human beings with a status of "common possession of the earth" (Derrida, 1997, p. 20). In other words, teachers and students do not consider one another as people whose rights to hospitable treatment should be undermined. Nevertheless, hospitality does not mean that one does not show hostility in the encounters; otherwise, one would merely listen to others without scrutinizing their claims. To rupture the encounter implies that one acts with a sense of hostility to awaken one another to see things anew (Derrida, 1997). In this way, hostility becomes a rupturing of pedagogical encounters whereby teachers and students are provoked to look at things differently.

My potential critic might pose the question as to how students and teachers are protected in deliberative encounters? Being protected implies that both students and teachers (as participants) have an equal opportunity to act autonomously and speak their minds. Equally, they are protected because they respectfully listen to one another without any form of subjugation and exclusion from pedagogical encounters. Teachers and students can be said to be protected by the autonomous requirements of deliberative pedagogical encounters on the basis that such encounters evoke their potentialities to come to equal speech actions.

6 Conclusions

In this contribution, I have analyzed the notion of democratic citizenship education and how it resonates with the notion of an African philosophy of education. The point about cultivating democratic iterations within pedagogical encounters on the African continent does not mean that such encounters merely "borrow" from Western ways of doing. Rather, talking about African pedagogical encounters as deliberative and equal actions is a way of showing that democratic education cannot be considered an exclusively Western practice. Instead, accentuating the significance of deliberative actions within African pedagogical encounters is a recognition that non-Western encounters are not out of tune with practices of democracy and iteration.

Considering that democratic citizenship education represents a form of educational activism, it would not be inappropriate to refer to an African philosophy of education as an activist practice. This is so because problems are not merely identified and undergo deliberation, but more poignantly, such problems on the African continent are critically scrutinized to avoid and eradicate inhumanity, autocracy, and irrationality. In this way, an African philosophy of education is commensurate with the philosophical underpinnings of an activist pedagogy.

Finally, I have shown how an activist pedagogy is manifested in an Education and Democracy module taught at a university in South Africa. I have accentuated the significance of advancing an activist pedagogy along the lines of deliberative iterations, compassionate imagining and cosmo-*ubuntu*. I concluded the chapter with an exposition of how activist pedagogy is manifested in teaching and learning concerning a university online module. My argument in defense of pedagogical encounters that are constituted by activism is threefold: teaching and learning promote non-violence; teaching and learning encourage teachers and students to engage with what seem to be "unforgivable" and "impardonable"; and teaching and learning advance hospitality and hostility so that teachers and students remain actively engaged in the encounters.

References

Aristotle. (1995). *Politics.* Oxford University Press.
Arendt, H. (1969). *On violence.* The Penguin Press.
Benhabib, S. (1996). Towards a deliberative model of democratic legitimacy. In S. Benhabib (Ed.), *Democracy and difference: Contesting the boundaries of the political* (pp. 67–94). Princeton University Press.

Benhabib, S. (2006). The philosophical foundations of cosmopolitan norms. In R. Prost (Ed.), *Another cosmopolitanism* (pp. 13–44). Oxford University Press.

Callan, E. (1997). *Creating citizens: Political education and liberal democracy.* Oxford University Press.

Cavell, S. (1979). *The claim of reason: Wittgenstein, skepticism, morality, and tragedy.* Oxford University Press.

Derrida, J. (1997). *On cosmopolitanism and forgiveness.* Routledge.

Greene, M. (1995). *Releasing the imagination: Articles on education, the arts, and social change.* Jossey-Bass.

Gutmann, A. (2003). *Identity in democracy.* Princeton University Press.

Manthalu, C. H., & Waghid, Y. (2019). *Education for decoloniality and decolonisation in Africa.* Palgrave-MacMillan.

Nussbaum, M. (2002). Education for citizenship in an era of global connection. *Studies in Philosophy and Education, 21*(6), 289–303.

Sherman, N. (1997). *Making a necessity of virtue: Aristotle and Kant on virtue.* Cambridge University Press.

Waghid, Y. (2010). *Education, democracy and citizenship revisited: Pedagogical encounters.* SUN Press.

Waghid, Y. (2014). *African philosophy of education reconsidered: On being human.* Routledge.

Waghid, Y., Waghid, F., & Waghid, Z. (2018). *Rupturing African philosophy on teaching and learning: Ubuntu justice and education.* Palgrave-MacMillan.

Young, I. M. (2000). *Inclusion and democracy.* Oxford University Press.

CHAPTER 5

Educating for Democratic Citizenship

Arabic in Israeli Higher Education as a Case in Point

Smadar Donitsa-Schmidt, Muhammad Amara and Abd Al-Rahman Mar'i

1   Introduction

Academia is acknowledged as playing a significant role in shaping society, directly and indirectly. Higher education institutions are central sources of knowledge and discourse design (Etzkowitz & Viale, 2010); they are a symbol of ethic and values (Bok & Bok, 2009); a place that cultivates economic, social, and political leaders (Astin & Astin, 2000); and the scene of social and political activism. Furthermore, formal education is known to influence social engagement and foster critical thinking. Over the years, the world has witnessed the involvement of academics and students who have protested regime injustices and reacted to social inequality, violent conflicts, and neglect of democratic values. Such involvement is, however, rare in the Israeli higher education system, and appears to be particularly low, almost nonexistent, when the issue concerns the struggle for the rights of Arabs in Israel (Amara, 2002, 2018).

The lack of symmetry and equality between the Hebrew and Arabic languages in Israel, reflected in various fields, such as the linguistic landscape, the education system, the media, public services, and the labor market, has long been documented (e.g., Ben-Rafael, Shohamy, Amara & Trumper-Hecht, 2006; Mendel, 2014; Saban & Amara, 2004; Yitzhaki, 2013). This asymmetry had existed long before Arabic lost its status as an official language in 2018. It is an expression of the tense relations between the Jewish majority and the Arab minority in Israel and an indication of dangerous processes of Arab exclusion from the social and political sphere. In a country that defines itself as the nation-state of the Jewish People, the Arabs necessarily become second-class citizens, and their culture and language have been demoted as well (Chaitin, Steinberg & Steinberg, 2019).

Promoting so-called "national interests" at the expense of humanistic values is not a unique Israeli phenomenon. Maintaining national strength and unity is a well-known justification for favoring the majority and for unequal allocation of resources, while ignoring the rights of other groups (Meadwell, 1989).

Nevertheless, the strength of a society lies in its ability to fight such social injustices and promote equal rights for all.

The purpose of this chapter is to demonstrate that educating for democratic citizenship is something to which Israel should aspire, regarding its Arab community, language, and culture. Here, we particularly focus on the higher education domain. The underlying assumption of the chapter is that universities and colleges are public spheres and civic institutions which should be dedicated to providing a public service to all, committed to addressing social problems, and educating future generations to be able to confront the challenges of a global democracy (Giroux, 2002). Furthermore, as noted by Giroux (2010), the role of academia is to educate young people in the spirit of a critical democracy by providing them with "the knowledge, passion, civic capacity, public value, and social responsibility necessary to address the problems facing the nation ..." (p. 187).

The chapter is comprised of four main parts. The first section reviews studies that have examined the role that higher education institutions worldwide have played in promoting civic, multicultural, and democratic principles. The second section describes the status of the Arabic language in Israel. The third part describes part of a research, conducted by the authors that investigated the place and role of Israeli higher education institutions in promoting the Arabic language and changing its status in Israel. Finally, the last section discusses possible reasons for the insufficient social and political engagement of Israeli higher education institutions and proposes ways to change the current situation of the Arabic language.

2   The Role of Higher Education Institutions in Promoting Democratic Citizenship

Maintaining social justice and a democratic community have become urgent concerns for many educational scholars and practitioners. This urgency springs from numerous factors, among them the strengthening winds of racism, fascism, intolerance, and discrimination, coupled with totalitarian and anti-democratic regimes and leaders worldwide. It becomes even more acute in divided societies struggling with ongoing social and political conflicts.

Although the strength of societies lies in their ability to fight social injustices and promote equal rights for all, this is a difficult and challenging task for many countries and societies, including Israel. It has been claimed that the idealized image of a democratic society that offers free and equal representation and participation to all its citizens has always been a fiction, predicated on the silencing of entire social groups (Holmwood, 2017). Moreover, following Antonio Gramsci, the nation-state has succeeded in realizing the hidden agenda of legitimizing its ideology and establishing it as the hegemony, while excluding certain social groups (Robinson, 2005). Contesting these tacit national motives, while striving to legitimize silenced social groups, is the mission of a civilized society and its true democratic citizens.

While the strength of societies, at large, lies in their ability to fight social injustice, it is the role of their institutions to promote equal rights for all and social values, in general. Academia is one such institution. Higher education institutions bear a profound moral responsibility for increasing the awareness, knowledge, skills, and values needed to create a just and sustainable future. They are also credited with an ability to realize, directly or indirectly, imperative societal agendas, such as democratization and social mobility, economic development, and innovation (Olsen & Maassen, 2007). After all, they train professionals who develop, lead, manage, teach, educate, work in, and influence society's infrastructure. Higher education is privileged with having unique academic freedom. It is a hub for diverse skills, it is ready to develop new ideas, comment on society and its challenges, and engage in bold experimentation in sustainable living.

A growing number of colleges and universities worldwide actively embrace the concept of the 'engaged campus' and give priority to civic education, utilizing varied avenues to promote this agenda (Butin, 2010). Thus, volunteerism, service learning, public interest internships, and community-based student practice and research all serve to bolster student civic engagement. There is growing acknowledgement that introducing such social involvement programs into the curriculum energizes the civic engagement of higher education (Clayton, Bringle & Hatcher, 2012). Such programs are likely to serve as catalysts for broader and deeper engagement and civic responsibility of colleges and universities. Active civic engagement can enhance students' critical thinking skills and help develop an understanding of the causes underlying social problems. It also allows students to acquire the democratic qualities of honesty, generosity, empathy, tolerance, cooperation, and social responsibility (Clayton, Bringle & Hatcher, 2012).

Nevertheless, while valuable, these efforts fall short of educating for democratic citizenship, since the design of civic engagement experiences is typically apolitical. Indeed, many campuses caution students to avoid political conversations in class. As noted by Thomas and Brower (2017), "Over the past few decades, colleges and universities have revitalized their efforts to advance student civic engagement. Unfortunately ... these initiatives are usually apolitical in nature" (p. 23). As a result, while students develop empathy for others and a sense of duty, they do not necessarily acquire the knowledge, skills, and commitment to address social and political problems (Thomas & Brower, 2017).

In addition to the initiatives that higher education institutions take to promote democratic citizenship, the students themselves have the power to promote these values. Although the era of student revolutions has been over for half a century, students continue to be active in politics and social events. They are often a key force in social and political change-seeking movements around the world (Altbach & Klemencic, 2014). Even if students might not comprise the backbone of the movements, they are often essential participants, helping to shape the messages, ideologies, and agenda behind those movements' actions and campaigns.

The university and college professors are a no less significant factor in the academic triangle. As intellectuals and key figures in society, they bear the responsibility, according to Chomsky (1967), for speaking the truth, exposing lies, and fighting against social and political injustices. In line with Chomsky's assertion, studies have shown that university professors tend to be more liberal than members of other professions and not as politically conservative (Gross & Simmons, 2014). Faculty ranks rarely include extreme right-wing and conservative voters. Moreover, a large proportion of university professors identify themselves as political activists and even radicals. They display liberal attitudes towards sex and gender, tend to be supportive of the welfare state idea, and favor government actions intended to reduce social inequalities. In terms of ethnic and racial minority groups, the majority of professors favors affirmative action in university admissions, agree that racial and ethnic inequalities result from ongoing discrimination, and support the incorporation of racial and ethnic diversity studies into the undergraduate curriculum. Nonetheless, professors broadly disagree about the extent to which politics should play a role in teaching, research, and general campus affairs (Gross & Simmons, 2014).

Campus context and organizational dynamics, academic curricula that grant credits for social and political involvement, and professors introducing their political commitment into their teaching – these can all pacify or energize the engagement of students in democratic citizenship (Morgan & Davis, 2019). Neutrality, avoidance, and evasion create, at best, a vacuum in the political education and democratic citizenship of students. At worst, they constitute a political stance that perpetuates established structures of social hierarchy and power.

3   Status of the Arabic Language in Israel

For 70 years, from the establishment of the State of Israel in 1948 to 2018, Hebrew and Arabic were both official languages in Israel. Hebrew is the language of the 74% Jewish majority, while Arabic is the language of the 21% Arab minority. The remaining 5% include non-Arab Christians and persons not classified by religion in the Population Register (Central Bureau of Statistics, 2019). Although Arabic is a minority language in Israel, it is the language of all the countries surrounding Israel in the Middle East. It is also considered to be part of the heritage of a large number of Israeli Jews, who immigrated from Arab speaking countries.

Despite having had an official status for so many years, the Israeli Jewish public has never wholly embraced Arabic. The local context and Israel's geo-political situation within the Middle East have had a direct impact on the linguistic preferences of Israeli society. By and large, the inner conflict between Arab-Palestinian society and the Jewish majority goes back to the late 19th century, when anti-Semitism and Zionism fueled the desire of Jews to establish a sovereign Jewish state. While before the establishment of Israel, and particularly before the British mandate, more positive attitudes were expressed toward Arabic by the Jews who lived in Palestine, many of whom spoke Arabic, a major turning point occurred in 1948 with Arabic gradually disappearing from the public sphere (Shenhav et al., 2015).

This conflict has been a major force in determining the attitudes and choices made, with regard to Arabic. Indeed, several research studies conducted over time have shown that Jewish adults display negative attitudes and little appreciation for the Arabic language (e.g., Donitsa-schmidt, Inbar & Shohamy, 2004; Kraemer, 1993; Yitzhaki, 2010). These negative attitudes were also found to be held by immigrants from Arab countries, and particularly by second and third generations, most of whom do not know or use Arabic any longer (Shenhav et al., 2015). Over the years, Israeli right-wingers have made numerous attempts to change the legal status of Arabic. They succeeded in 2018, with the passing of the Nation-State Law that declares Israel the national homeland of its Jewish citizens only. After 70 years, Arabic lost its status as a co-official language alongside Hebrew and was declared instead a language with special status, although its use in government documents and in the public sphere continues to be mandated by law.

Despite having had an official status for so many years, Arabic has never been a full-fledged official language in practice and has been inferior to Hebrew in almost every sphere of life (e.g., Amara, 2018; Saban & Amara, 2002; Yitzhaki, 2013). The hegemony of Hebrew is evident in all aspects of daily life and various social institutions legitimize it. Research has documented a consistent absence of Arabic from the public sphere. Hebrew is the language used in the *Knesset* (Israel's parliament), the law courts, and the government. It is the language of academic institutions, electronic media, business and finance, and most published books and newspapers. At the same time, Arabic has almost completely disappeared from the Israeli linguistic landscape, particularly the state-dominated one. Street signs, billboards, advertisements, warning signs, road signs, as well as the names of shops and public institutions, appear mostly in Hebrew and English. Moreover, many public services have no Arabic-speaking employees to help Arab customers in their own language, and most national events are held in Hebrew only. Given its marginality in cultural life, media, politics, and intra-community life, Arabic, for the most part, has not been treated as equal.

The only realm where the official status of Arabic is somewhat manifested is the K-12 education system. In this system, Arabs attend their separate schools in which the language of instruction is Arabic, while Jewish schoolchildren attend Hebrew-speaking schools. Nevertheless, despite the seemingly egalitarian situation, this is not entirely so. While Arab children are required to study Hebrew as a second language throughout their school years, this is not the case in the Hebrew-speaking schools.

Despite the Israeli Ministry of Education's efforts to promote the study of Arabic as a second language in Jewish schools, by making it compulsory for three years in grades 7 to 9, teaching Arabic to Hebrew speakers proves to be extremely problematic from various aspects. Among the problems encountered are negative attitudes and stereotypes that Jewish students and their parents hold toward the Arabic language and its speakers, resulting in low motivation and resistance to studying the language (Donitsa-Schmidt, Inbar & Shohamy, 2004). Those who study Arabic in school usually do not acquire sufficient language proficiency at the end of their studies and very few proceed with their Arabic studies in the upper grades. Furthermore, although Arabic is a mandatory school subject for three years, the Ministry of Education allows schools to replace it with French. Hence, while knowledge of Hebrew is a prerequisite for any academic studies in Israel, knowledge of Arabic is not required at all. Moreover, while Arabs are required to have a high level of Hebrew to integrate into society and the workplace, knowledge of Arabic is not essential for Jews.

In conclusion, the widespread use of Hebrew in the public sphere has helped establish Hebrew as the "national" and sole language for all practical purposes in everyday life, thus significantly marginalizing Arabic.

3.1   *Arabic in Israeli Higher Education Institutions*

The marginalization of the Arabic language in Israel is manifested in the setting of higher education institutions. Of the nine research universities and 33 academic colleges, none use Arabic as the primary language of instruction. Only three of the 21 academic teacher education colleges conduct their academic life in Arabic, for the benefit of the Arabic-speaking public. In other words, out of the 63 higher education institutions, only three use Arabic as the medium of instruction. A study that examined the prominence and visibility of Arabic in Hebrew-speaking universities showed that Arabic is completely absent from their public spaces, despite the large number of Arab students studying in them (Shohamy & Ghazaleh-Mahajneh, 2012). Another study that examined the presence and status of Arabic in university campuses and the visibility of Arab culture and social norms in them revealed that not a single campus has managed to meet targets set by Israel's Council for Higher Education to cater to the needs of Arab students. University websites did not offer an Arabic version; Arabic signage was rare on the campuses; computer keyboards did not carry Arabic lettering; campus services were not offered in Arabic; and very little of the campus cultural life or activity represented minority cultures and was held in Arabic. The study concluded that Arab students did not encounter their own linguistic, cultural, social, or religious background on campus. This led to ensuing feelings of social exclusion, cultural alienation, frustration, and helplessness, that did not promote a sense of belonging or ownership in academia (Abu-Ras & Maayan, 2014). Other researchers had similar observations and reached the same conclusions (e.g., Al-Haj, 2012; Arar, 2017).

Assuming that academia could bring about social change, The Van Leer Jerusalem Institute commissioned a study to examine whether higher education institutions were able to increase the prominence and status of Arabic within them (Amara, Donitsa-Schmidt & Al-Rahman, 2016). The study, which was conducted in 2015, shortly before the Arabic language lost its status as an official language in Israel, included two parts. A qualitative part dealt with the degree of presence of Arabic as an academic language in the Arab language department and as an official language on the institutions' websites. There was also a quantitative part that investigated how lecturers and students, Jews and Arabs alike, perceived and viewed the role of Israeli campuses in changing the situation of the Arabic language in Israel. The aim of the present article is not to present all the findings of this comprehensive study, but rather to focus on some of the responses of the 131 Jewish lecturers and 233 Jewish students, in order to make a case in point as to the ability of Israeli academia to promote democratic citizenship. For this purpose, we shall focus only on the Jewish students' and lecturers' responses to the following four topics: their attitudes and perceptions toward Arabic as an official language; the importance of Arabic in Israel; the visibility of Arabic in Israel and in the higher education institutions; and the role of Israel's academia in improving the status of Arabic. The majority of the research participants were Israeli-born and almost all of them defined themselves as native speakers of Hebrew. Most of them described themselves as secular and as having a left-wing political orientation (for the full report see Amara, Donitsa-Schmidt & Al-Rahman, 2016).

Findings showed that Jewish lecturers and students were both ambivalent about the status and place of the Arabic language in Israel. While most of them were supportive of preserving the official status of Arabic, not everyone, especially not all the students, agreed that both languages were entitled to equal status and rights. Although they perceived Arabic as an important language, they agreed unanimously that it had low instrumental value. The research results also showed that the Jewish lecturers, and even more so the Jewish students, were not keen on having an extensive presence of Arabic in Israeli society, especially the media, politics, and the internet. Furthermore, although they admitted that Arabic is almost completely absent from the public sphere, especially from Israel's institutions of higher education, many of them stated that they preferred it not to be overly visible in the institutions where they taught and studied, and thought it should be restricted to certain specific public spheres. They firmly objected to adding Arabic to the institution's logo and to holding social and academic events in Arabic.

The research also investigated the views regarding the role of academia in promoting the status of the Arabic language in Israel. The findings revealed that lecturers and students alike tended to agree that academia should have a part in bolstering the position of Arabic in Israeli society. At the same time, however, they doubted its ability to do so. These findings indicate quite clearly that the Jewish lecturers, and even more so the Jewish students, were not keen on having Arabic occupy a more significant and visible role in various spheres of life in Israel. Nor did they perceive the academic institutions as having the ability to influence or change the situation. Notably, they were not particularly inclined to pursue this goal themselves. In conclusion, this study denotes that Jewish lecturers and students both have a very weak tendency to engage in political activism.

The findings of this research contradict the opinions currently expressed in the literature, which attribute academia with having the power to promote democratic values and endorse social and political activism. The study shows that in Israel, the situation is quite the opposite: higher education institutions do not stand at the forefront when it comes to shaping the face of society, especially when related to the Arab minority in Israel.

4 Discussion

While students remain a potent political and social force in many countries, this is not the case in Israel, especially with regard to the Arab-Palestinian conflict (Amara, Donitsa-Schmidt & Al-Rahman, 2016). In an attempt to rectify the situation, in 2018, the Israeli Knesset enacted a law, "Encouraging Student Involvement in Social and Community Activities." The law aims to increase the involvement of students in activities on behalf of society, by entitling them to two academic credits during their studies for these activities. This law follows the Council for Higher Education's decision from 2004 to allow granting academic credits for social activities (Avgar, 2018). In addition to endorsing the Council for Higher Education, the law also allocates budgets to higher education institutions that encourage these social involvement activities. A study made public in 2015 claimed that a decade earlier, in 2005, one year after the Council for Higher Education had taken its decision, very few higher education institutions had formulated a comprehensive policy regarding the commitment of the institution, its students, and its lecturers to the community. Nor was there long-term planning on how to pursue this goal. In contrast, over the next decade, many higher education institutions formulated a comprehensive policy on this matter and set up social involvement units that partnered with the community (Golan & Rosenfeld, 2015). Despite this, a significant number of institutions do not allow granting credits for community work to this day. Higher education institutions' views are divided as to the type of activities deserving recognition for this purpose. The greatest disagreements concern involvement in politically oriented organizations (Golan & Rosenfeld, 2015).

Despite the increase in social involvement activities in some of the campuses, Israeli academia remains drowsy, indifferent, and complacent. The findings that emerged from the study presented above indicate that even individuals who identify themselves with the Israeli left-wing have no urge or motivation to promote the Arabic language on campus and in society at large. Jewish lecturers and students clearly preferred to maintain the hegemony of Hebrew and thus preserve the cultural, economic, social, and symbolic assets of Hebrew speakers. This may explain why the Nation-State Law that dramatically changed the status of Arabic passed so smoothly in the Knesset. The number of higher education institutions that protested the law at that time was negligible.

The lack of protest by higher education institutions regarding the Nation-State Law may seem surprising considering a unique program that was launched in 2016 in the academia as a new civic initiative of Israeli president Reuven Rivlin (Sachs & Reeves, 2017). The main thrust of the program, which was given the name, "Israeli Hope in Academia," was to establish a new Israeli civic order based on mutual recognition and cooperation between the four groups ("tribes") in the highly conflicted Israeli society. One of these groups is the Arab population. The three others are all Jewish – the secular tribe, the national-religious tribe, and the ultra-orthodox tribe. Since two of these groups – the ultra-orthodox and Arabs – do not serve in the Israeli military, academic institutions and the workplace are where the groups find themselves side by side. Since 2016, Israeli Hope in Academia has operated in more than 40 academic institutions, budgeted by the Planning and Budgeting Committee of the Council for Higher Education. To date, no comprehensive research has been conducted that examines the achievement of the program's objectives.

There are several possible explanations for academia conforming to the views of other spheres in Israel regarding the social and political advocacy of Arabic. These include generic reasons related to the massive access to higher education, such as widespread part-time studies, diversified student populations, a non-elite social background of most students, and an increasingly high cost of higher education, which causes students to be preoccupied with their livelihood, rather than engage with the problems of others (Altback & Klemencic, 2014). Another possible explanation may be that in the postmodern era, the focus of students and professors alike has shifted to becoming more individualistic and possibly more oriented toward their well-being, self-expression, and quality of life. It has also been argued that educational expansion, driven partly by an increase in white-collar job opportunities in the mid-twentieth century, has changed the sociology of intellectuals (Gross & Simmons, 2014). Along these lines, higher education has been accused of leading toward neo-liberal views, marketization, and privatization while abandoning its mission as a core political and civic institution (Giroux, 2010).

A different set of causes for the low levels of social and political engagement exists, that is unique to the Israeli context. These causes include the ongoing fragile security situation, political instability, and the Israeli-Palestinian conflict that directly affects the ideological perceptions of the political conflict. Of note is the fact that most Jewish students enter higher education after two or three years of military service, which could perhaps lead many of them to feel that they had already made their contribution to society. It has also been argued that the compulsory military service in Israel tends to increase the sense of nationalism and patriotism towards the state, while lowering humanistic and universal rights (Griffith, 2010). In a research study that explored Jewish-Israeli attitudes toward human rights activism and patriotism, it was found that human rights activism was often seen as unpatriotic, regardless of educational level and academic background. Furthermore, even the left-wing and centrists demonstrated unexpectedly highly emotional and negative attitudes (Chaitin, Steinberg & Steinberg, 2019), as was the case in Amara et al.'s (2016) research.

Lacking the leadership or support of the heads of the higher academic institutions, academia and its various mechanisms replicate the built-in inequality in Israeli society. To promote an effective democratic society, academia in Israel must become a civic model. Varied measures could remedy this situation, but undertaking them requires great determination and bold decisions on the part of the higher education institutions, especially given the current political and social climate in Israel. As the findings of the research conducted by Amara and colleagues (2016) show, it is doubtful that this is achievable under the existing circumstances. It is, therefore, worthwhile to incorporate teaching toward civic education, social involvement, and democratic citizenship in earlier stages of Israeli students' educational journey. Improving Arabic teaching programs in Jewish schools, making Arabic studies compulsory, opening more bilingual educational settings and integrating Arab teachers in Jewish schools are some of the possible steps in this direction.

References

Abu Ras, T., & Maayan, Y. (2014). *Arabic and Arab culture on Israeli campuses: An updated look*. Dirasat, The Van Leer Jerusalem Institute and Sikkuy. [in Hebrew].

Al-Haj, M. (2012). *Education, empowerment, and control: The case of the Arabs in Israel*. Suny Press.

Altbach, P. G., & Klemencic, M. (2014). Student activism remains a potent force worldwide. *International Higher Education, 76*, 2–3.

Amara, M. (2002). The place of Arabic in Israel. *International Journal of the Sociology of Language, 158*, 53–68.

Amara, M. (2018). *Language, identity and conflict: Arabic in Israel*. Routledge.

Amara, M., Donitsa-Schmidt, S., Al-Rahman Mar'i, A. (2016). *Arabic in the Israeli academy: Historical absence, current challenges, and future possibilities*. Dirasat, The Van Leer Jerusalem Institute, Sikkuy. [in Hebrew].

Arar, K. (2017). Academic spheres, students' identity formation, and social activism among Palestinian Arab students in Israeli campuses. *Journal of Diversity in Higher Education, 10*(4), 366–380.

Astin, A. W., & Astin, H. S. (2000). *Leadership reconsidered: Engaging higher education in social change*. W.K. Kellogg Foundation.

Avgar, I. (2018). *Recognition of student volunteering as an activity that grants academic credit points*. Government Research Center. [in Hebrew]

Ben-Rafael, E., Shohamy, E., Hasan Amara, M., & Trumper-Hecht, N. (2006). Linguistic landscape as symbolic construction of the public space: The case of Israel. *International Journal of Multilingualism, 3*(1), 7–30.

Bok, D. C., & Bok, D. C. (2009). *Beyond the ivory tower: Social responsibilities of the modern university*. Harvard University Press.

Butin, D. (2010). *Service-learning in theory and practice: The future of community engagement in higher education.* Springer.

Chaitin, J., Steinberg, S., & Steinberg, S. (2019). Jewish-Israeli attitudes toward human rights organizations and patriotism. *Ethnopolitics.* doi:10.1080/17449057.2019.1679488

Chomsky, N. (1967). A special supplement: The responsibility of intellectuals. *The New York Review of Books, 23.*

Clayton, P. H., Bringle, R. G., & Hatcher, J. A. (Eds.). (2012). *Research on service learning: Conceptual frameworks and assessment.* Stylus Publishing, LLC.

Donitsa-Schmidt, S., Inbar, O., & Shohamy, E. (2004). The effects of teaching spoken Arabic on students' attitudes and motivation in Israel. *The Modern Language Journal, 88*(2), 217–228.

Etzkowitz, H., & Viale, R. (2010). Polyvalent knowledge and the entrepreneurial university: A third academic revolution? *Critical Sociology, 36*(4), 595–609.

Giroux, H. A. (2002). Neoliberalism, corporate culture, and the promise of higher education: The university as a democratic public sphere. *Harvard Educational Review, 72*(4), 425–464.

Giroux, H. A. (2010). Bare pedagogy and the scourge of neoliberalism: Rethinking higher education as a democratic public sphere. *The Educational Forum, 74*(3), 184–196.

Golan, D., & Rosenfeld, Y. (2015). Learning from the successes of community-engaged courses in the Israeli academy. *Giluy Daat, 7,* 33–36. [in Hebrew]

Griffith, J. (2010). When does soldier patriotism or nationalism matter? The role of transformational small-unit leaders. *Journal of Applied Social Psychology, 40*(5), 1235–1257.

Gross, N., & Simmons, S. (Eds.). (2014). *Professors and their politics.* JHU Press.

Holmwood, J. (2017). The university, democracy and the public sphere. *British Journal of Sociology of Education, 38*(7), 927–942.

Israel Central Bureau of Statistics. (2019). *Media release: Population of Israel on the eve of 2020.* State of Israel.

Kraemer, R. (1993). Social psychological factors related to the study of Arabic among Israeli high school students: A test of Gardner's socio-educational model. *Studies in Second Language Acquisition, 15*(1), 83–105.

Olsen, J. P., & Maassen, P. (2007). European debates on the knowledge institution: The modernization of the university at the European level. In P. Maassen & J. P. Olsen (Eds.), *University dynamics and European integration* (Vol. 4, pp. 2–22). Springer, Dordrecht.

Meadwell, H. (1989). Cultural and instrumental approaches to ethnic nationalism. *Ethnic and Racial Studies, 12*(3), 309–328.

Mendel, Y. (2014). *The creation of Israeli Arabic: Security and politics in Arabic studies in Israel.* Palgrave Macmillan.

Morgan, D. L., & Davis III, C. H. (Eds.). (2019). *Student activism, politics, and campus climate in higher education*. Routledge.

Robinson, W. I. (2005). Gramsci and globalisation: From nation-state to transnational hegemony. *Critical Review of International Social and Political Philosophy*, 8(4), 559–574.

Saban, I., & Amara, M. (2004). The status of Arabic in Israel: Law, reality, and thoughts regarding the power of law to change reality. *Israel Law Review*, 36(2), 1–35.

Sachs, N., & Reeves, B. (2017). *Tribes, identity and individual freedom in Israel*. The Center for Middle East Policy at Brookings.

Shemhav, Y., Dallashi, M., Avnimelech, R., Mizrachi N., & Mendel, Y. (2015). *Command of Arabic among Israeli Jews*. Dirasat, The Van Leer Jerusalem Institute, Sikkuy. [in Hebrew]

Shohamy, E., & Ghazaleh-Mahajneh, M. A. (2012). Linguistic landscape as a tool for interpreting language vitality: Arabic as a 'minority' language in Israel. In D. Gorter, H. F. Marten, & L. V. Mensel (Eds.), *Minority languages in the linguistic landscape* (pp. 89–106). Palgrave Macmillan.

Thomas, N., & Brower, M. (2017). The politically engaged classroom. In E. C. Matto, A. R. M. McCartney, E. A. Bennion, & D. W. Simpson (Eds.), *Teaching civic engagement across the disciplines* (pp. 21–33). American Political Science Association.

Yitzhaki, D. (2010). The discourse of Arabic language policies in Israel: Insights from focus groups. *Language Policy*, 9(4), 335–356.

Yitzhaki, D. (2013). The status of Arabic in the discourse of Israeli policymakers. *Israel Affairs*, 19(2), 290–305.

PART 2

Enhancing Models of Shared Learning

CHAPTER 6

Turning Research into Policy

The Experience of Shared Education in Northern Ireland

Tony Gallagher, Gavin Duffy and Gareth Robinson

1   **Introduction**

This chapter looks at the Shared Education initiative in Northern Ireland (NI) that emerged in the context of the peace process in the early 2000s and has gone on to reshape our education system. The initiative involves local networks of schools, which provide opportunities for students and teachers to work collaboratively. In the context of a divided society, it has provided opportunities for sustained dialogic engagement between communities in ways that were previously transitory, uncommon or non-existent. The model has also been adapted for implementation in other divided societies. As currently over half of all schools in Northern Ireland are involved in school partnerships, the main purpose of the chapter is to examine why the initiative has been so successful.

Following this short introduction, we examine briefly the political context of political and religious divisions in Northern Ireland, before going on to explore how these were manifested in the education system. The outbreak of political violence in the late 1960s prompted a variety of educational interventions aimed variously at promoting reconciliation or equity. However, the interventions' limitations prompted the work that led to the development of the Shared Education initiative, the main tenets of which we then outline. Before considering some of the reasons for the success of this initiative, we examine the political structures put in place by the peace process and consider two education policy initiatives that became embroiled in political controversy and, consequently, failed to achieve their original aims. These provide a useful contrast to the way the Shared Education initiative was pursued, which we highlight as the main reasons for its success to conclude the chapter.

2   **Politics and Division in Northern Ireland**

Northern Ireland became a self-governing region within the United Kingdom in 1922, as an outcome of the struggle for Irish independence, which had been waged for several centuries. Throughout the 19th century, the relationship between political, national and religious identity in Ireland had grown stronger, so that the Irish nationalist demand for independence from the United Kingdom had generated growing opposition from the pro-Union, largely Protestant minority concentrated in the northeastern part of the island of Ireland.

A militant faction within the Irish independence movement had taken advantage of the First World War to launch a rebellion in 1916, termed the 'Easter Rising.' While the British Army defeated the rebellion, the spirit of the Rising re-emerged in a short War of Independence between 1919 and 1921, which resulted in a peace agreement that included the partition of the island. Parliaments were established in Dublin and Belfast, and each was given the option of leaving the United Kingdom or staying. The Dublin parliament opted for independence and the Belfast parliament opted to stay in the United Kingdom, albeit with new powers of regional self-government. Of the 32 counties on the island, the new Irish Free State (later Republic of Ireland) comprised 26 counties. The remaining six counties formed Northern Ireland.

The primary rationale for partition had been to create separate, economically viable jurisdictions that reflected, and would, hopefully, neutralize the religious-political division on the island. This plan was only partially successful. The population of the Irish Free State was overwhelmingly Catholic, Irish and committed to independence. In Northern Ireland, however, the Catholic community comprised approximately one third of the population, who, overall, shared much of the sentiment of their kin on the island. However, they now found themselves in a smaller polity governed by the Protestant majority, which was a strong supporter of the Union with Britain. Hence, they adopted the political label of Unionists, and were avowedly British in identity and outlook.

Thus, while the struggle between Ireland and Britain produced a majority-minority problem on the island of Ireland, the attempt to solve this through partition created a reversed majority-minority problem in Northern Ireland. Apart from the Unionists, in 1922, not many thought that Northern Ireland would last as a viable political entity. It has lasted, but at a cost: the Catholic, Irish minority was big enough to be perceived as a permanent threat to the security of Northern Ireland by many in the Protestant, Unionist majority. As a result, active attempts were made to consolidate Unionist political support around a single political party. In addition, draconian emergency legislation was enacted on a de facto permanent basis. The police force, the Royal Ulster Constabulary (RUC), adopted a quasi-military mode of operation, and an almost exclusively Protestant armed Special Constabulary was created to support the RUC. Militant Irish nationalists, or Irish Republicans, responded in kind by launching military campaigns against the authorities in Northern Ireland and, occasionally, bombing campaigns in England.

In the 1960s, a civil rights' campaign was established to protest alleged religious discrimination against Catholics by the political, civil and economic powers in Northern Ireland. Modelling themselves on the US civil rights' campaign led by Martin Luther King, the Northern Ireland campaign organized marches. These, however, soon descended into riots and the emergence of illegal paramilitary forces. The British Army was sent in by the government in London, ostensibly to restore order. However, this led to the quarter century of political violence, known as The Troubles, with over 3,700 deaths. The Troubles ended in 1998 with the Good Friday Agreement and the establishment of a new, shared system of government. From that point forward, the focus of attention was on trying to secure the peace (Darby, 1997).

3   Education in Northern Ireland

The religious traditions and divisions on the island of Ireland found expression in the structure of the education system. The first national system of schools was established in 1831, and while there was official preference for an integrated system of schools for Catholic and Protestant children, the system very quickly took on a denominational character, as the different Churches sought to assert their control over the new civil architecture of schools. When Ireland was partitioned in 1922, the dominant role of the Catholic Church was retained in the Irish Free State. It remained largely unchallenged until the end of the century (Akenson, 1970). Today, the Catholic Church continues to own and run the vast majority of schools in the Republic of Ireland, but the power of the Church has greatly diminished and is ebbing inexorably.

The new NI government had a somewhat different agenda, as well as a Minister of Education who wanted to set schools on a different course by promoting the assimilation of the Catholic minority. By holding this perspective, he risked tensions with the part of the Unionist movement that placed the religious principles of Protestantism at the heart of its identity, as compared to those, who placed British identity as its core concern. In 1922, while most schools in Northern Ireland were owned and run by the different Churches, the Minister of Education sought to follow the model adopted in England in the latter part of the 19th century, in which local authorities had largely displaced Churches as the main providers of education.

In pursuit of this goal, the Minister of Education established local authorities across Northern Ireland and invited the Churches to transfer ownership of their schools to these authorities. In the political environment at the time, there was little expectation that the Catholic Church would indeed embrace this opportunity. However, there was much more surprise when the Protestant Churches opted to take the same course. Over the next 10 years, the Protestant Churches lobbied successfully for a series of changes to the education legislation. This meant that the new local authority schools remained, for all practical purposes, as Protestant schools. The Churches retained a high level of influence and control, even if they no longer formally owned the school buildings. The Catholic Church watched all these developments from a distance, occasionally complaining that their schools were not treated fairly. However, they primarily focused on maintaining control of their schools and, through them, retaining a high degree of influence over the Catholic minority in Northern Ireland.

By the 1960s, the system of separate denominational schools for Protestants and Catholics in Northern Ireland was well institutionalized, and reflected the wider religious-political divisions within society. Apart from the Church itself, the Catholic schools provided the most significant set of civic institutions for the minority community: they were public spaces within which it was possible to express a sense of Irish culture and identity. On the concrete level, the teaching profession was one of the few middle-class occupations to which Catholics could realistically aspire. It is noteworthy, therefore, that unlike the US civil rights' campaign, the Northern Ireland civil rights' campaign did not challenge the system of separate schools and did not have school desegregation as one of its goals (Akenson, 1974; Farren, 1995).

3.1 Denominational Schools and Societal Division

The absence of a civil rights' call for school desegregation did not prevent a spotlight from shining on the system of separate schools, as Northern Ireland descended into the violence of The Troubles. Some suggested the political divisions in society were linked to, and perhaps even a consequence of, separate schools for Protestants and Catholics (Heskin, 1980). Therefore, creating a single system of schools for all would promote better community relations and contribute to reconciliation. The alternative perspective was that the problems in Northern Ireland were rooted in social injustice and a failure to provide equality for the Catholic minority (Aunger, 1975, 1983; Conway, 1970). From this perspective, inequality needed to be addressed as a first priority. A debate on this issue flared up in educational and policy circles for a while in the early 1970s, but there was no emergent consensus on whether separate schools reflected or contributed to wider societal divisions.

In the absence of consensus on the nature of the problem, two intervention programs were put in place over the next 30 years. The first focused on promoting reconciliation and tolerance, and included curriculum interventions (Arlow, 2004; Connolly et al., 2006; Francis & Greer, 1999; Malone, 1973; Smith, 2005), contact programs (O'Connor et al., 2002), and the development of new religiously integrated schools (Hayes et al., 2009; Moffat, 1993). The second focused on equality, the funding of Catholic schools, educational outcomes, and labor market opportunities (Gallagher et al., 1994).

There was significant learning from the interventions, which focused on reconciliation, but their impact was limited (Gallagher, 2004; Richardson & Gallagher, 2011). Thus, for example, many of the curricular reforms were innovative, but affected relatively few pupils. The contact programs were generally not used to address issues related to conflict or division and often lacked any real ambition to promote change. The development of integrated schools stalled at about seven per cent of the school age population.

There were many reasons why there was limited evidence of systemic change in education. The ideas behind the programs were generally quite good, but the quality of implementation was mixed. Too many projects were dependent on individual, committed teachers, thereby allowing others to abjure any responsibility for the issue. While education leaders generally identified the goal of reconciliation as a priority for schools, it was clear that it was only one among many priorities, most of which were more important in practice. Finally, the education system in Northern Ireland is risk-averse and has often encouraged, implicitly or explicitly, the avoidance of controversial or difficult issues (Gallagher, 2004, 2016).

The work on equality was more focused and emerged in the mid-1980s at a time where there was widespread debate on equal opportunity, or the lack of this, in the labor market. Evidence linked the differential outcomes from schools to the disadvantage of those leaving Catholic schools, and/or to lower levels of public funding for Catholic schools (Gallagher et al., 1994). This, in turn, may have been a contributory factor to differential labor market opportunity. At the time, government policy included a commitment to equal opportunity and, in the light of the evidence, it was agreed that Catholic schools should have access to full public funding. Since then, performance patterns have changed so that now students who graduate from Catholic schools achieve, on average, higher performance in comparison with students who graduate from Protestant schools.

3.2 *Shared Education*

The peace process and political agreement in the late 1990s allowed space for an extensive debate on community relations policy and the extent to which government should pro-actively work toward a shared society, or allow separateness to flourish in a managed way. The political model of consociationalism, which was eventually adopted, contained many elements of the latter approach and will be discussed below. The education model, which emerged from this, focused on the idea of supporting a shared society. After an extensive consideration of the evidence from education interventions in Northern Ireland during the Troubles, and a consideration of comparative experience, Gallagher (1998, 2004) suggested that structural solutions to schools would not, in themselves, guarantee positive outcomes. What was needed was a way to engineer greater opportunities for dialogue and engagement. The model accepted the right of communities to separate schools (Minority Rights Group, 1994), but sought ways to create connections between schools by making the boundaries between them more porous and establishing bridging processes to encourage engagement.

Cross ethnic connections between the institutions of civil society had proved to be beneficial elsewhere (Varshney, 2002), and connecting communities had been a feature of work on effective communities of learning (Granovetter, 1973; Lave & Wenger, 1991; Wenger, 1998, 2000). Flecha (1999) criticized approaches, which cast identity as immutable and fixed, in favor of a conceptualization, which saw identity as fluid, and encouraged dialogic processes aimed at the evolution of identity and hybridity. This was important in promoting ideas beyond a Manichean duality of common or separate schools as the only alternatives.

Gallagher (2005) proposed that school collaboration aimed at supporting participative dialogue might offer a way forward. This was later developed in a proposal for networks of locally based partnerships between Protestant, Catholic and integrated schools (Gallagher, 2016) in which pupils and teachers moved between schools to take classes on a regular basis to provide sustained contact (Hewstone et al., 2008), while protecting the ethos and existence of separate schools. Two large funding agencies, Atlantic Philanthropies and the International Fund for Ireland (IFI), supported a series of pilot projects between 2007 and 2013, which involved over 140 schools in 24 partnerships. Government funding supported an additional project that explored a form of partnership that extended beyond schools. This project included a range of external agencies, including the police, health and welfare services and community organizations (Duffy & Gallagher, 2015).

The model that developed was called 'shared education.' Today, there is an extensive corpus of research on its impact. This includes work on contact (Hughes, 2014); a consideration of its role in improving standards (Booroah & Knox, 2014); the sustainability of partnerships (Duffy & Gallagher, 2014); the dynamics of professional networks (Robinson et al., 2020); and the role of shared education in promoting tolerance or reconciliation in divided societies

(Gallagher & Duffy, 2016, 2017). There has also been a growing international interest in the shared education model with related work being undertaken in Macedonia, Israel and the United States (Kindel, 2015; Loader et al., 2018; Payes, 2013; Yitzhaki et al., 2020). Gallagher (2013) has further tried to locate this approach within the wider conspectus of structural and curricular initiatives in divided or diverse societies.

The shared education model contains five core elements:
- partnerships are based on bottom-up, locally tailored solutions, as each school partnership needs to address local circumstances, challenges and opportunities
- partnerships should involve teacher empowerment in order to create space for innovation (Hannon, 2008)
- contact between pupils should be regular, sustained and visible to the school and wider community
- shared education partnerships should pursue multiple goals, including economic, educational and social goals
- shared classes should involve core educational activities so that the partnership between the schools is explicit and visible (Gallagher, 2016).

One of the original goals of this work had been to mainstream shared education within the school system in Northern Ireland. The 2011–2015 Programme for Government in Northern Ireland contained specific shared education commitments and a Ministerial Advisory Group (Connolly et al., 2013) recommended further extension of the approach. The Shared Education Signature Programme (SESP) was established as an official government programme in 2014, effectively taking over from the pilot programs, while European Peace funds (Peace IV) expanded partnership work in schools. A Shared Education Act was passed by the NI Assembly in 2016. In a relatively short period of time, shared education seems to have transformed the educational landscape in Northern Ireland. At the last count, there were over 700 schools involved in shared education partnerships, with over 60,000 pupils participating in shared classes. The Department of Education informed schools that, because of the COVID-19 crisis, pupil engagement in shared classes would be suspended for the 2020/21 school year, but that online engagement between teachers would continue as part of the process for mainstreaming shared education fully in the school system from 2021 onwards.

By any measure, the shared education initiative has been successful in terms of its impact on the school system in Northern Ireland: it has attracted widespread political and societal support; teachers and pupils generally welcome the opportunities it provides; and there is plenty of evidence of its efficacy across a range of domains. Therefore, this raises the obvious question on how this has been achieved. Before addressing this issue, we need first to look at the political context for policy in Northern Ireland to consider the challenges, which this provides.

3.3   Education Policy and Government in Northern Ireland

As noted above, the political model for Northern Ireland that emerged from the peace process was based largely on consociational lines (Lijphart, 1975), the core idea of which is to accept the segmented nature of divided societies, but use coalition government, and non-majoritarian mechanisms for decision-making. Elites represent the interests of each of the communities as long as they are all involved in decision-making processes of government, while communities can maintain their own separate social institutions to provide an assurance that their identities will be protected. Perhaps the best know example of this arrangement is the Dutch system of 'pillarization' (Sniderman & Hagendoorn, 2009; Sturm et al., 1999).

There are a number of challenges with these arrangements. These include a concern that they lead to the institutionalization of difference (Assi, 2006; Parry, 1969) privileging political leaders, who seek to represent only their own community, over political groups, which seek support across a plurality of communities. There is also the possibility that it could descend into disputes over the allocation of resources, especially if the ethnic balance in the population changes over time. Thus, while the intention is to encourage cooperation and compromise, some think consociationalism risks institutionalizing and deepening divides, and encourages policy paralysis.

The NI Assembly established by the 1998 peace agreement contains many features of consociationalism that aim to encourage cooperation and the building of consensus. In practice, this has been difficult to achieve. In two major education debates in Northern Ireland, this concern about policy paralysis occurred. A review of the selective system of secondary education lasted for almost a decade, but failed to find consensus and ended up in a political limbo, with no decisions of any kind being made. As a result, an unsatisfactory status quo continued (Burns, 2001; Gallagher & Smith, 2000). A review of public administration sought significant efficiencies in the administration of education and began with apparent widespread agreement. However, after over 14 years of dispute, the level of change in an already bloated administrative system was minimal and there was no evidence of any financial savings and reinvestment in education (Knox & Carmichael, 2006a, 2006b).

Why then did the same challenges not confront shared education? When the pilot projects in school partnerships were established in 2007, the funders were keen that the work would lead to significant policy change. This presented a challenge to the research team as the education policy terrain involved a wide range of organizations and interests, in addition to the complexity arising from a form of government that involved a mandatory coalition of four or five political parties. In order to address these issues, the project infrastructure involved two distinctive strands (the wider project strategy is discussed in more detail in Gallagher, 2016).

The first of these was an Independent Governing Body (IGB) to which we invited representatives from as many different education interests as possible. The IGB was an attempt to ensure transparency and clarity among key education stakeholders on the goals and outworking of the project, and give them some influence over the shape and direction of the work. The IGB received annual reports from all the school partnerships and had an opportunity to make recommendations on future work. In addition, the operation of the IGB was designed to minimize the risk that some would attribute a 'hidden agenda' to shared education by being as open as possible on everything occurring within the partnerships and the wider policy discussions it was beginning to provoke.

The second element involved a public engagement strand for the project. Local newspapers were monitored for coverage on shared education work in schools, to try to gauge public awareness and perceptions of the work. A public affairs company was hired to monitor discussion on shared education in the NI Assembly and engagement activities were undertaken with the education spokespersons from every major political party and with members of the NI Assembly Education Committee. The primary intention was to ensure a steady flow of accurate information on the evolving character of the work. In addition, it provided us with an opportunity to identify individual Assembly members with an interest and enthusiasm for what was happening. This engagement meant that any concerns an Assembly member had about shared education could be identified and answered quickly, while at the same time a strong consensus of support for the initiative began to be built.

By the time the Ministerial Advisory Group reported (Connolly et al., 2013), there was clear momentum towards legislative support. This came in two stages. A bill to establish a new Education Authority came before the Assembly in 2014 and, after consultation with the research team, an independent Assembly member proposed an amendment that the Authority would have a statutory duty to 'encourage, facilitate and promote' shared education. Due to the high degree of support that developed in the Assembly over time, the amendment was carried and incorporated in the final act. As the 2014 Act did not provide a legal definition of shared education, a further piece of legislation was required. Thus, the 2016 Shared Education Act provided a legal definition of shared education and extended the statutory duty to encourage, facilitate and promote shared education to the Department of Education.

4 Conclusions

Shared education has had significant success in fostering new policy and practice across more than half of the school system in Northern Ireland. It also achieved, and held, a high level of political consensus, with all the main political parties supporting the 2016 Shared Education Act, which put a statutory duty on the Department of Education to encourage, facilitate and promote shared education. Perhaps the main difference between the shared education initiative to the two policy case studies of academic selection and the review of educational administration lies in its bottom-up character. Independent funding support from two foundations gave the project team a high degree of latitude in terms of how to pursue the work. Drawing on the notion of Next Practice (Hannon, 2008), the project empowered teachers to identify challenges and solutions for effective school collaboration, and to establish programs of work for individual school partnerships that addressed the problems and potential of their local context.

A key part of this was our ability to create a space for innovation in problem solving. This allowed teachers to identify and try out possible solutions, without requiring that every attempt would be successful, while affirming a commitment to learn from all successes or failures. This commitment to innovation, and a degree of tolerance of failure in the pursuit of innovative solutions, is, in our experience, uncommon in top-down official initiatives. These two features of teacher empowerment and locally tailored solutions emerged as keys to the success of the shared education model of school partnership.

References

Akenson, D. H. (1970). *The Irish education experiment: The national system of education in the nineteenth century*. Routledge and Kegan Paul.

Akenson, D. H. (1973). *Education and emnity: The control of schooling in Northern Ireland 1920–1950*. David and Charles.

Arlow, M. (2004). Citizenship education in a divided society: The case of Northern Ireland. In S. Tawil & A. Harley (Eds.), *Education, conflict and social cohesion*. International Bureau of Education.

Assi, A. (2016). *Democracy in Lebanon: Political parties and the struggle for power since Syrian withdrawal*. IB Tauris.

Aunger, E. A. (1975). Religion and occupational class in Northern Ireland. *Economic and Social Review, 7*(1), 1–18.

Aunger, E. A. (1983). Religion and class: An analysis of 1971 census data. In R. J. Cormack & R. D. Osborne (Eds.), *Religion, education and employment* (pp. 24–41). Appletree Press.

Borooah, V., & Knox, C. (2014). Access and performance inequalities: Post primary education in Northern Ireland. *Journal of Poverty and Social Justice, 22*, 111–135

Burns Report. (2001). *Education for the 21st century: Report of the post primary review body*. Department of Education (Northern Ireland)

Connolly, P., Fitzpatrick, S., Gallagher, T., & Harris, P. (2006). Addressing diversity and inclusion in the early years in conflict-affected societies: A case study of the Media Initiative for Children – Northern Ireland. *International Journal of Early Years Education, 14*, 263–278.

Connolly, P., Purvis, D., & O'Grady, P. J. (2013). *Advancing shared education: Report of the Ministerial Advisory Group*. Department of Education (Northern Ireland).

Conway, W. (1970). *Catholic schools*. Catholic Communications Institute.

Darby, J (1997). *Scorpions in a bottle: Conflicting cultures in Northern Ireland*. Minority Rights Group.

Duffy, G., & Gallagher, T. (2014). Collaborative evolution: The context surrounding the formation and the effectiveness of a school partnership in a divided community in Northern Ireland. *Research Papers in Education, 2*(2), 189–210.

Duffy, G., & Gallagher, T. (2015). Collaborative evolution: The context surrounding the formation and effectiveness of a school partnership in a divided community in Northern Ireland. *Research Papers in Education, 30*(1), 1–24.

Duffy, G., & Gallagher, T. (2017). Shared education in contested spaces: How collaborative networks improve communities and schools. *Journal of Education Change, 18*, 107–134.

Farren, S. (1995). *The politics of Irish education 1920–65*. Institute of Irish Studies, The Queen's University of Belfast.

Flecha, R. (1999). Modern and postmodern racism in Europe: Dialogic approach and anti-racist pedagogies. *Harvard Educational Review, 69*, 150–171.

Gallagher, T. (1998, August 27–30). *Religious divisions in schools in Northern Ireland* [Paper presentation]. The British Educational Research Association annual conference. http://www.leeds.ac.uk/educol/documents/000000904.htm

Gallagher, T. (2004). *Education in divided societies*. Palgrave/MacMillan.

Gallagher, T. (2005). Balancing difference and the common good: Lessons from a post-conflict society. *Compare, 35*(4), 411–428.

Gallagher, T. (2013). Education for shared societies. In M. Fitzduff (Ed.), *Public policies in shared societies: A comparative approach* (pp. 129–148). Palgrave.

Gallagher, T. (2016). Shared education in Northern Ireland: School collaboration in divided societies. *Oxford Review of Education, 42*(3), 362–375.

Gallagher, T., Cormack, R. J., & Osborne, R. D. (1994). Religion, equity and education in Northern Ireland. *British Educational Research Journal, 20,* 507–518.

Gallagher, T., & Duffy, G. (2016). Recognising difference while promoting cohesion: The role of collaborative networks in education. In I. Honohan & N. Rougier (Eds.), *Tolerance and diversity in Ireland, North and South.* Manchester University Press.

Gallagher, T., & Smith, A. (2000). *The effects of the selective system of secondary education in Northern Ireland* [Main report]. Department of Education (Northern Ireland)

Granovetter, M. S. (1973). The strength of weak ties. *American Journal of Sociology, 78,* 1360–1380.

Hannon, V. (2008). *'Next practice' in education: A disciplined approach to innovation.* Innovation Unit.

Hayes, B. C., McAllister, I., & Dowds, L. (2009). Integrated education, intergroup relations, and political identities in Northern Ireland. *Social Problems, 54,* 454–482.

Heskin, K. (1980). *Northern Ireland: A psychological analysis.* Gill & Macmillan.

Hewstone, M., Tausch, N., Hughes, J., & Cairns, E. (2008). *Can contact promote better relations? Evidence from mixed and segregated areas of Belfast.* OFMDFM.

Horowitz, D. (1985). *Ethnic groups in conflict.* University of California Press.

Hughes, J. (2014). Contact and context: Sharing education and building relationships in a divided society. *Research Papers in Education, 29,* 1–18.

Kindel, M. (2015). *Convening in contested spaces: The education success project* [Paper presentation]. The AERA Annual Conference, Chicago.

Knox, C., & Carmichael, P. (2006a). Bureau shuffling: The review of public administration in Northern Ireland. *Public Administration, 84*(4), 941–965

Knox, C., & Carmichael, P. (2006b). Improving public services: Public administration reform in Northern Ireland. *Journal of Social Policy, 35*(1), 97–120.

Lijphart, A. (1975). *The politics of accommodation: Pluralism and democracy in the Netherlands.* University of California Press.

Loader, R., Hughes, J., Petroska-Beshka, V., & Tomovska Misoska, A. (2018). Developing social cohesion through schools in Northern Ireland and the former Yugoslav Republic of Macedonia: A study of policy transfer. *Journal on Education in Emergencies, 4*(1), 114–140.

Malone, J. (1973). Schools and community relations. *The Northern Teacher, 11,* 19–30.

Minority Rights Group. (1994). *Education rights and minorities.* Minority Rights Group.

Moffat, C. (Ed.). (1993). *Education together for a change, integrated education and community relations in Northern Ireland.* Fortnight Educational Trust.

O'Connor, U., Hartop, B., & McCully, A. (2002). *A review of the schools community relations programme*. Department of Education (Northern Ireland)

Parry, G. (1996). *Political elites*. Allen and Unwin.

Payes, S. (2013). Separate education and hegemonic domination: Civil society challenges in the Arab-Jewish city of Jaffa. *Intercultural Education, 24*, 544–558.

Payes, S. (2015). *Shared education between Jewish and Palestinian Arab citizens in Israel* [Paper presentation]. AERA Annual Conference, Chicago.

Richardson, N., & Gallagher, T. (Eds.). (2011). *Education for diversity and mutual understanding*. Peter Lang.

Robinson, G., Gallagher, A., Duffy, G., & McAneney, H. (2020). At the boundaries: School networks in divided societies. *Journal of Professional Capital and Community, 5*(2), 183–197.

Smith, M. (2005). *Reckoning with the past: Teaching history in Northern Ireland*. Lexington Books.

Sniderman, P. M., & Hagendoorn, L. (Eds.). (2009). *When ways of life collide: Multiculturalism and its discontents in the Netherlands*. Princeton University Press.

Sturm, J., Groenendijk, L., Kruithof, B., & Rens, J. (1999). Educational pluralism: A historical study of so-called 'pillarization' in the Netherlands, including a comparison with developments in South African education. *Comparative Education, 34*(3), 281–297.

Varshney, A. (2002). *Ethnic conflict and civic life: Hindus and Muslims in India* (2nd ed.). Yale University Press.

Wenger, E. (1998). *Communities of practice: Learning, meaning, and identity*. Cambridge University Press.

Wenger, E. (2000). Communities of practice and social learning systems. *Organization, 7*, 225–246.

Yitzhaki, D., Tannenbaum, M., & Shohamy, E. (2020). 'Shared education' and translanguaging; Students at Jewish and Arab schools learning English together. *International Journal of Bilingual Education and Bilingualism*. doi:10.1080/13670050.2020.1740164

CHAPTER 7

"Moving into Hebrew Is Natural"
Jewish and Arab Teachers in a Shared Education Project

Dafna Yitzhaki

1   Introduction

This chapter explores a shared learning program of English among Jewish and Arab students in a mixed city in Israel, from the point of view of the *teachers*. As a rule, in Israel, Jewish and Arab students study in separate school systems in a context of a continuous political tension between the groups. The study closely observed a training course for Jewish and Arab English teachers aimed to guide them in the stages of preparing and carrying out the shared lessons with their students.

The aim of this study was to examine challenges and opportunities of shared learning, from both social and pedagogic aspects, in a participatory action research study. The analysis offers a general scheme for evaluation of the challenges and potential for teachers, working together in a conflictual context vis-à-vis three elements: (1) the shared field of study; (2) the experience of meeting the 'other'; and (3) the role of a teacher as a practitioner. These elements are exemplified with data from the meetings and raise the following general points. First, shared learning has the potential to empower teachers on both the personal and professional levels. Second, the tension between the two main goals of the program – meeting the 'other' and improving the field of study – is built-in. Therefore, creativity and teaching expertise can overcome this tension. Finally, teachers generally chose to focus on the similarities between the groups rather than dealing with complexities stemming from an imbalance of power. Nonetheless, the shared learning created numerous encounters with conflictual contexts, in general, and with the challenges of the minority group, in particular.

2   Background and Rationale of the Study

In deeply divided societies, such as Israel, contact between the divided groups is rare, due to fear, the desire to maintain the unique characteristics of each group, or for historic and geographic reasons. When the two groups study in two separate school systems, inter-group contact becomes even rarer. Based on the assumption that contact between groups is a desired goal that can reduce social tensions, various educational models for inter-group contact have developed over the years. The two main ones, which are very different from one another, are: (1) a system of integrated schools, which brings together students and teachers from both groups, and (2) short-term (sometimes even one-time) encounters.

These two very different models have their advantages and disadvantages. The integrative schools present in-practice coexistence, enable ongoing contact in an equal environment, involve the communities surrounding the students and have been found effective in promoting positive attitudes towards the 'other' (Ben-Nun, 2013). The main challenge facing these schools is that they are usually perceived as radical. In Northern Ireland and in Israel, where they began to operate at the same time during the 1980s, integrative schools have made great strides and have set an example of a unique educational model. However, they are still very far from the mainstream approach to schools, especially in Israel. In Northern Ireland, these schools have reached about seven percent of the student population, while in Israel they have grown into eight institutions throughout the country. However, they constitute an extremely low percentage of students (about 2000 out of a population of 2.3 million students) and they lack significant institutional support.[1]

The model of short term-meetings – programs that bring students together for a short period of time, sometimes singular events of social, cultural, sports or other activities – are, of course, much easier for broad implementation. However, they have been found to be limited in their ability to create meaningful change in the education system (Gallagher, 2016).

'Shared Education' offers a new outlook that can be placed between these two models (integrated schools and short-term social encounters). Shared Education is an educational approach that promotes partnerships among schools from different educational streams in the same geographic space. The model aims to enhance academic achievements and bring groups closer together. The model, which was developed in Northern Ireland in the context of the Catholic-Protestant conflict became a leading government policy within a decade (Duffy & Gallagher, 2017; Gallagher, 2016). A number of different models of Shared Education exist in various locations. The most prevalent one, implemented also in Israel, is one that joins two classes – one from each group (Catholic-Protestant; Jewish-Arab) – that meet alternately in the two schools and together study a subject that is part of the curriculum. In the current study, we examined the probability and effectiveness of this model in the Israeli context, while focusing on the role of the teachers and the shared field of study.

2.1 Israel

The Jewish-Arab division is the deepest and the most salient in Israel – a country divided over various social rifts, including ethnic, religious and others. Palestinian Arabs, who are Israeli citizens, constitute 21% of Israel's population (this figure does not include the Palestinian residents of Gaza and the West Bank, who are not Israeli citizens). Relations between Jews and Arabs in Israel are typical of minority-majority situations in terms of numbers, balance of power, and access to resources (Yiftachel, 2006).[2] Israel is defined as 'Jewish and democratic' – a description that reflects a constant tension between its characteristics as the home of the Jewish people and its commitment to the minorities living in its territory, especially the Palestinian population that became a minority once Israel was established as an independent state in 1948.

A grim reminder of the tension between the groups appeared in July 2018, when the Israeli parliament enacted a new Basic Law – the 'Nation-State Law,' which legally defined Israel as the nation-state of the Jewish people and terminated the status of the Arabic language as one of Israel's official languages (Yitzhaki, forthcoming). While there are public protests and petitions to overturn this decision (currently awaiting consideration in the High Court of Justice), the law still stands. Protesters do not usually oppose the claim that Israel is the home of the Jewish people, but rather criticize the fact that the law favors the Jewish elements over the democratic ones in Israel's definition. As a result, the law further destabilizes the imbalance between Jewish and non-Jewish citizens that already exists.

Almost all Jewish and Arab Israelis live in separate cities and villages. Approximately 10% of the Arabs live in what are termed 'mixed cities' – municipal entities in which Jews and Arabs live together, although, de facto, they are usually segregated in separate neighborhoods and they rarely live in shared spaces (Monterescu, 2015).

2.2 The School System and the Language Perspective

The division between Jews and Arabs is apparent in the Israeli school system. Historically, there have been two separate school systems – one for Jews and one for Arabs. As a result, most students from the two groups do not meet students from the other sector before attending higher education. The languages of the schools are the mother tongues of the students – Hebrew in the Jewish schools and Arabic in the Arab schools. Each system teaches the mother tongue of the 'other,' but in different scopes and manners. In the Arab school system, Hebrew is taught as a second language on a large scale from the first grades of elementary school (recently also in some kindergartens) throughout high school. The Hebrew language is compulsory, included in the matriculation exams, and it constitutes a required entry condition for higher education.

By contrast, in the Jewish system, Arabic is taught as a 'second foreign language' (after English), mostly in limited scope in junior-high school. Furthermore, it is not compulsory in the matriculation exams (Or & Shohamy, 2016). Moreover, Arabic studies in the Jewish sector have been characterized as being inspired by 'know your enemy' considerations and, often, the Israeli army is involved in pedagogic decisions (Mendel, 2014). Often, the desire on the part of students to serve in the Intelligence branch of the military functions as a key motivator in students' decisions to choose a more extended Arabic program at school.

In this respect, Shared Education offers an alternative to the tense social and linguistic reality of the Israeli school system. Theoretically, it rests on Allport's Intergroup Contact Theory (1954), claiming that direct contact is the most effective way of reducing tensions and prejudices (especially ethnic, religious, or racial tensions) between groups. Effective contact requires four conditions: equal status of participants in the encounters, common goals, collaboration between the groups, and institutional support.

The decision to focus on English as the shared field of study is very relevant to these conditions. Shared learning between Jews and Arabs would automatically lead to the use of Hebrew, based on the situation described above. English lessons, however, would require at least some of the content to be in English – a foreign language for both groups. Thus, would add equality to the context. In addition, the high prestige of English in Israel and other countries, in which it is taught as a foreign language (Crystal, 2012), was considered to be an element that would make it more probable that the program would be integrated into the system, since the school systems consistently seek to promote study of the language.

The study in the previous year evaluated the social and pedagogical experiences of the students. It was found that Shared Education creates an open environment for the students to meet the 'other' and provides a rich interaction between the three languages: Hebrew, Arabic and English (Yitzhaki et al., 2020). In this study, the focus was placed on the teachers, seeing them as central for exploration of the potential of a program to be integrated into the educational system (Lukacs, 2009). The aim of the study was to observe a Jewish-Arab shared learning environment in a politically charged context, from the point of view of the teachers. The research question was: What are the challenges and opportunities for teachers teaching in a bi-national shared learning program?

3 Methodology

The study was conducted as a participatory action research study (Kemmis et al., 2014). I acted as a co-facilitator of a professional training course for Jewish and Arab English teachers in a mixed city in Israel. Nineteen teachers took part

(10 Jewish and 9 Arab) from elementary and middle schools. Approximately half of the teachers had one to three years of experience in shared learning. The training course was 60 hours and included eight four-hour long face-to-face meetings, which ran from November 2019 to March 2020. The training course facilitated all stages of the shared learning – pairing the teachers from a Jewish and an Arab school, planning and implementing the shared lessons and the practice of shared teaching. The training was offered via the Israeli Ministry of Education and was accredited as an in-service course. Participation was voluntary. Data collected for the study included:
- field notes during course sessions
- field notes of meetings held between sessions with the co-facilitator, Ministry of Education (MOE) officials and municipal personnel
- course assignments and final assignments of the participating teachers
- in-depth joint interviews with teachers from one Jewish school and one Arab school.

4 Findings

Data from the different sources were merged and analyzed, employing Grounded Theory (Glaser, 1998) for locating relevant categories, including categories that had been decided upon prior to data collection (according to

TABLE 7.1 Challenges and opportunities for teachers in Shared Education in conflictual contexts

Regarding the shared field of study	Regarding meeting the 'other'	As practitioners
Curriculum	The other teacher	Personal (variety, interest in day-to-day work, workload)
Language	Negotiating the meeting of their students (with the 'other' students)	Professional (co-teaching, working with the professional community)
	Confronting the conflict (in the local community, the national conflict)	Social/political (getting involved in an educational program with social implications)
	The 'other' in my group	

the question asked) and other categories that emerged from the data. Overall, 25 categories were identified, with different levels of salience. The categories were organized according to the following three main ones: challenges and opportunities (1) regarding the shared field of study, (2) meeting the 'other' and (3) as practitioners.

In order to create a broad picture of the findings, the three main topics will be described, using examples from the data. The dynamics between the three topics will be exemplified using one relatively extensive segment from one of the course sessions.

4.1 The Shared Field of Study – English, a Foreign and Neutral Language

English, as the shared field of study, enabled *professional cooperation* among the teachers, created an *authentic pedagogic context* and gained *institutional support* from the professional and municipal authorities.

Unlike most fields of study, the English curriculum, including textbooks, is shared in Jewish and Arab schools in Israel. This made the shared learning more accessible. Moreover, the teachers used the group as a platform for the exchange of teaching resources and ideas, and even for practicing their own English skills.

I am a native speaker of Hebrew and my co-facilitator is a native speaker of Arabic: we both come from the field of teaching English as a foreign language. We stated at the beginning of the course that the lingua franca of the meetings would be English and that we would allow moving over into Hebrew or Arabic if and when necessary. The majority of the teachers in the group (all but two Jewish teachers) are not native speakers of English and their oral English skills varied considerably. Many of them, both Jewish and Arab, mentioned the fact that they did not have enough opportunity in their everyday lives to use English and that the training sessions created this opportunity for them. "Even as a teacher I practiced my English with the other teachers" (R., Arab teacher, final reflection).

The teachers reported that the shared lessons enabled them to get their students involved in practicing English oral skills, a task that is usually challenging for English teachers who teach large classes and need to find authentic context to motivate their students to speak. "I learned that it is really important for my pupils to speak in front of other pupils. It (the shared lessons) encourages them to improve their spoken English and gives them confidence" (N., Jewish teacher). The teachers also saw this as an opportunity to offer a unique content for the routine English lessons: "I think that the lessons were some kind of different approach to how to study English. It's some kind of 'out of the box' activity for the pupils. The pupils enjoyed it" (N. Jewish teacher, final reflection).

The city, in which the study took place, is socioeconomically below average and was designated by the Ministry of Education to receive additional support, due to students' poor achievements on English national exams. The Ministry of Education and the municipal authorities enthusiastically embraced the fact that the shared program was able to offer pedagogical context in English, which motivates the students. The municipality agreed to pay for the commute between schools and was willing to consider designating a weekly time slot for English shared lessons in the city to help the schools coordinate the different time schedules. Thus, the choice of English as the shared field of study was integrated into the institution's motivation to promote English and gave the teachers a feeling that the program would continue after the study as well.

4.2 Meeting the 'Other' – Moving between Numerous Conflictual Contexts

Meeting the 'other' took place on various levels: the Jewish and Arab teachers were paired with one another; all the teachers functioned as a group; and there was the need to negotiate the contact between both groups of students. This occurred while, in the background and below the surface, there were constant reminders of the conflict, on local and national levels.

The teachers' first task was to pair up to create the partnerships. In the second meeting, we encouraged teachers to look for partners to match their pedagogical needs (grade and level of students, etc.). For some of the teachers, this stage was carried out very smoothly, and resulted in effective contacts. These teachers referred to this in their final reflections as the central added value of the program and some reported they had established strong interpersonal connections beyond the professional level, such as exchanging messages and social encounters. Others mentioned specifically the moment in which their students first met and saw their teachers welcoming each other warmly, enthusiastically, and sometimes with a hug. They described the effect this had on their students, who were surprised to learn that their teacher had such close contact with someone from the 'other' group and said that this helped break the ice among the students.

This process, however, was not natural for everyone. In some cases, we, the facilitators, had to do the pairing. In one case, we agreed to the request of two Jewish teachers to create a partnership of three schools – two Jewish and one Arab – since the Jewish teachers did not feel comfortable working with an Arab colleague on a one-to-one basis. In another case, a Jewish teacher asked not to continue a partnership from the previous year and to pair up with another school. In a deeper discourse with the teacher, we learned that the situation was more complex. The Arab school is located in a neighborhood, which suffers from a very high crime rate. At the time, following an incident of shooting a police officer, unprecedented police force was present at the neighborhood. The Jewish teacher admitted that she was afraid the parents would not let their children go into that neighborhood. The partnership between those two schools started in a neutral place (a community center) and gradually moved to the schools. It was clear that curtailing the shared learning after it had begun would have had a negative effect. While trying to negotiate this issue with the Jewish school, the principal argued firmly that she was in favor of 'full cooperation' (field notes, December 2019) as long as the meetings would take place in the Jewish school or in a community center. The Arab school refused to view the meetings only in the Jewish school as 'full cooperation' and the meetings returned to the community center. This compromise enabled the partnership to carry on, despite the need to take a step back.

Another element of "conflict," though below the surface, was also relevant to the teachers participating in the program: there were Arab students studying in Hebrew-speaking schools. The education systems in the city, as in the rest of the country, are separate. Nevertheless, in mixed cities, there is a growing trend of Arab students studying in Jewish institutions. This is another perspective of the conflict – Arab parents view the Jewish schools as superior to the Arab schools. Since Jewish schools are not required to implement any type of accommodations, these students often fall through the cracks (Shwed et al., 2018). One of the Jewish teachers related to the issue of Arab children studying in her school:

> I'll tell you, they (the Arab students) are a minority. They are not the majority. Everything in the school is multicultural, but they are a minority. Sometimes they change their names, like Muhamad is Moshe. The girls too: they might change their names so they seem more … [hesitates] how do you want to call it, more Israeli. So maybe they'll feel more comfortable. I don't know.

The Arab students in the school were described as a "minority" and the school as "multi-cultural." The teacher related to this multi-culturalism mainly as a demographic issue, and not as an ideological issue. In other words, the school does not serve as a significant place for all groups. The teacher described situations in which the Arab students changed their Arabic names (e.g., Muhamad) to a Hebrew name (e.g., Moshe). Despite this reality, the issue did not arise at all during the in-service course. The issue that reflects a complex testament to the Arab-Jewish context, did not arise in discussion, whether unwittingly, or because of a lack of desire to confront it.

During the second meeting we, the facilitators suggested a preparatory classroom activity for the students that would deal with viewpoints of the 'other': the starting point being the different language backgrounds of the two groups. The Jewish teachers related the suggestion with reservations: one of the teachers left the group, and explained later that she had wanted to show her objection, since she could not "understand why it's necessary to talk about what's bad, when they have an opportunity to focus on the good" (field notes 2 Dec. 6). The Arab teachers did not express an opinion in this discussion. We, the facilitators, sensed dissension and settled it by saying that the activity was available to the teachers and it was up to their discretion whether to include it. At the same time, we encouraged them to think of the advantages of raising issues of the differences between the groups before the actual meeting.

In fact, it was quite clear that when the teachers related to the lesson plans they had prepared that related to the "other," the tendency was to emphasize the similarities. The activities/topics for discussion emphasized, for example, places in the city where everyone likes to "hang out" (a popular pizza place, playground, mall, etc.). The overall feeling, as some of the Jewish teachers claimed when asked about their insights regarding the joined lessons, was: "We should always remember that there are differences between people but there are also a lot of things in common. It's better to emphasize the things we have in common" (N. Jewish teacher, final reflection). "Emphasis was placed on recognizing what we share in the city and what we have in common in our cultures" (L., Jewish teacher, final reflection).

Thus, the program enabled meeting the 'other' at different levels, while in the background there were the ever-present reminders of the complexity of the situation: intensive crime-related police patrol in the Arab neighborhood, the "invisible" presence of Arab students in Jewish schools, etc. The teachers did not accept the strategy we had set out to employ – bringing the conflict to the table – and they chose to focus on what the two groups had in common.

4.3 *The Teacher as a Practitioner – Avoidance vs Initiative*

Participation in the program provided many opportunities for personal, professional and even socio-political growth. Teachers have a tremendous workload regardless of specialized programs, and it is natural that they would be busy with their everyday responsibilities. Participation in the program demanded overcoming the technical difficulties and investing a great deal of time. Most of the teachers in the group were prepared for this and used the program as an arena for empowerment and taking initiative.

On the school level, while some of the teachers joined the training course because the school principal required it, others joined the group on their own volition and they had to request the support of their principal. This took a toll on the teachers, as it demanded time, effort, energy, but it also gave the teachers a feeling of satisfaction for taking part in such a significant undertaking on their own, beyond their routine call of duty. For some of the teachers, the program gave them a special status that differed from the status of the rest of the teaching staff in their respective schools. Some of the teachers were asked to present the program at a general teachers' meeting, to lead the program in their schools on a wider scope, and involve more teachers in participation.

At the onset of the training program, a digital platform was created for the participating teachers and, throughout the entire program, the teachers used this platform in order to share materials, transfer relevant information, such as teaching opportunities and help each other with professional dilemmas. After the program ended formally, this platform remained open. It continues to be used on a daily basis for professional consultation, and for sharing holiday greetings.

In addition, the program introduced the teachers to officials in the municipality, the Ministry of Education and the Superintendent of English. In each of these encounters, the teachers were awarded direct contact with officials that they would not have encountered under ordinary circumstances. The teachers mentioned a number of times that the meetings served as a significant "foot in the door" in the system. Some shared that they felt proud of the fact that higher officials took the time to meet them personally and expressed appreciation for what they (the teachers) had accomplished. In one case, one of the teachers was offered a position as an English advisor for the city, due to her activity in the program.

On the local community level, teachers testified that this was an opportunity for them to be involved in an essential social activity, for them and for their students, and that the program enabled them to combine objectives beyond their regular curriculum.

> I don't live in this city but I have been teaching its children for the last 10 years! So, the importance of knowing the other side, is great for me, and I feel it's my job to pass it on to my pupils. (L., Jewish teacher, final reflection)

An opinion that was found at the opposite end of this scale, which did not see the program as a professional teaching opportunity at all, but rather only as a challenge, was heard clearly from only one teacher. However, it is necessary to present her opinion here. This teacher testified in her final reflection that she was not interested in continuing the program as it demanded too much effort and there was no monetary remittance. For other teachers in the group, it was actually the idea of being involved in a new program – whose limits, the level of depth, or the range of possibilities for teaching had not been defined – that aroused enthusiasm. Nonetheless, for this teacher, the benefit was not worth the amount of effort she felt she needed to invest in the project.

These three elements – field of study, meeting the "other" and the teachers as practitioners – were presented separately above in order to provide an overview. However, it is important to clarify the way in which the topics interconnected, and the tension that was generated among the various elements of the program as well. The following example describes an episode from one of the training sessions, and the tension that was found in the program.

4.4 *'Moving into Hebrew Is Natural': The Social, Linguistic and Pedagogic Aspects– An Analysis of One Episode*

In this session, we asked the teachers of one partnership to select a pedagogic dilemma that they encountered while carrying out their shared lessons and bring it up for discussion with the group. The teachers presented the following situation: their students were asked to sit in mixed (Jewish-Arab) groups and discuss questions about their everyday lives, getting to know one another while practicing English-speaking skills. When conversing, the students were very excited to learn about one another and they often stopped speaking in English and moved into Hebrew. The teachers were happy that the students wanted to chat with one another but felt that they were not achieving the aim of practicing English oral skills, as planned.

T. Jewish teacher: "When they move over to Hebrew, it's good for everyone. Moving over to Hebrew is natural."

N. and O., two Arab teachers who are sitting next to me, seem uncomfortable. One of them asks quietly, "Why is it natural that the Arab girls answer in Hebrew?"

One of the Jewish teachers suggests naming this dilemma 'switching to one's mother tongue.' The other facilitator and I explain that while moving over to Hebrew is moving over to L1 for the Jewish students, it is not so for the Arab students.

N. says that her spoken Hebrew is not good: "When you start speaking in Hebrew here, it's difficult for me to follow. I really have to make an effort."

O. joins in and says, "It's difficult for me too; our course here is English."

The Jewish teachers seem very ill at ease. For a moment, there is an uncomfortable silence.

O. speaks again and says: "When you use Hebrew here, in our discussions, it's disrespectful."

The atmosphere becomes quite tense. The teachers are interrupting each other. Some raise their voices in a way that has not yet been seen/heard in the previous sessions. The other facilitator and I try to get the floor in order to maintain a discussion, but are unsuccessful.

E., a Jewish teacher (in a very angry tone):

> I have Russian speakers in my class who can't speak Hebrew (new immigrants to Israel from former USSR). They have to deal with the situation. I'm sorry, Hebrew is the language of the state.

There is still a lot of tension in the room. We can hear comments left and right.

A. (an Arab teacher), who manages to get a word in edgewise, says that the point that persuaded the principal of her school to participate in the program was that this would be a good way to "get the students to learn Hebrew." This remark dissolved the tension and the discussion reverted to a quieter tone.

This episode was comprised of layers of complexity among the teachers and among the students, pedagogically and from an interpersonal point of view. First, within a linguistic-pedagogical context, the teachers described the transition of the students using Hebrew instead of English. Here is where the tension first arose between the social and pedagogic goals. The students were interested in one another and found that conversing in English was too difficult, so they moved over to Hebrew. The interaction continued, but the teachers felt that the objective of the program – speaking English – was being compromised. The Jewish teacher requested to define the issues as "reverting to the mother tongue," while being unaware that in doing this, only the Jewish students were using their mother tongue, and the Arab students were still on shaky ground, language-wise. Although Hebrew is the dominant language in Israel, and the Arab students learn it from a young age, not all Arab students or adults are proficient, even those who live in mixed cities. When a Jewish teacher defined this situation as "natural," she was unaware of the gap between the groups. English is a foreign language for both groups, though, at some levels, it is "more foreign" for some of the Arab students, since it is taught as their third language. Hebrew is the "comfort zone" for the Jewish students. Moving over to Arabic is not even up for discussion; even though the Jewish students in this city do learn Arabic from elementary school, they are not proficient in spoken Arabic at all, not even at the very basic level.

The Arab teachers, N. and O. moved the discussion from the student level to the teacher level. They both had a very basic knowledge of Hebrew and for them, English served as a bridge, not only at the symbolic level, but also at a practical level. While T. defined the transition to Hebrew as "natural," O. viewed it as disrespectful toward her and her Arab colleagues. The Jewish teachers were unwilling to accept this. The Jewish teachers who reacted so vehemently expressed a common Israeli perception that the Jewish symbols (the Hebrew language, the flag, the national anthem, all based on Jewish themes) represent the entire population and there is no place – in any forum – not even in one that is so ethnically diverse – that challenges this. A statement that claims that the use of Hebrew might demonstrate disrespect towards a minority that is not proficient in that language, is not up for discussion. The Arab teachers had an uncomfortable feeling when their students moved into Hebrew during previous discussions; however, this was the first time it was stated so blatantly. It is noteworthy that this was triggered by a discussion dealing with a student-oriented issue. The pedagogical discussion created a platform for the teachers to express their opinions.

The "solution" to this episode was offered by A: her statement dissolved the tension. It came from an unexpected place and added another layer of complexity to the discussion. A. did not delegitimize her colleagues' claim, but rather raised the fact that for the students and for the system (i.e., the school principal), what was perceived as disrespectful and demonstrated a lack of equality (by using Hebrew), was the true incentive that enabled carrying out the program. The Arab principal, who had objected to the meetings, agreed to have them only after one of the teachers pointed out that it was an opportunity for the students to practice their Hebrew, knowing that any subject taught would involve some use of Hebrew. A's statement highlighted the fact that when Arabs and Jews use Hebrew, this is not solely a marginalizing experience for the minority, but may also provide them with opportunities.

5 Discussion

This study provided a close look at a new, shared learning model in Israel. The research focused on the teachers' experiences of working together in their shared field of study, in a highly charged political reality.

The teachers – as individuals and as a group – served as the central links in implementing the shared learning and they made the work meaningful. Shared learning, as presented in this study, has tremendous potential for teachers on both the personal and professional levels. Teachers can make the program meaningful (or keep it superficial), they can enlist other teachers, as well as the principals (or succumb to the obvious difficulty of enlisting the system, or adding to their daily workload), turn the program into a platform for personal and professional growth, and generate a change in society. It was noted that the shared teaching positioned the teachers within a number of circles: her school community, professional staff, and her own community. In such a situation, the teachers are empowered, and feel that they are working toward meaningful goals. The teachers who joined because they had no choice, or were requested to do so by their principals, and were more passive at first, eventually embraced the project, as well. Teachers, who had especially high levels of motivation and initiative, can take advantage of shared education in order to broaden their activity outside of school limits, if they are inclined to do so.

In this study, it was shown that the tension between the two goals – getting to know the other and enriching the field of study – is inherent in activities of shared education. In this case, connection between the two goals was made through English. The teachers aimed to create an authentic context, in which the students and teachers could practice the use of the English language. Indeed, the program provided authentic engagement in English, creative ideas for pedagogical activities, reciprocal learning among the teachers and provided an experience for the students, which was different from their usual routine. The question "What is more important?" and "In what areas should we invest?" – so that the groups would develop a more positive connection than the one that existed before, or improve their English – was constantly in the air and required the teachers to draw on their professionalism and creativity.

Making a well-thought-out choice of the field of study, can help alleviate the tension. In this case, English was chosen for a number of reasons, including its potential to bridge the gap between each group's mother tongue. In situations in which the language is not the source of the obstacle, the field of study must be chosen according to the needs of the students, teachers and school system. This can keep the shared learning from becoming a fleeting episode. In situations in which the students do not share a mother tongue, it is possible to implement models that bridge the gap, such as reciprocal learning of the different mother tongues, or shared learning of a subject that demands less verbiage, while providing creative solutions for the subject of the languages.

The shared learning provided an opportunity for the teachers to encounter the conflictual contexts, in general, and the challenges of the minority group, in particular. The strategy chosen in most cases, mainly by the Jewish teachers, was to prefer to address the similarities in the groups instead of dealing with the difficulties that stem from the differences between the groups and the power imbalance. The teachers preferred to emphasize that we all eat pizza at the same place, hang out at the mall, and 'we are all human,' instead of emphasizing the 'other,' a discussion that has more possible "traps" that demand attention – issues such as equality, prejudice and stereotypes. The conflictual context included gaps related to the different languages and their status, the perception that the Jewish educational system is better than the Arab one, and a reality of crime, which is controlled by massive police forces, etc. All of the aforementioned issues were present during the meetings and appeared under and above the surface.

In situations, in which there is an imbalance of power, for example the Arab-Jewish context in Israel, constructing a balanced system (the number of participants, using a neutral language) is crucial and imperative. However, this does not change the general balance of power overnight, and does not abrogate the dominance of the stronger group. The recurring question in the literature that focuses on inter-group contexts is "What is the "right" thing to do when facing the elephant in the room, or the elephant behind the door?" The literature discusses when and how to bring these issues to the table, if at all, whether to initiate the discussion at the beginning of the meetings, to wait for a more solid relationship to form, or not to raise the issues at all, and to pay full attention to the task at hand (Hughes & Loader, 2021; Maoz, 2011).

Throughout the year, both groups related graciously and enthusiastically to the holiday greetings they received from the 'others,' during Ramadan, Hanukkah, or Easter. Nevertheless, certain heated issues remained unaddressed entirely (such as the desire to discontinue the meetings in crime-ridden neighborhoods) or were received as an insult or with anger. Discussing the "other" (such as, 'we have different languages') immediately reflected the power imbalance – there are two languages that are possible (Hebrew/English) and one that is not an option at all (Arabic). If the speakers of the minority language challenged the dominance of the symbols of the majority, this was perceived as an affront to the teachers from the majority group. It must be taken into account that if it is not possible to bring an issue to the table from the onset, the conflictual contexts teem under the surface. At any given moment, they can surface in situations, perhaps making them more difficult to manage.

Finally, we are left with two major questions: Can the practice of Shared Education challenge the power imbalance? And, is the effort entailed in carrying out this process worth the energy, pedagogically? This program points to a positive response to both questions.

In a social-political system characterized by an imbalance in power, a community of teachers working together collaboratively can be established. In the present case, partnerships were constructed between Arab and Jewish teachers: they were partners who presented a positive model of cooperation, warmth and mutual respect to their own students and to the "other" group. During the teachers' activities as a group, the Arab teachers brought forth a challenging perspective for discussion, regardless of whether it was accepted. They raised a topic that had been silenced and this cannot be taken for granted, given the gaps between the groups. We can only hope that the more the connection deepens and continues, it will be possible to raise other heated issues more easily and, perhaps, even create an atmosphere in which it will be possible to initiate the discussion of such issues, and not only as a response to a difficulty that arises in the field.

It is clear that the answer to the question concerning the benefit of the program depends on what is considered "success." From an interpersonal point of view, we can speak of friendship, warm interaction, long-term collaboration, and changing viewpoints. From a pedagogical point of view, we can speak of an appealing learning experience that raises motivation, improves levels of achievement, and deepens teachers' professional skills, because of the shared education. The level of expectation must correspond to the context. In highly volatile contexts, it is impossible to expect that conflict groups working together will immediately change the asymmetrical balance of power. However, making well thought out choices while facing realistic goals will certainly lead to a "worthwhile" experience. This is true from a pedagogical perspective, as well. The longer the shared learning continues, the more it will be possible to present measurable goals concerning the field of study, devised by the teachers, while, simultaneously, improving the students' knowledge as well.

Notes

1 In Israel, the integrated schools are usually labelled 'bilingual schools' since Jewish and Arab students speak two different mother tongues (Hebrew and Arabic). In practice, the schools operate more like the Northern Ireland integrated model than other bilingual/dual-language schools in the US and other places in the world. For a discussion, see Yuval and Yitzhaki (forthcoming).
2 This is of course a simplification, since both groups are very heterogeneous. Arab society is comprised of a Muslim majority and Christian, Druze and Bedouin minorities – each with its own characteristics and different opportunities for integration into mainstream Israeli society. Concerning Jewish-Israeli society, in 2015, Reuven Rivlin, the President of Israel, defined Israeli society as composed of four 'tribes' – secular Jews, national-religious Jews, Ultra-orthodox Jews and Arabs and called to overcome the tensions between the 'tribes' (Rivlin, 2015). While discussing the differences between the sub-groups within Jewish and Arab societies in Israel is beyond the scope of this chapter, it is important to acknowledge its value.

References

Allport, G. W. (1954). *The nature of prejudice*. Addison Wesley.

Ben-Nun, M. (2013). The 3Rs of integration: Respect, recognition and reconciliation; concepts and practices of integrated schools in Israel and Northern Ireland. *Journal of Peace Education, 10*(1), 1–20.

Crystal, D. (2012). *English as a global language* (2nd ed.). Cambridge University Press.

Duffy, G., & Gallagher, T. (2017). Shared Education in contested spaces: How collaborative networks improve communities and schools. *Journal of Educational Change, 18*, 107–134.

Gallagher, T. (2016). Shared Education in Northern Ireland: School collaboration in divided societies. *Oxford Review of Education, 42*(3), 362–375.

Glaser, B. G. (1998). *Doing Grounded Theory: Issues and discussions*. Sociology Press.

Hughes, J., & Loader, R. (2021). Building bridges: Dialogue and interaction between teachers from divided communities involved in a shared education project. In L. Caronia (Ed.), *Culture in dialogues: Language and interaction at home and school* (pp. 295–316). John Benjamins.

Kemmis, S., McTaggart, R., & Nixon, R. (2014). *The action research planner: Doing critical participatory action research*. Springer.

Lukacs, K. (2009). Quantifying 'the ripple in the pond': The development and initial validation of the Teacher Change Agent Scale. *International Journal of Educational and Psychological Assessment, 3*, 25–37.

Maoz, I. (2011). Does contact work in protracted asymmetrical conflict? Appraising 20 years of reconciliation-aimed encounters between Israeli Jews and Palestinians. *Journal of Peace Research, 48*(1), 115–125.

Mendel, Y. (2014). *The creation of Israeli Arabic: Political and security considerations in the making of Arabic language studies in Israel*. Palgrave Macmillan.

Monterescu, D. (2015). *Jaffa shared and shattered: Contrived coexistence in Israel/Palestine*. Indiana University Press.

Or, I. G., & Shohamy, E. (2016). Contrasting Arabic and Hebrew textbooks in Israel: A focus on culture. In X. Curdt-Christiansen & C. Weninger (Eds.), *Language, ideology and education: The politics of textbooks in language education* (pp. 109–125). Routledge.

Rivlin, R. (2015). President address to the 15th Annual Herzliya Conference. http://archive.president.gov.il/English/ThePresident/Speeches/Pages/news_070615_01.aspx

Shwed, U., Kalish, Y., & Shavit, Y. (2018). Multicultural or assimilationist education: Contact theory and social identity theory in Israeli Arab-Jewish integrated schools. *European Sociological Review, 34*(6), 645–658.

Yiftachel, O. (2006). *Ethnocracy: Land, and the politics of identity Israel/Palestine*. University of Pennsylvania Press.

Yitzhaki, D., Tannenbaum, M., & Shohamy, E. (2020). Shared education and translanguaging; Students at Jewish and Arab schools learning English together. *International Journal of Bilingual Education and Bilingualism.* doi:10.1080/13670050.2020.1740164

Yitzhaki, O. (forthcoming). Arabic and the nation-state law. In I. G. Or, E. Shohamy, & B. Spolsky (Eds.), *Multilingual Israel: Language ideologies, survival, integration, and hybridization.* Multilingual Matters.

Yuval, A., & Yitzhaki, D. (forthcoming). Separation and contact. In A. Yuval & D. Yitzhaki (Eds.), *Education and the Jewish-Palestinian conflict in Israel.* Resling. [in Hebrew]

CHAPTER 8

Shared Learning in the Context of Conflict

Shany Payes and Shula Mola

1   Introduction

In 2018, we published a call for schools in the central region of Israel – which is divided into separate Jewish and Arab cities and towns – to join a program of Shared Learning: Jewish and Arab schools forming partnerships for shared society and creative pedagogy. One of the respondents was a teacher from a Jewish village in the region. "Our home is five minutes away from an Arab town, but I never went there." She explained her interest in the program:

> … but in the last two years, my daughter participated in a Shared Learning program at her school, and made a close friend at the Arab town. She visited the town several times and keeps in touch with her friend. I am ashamed that, out of fear, I never even tried to enter the town. Seeing how my daughter's perception changed, I want to go through a similar experience myself and lead my students as they go through it with me.

As practitioners of Shared Learning in Israel, we find that breaking barriers of fear through effective, prolonged contact is one of this method's benefits. In 2014, the organization in which we work, the CET (Center for Educational Technology), a leading educational NGO in Israel, adapted the Northern Irish model to the Israeli reality, particularly to the Jewish-Arab context with its challenge of two separate languages and the ongoing Israeli-Palestinian conflict. With its partners in the Ministry of Education, municipalities, philanthropy and NGOs, CET supports 200 schools in implementing Shared Learning. Our context includes Jerusalem, where Palestinians are residents (but not Israeli citizens) of the State of Israel, mixed cities within Israel, where Jews and Palestinian-Arabs are both citizens and residents of the same city, and shared regions – where Palestinian-Arabs and Jews are citizens, and live in different localities.

This chapter draws on a six-year experience in those different geographic regions, disciplines, and age groups. It outlines some possible models for the implementation of Shared Learning in different contexts, in order to share our experience, since we believe that Shared Learning is a transferable, accessible and beneficial educational approach for the promotion of shared society.

Through details of the possible models, we encountered, and by sharing some of the challenges we met, and the lessons we have learned, we hope that this chapter will be useful for those of you who wish to lead activist educational practice of Shared Learning of different groups across divides, within your context.

The chapter is based on teachers' and principals' feedback in training courses, dozens of participatory observations in shared lessons, research of Shared Learning in Israel and abroad, and discussions with the Ministry of Education and municipalities' officers.

2 Theoretical Foundations of the Program

Our program's practices are case specific and adapted to changing, imperfect realities on the ground. However, we aim to base the practices on the following theoretical anchors. The first foundation of the program is the concept of *shared education*, which assumes that the collaboration of two or more schools, across a conflict divide, can improve community relations without threatening identity, while delivering educational benefits to learners of all schools involved. Shared Learning assumes that every group has different needs, but all groups share an interest in better education and may find shared interest in peaceful transformation of conflicts. Shared Education is underpinned by Social Network theory (add reference) and, as such, conceives of schools as working collaboratively in networks, and deriving benefits from the collaboration.

Additionally, shared education is underpinned by Intergroup Contact theory, which proposes that, under certain conditions, person-to-person contact is one of the most effective ways to reduce prejudice between majority and minority group members (Allport, 1954). These conditions include the equal status of participants, common goals, institutional support and the development of personal interaction with outgroup members (Forsyth, 2009; Pettigrew, 2006). Partner educators who practice Shared Education implement the theory by offering joint classes, mentoring, teacher exchanges, shared teachers and joint training days. Consequently, shared education results in a wider curriculum choice for students across the schools involved; it encourages pupil mobility between schools through shared classes and supports collaborative staff-development activities. Focusing on raising educational outcomes through partners in excellence, school collaboration aims for all schools, regardless of their students' background, to have the opportunity to improve (Connolly, Purvis & O'Grady, 2013; Gallagher, 2016).

The Shared Education Model in Israel is also based on the Narrative Approach (add reference) that provides an important opportunity to all participants to tell their stories and to make their voices heard. The Narrative Approach assumes that people can learn about a person's reality through the stories they tell and the personal experiences they share. When people tell their stories, the story reflects a perception on the reality in which the storyteller lives: the story confirms it, challenges it, explains it or gives information about it.

Therefore, the Shared Learning Program in Israel draws on the Israeli social psychologist Dan Bar-On's works (2004), in the context of the Israeli-Palestinian conflict. Group members are required to shed their judgmental and critical gaze and the conflictual discourse, and are invited to try and take the point of view of those who share their stories. Such a process increases the likelihood of dealing with painful and conflicting issues that arise from the stories.

We believe that the combination of these theoretical frameworks in Shared Learning action serves both the Jewish and Palestinian-Arab communities and informs meaningful activist pedagogies. However, their translation into action is dynamically challenging, as they meet the reality of separate educational systems for Jews and Arabs, as well as the asymmetrical power relations that exist between the groups.

In the following sections, we share our experience of leading various models of Shared Learning, with their benefits and challenges. This can serve as a guideline for educators, who are considering implementing the model in different contexts. We share with you – the reader – special stories on the creativity and commitment of teachers who succeed in practicing Shared Learning in the field, even in situations that seem impossible. We then elaborate on the challenges and dilemmas, through presenting insights based on a few telling anecdotes from our Shared Learning projects.

3   Theories Meet Practice: Work Frame and Challenges on the Ground

Implementation of the principles for engaging in Shared Learning practices in schools requires a systematic effort, as illustrated in the model in Figure 8.1. The model presents an optimal work frame, based on the four principles for best inter-group contact, as they are manifested in each of the relevant circles: from governmental and local authorities, through school principals, teachers and parents, to the students themselves. Support by each one of these partners is crucial for the success of the model.

To put this in words, in order to promote *equal status* across the system: *school management* should work on the two principals' shared vision and

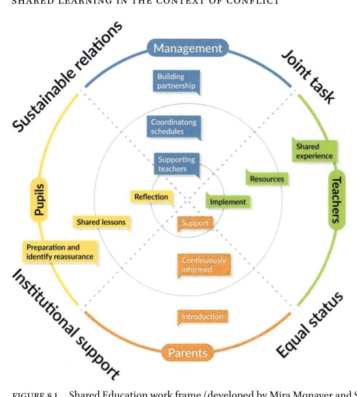

FIGURE 8.1   Shared Education work frame (developed by Mira Monayer and Shany Payes)

their mutual and committed reciprocity. They are the ones who enable Shared Learning logistically through coordinated schedules and provide support to teachers along the way. *Teachers* are at the heart of the Shared Learning process. They are the ones who both educate their students with the values of a shared society and train them with the skills they require in order to succeed in a multi-cultural context. They also facilitate the shared experience of the joint lessons through the setting of a joint pedagogical goal, development of appropriate teaching resources, and planning and teaching together. *Students* should be ready for the lessons, practice an attitude of respect for 'the Other,' learn about their own identity and that of 'the Other,' and speak their preferred language. Furthermore, *parents* should be meaningful partners.

To achieve *institutional support*: *management* should receive support from the Ministry of Education and local authorities, and give logistical and educational support to the teachers. *Teachers* should receive support from management to make Shared Learning a recognized part of their mission and, at the same time, give support to students (for example, through the creation of an environment that supports expression of opinions, concerns and expectations, encouraging relationships between students). *Students* should be prepared and supported by adults. Moreover, at least some of the *parents* should support the program, and resistance among parents should be diminished, through dialogue, over time, as everyone gains experience.

Sustainability of the process is a major goal of the program. Jewish-Arab intervention programs may be harmful and lead to disappointment, if they end within a short time frame. Focusing on a truly joint task that is important for both schools, is key to achieving sustainability. However, from our experience, sustainability over years is also driven by partnership and friendship of principals and/or teachers. Furthermore, it is based on the support of a sustainable systemic framework – for example, teachers' training courses that accompany Shared Learning and provide teachers with a space to collaborate, and cultivate professional development tools. They also receive financial compensation for the time needed for developing and implementing shared lessons.

Educators' agency is at the heart of the Shared Learning action. As long as routines are organized in advance, and respected by both partners, throughout the school year, there are numerous options for practical implementation that takes into account our recommended framework above. In our specific contexts, we have witnessed successful Shared Learning in:

- *Different age groups*: elementary schools can focus on early linguistic skills, for example, while high schools can focus on debates in mixed groups. Each age group can benefit from Shared Learning, if it is planned in accordance with its needs.
- *Online, face to face or hybrid meetings*: the current Covid-19 period, taught us that online Shared Learning can be powerful and effective and save money and time of travel. *In different subject matters*: shared projects in Civics, joint learning of English, Hebrew/Arabic, social skills, mathematics, art or science – all can be fruitful and manageable. *In mixed cities or between close towns*: and even conducted between two schools with mixed student populations, such as two Jewish schools in a mixed city that have a large minority of Arabs and use Shared Learning as an opportunity to discuss identity and cooperation within the schools.

As long as routines are agreed upon and preserved, and dialogue is ongoing, Shared Learning can be practical and manageable. The following examples demonstrate the flexibility of the model and the space it gives teachers to express their vision, creativity, and strengths.

Y. and L., for example, met each other at the teachers' training course. Both are 10th grade English teachers who identified their students' greatest difficulty as the acquisition of oral skills. The teachers, therefore, decided to focus the shared lessons on circles of introduction – beginning from hobbies and preferences, through family to culture and holidays. At the end of the process, L. suggested that each group of students would create a short video, introducing the diversity, similarities and differences, within their group. For this purpose, each lesson would be dedicated to the creation of a short video and uploaded to a shared drive, producing the complete video by the end of the year.

Y. loved the idea, but confessed that she had never used a shared drive with her students, nor had she created videos with them. "You can leave this to me," L. said. "I have a lot of experience with these methods." At the end of the year, when the teachers concluded their cooperation, Y. said: "For me, gaining confidence with technology was a pure bonus of this program. I learned so much from L. and implemented this, not only in the Shared Lessons but also in my other lessons." L. responded and said: "It was a pleasure for me to teach what I know. And I felt that my students gained a lot when they were taught by a native English speaker like Y., together with me."

When two schools collaborate, both teachers do not always specialize in the same area. However, interdisciplinary collaborations can also be very fruitful. Two of the participating junior high schools, for example, chose to lead a combined English and drama Shared Learning program, because one of the teachers was a theatre and drama teacher and her native language was English. The teachers from the other school, who wanted to participate, were English teachers. The teachers participated in Shared Learning training for two consecutive years and became good friends. Their lesson plans reflected their expertise and participating students benefitted from the enhancement of their English skills in creative, drama tools. At the end of the year, N., the principal of one of the schools, said:

> We are very proud of our English team and the level of English of our students. Using the English lessons as a platform to meet their Jewish peers on equal grounds is a wonderful experience for them. And the friendships of my teachers with their colleagues, as well as enhancement of the emotional-social aspect of learning embodied in drama, is an unexpected positive surprise.

Figure 8.2 shows an illustration of one task in a Shared Lesson of fifth graders in a mixed city, in the center of Israel. The students had to match the meaning of English emotions in English and Arabic, as a means of practicing vocabulary through social interaction. The students around the table are Jews and Arabs, but written Hebrew is not used, to encourage conversation and cooperation. Since the Arab students know Hebrew, everyone could manage to solve the task on their own, if the words were written in Hebrew. However, since the Jewish students do not speak Arabic, they had to consult their Arab

FIGURE 8.2   Mira Monayer, at the Eitan Frid (Darca) English Center, Ramle, 2017

friends in order to find the meanings. The creativity and educational depth of this task manifested itself, first, in making cooperation a must. Second, the task reversed the usual power dynamics in Israeli society. Usually, Jews hold the advantageous position in Jewish-Arab interactions, and their language – Hebrew – is the one that is used. This forces the Arabs to make more effort to communicate and places them at a social disadvantage. In this task, knowledge of Arabic was an advantage and a tool for success.

4   The Gap between Models and Realities

Shared learning is an ongoing, dynamic process. As practitioners of Shared Learning, we came to understand that what works well in one place might not be effective in another, depending on context and key stakeholders. While theories and principles underline the actions, most are contradictory to our daily reality of separation and conflict and, therefore, they can only serve as an aspiration, a lighthouse, which are important as a compass signifying our destination and informing our efforts, even if they are not fully realized. Given both the fundamentally unequal relations of Jews and Palestinian-Arabs and routine logistical constraints, meeting the goals reflected in this framework is challenging. In what follows, we share three particularly challenging case studies from our work, as means to highlight the underlining difficulties and possible solutions.

4.1   *Case Study 1: The Challenge of Equal Status against a Live Conflict*

Consider, for example, how difficult it is to get closer to achieving *equal status* in Shared Learning under conflict circumstances, in which a Jewish-Arab hierarchy is a given. Despite the best intentions of all partners, asymmetries and conflict are constantly present.

In 2018, we led a Jewish-Arab Shared Learning training course. Participants were teachers of Arabic in Hebrew schools and teachers of Hebrew in Arab schools, who came together to get to know each other on a personal and national level. They planned to create shared lessons of Hebrew and Arabic and then teach them together, in pairs, when their classes would meet. One of the pairs, Rania and Liat (pseudonyms), got on very well and had a wonderful plan to practice together Hebrew and Arabic vocabulary around garden and plants, and have the shared lesson in the schools' communal gardens – each lesson in a different school. The first shared lesson, in the Jewish school, was successful and fruitful, but as the second lesson got closer, tensions rose between the teams around the planned schedule, timetable and planned activities.

One evening, I (Shany) received a series of phone calls. First, Liat, the Jewish teacher, said: "I feel that I am doing all the planning, I don't feel the partnership" Then Rania called and said: "I don't know why they want to shorten the visit. It won't work if we give it such little time." The issues of work division and timetables may indeed be complicated when planning Shared Learning, but I felt that there was more to this case and asked about it. "Well," Rania said, "I feel that they may face resistance from parents and don't want to tell us." However, even that was not enough in order to understand why the two friendly teachers could not resolve the small differences between them. Phone calls continued. The Jewish teacher called again and said: "It is really frustrating; they are not willing to change anything in the plan, even though we have to go back to school a little earlier." Each phone call was long and elaborate, and it was hard to understand what went wrong. I kept feeling that disagreements were minor in comparison to the volume of emotions, and I asked about it. "You know what?" Rania told me, "It may be better if we collaborate with a city that is further away, you know. It's best if we don't work with our neighbors, because their [the partner's] city was built only recently on our land."

4.1.1   Discussion

The logistical issues, the timetables and activities, were all just symptoms, we realized. The root cause of the tension between the teams was the conflict between the cities. For the Arab teachers, visiting the modern city that had been quickly built on their lands was painful. For the Jewish teachers, the difficulty was having to cope with hostile and racist attitudes of some parents, and their own fears and concerns regarding the status of their city in the region, given the conflict over the land.

Despite our efforts, the teachers and principals of these schools were never willing to discuss these issues openly between them, and that partnership ended at the end of the year. The hardship was caused because, in those days, the confrontation was acute. From the perspective of the Palestinian partner, the expropriation of land was taking place in the present and through the direct involvement of the parents of the students, who were participating in the Shared Learning. This constituted a direct contradiction of the stated purpose of social cohesion and solidarity. In retrospect, we, the leaders of the program, did not take into account the element of topicality and the intense presence of the conflict, but focused on the potential of the partnership due to the geographical proximity between the communities.

4.2   Case Study 2: The Challenge of Friendly Relations against a Hostile Environment

This shared lesson of fourth graders was meticulously planned by the partner teachers around the subject of "family." In its first part, the children were divided into six groups of six children each, having a race to find as many words as they could from a bank of words that were placed in the middle of the gymnasium. In its second part, each group had scissors, glue, and crayons to create a collage with the words they found.

The children were happy and collaborating and all went well until the second part, when one of the Jewish children shouted: He stabbed me. "An Arab boy held his scissors up and looked puzzled. He did not even understand at first that the scream was directed at him, and when he realized it, he just murmured: "Sorry, I just wanted to cut the paper." It seems that the scissors unintentionally touched the Jewish boy. Soon, even before the teachers who were there realized that there was a situation, the boy's friends already gathered around him and the group was divided into two camps: Jews and Arabs. The teachers approached the group and investigated what happened. As the children were reluctant to relax, they called the school principals, who were present at the lesson, sitting outside the classroom, chatting between themselves.

The two principals were quick to respond. They stopped the activity and asked all groups to gather around. "We are stopping the work, because there is a misunderstanding between two children that seems to be getting out of hand," one of them said. "And we would like to ask you: what do we do in our classes when two people argue or when someone feels threatened by a friend?" The children all went quiet, and the principal continued: "Just as we listen to everyone, find out the facts and settle the argument in the class, this is what we'll do here." The accused child explained that he had no intention of stabbing, the child, who shouted, accepted the explanation, and the lesson continued.

4.2.1   Discussion

In those few minutes, the small interaction between the children was tightly connected to the national conflict between the groups. Unfortunately, despite the training that they undergo, the teachers told us that they did not know how to react during the first few minutes. They felt embarrassment, pain and confusion, while facing the situation. In this case, the principals were present and reacted well, but this, of course, cannot be the case in every interaction.

All educators, who were involved with this complicated interaction between Arab and Jewish students, know that the word 'stabbing' has a harsh meaning in Israeli-Palestinian relations. Therefore, the principals knew instantly that they had to react and move the discourse away from what could be interpreted as the national realm, to the educational realm. In other words, they normalized the interaction.

This story reveals the dilemmas and concerns that the program still faces – what level of discussion should take place with students on the issue of the conflict, and how to expose and cleverly deal with their prejudices and stereotypes, when the students meet one another. Additional concerns are related to the teachers and principals involved: do they have the skills to lead an honest discussion about 'the elephant in the room' – the Israeli-Palestinian conflict and its implications – on our interactions? Furthermore, if they do talk about it, how constructive is it for the task of Shared Learning?

The Shared Learning model assumes that working together can lead to new, better relations, just by means of the interactions. The joint task should have the power to get 'the elephant' out of the classroom. However, as this example shows, it is sometimes inevitable to talk about the big issues, even when the smallest, most mundane task is involved.

4.3 *Case Study 3: The Challenge of Institutional Support against the Norm of Separation*

The following example illustrates the potential challenges in receiving *institutional support*.

Amer (pseudonym), an English teacher in one of the remote villages in Jerusalem, came to the first teacher-training meeting without his colleague, who also registered for the same course. When we asked why, Amer just told the group that his friend could not come. During the break in the meeting, he approached me and said that, in fact, his friend did not come because there was no approval from the principal. "No approval from the principal?", I [who?] was surprised, "How can it be: your principal participates in the principals' training course himself." "You do not understand," Amer said:

> The principal participates without the approval of his inspector. The inspector knows he is participating, but has not formally approved it. So, the principal wants us to do the same thing. But, both my colleague and I

think it's not right. You need the approval of the principal and the inspector to participate, because I heard that not only do you have to attend this course, but you also must lead meetings with Jewish students. This is not something we decide upon. It's the decision of a principal and a supervisor. I also did not want to come today, but I said I would come and tell you so you can take care of it. To take care of it is not to call my principal and tell him. What you need to do is get the inspector's approval. Tell the principal he agrees. Otherwise, none of us can come.

4.3.1 Discussion

Since Shared Learning is a program that requires Jewish and Arab students meeting, alternatively in the schools or, as in the case of Jerusalem, in a neutral third place, the participation of adults in the process of training is a necessary, but not sufficient component. The program is not about dialogue between adults, but about recruiting and training adults to carry out the shared learning between students. Having a joint lesson cannot be a secret matter. It cannot exist 'under the radar.' Rather, it is an open matter, and the partners must take into account the risks – and the opportunities – involved in participating in the program. In the end, in the above example, we were unable to harness the supervisor for the move, so the two teachers dropped out of the training.

5 Conclusions

Shared Learning is a practice of interaction, which like all interactions, takes place in a context. It is this context – of conflict and inequalities – with which participants courageously challenge and deal in practicing their partnerships. Learning from case studies, such as those discussed above, highlight several points of emphasis throughout the Shared Learning process.

First, dealing with the challenges of Shared Learning requires a mechanism for safe dialogue between the partners. Educators often feel uncomfortable talking about the Israeli-Palestinian conflict. It seems to be out of their scope of influence, somewhere in the realm of high politics, and a source of uncomfortable disagreements. Enjoying that which is shared, such as hobbies, motherhood, or pedagogy, seems more productive and enabling for the execution of Shared Learning. However, the conflict is reflected in many levels of the schools' interactions – be they fights between children, such as those in the 'scissors incident,' or in teachers' and parents' objections, such as the 'land incident,' described above. To gain educational benefit from Shared Learning, such incidents should be frankly discussed, with the understanding that errors and disagreements are inevitable.

When examining conflict in Shared Learning, it can be understandable why the scissors incident was more easily resolved than the issues of the land. While fights between children can easily be conceptualized as part of the national conflict, skilled, trained teachers can re-conceptualize them to the educational realm, highlighting – as the principal in the scissors' incidents did – that children fight and make peace, and we should avoid making more of such routine incidents. When it comes to conflict over land, however, the solution is out of our hands and we cannot divert the discussion to the educational field per-se.

In all the cases described above, we firmly believe that frank, safe dialogue could have brought some relief to the pains and enabled the partners to continue working together. When this did not happen, it is clear that the dialogue mechanisms offered in the training course and the ongoing guidance were not effective enough. Therefore, such mechanisms are essential, and their methodologies, should be strengthened, and developed further.

As we can learn from the story of the teachers who demanded *explicit institutional support*, such mechanisms must be consistent and open. Implicit acceptance of Shared Learning is not enough. Teachers need their principals and inspectors to set the scene for them to have the required confidence to lead a disputed task, in order to succeed.

This chapter discussed both success stories and limitations of the Shared Learning program. Both success and frustration accompany educators who dare challenge personal and professional conventions. The reward of Shared Learning is that it allows us to experience a different, shared reality in the realm of education. Even when this alternative reality is challenging, it allows us to imagine and model Jewish-Arab cooperation, rather than segregation.

References

Allport, G. W. (1954). *The nature of prejudice*. Addison-Wesley.
Bar-on, D., & Adwan, S. (2004). Shared history project: A prime example of peace building under fire. *International Journal of Politics Culture and Society, 17*(3), 513–521.
Connolly, P., Purvis, D., & O'Grady, P. J. (2013). *Advancing shared education*. Report of the Ministerial Advisory Group.
Forsyth, D. R. (2009). *Group dynamics*. Cengage Learning.
Gallagher, T. (2016). Shared education in Northern Ireland: School collaboration in divided societies. *Oxford Review of Education, 42*(3), 362–375.
Pettigrew, T. F. (2006). A meta-analytic test of intergroup contact theory. *Journal of Personality and Social Psychology, 90*(5), 751–783.

CHAPTER 9

Jewish-Arab Bilingual Education in Israel

Assaf Meshulam

> Many people ask us, you've been around for 30 years and haven't changed anything, haven't brought peace ... I say, you're right. But we didn't take responsibility for the conflict or for its solution. We are alternative action. We want to be part of the reality. And so long as this place, including its educational institutions, exists and develops, that's enough for me. We exist.
> ABDESSALAAM (January 2009)

∵

Dedicated to the memory of Abdessalaam Najjar, Founding member and teacher at Wahat al Salam/Neve Shalom School

1   Introduction

Since the first Jewish-Arab bilingual (Arabic-Hebrew) school was established in 1984, the number of such programs has grown modestly to eight across Israel, operating under the auspices of three separate NGOs:[1] Wahat al-Salam/Neve Shalom (WAS/NS), the Center for Jewish-Arab Education in Israel (Hand-in-Hand), and the Hagar Association for Jewish-Arab Education for Equality (Hagar). A variety of terms are used to define this educational model, including bilingual, binational, multicultural, and integrated, as well as peace education and critical democratic education. This variation in terms represents the multilayered ideologies and educational traditions that characterize the different founders, teachers, and communities involved in the schools and those who research them.[2] Despite the small scale of Jewish-Arab education in Israel, a rich body of scholarly research has developed over the last decades, covering an array of topics. These include: school establishment, language, identity, co-existence, and parental choice (e.g., Amara et al., 2009; Arar & Massry-Herzalah, 2017; Bekerman, 2004, 2005, 2009; Bekerman & Shhadi, 2003; Dubiner et al., 2018; Feuerverger, 2001; Meshulam,

2011, 2012, 2015, 2019a, 2020; Nasser, 2011; Paul-Binyamin & Jayusi, 2018; Sitner & Meshulam, 2020). Notwithstanding the impressive research, there has been no comprehensive analysis of this unique educational model as a whole. Instead, studies tend to focus narrowly on one school or on a number of schools from a single NGO and not systematically on all the schools across all the NGOs.

This chapter seeks to fill this gap by offering a holistic overview of the Jewish-Arab schools as an educational model, including the pedagogy and curriculum development. I present the central educational models and approaches that shaped the development of the schools and propose that, despite the uncoordinated entanglement of influences, a unique, model of Jewish-Arab education can be identified. I contend that the hybridity in the types of programs that evolved is due to the variance in the fields of knowledge and approaches that influenced the schools' founders and developers. None of the Jewish-Arab schools was constructed on an existing educational model – bilingual or otherwise. However, notwithstanding the variance, all were founded on an ideological vision of shared education in Arabic and Hebrew for Jewish and Arab children, and all self-define as bilingual education. In addition, and significantly, all the schools share a similar integration of three primary educational approaches and implement similar key strategies and practices in developing their curricula and pedagogy.

The chapter is based on data collected in three case-studies conducted between 2008–2019 (Meshulam, 2011, 2019a, 2020; Sitner & Meshulam, 2020), which were supplemented by follow-up interviews and discussions with current staff and administrators at the schools and NGOs, and analysis of the research literature and publications produced by the schools and organizations. The chapter proceeds as follows: I begin by reviewing the background and development of Jewish-Arab schools in Israel. I outline the socio-historical contexts of the foundation and operation of the schools, as well as the impact of progressive education, peace education, and bilingual education on the formation of the educational model. I then discuss the practices and strategies that have emerged in all the schools, across all three NGOs for curricular and pedagogical development. I conclude with a consideration of the challenges the schools face in developing and realizing this model, particularly in conflict-ridden Israeli society.

2   Jewish-Arab Education in Israel: Background

2.1   *The Development of Bilingual Schools*
There are currently eight Jewish-Arab schools in the Israeli education system, in eight cities and towns across the country. They are operated and supported by three different NGOs (see Table 9.1): Wahat al-Salam/Neve Shalom ("WAS/NS"),

TABLE 9.1 Jewish-Arab bilingual schools in Israel 2019–2020 (updated data were provided by the Jewish-Arab NGOs)

Organization	Location	School name	Founding year	Status	Grades	No. of students
WAS/NS	WAS/NS	Wahat al-Salam/Neve Shalom	1984	Public/Special-Magnet	Childcare to 6th grade	299
Hand-in-Hand	Jerusalem	Max Rayne	1998	Public/Special-Magnet	Preschool to 12th grade	698
	Galil	The Galilee School	1998	Public/Special-Magnet	1st to 6th grade	250
	Wadi Ara	Bridge Over the Wadi	2004	Public/Special-Magnet	Preschool to 6th grade	271
	Haifa	Hand-in-Hand Haifa School	2012	Public/Special-Magnet Public	Preschool to 4th grade	180
	Jaffa	Tel Aviv-Jaffa School	2013	Public	Preschool to 5th grade	455
	Kfar-Saba	Hand-in-Hand Kfar-Saba School	2015	Private Recognized by MOE	Preschool to 2nd grade	89
Hagar	Beersheba	The Bilingual School	2006	Public/Special-Magnet	Childcare to 6th grade	372
Total						2614

the Center for Jewish-Arab Education in Israel ("Hand-in-Hand"), and the Hagar Association for Jewish-Arab Education for Equality ("Hagar"). The Jewish-Arab educational institutions serve a total of 2,614 students in a variety of childcare, pre-school, elementary-school, and high-school programs.

Jewish-Arab education began in 1984, with the opening of the first school, Wahat el-Salam/Neve-Shalom. The school was established by parents in a small cooperative village of the same name founded in the late 1970s by Jews and Palestinians as a model of coexistence between Jews and Arabs. The parents sought to create a school for their children that would promote and enable this vision. The village resembles a *kibbutz*-style[3] collective community in its egalitarian nature and structure, with the critical addition of Arabs and Jews living together as equal partners. As of 2019–2020, the WAS/NS frameworks serve 299 children in a daycare, pre-school, kindergarten, and elementary school. Today, only a minority of the pupils are residents of the cooperative village, with the majority commuting from neighboring Arab, Jewish, and mixed towns.

In 1997, the Hand-in-Hand organization was founded with the aim of creating a national network of Jewish-Arab bilingual schools. The organization's founders – a Palestinian educator and Jewish activist – sought to advance a "strong, inclusive, shared society in Israel through a network of Jewish-Arab integrated bilingual schools and organized communities" (Hand in Hand, n.d.) The largest Jewish-Arab education NGO, it operates six schools and educational frameworks in various areas of the country, serving 1,943 students. The first two schools were established in 1998 as regional bilingual schools in Jerusalem and the Galilee. The Max Rayne School in Jerusalem is currently the largest Jewish-Arab school in Israel and the only one that goes from preschool to twelfth grade. It serves 698 students, mostly from affluent families from Palestinian and Jewish neighborhoods in East and West Jerusalem. The Galilee school, located in Kibbutz Eshbal, runs from first grade to sixth grade, with 250 students coming from the neighboring Palestinian town Sakhnin, eight Palestinian villages, and 15 Jewish villages. In 2004, the NGO opened a third school, the Bridge-over-the-Wadi School, in Wadi Ara in northern Israel. A K-6 school, it remains the only Jewish-Arab school located in a Palestinian town and serves 271 students. The school began as a local shared-education initiative of Palestinian and Jewish parents from the Wadi Ara area and then joined the Hand-in Hand network for support and guidance. This type of educational action – parents who initiate a Jewish-Arab school in their locale and reach-out to the Hand-in-Hand organization for support – characterizes all the subsequent Hand-in-Hand schools: the Haifa, Jaffa, and Kfar-Saba schools are all local parental initiatives. All are small, growing both "upwards" (in grade levels) and laterally (in number of classes in each grade). The Haifa school, founded in 2012, runs from pre-school to fourth grade and serves 180 students. The Jaffa school, founded in 2013, runs from pre-school to fifth grade, with 455 students. The Kfar-Saba school opened in 2015 and includes only a pre-school, kindergarten, and first and second grades; it currently serves 89 students. All but the Kfar-Saba school are fully public magnet schools.

The third Jewish-Arab NGO, Hagar, was founded in the southern city of Beersheba in 2006 by parents and community activists seeking to build "an egalitarian civil society in the Negev and in Israel as a whole" (Hagar Jewish-Arab Education for Equality, n.d.). Initially operating in collaboration with Hand-in-Hand, Hagar became an autonomous organization with the establishment of its school. Nonetheless, the educational model implemented at the Hagar school was influenced by the Hand-in-Hand program. Hagar's pedagogical developer had worked at Hand-in-Hand prior to joining Hagar and brought some of the programs she had co-developed there. Supported by Hagar's founders and educators, the pedagogical developer developed a unique program that responds to the school's local contexts and particular vision. As of 2019–2020, Hagar operated three educational frameworks: a daycare, pre-school, and K-6 school, with a total enrollment of 372 children. The elementary school is a public magnet school, drawing students from neighborhoods in Beersheba, as well as from adjacent suburbs and towns, including Bedouin towns and unrecognized villages.[4] Beersheba, and the entire Negev region, in fact, are the geographical and socio-economic periphery of Israel: underserved and underdeveloped in terms of public infrastructures and resources, and suffering from a pronounced socio-economic gap and income inequality. Thus, Hagar's founders sought, from the outset, to form a school that "would produce a local story, of the Negev, of Beersheba, of the inhabitants" and address the socio-economic disparities characterizing the region.

2.2   *The Socio-Historical Context*

The emergence and development of the Jewish-Arab educational model must be understood in the context of the unique socio-historical conditions and circumstances in which it emerged and exists, particularly the persistent power inequality between Palestinian and Jewish citizens of Israel, at all levels of society. The schools operate in a public education setting that is de-facto segregated into two systems: a Jewish-dominated, Hebrew-language school system and a Palestinian, Arabic-language system. This makes it unlikely for Palestinian and Jewish children to learn together and is no mere coincidence.

Although there is no official segregation policy, since Israeli statehood in 1948, a policy of spatial separation of Palestinian and Jewish populations led to the geographic partitioning of Palestinian public schools from Jewish schools (Al-Haj, 1995). This longstanding educational reality has reinforced the ongoing socio-economic, cultural, and political discrimination and marginalization of the Palestinian minority (Abu-Nimer, 1999; Abu-Saad, 2006; Meshulam, 2015). There has been consistent subordination of the educational needs of Palestinian children and schools in terms of recognition, quality, resource distribution, and participation in setting the educational agenda and contents. The Palestinian schools have continually suffered from substandard infrastructure and facilities, inferior teacher qualification programs, triple dropout rates, and inadequate curriculum development (Abu-Asbah, 2007; Abu-Saad, 2006; Agbaria, 2018). Palestinian national and cultural contents are conspicuously absent from the official curriculum taught in the Palestinian schools, which promotes primarily Jewish-Western culture and narratives. This was the socio-historical background from which the Jewish-Arab educational stream emerged. Although developed by different individuals, with different educational orientations, and in different micro-level conditions, all are connected by a fundamental ideological basis and logic: the aspiration to create a framework for educating Palestinian and Jewish children together for social equality and justice, where the inequalities and tensions between the two communities are addressed and challenged.

2.3 The Emergence of the Jewish-Arab Education Model

Three interwoven premises guide my presentation of the formation of the Jewish-Arab education model. First, the model has not been developed in an organized, structured way and remains a work-in-progress. It is a fluid product of ongoing experimentation and dialogue between the schools' local communities, the NGOs, local education authorities, the Ministry of Education, and society-at-large. Second, although the schools are run by autonomous NGOs and have generally been the local initiatives of parents, educators, and activists responding to their communities' needs and conditions, there has always been a mutual exchange of ideas, practices, and experience across the schools and organizations. This has been in the form of loose cooperation in content development, for example, but also in the interchange of educators and educational administrators between the NGOs, who share and disseminate the knowledge and experience they bring with them. Third, three key – sometimes overlapping – stages can be identified in the model's formation: the early influence of progressive and peace education; the stage of gaining official public school status; and the integration of two-way bilingual education into the schools.

2.4 Progressive Education and Peace Education

As the pioneering school, WAS/NS laid the groundwork for the Jewish-Arab educational model. The founding educators, a Palestinian teacher and Jewish teacher – who had been influenced by two central educational streams, progressive education and peace education – developed its initial pedagogy and curriculum. In interviews with the teachers, both described a spontaneous development of the school's "clear and tangible" aims "to teach the two languages, to create a meeting between the two cultures, and to create a school where it will be fun to study" (Twenty Years, 2007, p. 15). To advance these goals, the school had always aimed for balanced representation of Palestinians and Jews, not only in the student population, but also in the teaching staff. The latter goal led to the development of a bilingual co-teaching practice at the school, adopted by all subsequent Jewish-Arab schools, where Arabic-speaking Palestinian teachers and Hebrew-speaking Jewish teachers teach alongside one another in their native languages in the same classroom.

The school's founding teachers were influenced by a different form of progressive education. The Palestinian teacher, who completed his elementary-school teacher training at the David Yellin College of Education in Jerusalem, was oriented towards the progressive open-school model developed there that was popular in Israel in the 1970s and 1980s as an experimental education method (David Yellin Academic College of Education, n.d.). The Jewish teacher trained at the Kibbutzim College of Education in Tel Aviv and was influenced by the kibbutz educational model, which was constructed on socialist, communal values (Kibbutzim College of Education, n.d.). Progressive, humanistic, and non-authoritarian in orientation, this educational approach is characterized by interdisciplinary, integrative thematic teaching, hands-on learning activities, and a deep connection to the local environment.

The Palestinian founding teacher described an organic integration of the two educational approaches at the school, which began as "open ... and democratic by definition. [W]e didn't sit down and think. That is how it evolved – a partnership between the children and the teachers ... open in the entire sense of the word." From the onset, a shared feature of both the open model and kibbutz model – project-based and thematic learning – was adopted in WAS/NS. Today, elements of these progressive education streams are present in all the Jewish-Arab schools, particularly in their child-centered pedagogy and project-based and thematic learning approaches.

The second educational model that influenced the Jewish-Arab model is peace education. This can be traced back to the WAS/NS adult-education school for peace, founded in 1979 prior to the elementary school, which aimed to "promote more humane, egalitarian and just relations between Palestinians and Jews" (The School for Peace, n.d.). This agenda, adopted also in the WAS/NS elementary school, is an integral feature in all the Jewish-Arab schools.

Peace education has a long history (Harris, 1988, 2010), in which various streams have evolved, based on different political, theoretical, and methodological tendencies (e.g., Bajaj, 2008; Salomon & Cairns, 2010). The Jewish-Arab model most closely follows what Bar-Tal (2002) terms the contextual approach to peace education. This approach integrates the universal dimensions of peace education emphasized by other approaches but emphasizes local contexts. In other words, peace education should reflect and respond to the socio-political conditions and contexts of the society in which it is implemented, and its curricula must reflect the dynamics, conflicts, and tensions of that society (Bar-Tal, 2002). Following this approach, the curricula in the Jewish-Arab schools address not only global universal peace concerns but also local socio-political tensions and inequalities between Palestinian and Jewish citizens of Israel and the geopolitical context of the Palestinian-Israeli conflict. Furthermore, the schools' aspiration to maintain symmetry between the two communities and languages can also be attributed to their peace education orientation, supported by the equal and egalitarian practices adopted from the kibbutz education model.

The structural and ideological goal of full symmetry between Palestinians and Jews in student composition and in the teaching staff was brought to the Hand-in-Hand schools by the NGO's Palestinian founder, who had taught at WAS/NS. This included the implementation of the co-teaching practice. The Hand-in-Hand pedagogy and curriculum continued to be influenced by the WAS/NS program, with variations developing over time. In the early years, there was even direct collaboration with WAS/NS. As recounted by the WAS/NS principal, during this period, "we kept in close contact with its directors [...] and even participated in and led joint seminars with Hand-in-Hand's educational team." This collaboration, however, was not maintained over time.

2.5 Becoming Official Public Schools and the Two-Way Bilingual Model

A notable turning point in the development of the Jewish-Arab educational model was the gradual transition of the schools to official public school status and the resultant incorporation of aspects that resemble the two-way bilingual education model prevalent in US bilingual education. Currently, with only one exception,[5] all the schools are public schools, officially recognized by the Ministry of Education (MoE).

The transition of WAS/NS to public school status meant that it gained the needed public financial support, but also subjected it to MoE supervision. The school now had to implement official guidelines and curricula, forcing it to make adaptions to its progressive curriculum, pedagogy, and structure. This created a need for a structured bilingual education model upon which to draw and led WAS/NS to the two-way bilingual (Arabic-Hebrew) model,[6] which best supports its education agenda and orientation in a public framework. Today, all the Jewish-Arab schools offer a similar bilingual education program.

In fact, none of the multiplicity of bilingual education models fully represents the Jewish-Arab education model. Although all the Jewish-Arab schools describe themselves as bilingual, none modeled themselves on any concrete bilingual educational approach at the outset. Their bilingualism was initially expressed in their aspiration for equal representation of the languages and cultures of the two communities at the school and not in the implementation of a particular bilingual model. However, of the existing models, the Jewish-Arab schools most closely resemble the two-way bilingualism model in key aspects: in the schools' structure, pedagogy, and curriculum and in their aim to equalize power relations between the minority-language group (Arabic-speaking Palestinian students) and the majority-language group (Hebrew-speaking Jews). Baker (2011) asserts that two-way bilingual education is the optimal program for minority-language students: they develop deep academic proficiency and cognitive understanding through their first language to compete successfully with native speakers of the second language.

At the foundation of the two-way model are three central features. (1) Classes comprise students from both language groups, ideally in equal numbers. (2) Classroom instruction is conducted in both the minority and majority languages, to facilitate bilingualism and biliteracy for both language groups. However, clear boundaries are maintained between the two languages. (3) The majority of the curriculum is taught in both languages, so that students experience instruction of content and not merely literacy in the two languages.

The Jewish-Arab schools generally meet the criterion of a balance of students from each language group, but struggle with the other two criteria. This is mainly because of the acute lack of support in the Israeli education system and in Israeli society for Arabic-Hebrew bilingualism and biliteracy. The co-teaching practice, which was developed to achieve symmetry in language-group representation, emerged as a challenge to two-way bilingualism by blurring the boundaries between the two languages: rather than lessons being taught alternatively in each language, as in the two-way model, they are taught in both languages simultaneously. Under this pedagogical approach, the lessons are taught in both languages simultaneously rather than alternatively in each language, as in the two-way model. However, in practice, this co-teaching pedagogy has not supported balanced bilingualism: it has only reinforced and reproduced the asymmetry between the two languages in broader society. The presence of a Hebrew-speaking teacher in each class enables the Jewish children to wait for Hebrew translation rather than making the effort to use Arabic. In contrast, Arab students, who were exposed to Hebrew as the hegemonic language, were able to communicate in Hebrew. Hence, Hebrew has remained the dominant language in the classroom and school in general. This troubling outcome is compounded by the lack of bilingual teacher training programs and bilingual curricular materials.

The two-way model has been lauded for its potential to equalize power relations between the minority-language and dominant-language groups and instill pride in students' native languages and cultures, alongside respect for other cultures (Cummins, 2001; Nieto, 1999, 2004; Skutnabb-Kangas & García, 1995; Valdés, 1997). However, as Valdés (1997) notes, developing and supporting bilingualism is not in itself sufficient to prevent reproduction of power inequalities and contribute to meaningful social change. Rather, in pursuing their ideological aspirations, two-way programs must be implemented with awareness of their inherent limitations (Palmer, 2007; Valdés, 1997) and an explicit agenda to produce new power relations (Nieto, 1999, 2004). This stands at the heart of critical educational studies, which strive to expose the manifestations, in education, of the various forms and combinations of power relations in society and to generate educational actions toward an egalitarian, just, and democratic society (Apple et al., 2011; Darder et al., 2017). It is also a fundamental element of the Jewish-Arab bilingual model: critical education that seeks to both expose and actively challenge unequal power relations in Israeli society.

2.6   *Shared Practices and Strategies: Developing Curricula and Pedagogy*

As seen from the above, Jewish-Arab bilingual education is comprised of an assortment of schools with a shared ideological vision and agenda, in which each local grassroots enterprise responds to specific needs, conditions, and circumstances. The schools' curricula and pedagogy are not constructed on a single educational model. Moreover, there has been no coordinated effort among the NGOs to develop such a model or form a database of shared knowledge on which such a model can be constructed. Nonetheless, out of the hybrid of influences, approaches, and contexts, an identifiable and distinct model of binational (Palestinian-Jewish) bilingual (Arabic-Hebrew) education has emerged. Despite the divergences between the NGOs and their respective schools, there is a certain symbiosis and coherence among them. These are produced through shared learning, partial joint development of curricular materials and pedagogical practices, and exchange of knowledge and experiences. I now consider how certain strategies and practices employed by all the schools in development of their curriculum and pedagogy have contributed to the crystallization and bolstering of this model.

2.7   *Bilingual Critical Education Curricula*

The Jewish-Arab schools contend with unique challenges in developing bilingual curricula that promote critical progressive education, peace education, and social justice. This is due to the lack of socio-political support for this mission and the resulting lack of critical resources. Since the establishment of the state in 1948, textbook design in Israel has been directed mainly at promoting "hegemonic national goals" (Hofman et al., 2007, p. 311) and a "specific national ethos" (Al-Haj, 2002, p. 181). The Arabic textbooks that had been used in Arab schools in Palestine since the 1800s were regarded by the Jewish state as a potential catalyst for Arab-Palestinian national awareness and national identity. Therefore, they were replaced with Israeli, Hebrew textbooks translated into Arabic. All curricula were designed and implemented under Ministry of Education supervision. This prevented the inclusion of Palestinian national or cultural content.

Oral literature with Arab and/or Palestinian national context and Arab history and geography contents, deemed nationally-oriented, were banned and removed from the curriculum. Instead, a core curriculum of Jewish-Western history, literature, and culture was taught in the Arab public schools. While a new wave of official textbook design arose in the 1990s, and a "more open and complex perspective" on the Arab-Israeli conflict and relations was presented in the newer curricula, there remained a single narrative that "reflects the dominant ethno-national culture that is controlled by the Jewish majority" (Al-Haj, 2002, p. 181). For the Jewish-Arab schools, this means that they must develop curricular materials that counter and balance the Jewish-Israeli ethnocentricity of the official curricula. The MoE offers no support to develop official textbooks and materials suited to Jewish-Arab educational goals and needs. Hence, the burden of developing the materials is borne by the NGOs, and the schools and teachers, who often must rely on external sources of funding and resources, such as the EU and USAID. In this process, the schools are in a constant state of struggle, negotiation, and compromise with the education authorities over the adaptations they make to the official textbooks and the new curricula they develop.

Existing studies on the bilingual schools tend to describe their curricula simply as "the standard curriculum of the state non-religious school system" (e.g., Bekerman & Nir, 2006, p. 330). However, the curricula are in no way "standard," and the outcomes of their curricular development are far from uniform. Three distinct practices and strategies can be identified, in some form and to some extent, in all schools for developing curricula that build on, expand, and, at times, deviate from the official curriculum, with varying products.[7]

(1) *Curricular adaptation* – relies on official textbooks with some adjustment of contents. This practice is most prominent in developing curricula for math, science, and English and Hebrew language arts. As a teacher at one school explained, "We take the Ministry's ... curriculum and adjust it to the school's needs and orientation." A teacher from a school at another organization

similarly stated, "We adapt the Education Ministry's textbooks. We use what suits us. What doesn't suit us is adapted ... to the complexities of our life."

(2) *Curricular supplementation* – relies on official textbooks but is supplemented with other sources. This is a prominent practice, for example, with the curricular materials used for Arabic language arts. The schools generally use the official Arabic language arts curricula for native-Arabic speakers, but must develop new curricular materials for Hebrew-speakers. The schools seek to develop spoken bilingualism in Arabic for Jewish students, to promote equalized communication and interaction between the two groups. However, no official materials exist for teaching the colloquial dialects used in daily communication. The schools, thus, supplement the official curricula with colloquial Arabic learning materials they design.

(3) *Curricular innovation* – reflects development of new curricula that meet MoE guidelines. In certain subject areas, the Jewish-Arab schools have found it necessary to develop completely new curricula, when adapting or supplementing the official curriculum would not suffice to support bilingual critical education. The only curriculum collaboratively designed by the three NGOs is the Religious Cultures and Heritage program.

A team of Palestinian and Jewish teachers and curriculum developers from four Jewish-Arab schools developed the curriculum over a decade ago, to replace the official religious studies curriculum. In the absence of official multicultural materials for teaching simultaneously the religious traditions, narratives, and scriptures of all three monotheistic religions, represented at the schools to all the students, the NGOs collaborated to form a team to develop a curriculum that responded to their common need but also followed MoE guidelines for religious studies. A team member described the sensitivity and balance of the process:

> We had to come up with a completely new title for the curriculum, not religious studies or scriptures studies. Something that also reflects what we want to do. So, we decided to emphasize first the culture of the religions and then the heritage and customs.

Thus, the team designed a reader, as the basis of the curriculum, entitled "BARAKAT" – the Hebrew acronym for the New Testament, Koran, and Bible – containing central contents from each of the sources.

The Jewish-Arab schools have also developed innovative curricula for mandatory social studies subjects, albeit following MoE guidelines: Homeland Studies, History, Civics, and Geography. The official curricula for these subject-areas tend to present Western-Jewish dominated narratives and "official knowledge" (Apple, 2014). The materials in Arabic for these subjects are almost wholly translations from the original Hebrew-language texts and not adapted for local context or cultural relevance. Against this background, the Jewish-Arab schools developed social studies curricula that combine the subjects into unique programs on identity and Culture, from a humanistic perspective. However, they still follow MoE guidelines for weekly hours of instruction and the general topics to be covered.

2.8 Bilingual Critical Education Pedagogy

Two pedagogical practices emerged and were developed in all the Jewish-Arab schools. The first one is co-teaching, a unique practice, in Israel, and bilingual education, in general. This practice was adopted to support the bilingual, binational symmetry to which the schools aspired. The second practice is inquiry-based learning and project-based learning, stemming from the influence of the progressive kibbutz and open school models. The latter practices are not unique to the Jewish-Arab schools or bilingual education: project-based learning has become common in Israeli mainstream public education. However, they have been featured in Jewish-Arab pedagogy from the outset.

Binationally and bilingually balanced co-teaching was implemented in all the schools to support their bilingual critical education agenda. Ideally, all lessons are co-taught by a Palestinian teacher and a Jewish teacher in their native languages. WAS/NS initiated the practice to maintain the balanced relations between the Palestinian and Jewish families and languages in the village. A founding member of the school stated, "It was clear to us from the beginning that we need to have an Arab teacher and a Jewish teacher and that each should use his own language." When Hand-in-Hand opened its first two schools in 1998, the organization adopted the practice, setting it as a hallmark of the Jewish-Arab bilingual model. Alongside promoting balanced relations between the groups and languages, Hand-in-Hand viewed co-teaching as a means of advancing peace education: "Arab and Jewish staff work together to teach tolerance, respect and coexistence."

Implementing co-teaching has been challenging and, therefore, has been adjusted over the years in all the schools. The pedagogical developer at one of the schools reflected, "It is not a simple task, and we have to get better at it." Since co-teaching is not practiced in any other stream in Israeli education or taught in teacher education programs, the Jewish-Arab schools are continuously engaged in rethinking the practice and developing the necessary pedagogical training and support for their teachers. Recently, some schools began to reevaluate the practice and decided to use it selectively for only certain classes and for instruction in only certain subjects.

3 Concluding Remarks

This overview of Jewish-Arab bilingual education in Israel points to the varying goals and factors the schools must navigate in developing and implementing their curricula, pedagogy, and educational visions. The schools aspire to operate within the formal public education framework to broaden the scope of their impact, while challenging the official knowledge and the spatial educational reality that separates the Palestinian and Jewish populations. Moreover, the schools do not confine their challenge to the boundaries of the education system; rather, they seek to counter the unequal power relations in Israeli society, generated by racism and the protracted Palestinian-Israeli conflict, with the ultimate goal of promoting peace and equality. Public school status has afforded not only public resources and stability, but also has social and political significance, despite the compromises it has entailed.

As described above, the Jewish-Arab schools draw insights and practices from various educational models and traditions, including two-way bilingualism, progressive education, peace education, and critical education. At the same time, they have adopted practices and strategies for developing their curriculum and pedagogy to "work from within" a discriminatory educational system and transform it into a system that educates for a just and egalitarian society. The schools and NGOs must navigate between an array of forces, contexts, and stakeholders: education authorities, local superintendents, local communities and needs.

In addition to official pressures and challenges, the schools often contend with parental concerns over the pedagogy and curriculum. Parental involvement in schools is a common phenomenon, and the Jewish-Arab schools are uniquely positioned in this respect: they are community schools, often parental initiatives, in which parents are partners and deeply involved in the schools' development and operation. For many parents, learning the official curricula is seen as vital for their children's success. Acceptance into prestigious high-school programs is contingent on passing conventional admission exams, and acceptance into university, on excelling in the high-school matriculation exams. Thus, parents bring considerable pressure to bear on the schools to align the pedagogy and curriculum with the official curriculum. On the other hand, conflicting pressure comes from parents, who are ideologically invested in creating counter-knowledge and rejecting the official knowledge. The schools must maneuver between these different needs and demands, through compromise that is not always successful. These different needs demonstrate that these schools do not hide contradictions but, rather, reflect tensions in Israeli society.

What may emerge from this presentation of Jewish-Arab bilingual education in Israel is an amalgam of non-uniform educational models, with a common ideological base and certain shared practices, but limited collaboration to consolidate knowledge and experience. The latter is not for want of trying and or desire. A multiplicity of macro-level tensions and dynamics undermine the schools' abilities to form a cohesive body. There is lack of official support, not only for curricular development, but also for developing bilingual teacher training programs that could advance a unified educational model. The struggle for MoE recognition and approval, alongside local and internal pressures, forces the schools to make ideological, curricular, and pedagogical compromises. Finally, the tensions deriving from the Palestinian-Israeli conflict and internal racism in Israeli society have positioned the two populations as "enemies" and Arabic as "the language of the enemy." All the schools are affected by different challenges, and all are affected differently by the same challenges. Thus, the hope is that with the growing acceptance and prevalence of the Jewish-Arab model in Israel and the mainstream education system's incorporation of some of the schools' practices, support for this educational endeavor will grow as well – from the public and the state.

Acknowledgments

I would like to thank Moran Ofek for insightful comments on an earlier draft as well as the teachers, administrators, founders, and community members who generously contributed their time.

An earlier version of this article was published as: Meshulam, A. (2019). Palestinian-Jewish bilingual schools in Israel: Unravelling the educational model. *International Journal of Educational Development*, 70. doi: 10.1016/j.ijedudev.2019.102092

Notes

1 Some private Jewish-Arab initiatives operate pre-schools and early childhood education. These include the YMCA in Jerusalem, the Orchard of Abraham's Children frameworks, and the Ein-Bustan School in Lower Galilee Hilf.
2 I tend to follow Bekerman's term "Palestinian-Jewish" (e.g. Bekerman, 2005), which is sensitive to the cultural politics around the identities of the two communities. However, in this chapter, I use the more commonly used term "Jewish-Arab" to describe the schools, which is also used by two of the organizations that established some of the schools.
3 The *kibbutzim* were collective communities formed in Palestine/Israel from the early 1900s. The *kibbutz* education system was influenced by Dewey, Marx, and Freud, as well as by A.D. Gordon and B. Borochov, prominent Jewish leaders and thinkers in pre-state Israel.

4 The Bedouin are an indigenous Palestinian community and one of the most marginalized communities in Israel. About one-third live in villages that are unrecognized by the State, and lack access to basic services and infrastructures, such as connection to the electrical grid and water mains. The other two-thirds live in urban-style towns to which they were resettled by the State in the late 1960s and early 1970s.
5 The Kfar-Saba school has applied for full public status.
6 Various terms are used interchangeably to describe this model, including two-way bilingualism, two-way immersion, and dual-language.
7 For a more elaborated presentation, see Meshulam (2019b).

References

Abu-Asbah, K. (2007). *The Arab education in Israel. Dilemmas of a national minority.* Floersheimer Institute for Policy Studies.

Abu-Saad, I. (2006). State-controlled education and identity formation among the Palestinian Arab minority in Israel. *American Behavioral Scientist, 49*(8), 1085–1100.

Agbaria, A. K. (2018). The "right" education in Israel: Segregation, religious ethnonationalism, and depoliticized professionalism. *Critical Studies in Education, 59*(1), 18–34.

Al-Haj, M. (1995). *Education, empowerment, and control: The case of the Arabs in Israel.* State University of New York Press.

Al-Haj, M. (2002). Multiculturalism in deeply divided societies: The Israeli case. *International Journal of Intercultural Relations, 26*(2), 169–183.

Amara, M., Azaiza, F., Hertz-Lazarowitz, R., & Mor-Sommerfeld, A. (2009). A new bilingual education in the conflict-ridden Israeli reality: Language practices. *Language and Education, 23*(1), 15–35.

Apple, M. W. (2014). *Official knowledge: Democratic education in a conservative age.* Routledge.

Apple, M. W., Au, W., & Gandin, L. A. (2011). *The Routledge international handbook of critical education.* Taylor & Francis.

Arar, K., & Massry-Herzalah, A. (2017). Progressive education and the case of a bilingual Palestinian-Arab and Jewish co-existence school in Israel. *School Leadership & Management, 37*(1–2), 38–60.

Bajaj, M. (Ed.). (2008). *Encyclopedia of peace education.* IAP.

Baker, C. (2011). *Foundations of bilingual education and bilingualism* (5th ed.). Multilingual Matters.

Bar-Tal, D. (2002). The elusive nature of peace education. In G. Salomon & B. Nevo (Eds.), *Peace education: The concept, principles and practice in the world* (pp. 27–36). Lawrence Erlbaum.

Bekerman, Z. (2004). Potential and limitations of multicultural education in conflict-ridden areas: Bilingual Palestinian-Jewish schools in Israel. *Teachers College Record, 106*(3), 574–610.

Bekerman, Z. (2005). Complex contexts and ideologies: Bilingual education in conflict-ridden areas. *Journal of Language, Identity, and Education, 4*(1), 1–20.

Bekerman, Z. (2009). Identity versus peace: Identity wins. *Harvard Educational Review, 79*(1), 74–83.

Bekerman, Z., & Nir, A. (2006). Opportunities and challenges of integrated education in conflict-ridden societies. *Childhood Education, 82*(6), 327–333.

Bekerman, Z., & Shhadi, N. (2003). Palestinian-Jewish bilingual education in Israel: Its influence on cultural identities and its impact on intergroup conflict. *Journal of Multilingual and Multicultural Development, 24*(6), 473–484.

Cummins, J. (2001). *Language, power and pedagogy: Bilingual children in the crossfire.* Multilingual Matters.

Darder, A., Torres, R. D., & Baltodano, M. P. (2017). *The critical pedagogy reader.* Routledge, Taylor & Francis Group.

David Yellin Academic College of Education. (n.d). *Chofen.* https://www.dyellin.ac.il/re_training/chofen

Dubiner, D., Deeb, I., & Schwartz, M. (2018). 'We are creating a reality': Teacher agency in early bilingual education. *Language, Culture and Curriculum, 31*(3), 255–271.

Feuerverger, G. (2001). *Oasis of dreams. Teaching and learning peace in a Jewish-Palestinian village in Israel.* Routledge Falmer.

Hagar Jewish-Arab Education for Equality. (n.d.). http://www.hajar.org.il/index.php/en

Hand in Hand. (n.d.). *Why we exist.* https://www.handinhandk12.org/inform/why-we-exist

Harris, M. I. (1988). *Peace education.* McFarland & Company.

Harris, M. I. (2010). History of peace education. In G. Salomon & E. Cairns (Eds.), *Handbook on peace education* (pp. 11–20). Taylor & Francis.

Hofman, A., Alpert, B., & Schnell, I. (2007). Education and social change: The case of Israel's state curriculum. *Curriculum Inquiry, 37*, 303–328.

Kibbutzim College of Education. (n.d.). *About us.* https://en.smkb.ac.il/about-us/

Meshulam, A. (2011). *What kind of alternative? Bilingual, multicultural schools as counterhegemonic alternatives educating for democracy* [Doctoral dissertation]. University of Wisconsin-Madison.

Meshulam, A. (2012). "We had a dream": Lessons from an Israeli Palestinian-Jewish school. In M. Knoester (Ed.), *International struggles for critical democratic education* (pp. 9–30). Peter Lang.

Meshulam, A. (2015). The "two-way street" of having an impact: A democratic school's attempt to build a broad counterhegemonic alternative. *Teachers College Record, 117*(3), 1–44.

Meshulam, A. (2019a). Cross-national comparison of parental choice of two-way bilingual education in the US and Israel. *Comparative Education Review, 63*(2), 236–258.

Meshulam, A. (2019b). Palestinian-Jewish bilingual schools in Israel: Unravelling the educational model. *International Journal of Educational Development, 70*, 1–9.

Meshulam, A. (2020). Critical practices in education and their implementation in bilingual schools in Israel. In M. Krumer-Nevo, I. Weiss-Gal, & R. Strier (Eds.), *Critical theory in action: Critical practices in the social sphere in Israel* (pp. 33–67). Resling.

Nasser, I. (2011). Perspectives of Palestinian and Jewish parents in Israel on bilingual education. *International Journal of Bilingual Education and Bilingualism, 14*(3), 301–318.

Nieto, S. (1999). *The light in their eyes: Creating multicultural learning communities.* Teachers College Press.

Nieto, S. (2004). *Affirming diversity: The sociopolitical context of multicultural education* (4th ed.). Pearson.

Palmer, D. (2007). A dual immersion strand programme in California: Carrying out the promise of dual language education in an English-dominant context. *International Journal of Bilingual Education and Bilingualism, 10*(6), 752–768.

Paul-Binyamin, I., & Jayusi, W. (2018). The bilingual school – an educational model for civic equality in a divided society. *Intercultural Education, 29*(3), 340–362.

Salomon, G., & Cairns, E. (Eds.). (2010). *Handbook on peace education.* Taylor & Francis.

Sitner, Z., & Meshulam, A. (2020). Gentle cultural dripping: Reflections of multiculturalism in shaping the learning space in a bilingual pre-school. In I. Paul-Binyamin & R. Reingold (Eds.), *Shared spaces in the education system and academia* (pp. 21–39). Mofet.

Skutnabb-Kangas, T., & García, O. (Eds.). (1995). *Multilingualism for all? General principles.* Swets & Zeitlinger.

The School for Peace. (n.d.). *About.* http://sfpeace.org/about/

Twenty years of activity: The binational bilingual school [Twenty Years]. (2007). Emerezian.

Valdés, G. (1997). Dual-language immersion programs: A cautionary note concerning the education of language minority students. *Harvard Educational Review, 67*, 391–429.

CHAPTER 10

Minority EFL Teachers on Shared-Life Education in Conflict-Ridden Contexts

The Subaltern Speaks Back

Muzna Awayed-Bishara

1   Introduction

This chapter examines how the teaching of English as a Foreign Language (EFL) in conflict-ridden contexts could offer a unique discursive terrain for minority teachers to negotiate conflicts and advance a justice-oriented dialogue. Scholarship in foreign language education in the last two decades has accentuated the transformative role language pedagogies must play in advancing global cultural consciousness and intercultural competences (Byram, 2011; Kumaravadivelu, 2008). The idea is that in teaching English as a global/foreign language, there is a need to shift the goal "away from its focus on the development of native-speaker competence towards more realistic competencies to facilitate communication between speakers from a wide range of cultural backgrounds" (Sharifian, 2013, p. 2). Nevertheless, EFL discourses still play a leading role in reproducing Anglo-centric hegemonies and essentialist binaries such as Self/Other, Native/Nonnative, or Western/Nonwestern (Awayed-Bishara, 2020). Native-speakerism is arguably one pervasive ideology that is associated with the global spread of English and which is "characterized by the belief that native-speaker teachers represent a Western culture from which spring the ideals both of the English language and of English language teaching methodology" (Holliday, 2006, p. 385). The hegemony of native-speakerism has been recently viewed from a broader sociocultural perspective, which Houghton and Rivers (2013) describe as "a conviction that non-Western cultural realities are deficient" (p. 17). Against this backdrop, this chapter sets out to critically examine how non-hegemonic understandings and knowledge could offer new epistemic spaces for increasing the commitment of EFL pedagogies to transformative politics.

Drawing upon de Sousa Santos' (2014) notion of the "abyssal line" – which has long separated the hegemonic and the marginal – this chapter shares voices from the marginal side of that line in order to offer a counterhegemonic model for EFL education in conflict-ridden contexts. On the hegemonic side of the abyssal line lie the culture, values, languages, and knowledge of metropolitan societies (i.e. those of the Global North); on the other side of the line, lie those of colonial/marginal societies (i.e. those of the Global South). Rather than being ontological or geographical reference points, North and South are understood in this study as two epistemological sites involved in relations of power. Crossing to post-abyssal lines requires, according to Santos, that the South talks back. This "does not mean discarding the rich Eurocentric critical tradition" (2014, p. 44) but that the subaltern South is also entitled to add their voices for the sake of balancing and enriching knowledges.

The case of Israel offers a unique avenue for exploring how marginal voices could be brought into a productive dialogue with hegemonic models of EFL, since the ubiquitous intersections between social categories and power structures take on a particular dimension in the context of an educational system that is almost entirely separate for the Jewish majority and the Palestinian-Arab minority. Segregation notwithstanding, the English curriculum is exceptionally uniform for the *entire* population, rendering EFL a potentially unique educational opportunity for bringing together groups in conflict (Awayed-Bishara, 2018, 2020). While English teachers are generally employed in the school system that matches their ethnic affiliation (i.e. Jews in Jewish schools and Arabs in Arab schools), the last decade or so has marked a major change in the increasing number of Arab teachers who are employed in Jewish schools (Gilat, Gindi & Masri, 2020).

Considering Israel's ethnic diversity, integrating Arab teachers into Jewish schools might falsely appear to accommodate cultural differences, educational pluralism, or even to encourage assimilation. However, the separation is meant to strengthen and maintain Jewish identity among the Jewish minority (Gilat, Gindi & Masri, 2020). Hence, this new educational arrangement mainly serves practical agendas as it offers a path around two impasses: a high proportion of unemployed Arab teachers in Israel and the difficulty Jewish schools have in filling vacant positions (Agbaria, 2011). While I argue that teaching English by Palestinian-Arab teachers in Jewish schools offers a particular vantage point from which to understand power relations and epistemological tensions between the hegemonic and the marginal, I also contemplate that it could potentially inspire educational solutions for the manifold forms of shared life within the educational context.

For this purpose, in this chapter, I present a case study that examines the dynamics between the way a Palestinian-Arab EFL teacher, who works in a Jewish school, negotiates her identity and exercises her agency to contest hegemonic, discriminatory, and unjust representations related to her English proficiency and ethnic background. To examine how minority teachers, who work in majority-based contexts, use English to speak back to hegemonic (language) educational policies, I focus on their agency as a speaking community struggling "to survive in [what might be] hostile contexts in an exclusionary society" (Santos, 2016, p. 25). In this regard, Kumaravadivelu (2014) calls not only for "the unfreezing of the subaltern's potential for thinking otherwise," (p. 79) but also for them to "activate [their] latent agentive capacity" (p. 81).

In a recent study, I examined the dynamics surrounding the way pre-service Palestinian-Arab teachers in Israel respond to imposed linguistic and educational subjectivities, and their political agency in contesting unequal EFL policies (Awayed-Bishara, forthcoming). Findings indicate that contesting exclusionary ideologies in EFL textbooks, fostering dialogicity (i.e., the ability to construct knowledge through engaging in dialogue) in EFL classrooms, and increasing students' agency and reflexivity in EFL programs strategically promote the discursive role of English as an instrumental tool for implementing local-global understanding and social justice. The study concludes that what EFL teachers *do* to contest hegemonic language policies and practices constitutes an agency that could be understood within Christopher Stroud's (2018) theoretical notion of *linguistic citizenship* (Awayed-Bishara, 2020, 2021). Linguistic citizenship (LC) "refers to what people do with and around language(s) in order to position themselves agentively, and to craft new emergent subjectivities of political speakerhood" (Stroud, 2018, p. 4). By focusing on what people *do* around languages, LC stresses the importance of grassroots activity on the ground and helps to resituate "practices whereby new actors, seeking recognition in the public space in order to determine a new course of events, shift *the location* of *agency* and *voice*" (Stroud, 2018, p. 21, original emphasis).

Situated within the theoretical frameworks of linguistic citizenship and Santos' notion of the abyssal line, this chapter offers a nuanced method for investigating how minority teachers working in majority-controlled educational contexts respond to hegemonic practices related to their role as minority language teachers (e.g. EFL). In this sense, the chapter initiates a productive dialogue "on critical topics of importance to a more equitable and ethical engagement with marginalized and vulnerable speakers" (Stroud, 2018, p. 12). To gain nuanced insights on how EFL pedagogies could push toward social transformation in a conflict-ridden place, such as Israel, I examine this question *with* and not on the people to whom this question matters. In this regard, Paulo Freire encourages educators and scholars working in contexts characterized by asymmetrical power relations not to "expect positive results from an educational or political action program which fails to respect the particular view of the world held by the people" (1970/2005, p. 95).

I begin by outlining EFL pedagogy as a cultural discourse that reproduces hegemonic and Anglo-centric ideologies, and then move to a different understanding of EFL, by offering an alternative transformative model for advancing a cultural politics of social justice and equity (Awayed-Bishara, 2020). To demonstrate what insights could be gained from this transformative model, I draw upon a case study with Mona (pseudonym) while reporting on her one-year experience as a Palestinian-Arab EFL teacher in a mainstream non-religious Jewish elementary school in the Haifa District. Through a detailed critical analysis of five interviews I held with her at different stages of this year, I will locate how minority teachers use English to speak back to hegemonic and discriminatory practices that aim to maintain their subaltern subjectivities.

2   EFL Pedagogy as a Cultural Discourse

The continued spread of English worldwide motivates the examination of how the teaching of English could capture the dynamic link between the cultural multiplicity of its speakers and its globalizing, albeit often still Anglo-centric, nature. The globalization of English, the increasing number of its non-native speakers, and the role cultural representations play in shaping ideologies of Self and Other, among speakers of different languages, constitute the basis of my understanding of EFL pedagogy as a cultural discourse (Awayed-Bishara, 2020). Investigating the cultural and ideological aspects of EFL discourse in a conflict-ridden place, such as Israel, is contemplated in light of a number of critical observations. For one, insofar as the English curriculum in Israel is uniform, the learning populations use the same EFL materials and equally comply with the state's general EFL policy. Despite the uniform curriculum, there is divergence in the way both populations learn English. While most Hebrew speakers study English as a second language, to speakers of Arabic, English might be considered a fourth language after Spoken Arabic, Modern Standard Arabic, and Hebrew (Awayed-Bishara, 2020). The second critical observation is that the curriculum adopts a global rather than an Anglo-centric approach that takes into account how English is no longer considered the sole asset of Anglophone countries, such as the United States or Britain.

However, native speaker competence is still treated as the international norm (Davies, 2003) and in Israel, the ideological dominance of native speaker models constitutes a hegemonic discourse of native speakerism within the architecture of EFL policy (Awayed-Bishara, 2020). This tendency continuously results *inter alia* in prioritizing native speaker teachers over non-native ones, often overlooking the serious implications of the false assumptions about how English teaching professionalism is assessed. In this regard, Holliday (2013, p. 18) postulates:

> There is therefore something deep within the profession everywhere which makes it possible for 'native speaker' and 'non-native speaker' to continue as a basic currency not only for labeling teachers but also for judging them through forms of chauvinism of which we are largely unaware and easily put aside.

Critical discourse analyses of Israeli EFL policy and textbooks also suggest how the ideological role of EFL discourse exceeds its pedagogical and educational makeup. Instead of facilitating learning processes about mutual understanding and enabling the growth of a multicultural learning community, EFL discourse perpetuates ideologies of dominance, native speakerism, Anglo-centric superiority, and Western hegemony (Awayed-Bishara, 2015, 2018, 2020). Such a tendency contributes to maintaining Western and Jewish hegemony while reinforcing the marginalization of the Palestinian-Arab minority. It could be also argued that native speakerism in Israel is quite oppressive for other Jewish teachers who are not native speakers of Hebrew (e.g. speakers of Russian or Amharic).

In light of the current emphasis on developing critical intercultural competences (Byram, 2011), and the role of English as *the* global language, the ideological orientation of EFL discourse risks replicating the power structures it sets out to subvert: namely, it paradoxically reinforces its Anglocentric hegemony and native speakers' ownership while stifling the voices of marginalized populations. Notwithstanding its exclusionary nature, this chapter contemplates that EFL pedagogy, as a cultural discourse – particularly in conflict-ridden places, such as Israel – might still constitute a potentially unique educational platform for advancing a cultural politics of equality and social justice. Understanding EFL discourse as a socio-political practice focuses on meaning-making as the site of a power struggle for contesting hegemonic practices (Awayed-Bishara, 2020). In other words, discursive practices make use of certain conventions that work for the naturalization of certain power relations and ideologies. In this sense, the ways in which different actors articulate these conventions, are themselves a focus of struggle (Fairclough, 1992).

Moving from ideological reproduction to social transformation in EFL education requires, then, the examination of different forms of struggle, since "sometimes the struggles are very different from what we think they are" (Santos, 2016, p. 25). While questioning the core notion of "struggle," Santos brings our attention to how people, who are engaged in daily struggles in conflictual settings, often take a form of a passive or silent struggle, out of fear of confrontation with the legal powers. Teachers who have been trained to work under oppressive conditions – e.g. Arab teachers in the state-controlled school system in Israel (Abu-Saad, 2006) – might prefer a passive form of resistance. Whether the daily struggles of Palestinian-Arab EFL teachers in Jewish schools could make a case for transformative politics is what the following section on Mona's experience will try to tackle.

3 Viewed from Their Eyes: Minority EFL Teachers on Shared-Life Education

3.1 *The Case Study*

The analysis in this chapter is based on data collected from five interviews I held with Mona at various stages of the school year 2019/2020. This year was Mona's first experience of teaching English to sixth graders in a mainstream non-religious Jewish elementary school in the Haifa District. Mona's previous teaching experience was only within her practicum as a pre-service teacher that took place at Palestinian-Arab middle schools in the Northern District. After graduating from high school, Mona won an academic scholarship from the Ministry of Education for her distinguished achievements on the psychometric and matriculation exams (national tests required for entering tertiary education). This achievement, she reports, basically paved her way into the Jewish school. The interviews were conducted in Arabic – Mona's first language – and are presented here in English translation. Mona is Muslim and wears a hijab (veil).

In the interviews, Mona describes and interprets her experience, both as a Palestinian-Arab teacher working in a Jewish school and as an EFL teacher. Drawing upon Stroud's (2018) notion of linguistic citizenship and Santos' (2014) notion of the abyssal line, I focus on what Mona, a minority teacher, does with and around language so as to situate herself *agentively,* and how she speaks back to hegemonic (educational) practices that aim to maintain her subaltern subjectivity. I now present an analysis of the dynamics surrounding the way Mona responds to imposed discriminatory practices related to her EFL teaching position and her political agency in *contesting* unequal educational practices.

4 Findings and Data Analysis

4.1 *Struggling in a Hostile Environment*

Studies on the experience of Palestinian-Arab teachers who work in the mainstream non-religious Jewish school system underscore the conflict these teachers have between their professional and national identities (e.g. Gilat et al., 2020; Saada & Gross, 2019). Analysis of the way Mona describes her experience as an Arab EFL teacher in a Jewish school indicates that she perceives her teaching experience as an ongoing struggle in a hostile environment (Santos, 2014). In the first interview that I held with her shortly after the beginning of the school year, Mona states:

> I was actually trying to be mentally prepared. Why would I talk about being mentally or psychologically prepared for working in a Jewish school? Maybe because we, Arabs, if we were to start working in a Jewish surrounding, we would work harder to prove to them, Jews, that we know. We have to prove that we know what we are doing and that we are different from what they think of us: we don't really live in tents or aren't always cooking hummus. (Interview 1:1)

Mona states that starting a new job at a Jewish school entails mental or psychological (translated from the Arabic word *nafsi*) preparation, suggesting that she could preconceive the hardship of the experience that was awaiting her. Responding to what she perceives as dominant Jewish-Israeli ways of thinking about what Arabs are or can do, is perhaps a practice to which she is accustomed. Mona specifically mentions that she needs to prepare herself for having to prove to the "Jewish" others in her new school that she knows what she does (i.e. is knowledgeable), leads a non-nomadic lifestyle (i.e. is "developed"), and has "professional" skills (i.e. is professional). In other words, the most pressing matter for Mona when she begins her new job is to contest an Orientalist construction (Said, 1978) of the Arab as lazy (thus, there is the need "to work harder"), unknowledgeable (thus, there is the need to "prove that we know"), or underdeveloped (thus, she needs to "prove that we don't live in tents"). Instead of navigating ways for learning and living together in the new school year, as one would expect from a new teacher preparing back-to-school activities, Mona is "mentally and psychologically" preoccupied with how breaking the walls of preconceived stereotypes of herself as an Arab might be achieved. Despite these difficulties, Mona describes how she eventually responded:

> I have gone through this a long time ago because I have already been in Jewish surroundings before, and now I have no intention to impress anyone or to prove anything to anyone. This is something that many Palestinians or minorities go through and you must have a name to describe this phenomena [Mona uses "you" (*inti* in Arabic) to address me as the researcher]. (Interview 1:2)

Based on previous experiences that she had in other Jewish surroundings, Mona states that she has no intention to acquiesce to hegemonic practices that construct her as "lazy," "unknowledgeable," and "underdeveloped," by default. Hence, her *great refusal* (Marcuse, 1964) to "impress anyone" is basically a conscious refusal to take part in the reproduction of these stereotypes by proving them otherwise. Elsewhere, Mona explicitly criticizes other Arab teachers who try, in her words, "to beautify" (she uses the Hebrew word *liyafyef*) things for the sake of satisfying the other, who sees them as inferior. Not only does she relate to her individual experience, she also situates herself within the larger community of other Palestinians and minorities who often face injustices. By addressing the researcher (using the direct pronoun "you"), Mona makes her subaltern voice, as well as that of others in her position, heard about the need to transform the underlying frameworks that maintain unequal practices toward minorities. It seems that Mona perceives the researcher as someone capable of amplifying her voice. Apparently, the "mental preparations" seem to be justified:

> Well, my first encounter with the school is not different than any other encounter with other ignorant [she used this word in English] Jewish surroundings where I was asked all sorts of stereotypical questions like if I were the new cleaner because I cover my hair. Should all the Arab women who work in Jewish schools be cleaners? Or, they would ask if I were an Arabic teacher, or if I were married, also because of the hijab. Since I am "prepared" [gesturing the quotation marks and referring to her earlier attempt to be mentally prepared] I wasn't really going crazy to prove other things like: Arab women aren't only cleaners, but can be also other things. I was more disgusted than angry and so, I would answer things like: No, I am not married, it's not like in Judaism where the woman covers her head only when she gets married, and I don't have to shave my head. I was explaining a lot because some of them didn't know much about Judaism. (Interview 1:3)

Mona voices her discontent with the stereotypical questions that she had to answer in her first encounter in the Jewish school and that she attributes to "ignorance." An analysis of how learners discursively relate to cultural content in EFL textbooks about the Palestinian-Arab community indicates that most of the Jewish participants interviewed in the study demonstrate not only how superior they feel toward Arabs, but mainly how they lack knowledge about them (Awayed-Bishara, 2020). Her ability to answer these "ignorant" questions by drawing on her own "knowledge" of the marital practices of some religious

Jewish women (specifically ultra-orthodox women who shave and cover their heads after they get married) constructs Mona as "knowledgeable" of the Other. While not intending to "prove" that she knows (as she explicitly stated earlier), she ends up demonstrating that she knows more about "Judaism" than the secular Jewish students themselves who apparently not only lack knowledge about Arabs, but also about Other "different" groups within their own Jewish community (spelled out by Mona as "don't know much about Judaism"). Beyond her knowledge of the Other, not only does Mona reject the categorization of Arab women as "cleaners," but she also acts against the degrading attitude that people, on both sides (Jewish and Arab), have about women whose work entails cleaning:

> If I were the cleaner? I would sometimes answer: Yes! because I have a deep respect for the cleaners who work in Jewish schools. This is a different story in itself: how women are oppressed inside our community and theirs [Jewish] as well. They are called "the cleaner," as if she has no name or a personality, whereas the maintenance men or the guards have names and are respected. Or, when anyone wanted to talk to them [the "cleaners"], they would come to me and ask me to talk to them, as if they weren't able to communicate normally. They don't speak Hebrew well, so what? (Interview 1:4)

Mona exercises her agency by acting against the stereotypical and degrading treatment of Arab women who work in the cleaning business by means of proudly and respectfully accepting to take on the role of "the cleaner." By the same token, she contests both the Other's and her own community's practices toward women. She speaks up against the gender-biased and unequal treatment of women who are also dehumanized (they "have no name" and you cannot talk to them) as opposed to the men who, despite belonging to the same ethnic community, are called by their names and respected. Since the practices which Mona is contesting are framed within an educational setting (i.e. school), this compels us to consider what are the desired ethical values and transformative pedagogies that might bring about the deconstruction of such harmful categories and systems of othering. Paulo Freire's perception of human misery as a social construction, and not as a sad determined destiny, inspires an understanding of dehumanization that results from an unjust order, not as "a cause for despair but for hope, leading to the incessant pursuit of humanity denied by injustice" (Freire, 1970/2005, p. 92). In this sense, Mona's agentive acts against the injustices that she, and other minority members, encounter in hegemonic contexts that feed on Self-Other distinctions and unequal power relations suggest that our strength as teachers lies in our ability to speak up and act against structural inequality. To become transformative pedagogues requires that teachers intervene ethically in what happens inside their school communities. In a conflict-ridden place, like Israel, students and teachers that are exposed to justice-oriented practices might take these acts out of the school and become agents of social change.

4.2   *Speaking Back to Native-Speakerist Ideologies in EFL Teaching*
Constructing the native speaker as the ultimate English teacher and professional is dominant in EFL policy discourse in Israel (Awayed-Bishara, 2020). Mona's ongoing struggle in a hostile school environment is evident, not only in the way she speaks back to hegemonic views related to her ethnic background (as we have seen in the previous section), but also in the way she responds to practices that attempt to undermine her English proficiency as a non-native speaker of English. In this regard, Mona states:

> When the school principal observed my lessons, her comments had nothing to do with my professional knowledge of English. My biggest problem was my English pronunciation. She didn't comment about the other positive things, such as my relationship with the children, my teaching skills, or the number of people who really appreciated my work. I used to receive text messages from parents thanking me for what I was doing with their children. For the principal, the fact that I didn't pronounce "water" as "warer" [as she thought Americans pronounced it] was a problem. She told me that my pronunciation makes things harder on the students. (Interview 2:1)

What this excerpt demonstrates is that the well-meaning statements that English is no longer 'owned' by American English (as stated in the English curriculum) are undermined by the way the school principal assesses the professionalism of her English teachers. Mona's account of the messages that she continuously receives from parents praising her skills and investment in their children, and the fact that she was recognized as a student with outstanding academic achievements, do not construct her as a "professional" English teacher in the eyes of the principal. That is, the principal seems to be ideologically subjugated by native speakerist values, dominant in Israeli EFL discourse (Awayed-Bishara, 2020). The way the principal perceives Mona's non-American pronunciation as an obstacle that "makes things harder on the students" reinforces the Anglocentric hegemony of EFL educational practices and the chauvinistic forms for labeling non-native English teachers (Holliday, 2013).

The way Mona responds to these unjust practices offer, however, a nuanced insight:

> Frankly, I don't really care. What I want to say is that I work really hard to master English and never really cared about having an accent. What they want is that if you want to become an English teacher, you need to adapt your tongue to the American way of pronunciation [i.e. adopt the American accent]. For the school principal, this was a very important issue. For me, I want to use English for learning new things about the world and help my students learn new things, so they can better understand problems in the world. (Interview 2:2)

Mona activates her agency to contest hegemonic attempts to Americanize the teaching of English, which it could be argued, contradict the goals set for EFL pedagogies in the last two decades, i.e. developing intercultural competencies and becoming transformative (see Byram, 2011; Kumaravadivelu, 2008). Mona repeatedly speaks back to these prevalent hegemonic practices through refusing to comply with top-down demands (e.g. of the school principal) to adopt an American accent. Instead, she offers a counterhegemonic model for using English that enables her, as a teacher, to learn more about the world and facilitate the way for her students to learn about the world through negotiating problems.

Her perception of the role English plays in advancing a problem-posing education, contrasted with one-way "banking" education (Freire, 1970/2005), is underscored in her understanding of learning as an ongoing process that involves both the teacher and the students in epistemological curiosities about the world. The following excerpt demonstrates how Mona translates her perception of her role as an EFL teacher in a Jewish school, not only to foster students' intercultural competences, but also to promote peace-building values in the conflict-ridden context of Israel:

> It was a teaching unit that we called: Travel Aaround the World. Every day we would take a virtual tour to a different country and learn about its people, culture, etc. One day, the English coordinator informed us that we need to make a connection stop in Israel. That meant that I had to plan activities for Israel. While I had many different possibilities with the other countries, I wasn't sure what could I, as an Arab, do in this day. I then decided to start from Judaism, Judaism and not Zionism. I decided to focus on *V'ahavta L'Reacha Kamocha* [Hebrew for: "You should love your fellow as yourself," which is a basic principle of the Torah]. I continued by focusing on what love is in Christianity and Islam. (Interview 2:3)

Through resisting the negative framing of her non-native proficiency in English, Mona adopts a non-hegemonic approach (spelled out as "Judaism and not Zionism") whereby she uses English to teach her Jewish students an ethical lesson about love, as it is conceived in the three monotheistic religions. It could be argued that choosing "Judaism and not Zionism" is another way through which Mona contests non-native proficiency in English. This observation is supported by a study that shows how EFL policies in Israel tend to situate the EFL context in Jewish-Zionist frameworks "through a systematic use of Jewish-Zionist vocabulary, national symbols, and the centering of *Aliyah* as a typical NS [native speaker] teacher experience" (Awayed-Bishara, 2020, p. 127). As opposed to the principal's skeptical view of her professionalism as an EFL teacher, Mona's knowledge of what might be considered a fundamental principle in Judaism demonstrates an ability to think beyond her personal reality of injustice and oppression (that she discussed earlier). It is important to mention that, elsewhere, Mona describes how her decision to focus on Judaic values was partially made in response to her Jewish colleagues' activities on Israel. The other teachers, together with their students, decorated the classrooms with Israeli flags, pictures of Herzl, Jabotinsky and other influential Zionist leaders, as well as pictures of the current Israeli prime minister and president. Conversely, Mona's focus on teaching about the multireligious conception of the notion of love constructs a new cultural discourse that rarely appears in Israeli educational materials that tend to exclude the Palestinian-Arab minority, its history, and its communal practices from public discussions of Israel (see Abu Saad, 2006; Awayed-Bishara, 2015, 2020; Yiftachel, 2006).

To wrap up this section, Mona's acts entailed a resistance of hegemonic attempts that aimed to construct her as inferior both as a minority member (as we have seen in the previous subsection) and as a non-native speaker English teacher. Her agentive acts enabled her, on the one hand, to situate herself cleverly and *proudly* in the asymmetrical minority-majority context, in/with which she had to cope, and to contribute to the ethical development of her students, on the other hand. This chapter set out to examine potential solutions for the manifold forms of shared life within conflict-ridden educational contexts and, thus, suggests that the way Mona planned and executed the assignment about Israel, which was indeed part of an English lesson, could inspire the way teachers of other subjects design intercultural communicative activities in many other lessons. By engaging her students in an EFL activity about love, as conceptualized in the three religions, Mona reclaims her position as an equal participant in the EFL educational context, acting, according to Stroud (2018) as a linguistic citizen. The acts of speaking back to imposed educational subjectivities in EFL contexts can be captured through the transformative conception of linguistic citizenship (Stroud, 2018) that seeks to remedy some forms of misrecognition. These counterhegemonic acts could also contribute to blurring the borders of the abyssal line, through bringing voices from the hegemonic North (e.g. the Jewish school principal) into a productive, more just dialogue with the marginal South (e.g. Palestinian-Arab teachers in Israel).

5 Conclusions

To conclude, the case study offered in this chapter suggests that alternative voices inserted into the conceptualization of the justice-oriented goals of EFL pedagogies, which could be otherwise alienating, offer a counterhegemonic model of EFL. Educational initiatives that conceptualize the role of educators as agents of social change must build on the capacity of marginalized teachers (e.g. Palestinian-Arab teachers in Israel) to take an active part in the struggle for social transformation and educational justice. Transformative educational programs must aim at restructuring the underlying frameworks that generate unequal educational opportunities (Fraser, 1995), and focus on the agency of marginalized communities and their ability to actively design and critically consider shared-life possibilities. This requires a view of the people in conflict-ridden settings as *partners*, whose epistemological knowledge contributes to better conceptualizations of education as a possible arena for mitigating tensions and bringing divided and diverse societies together. Future research is needed to examine whether this insight could become a part of a transformative project toward equality and social justice.

References

Abu-Saad, I. (2006). State-controlled education and identity formation among the Palestinian Arab minority in Israel. *American Behavioral Scientist*, 49(8), 1085–1100.

Agbaria, A. K. (2011). "Living in enduring expectation": In the shadow of inevitable unemployment. How the teacher training policy in Israel contributes to generating an excess of Arab graduates from the teacher training colleges. *Studies in Education*, 4, 94–123. [in Hebrew]

Awayed-Bishara, M. (2015). Analyzing the cultural content of materials used for teaching English to high school speakers of Arabic in Israel. *Discourse & Society*, 26(5), 517–542.

Awayed-Bishara, M. (2018). EFL discourse as cultural practice. *Journal of Multicultural Discourses*, 13(3), 243–258.

Awayed-Bishara, M. (2020). *EFL pedagogy as cultural discourse: Textbooks, practice, and policy for Arabs and Jews in Israel*. Routledge.

Awayed-Bishara, M. (2021). Linguistic citizenship in the EFL classroom: Granting the local a voice through English. *TESOL Quarterly*. https://doi.org/10.1002/tesq.3009

Byram, M. S. (2011). Intercultural citizenship from an international perspective. *Journal of the NUS Teaching Academy, 1*(1), 10–20.

Davies, A. (2003). *The native speaker: Myth and reality*. Multilingual Matters.

Fairclough, N. (1992). *Discourse and social change*. Polity Press.

Fraser, N. (1995). From redistribution to recognition? Dilemmas of justice in a 'post-socialist' age. *New Left Review, 212*, 68–91.

Freire, P. (2005). *Pedagogy of the oppressed* (M. B. Ramos, Trans.; 30th anniversary ed.). Continuum. (Original work published 1970)

Gilat, I., Gindi, S., & Massri, R. (2020). "I am living proof of coexistence": The experience of Israeli-Arab teachers in Jewish schools. *International Studies in Sociology of Education*. doi:10.1080/09620214.2020.1766374

Holliday, A. (2006). Native-speakerism. *ELT Journal, 60*(4), 385–387.

Holliday, A. (2013). "Native speaker" teachers and cultural belief. In S. A. Houghton & D. J. Rivers (Eds.), *Native-speakerism in Japan: Intergroup dynamics in foreign language education* (pp. 17–28). Multilingual Matters.

Houghton, S. A., & Rivers, D. J. (Eds.). (2013). *Native-speakerism in Japan: Intergroup dynamics in foreign language education*. Multilingual Matters.

Kumaravadivelu, B. (2008). *Cultural globalization and language education*. Yale University Press.

Kumaravadivelu, B. (2014). The decolonial option in English teaching: Can the subaltern act? *TESOL Quarterly, 50*(1), 66–85.

Marcuse, H. (1964). *One-dimensional man: Studies in the ideology of advanced industrial society*. Beacon Press.

Saada, N., & Gross, Z. (2019). The experiences of Arab teachers in Jewish schools in Israel. *Teaching and Teacher Education, 79*, 198–207.

Sharifian, F. (2013). Globalisation and developing metacultural competence in learning English as an International Language. *Multilingual Education, 3*(1), 7. https://doi.org/10.1186/2191-5059-3-7

Sousa Santos, B. (2014). *The epistemologies of the South*. Paradigm.

Sousa Santos, B. (2016). Epistemologies of the South and the future. *From the European South, 1*, 17–29.

Stroud, C. (2018). Linguistic Citizenship. In L. Lim, C. Stroud, & L. Wee (Eds.), *The Multilingual citizen: Towards a politics of language for agency and change* (pp. 17–39). Multilingual Matters.

Yiftachel, O. (2006). *Ethnocracy: Land and identity politics in Israel/Palestine*. University of Pennsylvania Press.

PART 3

Nurturing Intercultural Competencies

CHAPTER 11

Contestation as an Innovative Construct for Conflict Management and Activist Pedagogy

Zehavit Gross

1   Introduction

For the past 25 years, I have been facilitating dialogue groups between Arab and Jewish students on campus. In one of the classes, I asked each of the students to share with us something good that had happened to them during the week. Hiba, a veiled Arab student who was one of the nicest and most pleasant students in the class, stood up and asked if she could share something bad that happened to her during the week, and then she burst into tears. We tried to reassure her and she explained:

> This week I was fired. I worked at the mall, at a store selling hats, bags and accessories. Earlier this week, a shopper came into the store who looked a little strange and started talking to me. He said to me: 'Why should an Arab woman work in a Jewish mall?' He was being provocative, but I decided to ignore him. I called my girlfriend on my mobile phone and spoke to her in Arabic. I was upset and told her what had happened. Two minutes later, he called the police and two policemen entered the store. The frightened shop owner ran up to them and asked what had happened and what they were doing there. They replied that they had received a call from a man who was in the store. The man approached us and said that he had called the police because I was talking on the phone in Arabic and I had a strange expression and he thought I was going to carry out a terrorist attack.

I asked the students in the class what they thought about the incident. The students were upset and expressed disgust at that person's behavior, and there was a consensus in the class that it was inappropriate. The discussion on the subject could have ended at that point. All the participants were in agreement, and an atmosphere of unity was ostensibly created, which is good for starting a class, and that would have been that.

However, I felt that something was wrong and I was not sure that all the Jewish students had expressed what they really felt about the incident. I turned to one of the Jewish students, who I knew had very right-wing views, and asked him what he thought about what had happened at the store in the mall. I asked him to be authentic and not politically correct and to tell me what he really thought about what had happened. He felt uncomfortable at first, and then he said:

> If we lived in Switzerland this story could have ended then and there, but since we live in the State of Israel where there are murderous attacks on a weekly basis, it is clear that if a citizen suspects that he is in mortal danger in a store in a mall, it is his duty to call the police.

The class erupted with students shouting: "If that's what you think you should be ashamed of yourself. This is a Hiba, a classmate of ours ... How dare you talk like that?"

One of the questions that I grapple with, as a conflict group facilitator, is whether to employ a harmonious approach in class that unites the participants or a conflictual approach that offers confrontation and deliberately creates a conflict representing the range of authentic opinions that exist in the conflictual site of the dialogue. At the beginning of my career as a conflict group facilitator, I thought that the purpose of meeting the other was to create an atmosphere of harmony with the other, and develop consensus in order to connect with them and to get to know them better. This pedagogical starting point claims that if we get to know the other and merge with them – we will bring good to the world. Merging with the other was seen as an ideal and as the purpose of an encounter that may also be of great benefit to the individuals who belong to the conflict groups, on both the macro and micro levels.

In retrospect, it seemed to me that what actually happened in the classroom was that the encounters were artificial and forced, and that only some students really connected with the classes. This was despite their ostensibly unifying nature and the message that connections should be forged between the various sectors of Israeli society. The Jewish students argued, "How do you want us to unite when the Arabs are constantly carrying out terrorist attacks?" whereas the Arab students argued, "How do you want us to connect with them when the Jews are so racist, discriminate against us, deprive us of full equality and say such racist things in class." The classes were interesting, but they ended with a predetermined message: "We have to find a way to connect." They were deliberately designed to reduce conflicts and generate unity on a human basis, "We are all human beings and therefore we are all equal." When I was just starting out in the field of intergroup dialogue of conflict groups, and tried to understand what was bothering the students, I discovered that the inability of some students to connect to the class stemmed from a feeling of a lack of authenticity. This was because the ostensible demand for unity created a distorted feeling among the students. They felt that it was necessary to create unity and agreement among everyone so that we could connect the various members of the group and ostensibly manage to create one single Israeli civil society.

Jacques Derrida (1967) talks about the crisis of representation in the modern world, which breaks down language into a collection of signs that create a revelation of the ultimate true meaning. In an era, that has experienced the disintegration of great truths and ideas, a void has been created, along with the inability to express and represent the seemingly hidden truth in words that have ceased to represent the apparent content that they were meant to represent. Therefore, it seems that the realities or truths of individuals or groups cannot be described in words, since each word creates substitutes for truth and creates a new "exile" that threatens the existential existence of humankind.

The crisis of the representation of language in the dialogue group classroom created a new element of difficulty that joined together additional elements of the inability to produce virtual fictions, for the sake of unity. The obsessive need to create common denominators in the dialogue process created "saccharine" encounters devoid of authenticity and, in some respects, lifeless. There was a group consensus that conflict is a bad thing that must be eliminated. Hence, beyond the fact that the sessions lacked any real action, a herd mentality atmosphere was created in class, with everyone feeling the need to appease everyone else and give up their true authentic selves for the sake of creating a cohesive whole.

Over the years of facilitating these dialogue groups in a conflict situation, I found that an encounter, which aimed at creating integration and symmetry, undermines the participants' authenticity. The need to create integration required my students and me to adopt a unifying language. However, this "exiled" the participants and made them strangers, in their own eyes, as well as in the eyes of others. The participants and I, the facilitator, were very frustrated, and I felt the need for a different pedagogic approach. For this reason, I developed a new concept that I called contestation. Instead of aiming for artificial harmony, I used this approach because I realized that rather than forcing the students to pretend that there are actually no gaps, with the goal of creating group cohesion, a different methodology could be more successful. With the help of this concept, I began to balance the class sessions with content whose nature was divisive rather than unifying, as described in the story above with the right-wing student's comments, but which reflected the authentic reality of the various stakeholders in the conflict group. Through the contestation approach, students can express their views more openly and with authenticity, creating difficult situations and knowledge. However, by the end of the course, the students come to understand that they can disagree, but still respect the 'Other.'

The aim of this chapter is to describe and analyze this pedagogic approach of contestation in the discourse of conflict education. First, Judaism's approach to disagreements and contestation between different and opposing opinions is presented. This is pivotal to conflict discourse in Israel and for Jews worldwide, and can serve as a starting point for debate due to its wider relevance. The discussion then examines several factors that accelerate the contestation component in educational discourse in conflict regions, more generally. A critical analysis is then undertaken of research studies that have explored the nature of discourse between conflict groups. The reasons for their failure to address the concept of contestation is analyzed. Finally, the development of a culture of contestation in educational research and practice is proposed.

2 Contestation between Different Voices and Truths: The Approach in Judaism

Education is a space with room for competing voices that represent different forces and starting points of debate. The world of Judaism and the Talmudic corpus are based and structured on contestation between different voices. Judaism distinguishes between two types of disagreements in contestation: between different voices defined as *'le'shem shamayim'* (for the sake of heaven), and those that are not *'le'shem shamayim.'* We read in the *Mishna, Masechet Avot* 5:17 that,

> Every argument that is for the sake of heaven's name, it is destined to endure. But if it is not for the sake of heaven's name – it is not destined to endure. What is an example of an argument for the sake of heaven's name? The argument of Hillel and Shammai. What is an example of an argument not for the sake of heaven's name? The argument of Korach and all of his followers.

An interpreter of the Mishnah, known as Bartenura, wrote that in an argument for Heaven's sake, "the objective, and our end goal in that argument, is to arrive at the truth … but in an argument that is not for Heaven's sake, the goal is control over others and winning the fight." In other words, argument, for the sake of heaven, is a practical argument aimed at seeking the truth, and since it deals with truth, its content will remain relevant even after the argument is concluded (like the disagreements of principle between the House of Shammai and the House of Hillel, that are discussed below).

An argument, whose background is personal, reflects a struggle for power, and the desire to rule and will not remain relevant when it is concluded (like the dispute of Korach and his followers). Korach and his followers came to Moses, intent on taking over the leadership in the name of equality and democracy. They argued that the entire congregation is holy and asked why Moses and Aaron should exult themselves over everyone. Since their request for leadership was driven by material personal interest, by the desire to rule, not out of the desire to serve the people of Israel, they were swallowed up and buried deep in the earth. In Judaism's pantheon of ideas and opinions, no one remembers the components, character and nature of a disagreement with a negative and non-constructive nature; people only remember the bitter end of being swallowed up by the earth.

It seems, then, that Judaism's perception of argument is not necessarily a negative one. One finds in Judaism and in the Talmud substantive disagreements between different worldviews and perceptions. Judaism sees nothing wrong in arguments: the Sages said of contesting arguments that "both this and that are the words of the all-powerful God." In other words, two contesting opinions possess inherent quality, which can be considered holy. However, it is noteworthy that Jewish law ultimately rules according to only one of the opinions (usually in accordance with the House of Hillel, which takes a more pragmatic and lenient line). According to Judaism's perception, two differing opinions do not imply that one is wrong.

Furthermore, the perception of *halacha* (Jewish law) stems from an overall worldview that differs from the reality. For example, there is a disagreement in *halacha* between the House of Shamai and the House of Hillel concerning the way in which candles should be lit during Hanukkah. Hillel says *mosif va'holech* (adding on to the candles). On the first night, you light one candle; on the second night two candles, and so on, until the full number of eight candles are lit. Shamai believed that the candles should be lit according to *pochet v'holech* (lighting fewer candles every night). On the first night, you light eight candles, on the second night seven, and so on.

The Sages argued that, fundamentally, that disagreement is rooted in an overall worldview regarding how we deal with evil. Shamai said that all the forces of evil must be burned by fire: "So shalt thou put the evil away from among you" (Numbers 17: 7). Hillel says that in order to battle evil, we must add light. In this approach, it is light and more light that will bring the great light, as we can see on the final day of Hanukah, when all eight candles are lit. Hillel perceived the battle with evil as a progressive process of adding goodness, and objects to the radical approach of burning evil. The two approaches express two contesting worldviews. The *halacha* ruling does not aver that one opinion is incorrect. For pragmatic reasons, the more lenient approach is chosen, not the more rigorous one, unconnected to the quality of the other approach.

Judaism views contesting opinions as typifying the society that breaches them, and allows for the accommodation of alternative options. Moreover, Rabbi Kook saw contesting opinions, and the basis for the contestation, as a condition for shaping real peace. He wrote:

> There are those who think wrongly that world peace will come about only through one kind of thinking, opinion, and characteristic. So, when they see scholars studying the wisdom of Torah, and thus the varieties of approaches increase thereby – they think that the variety causes disagreements, and the opposite of peace. It is truly not so. Because true peace can only come to the world by various streams – peace will grow when everyone can see everyone else's methods, and it will become clear that there is room for each one, each according to its place, value, and theme. And, in the case of matters that seem unnecessary or contradictory – once the veracity of that wisdom is revealed from all sides – it is only by bringing together all the parts and details, all the apparently different opinions, all the different streams – it is through them that the light of truth and justice will be revealed, and the Word of God, fear of God, love of God, and the light of the Truth. So it is the scholars who bring peace, not dissension, because by widening scholarship, by interpreting and generating new wisdom from different approaches, from numerous perspectives – it is they who engender peace. For as it is written: 'All thy children shall be taught of the Lord' (Isaiah 54:12). Because the world will see that everyone, even those whose opinions differ, all serve the Lord.

Rabbi Kook's approach is that genuine peace will arrive only once all rival opinions co-exist, without narrowing or minimizing other opinions. One can find an approach that explains the variety of competing approaches in *halacha* because of the individual's weakness that impels her/him to create a biased or unclear view of reality, because of her/his inability to see. Different approaches are required, that examine reality from different perspectives, as well as an approach that explains that differing opinions derive from the pluralistic character of Divine will. Here, the divide between the religious pluralistic approach and the democratic pluralistic secular approach can be bridged, even though it is a matter of two different sources of authority.

Tova Ilan (2002) (a central figure in the introduction of religious reforms and pluralism into Judaism) explains how one can bridge between outlooks, which appear to contradict one another. She maintains that,

> In the idea of modern democracy, there is in fact a similar idea, that laws and civil freedoms are actually the result of compromise between opposed opinions. Although they do not always represent what seems to us just and true, at the end of that process, they create a balance. Stemming from this is the need and duty to criticize government, but also the need to understand the partial nature of the truth that we represent. There is a need for humility, for perhaps our truth is not the absolute truth. That sort of humility will lead not only to attentive listening to the opponent's words, not only to refraining from belittling him, but also to an attempt to ponder the inherent contradictions of the matter – any matter – and to bring up proposals for solution, that deal proactively with the rejected side. (p. 24)

In fact, according to Ilan's approach, both the religious and secular approach are aware that human consciousness will always be partial and limited to time and place. Thus, there is a need to apply critical approaches and, most of all, humility that leads, in turn, to listening, and not belittling the other. Conflict education that enables the conscious introduction of contesting opinions allows the creation of true freedom and choice, creativity and innovation.

3 The Nature and Character of the Educational Discourse between Conflict Groups

Research into encounters of conflict groups in secondary and higher education has accumulated substantial knowledge on the importance of contact, and the effectiveness of contact between conflict groups. It has provided knowledge on stages in the development of discourse between the groups and on the distinction between the character and nature of the discourse (collective or individual).

3.1 *The Encounter between Conflict Groups from the Perspective of Contact Theory*

Allport's intergroup contact theory (1954) was one of the theories that created a turn in the field of research that explored intergroup encounters. The theory maintains that contact between conflict groups is likely to decrease prejudice and build greater willingness for proximity. It also provided the basis for reconciliation programs for conflict groups across the world. Allport averred that there are four criteria for contact, which lead to interaction: the groups must have equal status at the time of contact; there must be shared goals; there must be collaboration between the groups; and there has to be institutional support for contact. In his research, Pettigrew added another criterion – that there should be some potential for friendship between the participants.

Contact theory argues that conflict groups, which created opportunities for some kind of contact, were able to soften and moderate intergroup hostility, and could sometimes create friendship and empathy, at different levels. The theory completely ignores the element of contestation between the groups, and its impact on the nature and quality of contact: it tends to focus on the elements, which enable societal uniformity.

Many research studies have validated contact theory, though, in tandem, other researchers note that the impact is mostly effective in the short- and immediate-term. If the meetings do not continue, the contact's impact disappears, as does the sense of empathy and the negative form of contestation surfaces constantly. In fact, the absence of a facilitated encounter, as in educational intervention programs that monitor contact, the contestation element takes over the discourse, and its true or virtual impact of the contact fades away. It is, however, worth noting that most of the research studies were short- and immediate-term. As a result, long-term research is needed to examine the impact of the contact, and especially the retrospective impact of the contestation element in contact between conflict groups. Contact between conflict groups is a complex event, with several stages, as we show below.

3.2 *Stages in Developing Educational Discourse between Conflict Groups*

Steinberg and Bar-On (2002) examined encounters between Jews and Arabs in Israel and explored the structure of the discourse and changes that occurred in the process. They identified seven development stages in the discourse between conflict groups, in the transition from an ethnocentric discourse to a dialogic one, as follows. In Stage 1, there is *lack of contact*, where an ethnocentric dialogue takes place, in which each side clings to its position; the other, who was meant to be a partner in the dialogue, is not addressed. In Stage 2, there is *attack* – each side, or sometimes one side, attacks the other in a hostile, accusation-laden style. Though this stage consists of an attack on the opponent, it does pay some attention to the opponent. In Stage 3, *a window opens* – the sides start expressing emotions and try to share their own personal experiences with the other side. At this stage, each side remains entrenched in its positions, and cannot understand the other side's perspective. In Stage 4, initial *assumptions are undermined* – each side recognizes the existence of possible other options, and the basic need to listen to and understand them. In Stage 5, *intellectual discussion* occurs – people listen to the opponent's arguments, and there is a preliminary attempt to reach agreement. In Stage 6, there is *accommodation of the other* – participants not only listen to the other side, but also talk reflectively about their thoughts. Each side asks the other side clarifying questions, in order to try and better understand them. Finally, in Stage 7, there is *a moment of dialogue* – a moment with some emotional and cognitive understanding. There is genuine contact between opponents that makes it possible to grant legitimacy to the other's narrative. At this stage, there are some moments of empathy between groups.

Most researchers have found that dialogue in conflict situations chiefly remains at the ethnocentric stage, that the participants only think about their own narrative and pain; occasionally the groups reached the dialogue stage. Ethnocentric discourse delegitimizes the opponent and often creates dehumanization processes: when the opponent is perceived as less than human, it follows that their lives are less valuable, their pain less than ours, their children not as precious, and their lives are less important. To move beyond the ethnocentric stage, each side needs to recognize and understand the narrative and pain of the other. This is not an easy process. Most conflict resolution programs seek to achieve consensus, but the tensions between the conflict groups, and the frustrations, anxiety and anger all prevent significant progress towards dialogue. In my opinion, a pivotal failing of this educational approach is that it disregards the contestation aspect between conflict groups. The objective of the educational intervention programs, which seek to reach social consensus, is that one side, or both, have to suppress their true feelings. The major weakness with this proposed dialogue process is that it can lead to a sense of dissatisfaction and alienation, in spite of apparent agreement in the classroom. The educational approach of seeking resolution of the competition/conflict ignores the unchanging reality outside the classroom, in which the conflict is a permanent structural foundation. Therefore, it is important that educational intervention programs train students to express, through contestation, their true feelings and through that process, learn to co-exist with the other through listening to and understanding the narrative of the Other, while continuing to hold opposing opinions.

3.3 *Personal Orientation and Collective Orientation in Conflictual Encounters*

In addition to the educational research that analyzes contact between groups in the educational arena and the stages in which conflict groups develop, there is research that has also focused on encounters between individuals, and between groups. There are two fundamental and different approaches, discernible in the literature that describe how interaction unfolds during contact between two conflict groups, in the course of an educational intervention process (Salmon, 2002).

One approach describes a process of transition from the micro to the macro: that is, a process in which dialogue takes place that tries to develop interpersonal relationships with people from different ethnic and cultural backgrounds, the conflict's basis. According to this approach, creating interpersonal understanding and empathy in an interactive process tends to result in a better understanding of the other's collective (see Gross, 2013). The individual, in this approach, who participates in a dialogue in the framework of an intervention program, will be able to perform transformative processes that will project the feelings of the individual from the individual sphere toward the public sphere, and the collective. In turn, this paves the way to reconciliation between collectives (in other words – peoples), not just successful dialogue between individuals.

Another approach (Sagy, 2002) describes a process of transition from the macro to the micro. This approach maintains that because what is at stake is a conflict between historical narratives of different, hostile collectives with inherent sets of beliefs, values, worldviews, and identities, the focus in an interactive intervention process should be on analyzing those narratives and the basic conflict that divides the different groups.

The literature also offers a third approach which links together the two previous ones (see Bar-On & Kassem, 2004) – asserting that a meeting in the framework of an educational intervention program should be based on the personal narrative and family story of each participant. The way in which the individual experiences and conceptualizes the conflict in the intervention program helps to move toward perceiving the conflict simultaneously from both the personal and collective viewpoints.

Researchers have found that processes of reciprocal empathy between participants from rival groups developed in groups in educational intervention programs. In turn, this led toward a shift away from an interpersonal discussion to a collective one. It enables a dialogue in which, a prior, it is possible to grant legitimacy to the collective narrative of the other and, this contains, of course, the personal input described and expressed in the personal life-story, which the participant presented during the educational intervention process.

I believe that what the three approaches have in common is disregard of the contestation aspect of conflict. Underlying the three approaches is the assumption that eradication of the dispute (at the micro level and the micro level, and at both levels combined) will make it possible to resolve conflicts by the stronger side becoming ready to 'accommodate' the narrative of the weaker side, and, thus, to end the dispute. Focusing research on the personal or group point of origin has a functional nature that does not invalidate the dispute between conflict groups, and does not change the broader perspective of studying the phenomenon. This approach proposes a 'thinner' examination of conflicts, with the naive and unrealistic belief in removing the competitive basis, which while having lethal potential, also has the potential for rebirth and productivity. The three approaches outlined above represent, at the principled level, a differing perception of the concept of conflict described below.

4 Conflict – Problem or Challenge? – As Well as a Lever for Building a Just Society

Underlying the three educational intervention processes described here is a fundamental worldview that sees conflict as a challenge, and as a form of leverage for constructing a just society. However, it also perceives ignoring the element of dispute that is integral to the conflict as a problem or source of threat. While in the past, conflict was perceived as the root of all social maladies, research literature in the last decade reveals the attempt to see conflict as a fundamental phenomenon that is inherent in healthy and just social life. This innovative approach to conflict (Pinson, Levy & Soker, 2010) contends that we cannot describe social relationships without addressing the existence, as an integral part of society, of conflicts of interest, clashes of identities, contestation, disagreements and disputes connected to power relations. This approach, therefore, does not address the various parties' positions and images of the conflict, in terms of bias and deviation (which is found, for example, in the use of stereotypical and prejudicial concepts), but rather as components of different types of discourse on the conflict. The approach, furthermore, reflects a dynamic perception of the social reality and does not see struggles and conflicts as situations set in stone, but rather as a source of changes and new struggles. It is an approach based on the constructivist approach to social identities (Benhabib, 1994, p. 28).

Later, Davies' research (2011) proposed a wide-ranging typology of educational approaches to conflict, which has two axes: active-passive and positive-negative, which result in four quadrants. Active-negative approaches teach stereotypes, defense and even hatred of Others. Passive negative approaches teach acceptance of war and conflict as normal, or ignore the inclusion of recent conflict in their citizenship curriculum. Passive positive approaches will emphasize tolerance and personal problem solving; but it is not until one reaches active positive approaches that one finds contentious dialogue, encounter and the encouragement of action to challenge violence and injustice.

This typology, then, makes it possible to examine schooling perceptions, positions, and practices regarding how historical and current conflicts, nationally and internationally, are tackled. More particularly, it provides the option to evaluate the significance of the discourse that develops, in terms of its contribution to empowering the material nature of the conflict or to developing a more complex and realistic position regarding contestation. This position, which takes its inspiration from Davies (2011), is likely to encourage pupils to acknowledge the existence of contestation, and to develop practices based on active involvement, in the search for positive approaches to it. This is antithetical to the common tendency of pupils to develop a passive approach to conflict, or even an approach that disregards completely its contested aspect.

To sum up, we have seen that conflict education previously focused on preventing or reducing conflicts and contestation, usually at the interpersonal level, and in particular eradicating or minimizing the contestation aspect in the complex responsibility for national and global conflicts. Conflict was perceived, a priori, as negative. However, alternative approaches have been developed more recently, maintaining that positive conflict (as in the workings of democracy) becomes a major factor in generating productive discourse in education, relevant to current global crises in conflict and extremism (see Davies, 2004, 2008). It is the basis of education and the foundation of a society granted on equality and justice. The approach enables response to the complex postmodern reality in which attempts are not made to find solutions, but rather to structure a mechanism that can accommodate and institutionalize conflict and contestation – allowing the conflict to be managed, rather than resolved.

5 Creating a Culture of Contestation: A New Pedagogical Approach

The objective of this chapter is to suggest a different approach to the concept of contestation, one that neutralizes the negative aspect of contestation and addresses its positive and productive potential to promote contestation as a constructive way of managing conflict. Today, in educational research, we must discuss and practice the shaping of a culture of contestation. Contestation also has an educating aspect, since it nurtures the inner balance (homeostasis) of the individual. This creates curiosity and a sense of criticism, a positive significance that, in turn, creates learning and new insights (Shulman, 2000). Life without disagreements is a frozen form of life that can result in stagnation and corruption. In comparison, life with ongoing contestation between foundations that do not mesh with one another creates a dynamic world that strives for regulation and response to the new cognitive and emotional challenges that arise.

Educating for a culture of contestation and for life, in which clashing forces are a given aspect, encourages better, more authentic coping with the complex and conflicted reality in which we live. In order to encourage educators to employ positive contestation in the educational system, we must develop a culture of contestation within this system. The notion of a culture of contestation is inspired by the United Nations' definition of a culture of peace: a set of values, attitudes, modes of behavior and ways of life that reject violence and prevent conflicts by tackling their root causes in order to solve problems through dialogue and negotiation among individuals, groups and nations. A culture of contestation is a hermeneutic process that involves continual adaptation, criticism and reflection.

Kluckhohn (1951, p. 86) argued that:

> culture consists of patterned ways of thinking, feeling and reacting, acquired and transmitted mainly by symbols, constituting the distinctive achievement of human groups, including their embodiment in artifacts, the essential core of culture consists of traditional (i.e. historically derived and selected) ideas and especially their attached values.

Hofstede has enlarged the scope of this definition to adapt it to different settings and contexts. Hence, culture is perceived in his terminology as "the collective programming of the mind that distinguishes the members of one group or category of people from another" (Hofstede, 1991, p. 5). This conception implies that culture is a multi-layered entity that is contextually bound.

A culture of contestation means the acknowledgement of the fact that two (or more) contesting opinions possess an inherent quality. While educating about contestation previously constructed conflict as negative, more recently, alternative approaches have been developed, maintaining that contestation among people and ideas is a major factor in generating productive discourse. It is the basis of a society founded on equality and justice. The approach enables response to the complex postmodern reality in which attempts are not made to find solutions, but rather to structure a mechanism that can accommodate and institutionalize contestation, and allow it to be managed rather than solved.

5.1   *How to Enhance a Culture of Contestation*

As discussed at the start of this article, for many years I wondered whether it is time to put an end to politically correct approaches that stress the issue of culture and interculturality. This ensures a positive atmosphere, which we need to cultivate in encounters with 'the Other.' However, it is achieved at the expense of digging deeper and truly coping with this difficult knowledge and the complicated situation, which we face in Israeli society, in general, and especially within this specific academic setting. As demonstrated in the analysis, which presented a picture of the reality of the Israeli-Palestinian conflict, the contestation approach presents a new platform for inter-religious, multicultural and multiethnic conflict discussion.

The strategic shift to contestation initially created a great deal of reluctance and a sense of anxiety in some participants; but it was gradually perceived as more fascinating and interesting, and the class sessions became more dynamic. Whereas in sessions of a unifying nature, the end of the session is predictable and predetermined, in sessions of a divisive nature, in which I employed the pedagogy of contestation, the ending was enigmatic, unknown and intriguing. The sessions become far more interactive and dialogical in the deepest sense of the word. Some of the students were resentful at the end of the sessions in which I employed the strategy of contestation, and the atmosphere of artificial optimism that prevailed in the sessions focusing on harmony was initially replaced by a pessimistic atmosphere for some participants in the sessions of a divisive nature. However, the interactions between the students gradually became more balanced and more realistic.

The major challenge is how to enhance a culture of contestation in a way that will not offend anyone, since the students come from different cultures in Israeli society and there are some major intercultural concerns that need to be taken into account (Gross & Maor, 2020). One of the dangers of the critical approach is that it makes people resentful and bitter. Therefore, as part of the educational process, they need to be taught to distinguish between critical observation of life and criticism as a way of life – criticism for the sake of criticism. Critical observation means that you look at things, and understand the complexities of the human endeavor. The obsession of constantly looking at the gloomy and negative things, without seeing the big picture, also creates a false reality that should be avoided in educational activities, in general, and conflict group meetings, in particular.

Contestation is not merely a technique for working with conflict groups, but rather a pedagogy and a worldview. It requires honesty and does not allow participants to be bystanders or apolitical. As Peter McLaren (1995) argues, it perceives a politically neutral approach as an immoral approach. The pedagogy of contestation is an enabling and dialogical approach. It is authentic because it allows a person to return to her/himself from the "place of exile," to use the term coined by Jacques Derrida (1967). It makes it possible to engage in parallel and contradictory narratives without the need to reconcile them. It is an approach that sanctifies and empowers the subjective and enables an empowering dialogue between real participants that transforms the discourse from a narcissistic monologue to an inclusive, humanistic and loving dialogue. It is a dialogue that restores people's humanity and turns the group into people who seek truth and authenticity and want to work together to improve the world.

References

Abu-Asba, H., Jayusi, W., & Sabar-Ben Yehoshua, N. (2011). The identity of Palestinian youngsters who are Israeli citizens: The extent of their identification with the state and with Jewish culture, and the implications for the education system. *Dapim: Journal for Studies and Research in Education, 52*, 11–45. [in Hebrew]

Al-Haj, M. (1998). Education for multiculturalism in Israel in light of the peace process. In M. Mautner, A. Sagi, & R. Shamir (Eds.), *Multiculturalism in a democratic and Jewish state* (pp. 703–714). Ramot. [in Hebrew]

Allport, G. W. (1954/1979). *The nature of prejudice*. Addison-Wesley.

Bar-On, D., & Kassem, F. (2004). Storytelling as a way to work through intractable conflicts: The TRT group in the German-Jewish experience and its relevance to the Palestinian-Israeli context. *Journal of Social Issues, 60*(2), 289–306.

Benhabib, S. (1994). From identity politics to social feminism. In *Philosophy of education: Proceedings of the annual meeting of the philosophy of education society* (pp. 22–35).

Derrida, J. (1967). *Voice and the phenomenon: Introduction to the problem of the sign in Husserl's phenomenology* (L. Lawlor, Trans.). Puf.

Davies, L. (2004). *Education and conflict: complexity and chaos*. Routledge Falmer.

Davies, L. (2011). Teaching about conflict through citizenship education. In H. Alexander, H. Pinson, & Y. Yonah (Eds.), *Citizenship, education and social conflict: Israeli political education in global perspective* (pp. 114–133). Routledge.

Gonzalez, K. V., Verkuyten, M., Weesie, J., & Poppe, E. (2008). Prejudice towards Muslims in the Netherlands: Testing integrated threat theory. *British Journal of Social Psychology, 47*(4), 667–685.

Gross, Z. (2003). State-religious education in Israel: Between tradition and modernity. *Prospects, 33*(2), 149–164.

Gross, Z. (2013). Educating for harmony in conflict settings – A case study. In J. Arthur & T. Lovat (Eds.), *The international handbook of religion and values* (pp. 326–336). Routledge.

Gross, Z., & Gamal, E. (2014). How Muslim Arab-Israeli teachers conceptualize the Israeli-Arab conflict in class. *Studies in Philosophy and Education, 33*(1), 267–281.

Gross, Z., & Maor, R. (2020). Is contact theory still valid in acute asymmetrical violent conflict? A case study of Israeli Jewish and Arab students in higher education. *Peace and Conflict: Journal of Peace Psychology*. Advance online publication. https://doi.org/10.1037/pac0000440

Ilan, T. (2002). On education for truth. In A. Sagy & T. Ilan (Eds.), *Jewish culture in the eye of the storm tribute to Yoske Ahituv* (pp. 13–36). The Yaacov Herzog Center.

Jamal, A. (2007). Education toward peace and multiculturalism in a multi-conflict society. *Interdisciplinary Thought in Humanistic Education, 2*, 11–16. [in Hebrew]

Kosic, A., Phalet, K., & Mannetti, L. (2012). Ethnic categorization: The role of epistemic motivation, prejudice, and perceived threat. *Basic and Applied Social Psychology, 34*(1), 66–75.

Lewis, B. (1998). *The multiple identities of the Middle East.* Schocken Books.

McLaren, P. (1995). *Critical pedagogy and predatory culture: Oppositional politics in a postmodern era.* Routledge.

Pinson, H., Levy, G., & Soker, Z. (2010). Peace as a surprise, peace as a disturbance: The Israeli-Arab conflict in official documents. *Educational Review, 62*(3), 255–269.

Pettigrew, T., & Tropp, L. (2006). A meta-analytic test of intergroup contact theory. *Journal of Personality and Social Psychology, 90*(5), 751–783.

Raijman, R. (2013). Foreigners and outsiders: Exclusionist attitudes towards labour migrants in Israel. *International Migration, 51*(1), 136–151.

Salomon, G. (2002). The nature of peace education: Not all programs are created equal. In G. Salomon & B. Nevo (Eds.), *Peace education: The concept, principles and practices around the world* (pp. 3–14). Lawrence Erlbaum Associates.

Sagy, S. (2002). Intergroup encounters between Jewish and Arab students in Israel: Towards an interactionist approach. *Intercultural Education, 13*, 259–274.

Steinberg, S., & Bar-On, D. (2002). An anlysis of the group process in encounters between Jews and Palestinians using a typology for discourse classification. *International Journal of Intercultural Relations, 26*, 199–214.

Stephan, W. G., & Renfro, L. (2003). The role of threat in intergroup relations. In D. M. Mackie & E. R. Smith (Eds.), *From prejudice to intergroup emotions* (pp. 191–208). Psychology Press.

Stephan, W. G., & Stephan, C. W. (1996). Predicting prejudice. *International Journal of Intercultural Relations, 20*(3–4), 409–426.

Tur-Kaspa Shimoni, M., & Schwarzwald, J. (2003). Perceived threat and prejudice in three domains of inter-group rivalry in the Israeli society. *Megamot, 42*, 549–584. [in Hebrew]

CHAPTER 12

"Thou Shalt Not Be a Bystander"

Holocaust and Genocide Education with a Gendered, Universal Lens, as a Path to Empathy and Courage

Lori Weintrob

1   Introduction

"During the armed resistance, the women were armed like the men," wrote Nazi Waffen-SS Major General Jurgen Stroop of the Warsaw Ghetto Uprising. In his April 1943 report to Heinrich Himmler, *The Warsaw Ghetto is No More*, Stroop lamented: "It happened time and again that these women had pistols or hand grenades … to use against the men in the Waffen SS, Police or Wehrmacht …". (Arens, 2011, p. 375). The role of armed women in the most significant Jewish uprising of the Shoah was confirmed by Zivia Lubetkin, who was the highest-ranking woman in the command of the Jewish Fighting Organization (or ZOB). Early in the battle, Lubetkin explained: "One of the women in the unit, Zippora Lerer, leaned out the window and hurled bottles of acid onto the Germans below. The Germans were so shocked to see a woman fighting they shouted: *Ein Frau Kampft* [A woman is fighting]" (Lubetkin, 1981, p. 187). As she escaped the inferno of the ghetto, Zivia held her gun, while crawling through the sewers for 20 hours (Gutterman, 2015, p. 247).

In the armed resistance during the Holocaust, as in other historic instances of guerilla warfare, women played a vital role in surveillance operations, collecting funds for weapons, forging documents, as underground couriers, in battles in ghettos and death camps and in vital forms of non-violent resistance (Baumel-Schwartz, 1998; Laska, 1983; Ofer, 1999; Peto, 2015; Ronan, 2011). Three thousand women, an estimated 10% of Jewish partisans, escaped to the forests (JPEF, 2013). Nevertheless, the courage of these thousands of Jewish women, as well as other non-Jewish women, often remains invisible among the lessons of the Holocaust and other genocides. While we admire those who challenged Nazi ideology with rifle, hand grenade or pen, many find it difficult to name individuals who rebelled.

Why can we name the perpetrators – Heinrich Himmler, Joseph Goebbels, Adolf Eichman, Hermann Goring, Josef Mengele or Adolf Hitler – and not the resisters? Extraordinary efforts to fight fascism marked the war years of

Zivia Lubetkin, Vitka Kempner, Roza Robota, Marianne Cohn, Friedl Dicker-Brandeis, and many others (Baumel-Schwartz, 1998; Paldiel, 2017; Weintrob, 2020). We move closer to understanding hurdles to resistance by examining those Jews and "righteous gentiles," who stood up: from the Jewish educators, Janus Korczak and Stefa Wilczynska in the Warsaw ghetto to the Japanese diplomat Chiune and Yukiko Sugihara, to the Muslim community in Albania, which hid 2,000 Jews (Afridi, 2016; Gershman, 2008). Attention to Afro-Germans, homosexuals, people with disabilities, or non-Jewish victims of Nazi persecution also offers opportunities for new perspectives and criticality among diverse students. The study of the Holocaust and genocide is enhanced when it promotes empathy, courage and ethical choices.

This essay also argues for a focus on witnesses, individual stories and, when possible, the precise words of testimony of perpetrators, bystanders, rescuers, resisters and victims. Amplified by use of the arts, and particularly theater, the study of testimony represents a departure from my own training and over two decades of teaching about the Holocaust, which prioritized written, often German, documents. The official documents created by perpetrators remain a valuable source of study. However, readings of testimony offer a profound impact and new insights into Nazi brutality and Jewish survival, by studying the exact words of survivors, whether born in Germany, Poland, Slovakia or Romania. Film and theater also offer the potential for engaging ever-larger audiences and making a larger impact. The arts have the potential to convey historical empathy and critical reflection on the difficult lessons of genocide.

To begin with, the pedagogy of Holocaust and genocide education should aim not to address the question "What happened," but rather, "How did it happen?" and "Why does it matter?" We should not detract from the central issue of the Nazi mass murder of six million European Jews and the role of a hate-filled ideology of, in Saul Friedlander's words, "redemptive anti-Semitism" (Friedlander, 2007). Our students should examine such critical issues as how the prejudices of the 1930s escalated to "industrial-style killing" (Bartov, 1996).

Nonetheless, we can benefit from an open-endedness in our approach. A central goal of teaching the Holocaust should be to encourage our students to ask questions: How was the Holocaust different in France compared to Hungary or Denmark? To what extent were the stages of genocide planned in advance, or subject to improvisation? Which non-Jewish victims were targeted? Who stood silent and why? This approach takes its inspiration, in part, from the wisdom of Israeli historian Yehuda Bauer (2001, p. 67): "Thou shalt not be a perpetrator. Thou shalt not be a victim. But above all, thou shalt not be a bystander." This call to action, a moral imperative, demands that we turn out attention to those who did not stand silent, to examine resistance, in all its complex forms.

However, it is not only this historical understanding we seek. Insight into the escalation of racial anti-Semitism toward the "Final Solution to the Jewish Question," in comparison to other atrocities, ought to be, as Bauer (2001, p. 3) proposes, "a warning, not a precedent." The "ultimate purpose" of analyzing crimes against humanity "is to help lessen and, in some future perhaps, do away with such horrors" (Bauer, 2001, p. 12). Using a universal and gendered pedagogy raises new questions and new perspectives of the Shoah and crimes against humanity.

2 Empathy and Holocaust Education

The pedagogical effort to create empathy contrasts with the Nazi campaign of dehumanization. As an ethical response to trauma and suffering, empathy can deepen our understanding of genocide. Empathy offers a foundation to understand the actions of others, which is particularly relevant to a historical approach that emphasizes human agency. In terms of Holocaust studies, Katherine Hall (1999, p. 42) argues,

> The dominant presence of first-person memory within the history of the Holocaust actively invites readers to identify with a particular individual, group or perspective. Identification ... is typically marked by the presence of an empathy that allows the subject to enter imaginatively into feelings and experiences of the other.

Hall points out that awareness of the value of individual stories can be traced back to the war years, as Jewish men, women and children wrote diaries. Emmanuel Ringelbaum and Rachel Auerbacher collected eyewitness accounts for the Warsaw ghetto's invaluable underground archive, the *Oneg Shabbat*. It is a worthwhile reminder that Jews in Nazi-occupied Europe were conscious of their humanity.

Empathetic understanding allows a subject to cross boundaries of nation, ethnicity, class and gender, to move beyond the limits of his or her own lived experience, which might otherwise impede an understanding of the other. As Martha Nussbaum (2001) writes in *Upheavals of Thoughts*,

> The pain of another will be an object of my concern, a part of my sense of my own well-being, only if I acknowledge some sort of community between myself and the other, understanding what it might be for me to face such pain. (p. 317)

For Nussbaum, "empathy" represents "an imaginative reconstruction of another person's experience" and "is "psychologically important as a guide" to prevent "sublime indifference." It is "a very important tool … in establishing concern and connection" which might lead to compassionate action (Nussbaum, 2001, p. 317).

Coined in 1908 from the German word *Einfühlung* (literally, "in feeling"), empathy was linked to aesthetics. Lines moving upward or a bird in flight, for example, expressed uplifting feelings. In the 1930s, psychologists broadened its meaning to include understanding others more deeply, including feelings of sadness. By the Second World War, social psychologists began devising experiments to gauge a subject's ability to grasp other's feelings and gain motivation to act in a more caring manner.

The potential force of empathy can be strong in pulling together, while still allowing for distance. Sympathy "seems to stop at the necessary externality of two people to one another," while, in contrast, empathy "suggests the possibility of a self-transformation that allows partial internality" (Moyn, 2006, pp. 399–400). As Dominick LaCapra has proposed, empathy is a form of "affective investment" that allows for the recognition of the other's point of view, while preserving a space for thinking critically about that point of view. This is not empathy as "fusion," but as an "affective relation, rapport or bond with the other, recognized and respected as the other" (LaCapra, 2001/2014, pp. 212–213).

Some historians raise concerns about empathy and history, with regard to both emotional manipulation and the dangers of identifying with perpetrators. In *The Fragility of Empathy after the Holocaust,* Carolyn Dean credits historian Omar Bartov with resolving that dilemma by pronouncing the difficulty of the task. His empathy with the victims is not only a recognition of their human nobility, but also "the fragility of human dignity" (Dean, 2004, pp. 71–72; Bartov, 1996). Empathy is a path to recognizing our own responsibility to others. Empathy can be a key to understanding intergroup relations in a pluralistic society and a tool for combatting racism.

3 Eyewitness Testimony and Theater

There is no holocaust history without attention to eyewitnesses. Claude Lanzmann's monumental documentary film *Shoah* is a tour-de-force of eyewitness testimony, heightened by juxtaposition with sites of trauma (Lanzmann, 1985). In the seminal *Women in the Holocaust,* edited by Dalia Offer and Lenore J. Weitzman, personal narratives of female resisters and survivors were placed alongside scholarly analysis. Saul Friedlander's Pulitzer-prize winning *Nazi*

Germany and the Jews: The Years of Extermination, 1939–45 (2007) combined the voices of victims with the structures of persecution. Beyond testimony, eyewitness voices were found in diaries, letters and other sources written during the war. Agnes Grunwald-Spier edited *Women's Experiences in the Holocaust in Their Own* Words (Grunwald-Spier, 2018), with extensive space given to testimony in memoirs or letters. Omar Bartov's most recent Holocaust course at Brown University (taught, by coincidence, during the COVID-19 pandemic) is entitled "First-Person History in Times of Crisis: Witnessing, Memory, Fiction" (Klein, 2020).

A significant part of my teaching in recent years has been using the narratives of resilience by survivors of Nazism from my own community – "ordinary Jews" from Krakow, Warsaw and Auschwitz. We have woven these stories into research papers and theatrical performances. Our college students select an impactful few minutes of testimony, study it in context and then learn it by heart. Students practice the gestures, body movements, expressions and accent with theater professor Theresa McCarthy, honing a theatrical technique developed by Anna Devere Smith (1992). One non-Jewish student Jessica Vincello said to our class: "I feel as if I know the survivor Margot Capell better than my parents, because I took the time to listen to her breathe." For youth of all faiths, listening to Margot as an eyewitness to Kristallnacht is transformative.

Students frame their presentation around questions such as, "Why would the Nazis prevent a young Jewish girl from watching her favorite movie star, Shirley Temple?" or "What enabled a 14-year old religious yeshiva boy to disguise himself as a Nazi and join the partisans?" The journey of 15-year old Egon Salmon on the S.S. St. Louis triggers questions about the U.S. immigration policies in the 1930s. The inaction of bystanders, and how the world stood silent, is also provocative for discussion of ethical choices made during World War II and since.

This theater project led us to co-author a Holocaust play with playwright Martin Moran centering on testimony from six survivors, *Rise Up: Young Holocaust Heroes*. It includes an original song, *Tali's 100 Questions*, written by David Dabbon that poses questions such as:

> When did refugees arrive in your town?
> When they needed food who turned them down?
> Do you often ask questions like who could have done more?

First performed in the presence of the survivors and their families, the play has been seen by over a thousand students of all faiths, as well as community members. In contrast to the impressive, therapeutic Self-help Witness Theater, our actors are a multi-racial cast, primarily not Jewish. Our work inspired a

New York Emmy award-winning series of films about Staten Island's Holocaust survivors, including *Rise Up* and *Where Life Leads You*, by Shira Stoll, supported by our local newspaper the *Staten Island Advance*. Over 100,000 viewers on the U.S. Public Broadcasting Station or PBS (Stoll, 2018) have seen it.

Narrative and explanation offer a strong pedagogical model, according to psychologist Deena Weisberg of Villanova University. "We learn best through things that are interesting to us. And stories by their nature, can have a lot of things in them that are much more interesting in a way that bare statements don't" (NPR, 2019). Amid concern of the relevance of testimony with the passing of a generation of survivors, theater performance, which is focused on eyewitness testimony, can be meaningful. The vast Holocaust Theater Catalog, organized by Arnold Mittleman, as well as our collaborative work with his organization, the Holocaust Theater International Initiative, suggests the possibilities and potential impact of this approach (See: National Jewish Theater Foundation). Our students also study several powerful theatrical works, such as Tony Kushner's *Bright Room Called Day*, Charlotte Delbo's *Who Will Carry the Word?*, and Abby Mann's *Judgement at Nuremberg*, among others. Delbo's play testifies to her daily life in Auschwitz, along with other non-Jewish women in the French resistance who were deported.

Scholars have raised concerns that "a pedagogy of remembrance," in which testimonies are treated as a "sacred ultimate source" and "absolute truth," has "moved teachers to put aside their critical tools," particularly in Israel (Bornstein & Naveh, 2017, p. 5). They "strongly reject the use of survivor testimony to produce or intensify identification with the trauma of the Holocaust" (Bornstein & Naveh, 2017, p. 19). Paying attention to situational context, and cross-referencing sources, instead, as these authors point out, enables a return to a critical pedagogy. These techniques enable educators to move beyond "competitive victimization" to "multidirectional memory."

> Connecting the study of Holocaust testimonies to the surrounding reality, and using the classroom setting to reflect and deepen the meaning of testimonies, also mitigates feelings of privilege and victimhood. The creation of "multidirectional memory" takes the Holocaust out of the realm of an exclusive concern of Israeli Jews, framing it in universal ethical terms ... personal and emotional experience can serve as an opening to academic learning. (Bornstein & Naveh, 2017, p. 21)

Among the ways to achieve this, they propose, is by incorporating the testimony about non-Jewish rescuer Chiune Sugihara, his wife Yukiko, and their son Nobuki Sugihara.

4 Muslim Rescuers and Afro-German Victims: A Universal Lens

The inclusion of non-Jewish voices, particularly of those who risked their lives to save Jews, is one way to introduce connections and empathy. Another important project I have worked on involved Muslims who rescued Jews. BESA is an Albanian word, a code of honor that demands that one take responsibility for the lives of others in their time of need. The Albanian rescue of 2,000 Jews meant that Jews that fled there were 10 times more likely to be saved than in other nations. This history has been told on film and in photography. When I took a local high school class to visit the BESA exhibit at the Albanian Islamic Cultural Center, one Palestinian student said she found it transformative to see, for the first time, a positive example of Muslim-Jewish relations (Weintrob & Ghosh, 2017).

One example that I find particularly moving is Nazlie Alla, who with her husband, a partisan in WWII, sheltered three Jewish families from Greece, Slovakia and Germany, as well as many partisans. She said: "As Muslims we welcomed them all. We welcomed them with bread, salt and our hearts" (Gershman, 2008, p. 42). A second example comes from another rescuer, Drita Veseli, who hid four family members of the Jewish photographer, who had taught her husband his profession. He and his family had been deported from Pristina to Tirana (the capital of Albania). Drita said: "Our home is first God's home, then our guest's home and finally third our family's home. The Koran teaches that all people – Jews, Christians and Muslims, are under one God" (Gershmann, 2008, p. 71).

Another interesting way to integrate Muslims into Holocaust education is by discussing the female resistance fighter, Noor Inayat Kahn (Afridi, 2016). A Muslim woman who served as a British spy, Kahn was the first female Special Operations Executive (SOE) sent into occupied France, who was later killed at Dachau concentration camp. In 2012, a bronze bust of Kahn was unveiled in London and, two years later, she was commemorated on a British stamp series of "remarkable lives." The inquiry into why any non-Jewish person would risk their lives to assist and save Jews offers important lessons in empathy and human rights leadership. As when discussing Danish, French or any rescue efforts, contextual factors should be invoked as well.

Furthermore, the study of the Holocaust is enriched by gaining a closer look at the range of victims of Nazi violence. To explain how the Holocaust began and the emergence of the "Final Solution to the Jewish Question," most historians and museums would consider it necessary to explain the persecution of people with disabilities, known as Operation T-4. A key step in the escalation of genocide was the first use of gas in showers and the training of SS personnel, like Christian Wirth, later the first commander of Belzec. The sterilization in 1937 of over 300 Afro-Germans and the mounting arrests and deportations of homosexuals in that period are equally important signposts of transforming Nazi power (Burleigh & Wippermann, 1991).

In teaching about non-Jewish victims, how do we compare the persecution and arrest of 100,000 homosexuals, and the death of 8,000 of these men, to the six million Jews who were killed? This lesson is invaluable for observing limited similarities, including pre-existing prejudices, discriminatory legislation, and a bureaucracy of enforcement. We are able to observe how the establishment of the Office against Homosexuality and Abortion by Heinrich Himmler affected his power and popularity in a critical period from 1934–1938.

The stigmatization of Afro-Germans in the interwar era, particularly the 1921 scandal of the "Black Horror on the Rhine," demonstrates that many Germans held racist prejudices or feared black men. This study enables us to understand better the dynamics of the Weimar Republic and the role of pre-existing prejudices in genocide. Doris Bergen has referred to this as the "dry timber" that enabled persecution and violence to develop during the Holocaust (Bergen, 2016, p. 13). Gert Schramm, the only Afro-German sent to Buchenwald at age 15, number 49489, survived, in part, due to the protection of communists there. His tragic experiences deserve to be remembered (Campt, 2003).

The industrial-style killing at Auschwitz-Birkenau is unique; however, in the 1920s, German newspapers proposed brutally lynching African troops in the Rhineland, a connection that raises questions of comparative racism in the U.S. and Germany. A new museum, dedicated to 4,400 black men and women lynched in the United States, was inspired by Berlin's Memorial to the Murdered Jews of Europe, and bears a striking resemblance. Its founder Bryce Stevenson points out, "When you leave these places, you want to say, 'Never again should we commit this kind of suffering and abuse'" (Sales, 2018, p. 1). In contrast, "When you come to the United States, the landscape is largely empty of any reckoning, any acknowledgement of the horrors of our history" (Sales, 2018, p. 2). Similarly, as President Barack Obama said during a tour of the Elmira Slave Castle in Ghana:

> It is reminiscent of the trip I took to Buchenwald because it reminds us of the capacity of human beings to commit great evil. One of the most striking things that I heard was that right above the dungeons in which male captives were kept was a church, and that reminds us that sometimes we can tolerate and stand by great evil even as we think that we're doing good. (CNN, 2009)

Comparative history can promote empathy, deepen interest in the Holocaust and encourage fighting anti-Semitism and racism.

5   Comparative Genocide: Armenia and Rwanda

In a course focusing on the Holocaust, patterns of persecution can become more visible when this era is framed between the genocide in Armenia and the genocide in Rwanda. In the case of Armenia, the motives of the Minister of the Interior Mehemed Talaat and the other Young Turks (Committee on Union and Progress) drew on political, economic, cultural and religious ideology. The starting point of the killing of one million Armenians is identified as April 24, 1915. On that day, 250 leaders were rounded up and executed, to undermine resistance. In a single class, students read two short eyewitness testimonies, including one by U.S Ambassador Henry Morganthau, and watch a 60 Minutes profile on killing sites, such as Deir ez-Zor (CBS, 2010). For Rwanda, the film *Sometimes in April* (2005), directed by Raoul Peck, provides an opportunity to hear testimony about how hate propaganda on the radio escalated into mass killings and rape. We discuss the debates on defining "genocide" in the United Nations during the 100 days of the genocide in 1994 that occurred while 800,000 Tutsis and moderate Hutus were murdered.

A moving part of the class is the testimony of genocide survivor and activist Consolee Nishimwe (2012) – a survivor who lost her father and two brothers in the genocide. Author of *Tested to the Limit: A Genocide Survivor's story of Pain, Resilience and Hope*, Nishimwe was recently named one of 50 "global heroes who speak up against sexual violence against children" (*Safe Magazine*, 2013, p. 54). The parts of Nishimwe's memoir that focus on rescue are particularly interesting. *Pillar of Strength* documents her mother's efforts to save the family during the genocide. Knocking on the door of her Hutu neighbors, Consolee's mother Marie-Jean Mukamwiza was turned away by the parents. However, rather than denouncing them, the children in the household begged their parents to allow their teacher and her family to hide there. Another section describes how they were sheltered by a Muslim neighbor Saidi, who is among the very few "truly good at heart," and protected them, despite direct threats from the *Interahamwe* militia. These chapters highlight the courage and persistence needed to survive and the example of rescue. Like Elie Wiesel's condemnation of "when the world stood silent," her words represent a protest against global inaction to prevent genocide and a plea for remembrance (Powers, 2002; Weintrob, 2017).

6 Resistance: Women, Memory and Leadership

In 1951, the first official Holocaust and Heroism Remembrance Day (in Hebrew, *Yom ha'Shoah v'ha Gevurah*) was held on Mount Zion in Israel, on the 27th of Nissan, a date chosen as a connection to the Warsaw Ghetto Uprising (Baumel-Schwartz, 1998). A bronze statue of the ZOB leader Mordechai Anielewicz was unveiled at Kibbutz Yad Mordechai in his honor. Even today, a reproduction of Nathan Rappaport's Warsaw Ghetto monument is the backdrop to the official ceremonies at Yad Vashem. Outside Israel, Hirsch Glik's partisan song, *"Zog Nit Keynmol"* ("Never Say") is often performed at Holocaust remembrance ceremonies. However, organized violent and non-violent resistance and, in particular, the contributions of female strategists and fighters, are rarely taught or discussed in depth. More than ever, the lessons of how to stand up to hate and anti-Semitism offered by young Jewish women and men in the resistance remain critical lessons for human rights today.

Eyewitness testimony of the heroism and vital role of women that is relevant to understanding the "Final Solution" is abundant and in plain sight. 24-year old Abba Kovner of Vilna identified the systematic nature of Nazi policy and replied with a call to "Rise up until your last breath!" and the founding of the United Partisan Organization (*Fareynegte Partizaner Organizatsye*; FPO). Consider the less well-known words of Kovner at the 1961 trial of Adolf Eichmann:

> In this courtroom, there sits a woman who spent a certain time outside the ghetto with Aryan papers living as a teacher of Catholic children in a secure place. And she, and others like her, were asked whether they were prepared to return to the ghetto; they were asked by comrades in the underground to leave their place of security in order to be partners in our fate in the War and to sacrifice themselves, with no chance of returning. And through this gate – where according to the announcement, according to this document, whoever went through it in order to buy food and to bring in a kilogram of potatoes was shot to death – on her person she transferred explosives, dynamite .... (Kovner, 1961)

Thus, Kovner presents Vitka Kempner (1922–2012), a young Jewish woman in Vilna, credited with the first act of sabotage of the Jewish underground of Lithuania – when she smuggled a homemade bomb out of the ghetto and blew up a Nazi train line. Her partisan team killed over 200 German soldiers and she became a chief FPO lieutenant. Indeed, as early as 1943, one of the most famous Yiddish poets, Hirsh Glik, paid tribute to her bravery in his poem, *Shtil, Di Nacht Iz Oysgeshternt* (*Quiet, the Night is Full of Stars*). Glik wrote of a "girl in a short coat and a beret" with "a face as soft as velvet" who watched for and stopped "a truck loaded with ammunition" (Yad Vashem, 2020). Perhaps because she later married Kovner, her own deeds were overshadowed. Vitka Kempner-Kovner deserves more recognition for her risk-taking.

Indeed, Glik's poem addresses the courage of over 3,000 Jewish women partisans and ghetto fighters, who participated in the resistance movements of World War II. Many are the "heroines of the Holocaust" whose names must be written into the history books, and not only by feminist historians, but by all Holocaust historians, who seek to explain the Jewish response to genocide. Another partisan in Lithuania, Sara Ginaite, gave a detailed description of her commitment to battle the Nazis at a speech to Jewish and non-Jewish partisan groups for International Women's Day, March 9, 1944:

> Nobody taught us how to fight or to perform our duties. We learned by ourselves not only how to clean and use a gun, but how to conduct ourselves in combat and battle, how to blow up a bridge or a train, how to cut communication lines and how to stand on guard. (Ginaite, 2005, p. 176; Grunwald-Spier, 2018)

Ginaite's strategy to smuggle guns into the ghetto at age 19 involved the complicity of Jewish police in Kovno, language skills, work choices and separation from family. Her powerful memoir reveals the transformation of a 17-year old eyewitness to mass killing into an effective member of the underground to a fighter in the Rudniki forest, where women made up 15% of the detachment (Ginaite, 2005; Grunwald-Spier, 2018).

The focus on resistance and rescue efforts by thousands of Jewish women raises many questions about motives, methods and constraints in human rights struggles. Historians understand resistance in the Holocaust as a broad term, often referred to as *Amidah*, which translates in Hebrew into "stand up." This concept of defiance encompasses the anti-fascist artist Friedl Dicker-Brandeis' dedication to the children of Terezin, as well as Roza Robota's organizational work in Auschwitz to aid in smuggling gunpowder (Weintrob, 2020; Wix, 2010). Another notable woman who rebelled against the Nazis was Marianne Cohn who rescued 200 children. After a brief internment in Gurs, France, Marianne was captured near the Swiss border with 28 children. During her time in prison, she penned the chilling poem "I shall betray tomorrow." The local French mayor, who was able to rescue the children, was named a "Righteous Gentile," while Marianne endured brutal torture by the German military officers (Paldiel, 2017). She has since been honored by a garden in her name at Yad Vashem.

Zivia Lubetkin's chronicle of the Jewish underground in Poland, and its transformation from non-violent to violent resistance, is among the most compelling sources on the Holocaust. The highest-ranking female commander in the Warsaw Ghetto Uprising, Lubetkin's analysis of the underground Jewish communication networks explains that "danger awaited the *liasons* at every turn," as they circulated information on massacres and resources between ghettos (1981, p. 80). How did they find the courage to not only sustain their dignity but also organize resistance? Zivia Lubetkin (1981) explained:

> It would be wrong, painfully wrong, to assume that the resistance displayed by the youth during the stormy days of destruction was the response of a few individuals, of Yitzchak, or Zivia, or Mordechai, or Frumka ... the feeling that there was a community of people who cared about each other, who shared ideas and values in common, made it possible for each of us to do what he or she did. This was the source of our strength. (p. 276)

One lesson of the resistance is that it was not the work of individuals, but rather emerged from meetings, discussion and planning that began in 1940, or even earlier (Einwohner, 2003). A full chronology of the Holocaust must take into account not only the timing of the decision of the Final Solution, but also a range of Jewish and non-Jewish actions of resistance and rescue, by both male and female leaders. We must heed the words of Yitzhak Zuckerman on the anniversary of the Warsaw Ghetto Uprising: "If there's a school to study the human spirit, there it should be a major subject" (Zuckerman, 1993, p. xiii). We have much to learn from this community of shared values, acknowledging publically the roles of women and men. Whether individual acts of defiance, altruism or guerilla movements, the courage and moral choices of those in resistance and rescue efforts offers many lessons.

7 Conclusions: The Centrality of Resistance

In Stroop's report on the Warsaw Ghetto Uprising, he attaches a photo of three "captured armed females of *He-Halutz*," a Jewish youth group "the Pioneers." Dressed without the Jewish armband, Bluma Wyszogrodzka was shot, while her sister Rachela Wyszogrodska and Małka Zdrojewicz were sent to Majdanek. Only Malka survived (Ghetto Fighter's House, 1943). While the world stood silent, individuals worthy of our emulation acted with compassion and courage. In the face of horrific constraints, varying within their national context, a minority of "righteous gentiles," including Muslims, and ghetto fighters, made moral and ethical choices that enable us to understand better Nazi policy and human nature. They often put the needs of others before that of their own families – in acts of empathy, solidarity and defiance. Highlighting less visible parts of the history of genocide, using a gendered and universal lens, is a valuable and impactful undertaking.

The role of resistance and rescue, by Jews and non-Jews, is often portrayed as less important to understanding genocide than the work of perpetrators. However, the centrality of resistance and rescue is critical if our key aims are both the historical understanding of the Holocaust and the prevention of future genocides. If we are to commit to the pledge: "Thou shalt not be a bystander," our next task is to demonstrate how it was done and how to be an upstander (Bauer, 2001). The term, "upstander," coined by diplomat Samantha Powers and popularized by Facing History and Ourselves, was added to Oxford Dictionaries in 2016 (Powers, 2002; Zimmer, 2016).

In emphasizing the misrepresentation of the Nazi's industrial-style killing, Omar Bartov points out how "the heroic qualities of the individual warrior" with courage masks the reality of mass, anonymous death and the suppression of individual actions amid the "blood and gore" (Bartov, 1996, pp. 18–19). The six million Jews who perished, and those who fought back or survived with quiet acts of defiance, were individuals. Each one has a unique story of heroism that rivals the courage of those in military units. Jewish and non-Jewish leadership, who resisted Nazism against all odds, was an integral part of the battle against anti-Semitism and Nazism.

Theater and the arts are not simply entertainment; they enhance the levels of inquiry and empathetic understanding. They allow us to hear the voices of victims and survivors in perpetuity. Inclusion of non-Jewish victims and other genocides, as well as perpetrators and bystanders, can be achieved, while strengthening the inquiry into anti-Semitism and the range of Jewish experiences. If even under wartime brutalization and genocidal persecution, individuals could resist, we can make lesser sacrifices too, and commit to compassion. While bringing survivors and students face-to-face will become increasingly difficult in the next generation, new challenges and opportunities await to inspire empathy for one another.

References

Afridi, M. (2016). *Shoah through Muslim eyes*. Academic Studies Press.
Bartov, O. (1996). *Murder in our midst*. Oxford University Press.

Bauer, Y. (2001). *Rethinking the Holocaust.* Yale University Press.

Baumel-Schwartz, J. T. (1998). *Double jeopardy: Gender and the Holocaust.* University of Michigan Press.

Bergen, D. (2016). *War and genocide: A concise history of the Holocaust.* Rowman and Littlefield.

Bornstein, L. N., & Naveh, E. (2017). From empathy to critical reflection: The use of testimonies in the training of Holocaust educators. *Journal of International Social Studies, 8*(1), 4–36.

Browning, C. (2004). *The origins of the final solution: The evolution of Nazi Jewish policy, September 1939–March 1942.* University of Nebraska Press and Yad Vashem.

Burleigh, M., & Wippermann, W. (1991). *The racial state: Germany, 1933–1945.* Cambridge University Press.

Campt, T. M. (2003). Converging spectres of an other within: Race and gender is prewar Afro-German history. *Callaloo, 26*(2), 322–341.

Dean, C. (2004). *The fragility of empathy.* Cornell University Press.

Delbo, C. (1982). *Who will carry the word?* In R. Skoot (Ed.), *The theater of the Holocaust, Vol. I* (pp. 267–325). University of Wisconsin Press.

Einwohner, R. L. (2003). Opportunity, honor and action in the Warsaw Ghetto Uprising of 1943. *American Journal of Sociology, 109*(3), 650–675.

Friedlander, S. (2007). *Nazi Germany and the Jews, 1939–45: The years of extermination.* Harper Collins.

Gershman, N. (2008). *Besa: Muslims who saved Jews in World War II.* Syracuse University Press.

Ghetto Fighter's House. (1943). *Jewish women fighters in the Warsaw Ghetto Uprising who were captured by the Nazis.* 01567P, photo archives, catalog 1893.

Ginaite, S. (2005). *Resistance and survival: The Jewish community in Kaunas, 1941–44.* Mosaic Press.

Grunwald-Spier, A. (Ed.). (2018). *Women's experiences in the Holocaust in their own words.* Amberley Publishing.

Gutterman, B. (2015). *Fighting for her people: Zivia Lubetkin, 1914–1978.* Yad Vashem Publications.

Hall, K. (1999). The politics of memory: Memory and the dynamic of empathic identification within historical accounts of National Socialism and the Holocaust. *The Journal of Holocaust Education, 8*(3), 41–70.

Jewish Partisan Educational Foundation (JPEF). (2013). Jewish female partisans. In *Jewish virtual encyclopedia.* https://www.jewishvirtuallibrary.org/holocaust-resistance-female-jewish-partisans

Klein, J. (2020). Eyewitness history: An interview with Omar Bartov on first-person accounts in global crises. *Brown Alumni Magazine.*

Kovner, A. (1961). *Session 27, Trial of Adolf Eichmann.* Film #2038. United States Holocaust Memorial Museum.

LaCapra, D. (2014). *Writing history, Writing trauma*. John Hopkins University Press. (Original work published 2001)

Laska, V. (Ed.). (1983). *Women in the resistance and Holocaust: The voices of eyewitnesses*. Greenwood Press.

Lubetkin, Z. (1981). *In the days of destruction and revolt*. Lochamei Ha'Getaot: Ghetto Fighter's House.

Moyn, S. (2006). Empathy in history, empathizing with humanity: A review essay. *History and Theory, 45*, 397–415.

Nishimwe, C. (2012). *Tested to the limit: A genocide survivor's story of pain, resilience and hope*. Balboa Press.

NPR. (2019). Storytelling instead of scolding: Inuit say it makes their children more cold-headed [Interview].

Nussbaum, M. (2001). *Upheavals of thought: The intelligence of emotions*. Cambridge University Press.

Ofer, D., & Weitzman, L. (Eds.). (1999). *Women and the Holocaust*. Yale University Press.

Paldiel, M. (2017). *Saving one's own: Jewish rescuers during the Holocaust*. University of Nebraska Press.

Pető, A., Hecht, L., & Krauska, K. (Eds.). (2015/2017). *Women and Holocaust: New perspectives and challenges*. IBL and CEU Press.

Powers, S. (2002). *The problem from Hell: America in the age of genocide*. Basic Books.

Ronan, A. (2009). Women leaders in the Polish underground during the Holocaust. *Jewish Women's Archive*. https://jwa.org/encyclopedia/article/poland-women-leaders-in-jewish-underground-during-holocaust

Ronen, A. (2011). *Condemned to life: The diaries and life of Chajka Klinger*. University of Haifa and Yedioth Books.

Safe Magazine (2013). Issue 1. https://issuu.com/safemag/docs/safe_issue_1

Sales, B. (2018, April 26). What a new memorial for black lynching victims learned from Holocaust commemoration. *Jewish Telegraphic Agency*.

Smith, A. D. (1992). *Fires in the mirror: Crown Heights, Brooklyn and other identities*. Dramatists Play Service.

Stoll, S. (2019, October 19). Rise up: Students carry the word of Holocaust survivors through performance. *Staten Island Advance*. https://www.youtube.com/watch?v=P2QTGb9qYRE&feature=emb_logo

Stroop, J. (1979). *The Stroop report: The Jewish quarter of Warsaw is no more* (S. Milton, Trans.). Pantheon/Random House.

Stroop, J. (2011). Summary report, May 16, 1943. In M. Arens (Ed.), *Flags over the Warsaw Ghetto: The untold story of the Warsaw Ghetto uprising* (pp. 370–378). Gefen Publishing House.

Tec, N. (1997). *Jewish resistance: Facts, omissions, distortions*. Miles Lehman Center for the Study of Jewish Resistance.

Weintrob, L. (2017). Elie Wiesel's plays as kaddish: The sacred duty to remember and resist. *Holocaust Theater Catalog.* National Jewish Theater Foundation. https://htc.miami.edu/elie-wiesels-plays-as-kaddish-the-sacred-duty-to-remember-and-resist/

Weintrob, L., & Ghosh, C. (2017). Whose dreams? Debates on immigration in the mosque, museum and classroom. In N. Aloni & L. Weintrob (Eds.), *Beyond bystanders: Educational leadership for a humane culture in a globalizing reality* (pp. 117–129). Sense Publishers.

Zuckerman, Y. (1993). *A surplus of memory: Chronicle of the Warsaw Ghetto uprising.* University of California Press.

CHAPTER 13

Internationalization for Nurturing Intercultural Communicative Competencies in Pre-Service Teachers

Beverley Topaz and Tina Waldman

1   Introduction

This chapter seeks to add to the current discourse on internationalization, "the process of integrating an international, intercultural or global dimension into the purpose, functions or delivery of post-secondary education" (Knight, 2004, p. 11), in teacher education by reporting on a grassroots development of an internationalization program. It attempts to respond to one of the questions posed by Quezada (2010, p. 1) concerning the ways of preparing teacher education candidates to be, "… competent and have the knowledge, skills, and dispositions to be effective intercultural teachers in an era of globalization." One of the features emphasized in the literature on internationalization of teacher education is the intercultural competence of pre-service teachers. Sieber and Manetl (2012) point out that this emphasis is a necessary response to the social cultural complexity in education due to multiculturalism, migration, globalization and the necessity of best pedagogical practices to meet the needs of these developments.

In tandem with developing appropriate pedagogy, is the requirement for pre-service teachers to develop the human touch: to care for the wellbeing of prospective pupils, to be able to form connections with them and embrace their cultural diversity. Furthermore, specifically among educators of additional languages, there is a consensus that a primary goal of teaching EIL should be to facilitate intercultural communicative competence (ICC) because of the reciprocal relationship between language and culture. ICC can be defined simply as communicating appropriately in various cultural contexts. However, it also implies that language learners and language users be sensitive to their interlocutors' cultural norms, and be openly curious and non-judgmental during interaction (Byram, Gribkova & Starkey 2002). Thus, pre-service EIL teachers are required to develop ICC skills, so they can model and instruct their prospective pupils to communicate and develop relationships with people from other cultures and thus mitigate possible tensions arising from cultural differences.

In response to this context, the English teaching department at the Kibbutzim College of Education in Israel, has developed an internationalization program that focuses on bilateral relations with Karlsruhe University of Education in Germany. A bilateral agreement was signed by both institutions of teacher education, as they are similar in size, curricula, pedagogy and practical field experience. Cooperation between the institutions involves SA and VE, also known as internationalization at home. This chapter reports on both modes of internationalization initiatives, including how they affect the pre-service teachers' development of ICC.

2   Intercultural Communicative Competence

Within teacher education, and especially language teacher education, a definition of ICC may be better served by remaining fluid and open to change in order to meet the variety of contexts in which 21st century teachers will teach. Byram's (1997) landmark model of ICC comprises five dimensions: knowledge, attitude, critical awareness, interpretation and skills of discovery and interaction. Though this ICC model is still relevant, it should be remembered that it predates the rapid development of digital communication, the popularity of social media, the increase in multi-modality, and the current explosion in distance learning, due to the Covid-19 pandemic. Recent descriptions of ICC center less on knowledge of particular cultures, and emphasize both affective and behavioral components of communication. Today, studies in ICC emphasize understanding of intercultural differences, avoidance of stereotyping, curiosity about others and frank openness about oneself (Byram, Gribkova & Starky, 2011).

ICC, then, is the nexus of a number of interrelated dynamics, one of which is the speakers' identity, which involves, "the social positioning of self and other" (Bucholtz & Hall, 2005, p. 586). Since language learners must learn to speak in various contexts, employ different registers and interact in culturally appropriate ways, language learning and identity are bound to one and other (Thorne, Sauro & Smith, 2015). Zimmerman (1998) provides a model of identity comprising several aspects. Of relevance here is what she calls 'situated identity,' which describes the expected behavior for a specific context of communication, and 'transportable identity,' which involves aspects of one's identity that can be transported across contexts. These could include aspects of one's religion or culture, like a religious Jew wearing a skullcap, or a Muslim woman wearing a hijab. These transportable elements may be made salient by the wearer to align them to their identity, or they may not be made relevant to the interaction by any of the participants. The disclosure and recognition of identity is an integral aspect of intercultural competence.

3 Internationalization

Although we make the argument that internationalization is an opportunity to expose students to diverse peoples and cultures, and, thereby, develop their ICC, we are also aware that internationalization is not a neutral process. On the one hand, it is a response to globalization influenced by rapid technological advances, economic global markets and massive migration, among other factors. On the other hand, it is also a response to economic competition between higher education institutions to attract students in the global market (Marginson & van der Wende, 2006). Richer economies have more access to internationalization opportunities creating an unequal playing field, possibly creating both "victims" and "agents" (Larsen, 2016).

3.1 *Internationalization and Study Abroad*

Internationalization, in the form of studying abroad in higher education (HE), has become one of the priorities of the European Council and is perceived as "one of the fundamental ways in which young people can strengthen their future employability, as well as their intercultural awareness, personal development, creativity and active citizenship" (EU, 2011, p. 3). SA programs in teacher education can range from participating in an academic course, an entire semester of studies and practical teaching placements. In 2011, the EU established a benchmark for SA. This required that by 2020, at least 20% of higher education graduates would have participated in some form of SA program, defined as either having a minimum of 15 European Credit Transfer System (ECTS) credits or having studied abroad for a minimum of three months. The number of international students in Europe increased by approximately 114% from 2000 to 2010 (Barrioluengo & Flisi, 2017).

3.2 *Internationalization and Virtual Exchange*

Virtual exchange (VE,) as an "internationalization at home" initiative, is slowly gaining popularity in higher education (O'Dowd, Sauro & Spector-Cohen, 2019). It is described as:

> ... a form of learning which consists of virtual components through an [information and communications technology] supported learning environment that includes cross-border collaboration with people from

different backgrounds and cultures working and studying together, having, as its main purpose, the enhancement of intercultural understanding and the exchange of knowledge. (Bijnens et al., 2006, p. 26)

Recently VE has been promoted by several support platforms and Erasmus supported projects, such as EVALUATE[1] 2017–2019 and EVOLVE[2] 2019–2021. Despite this move toward the recognition of VE as a viable alternative to SA, it is nevertheless slow in being considered as a practical means for internationalization in HE. A survey, conducted by EVOLVE in 2019, showed that only 57% of European HE management and faculty would consider implementing VE for internationalization. One of the main reasons for the fairly low interest in VE is the challenge of creating sustainable partnerships. Contributing factors include time constraints and scheduling differences; language differences, lack of institutional support, lack of technical support, and an absence of mentoring for faculty members.

VE in language education is also known as telecollaboration, which is principally informed by socio-cultural and interactionist theories of language learning with the principal goal of providing authentic, intercultural communication experiences among language learners (O'Dowd, 2015; O'Dowd et al., 2019; Sadler & Dooly 2016). Much of the literature argues that telecollaboration facilitates ICC through a number of conditions associated with Allport's (1954) contact theory hypothesis including equal status, common goals, and cooperation of the partners. Some studies have shown that communication and collaboration within the framework of telecollaboration results in the weakening of stereotype impressions and strengthening of intercultural sensitivity and understanding. It has been argued that language learners "create a sense of transnational identification with learners in another country" (Porto, Houghton & Byram, 2018, p. 486) through collaborating on international projects. However, others argue that intergroup communication through telecollaboration, which aims to increase intercultural communication skills, remains debatable. Kern (2016) suggests that technology based communication is likely to "quash difference" (p. 339). Similarly, Kramsch (2014) claims that much of the interaction downplays cultural difference, because it is "phatic communication" (p. 300) with students skirting around difference, avoiding sensitive issues and being polite.

4   SA and VE in the Context of the Study

The form of SA that the Kibbutzim College of Education has employed is that of credit mobility, where students study a semester abroad at Karlsruhe

University of Education and, in return, receive academic credit from their home institution. The first SA exchange took place in the 2018–2019 academic year. One student from Karlsruhe University of Education spent the fall semester at the Kibbutzim College of Education and two students from the Kibbutzim College spent the spring semester in Germany. The students were selected, based on their grade point average, faculty recommendations and their desire to undergo an intercultural experience and be immersed in another culture. The student from Germany spent her semester in Israel residing with an Israeli family, whereas the students from Israel resided in the residence for international students.

The SA students studied in courses in the English department in the host institutions, based on a previously approved learning agreement. In the Israeli context, the student from Germany took all her courses with local students whereas the Israeli students studied with both local German students and other international students. Karlsruhe University provided SA students with an intensive course in German prior to the beginning of the semester, whereas no such course in Hebrew was available for the student from Germany.

The first VE took place in the fall semester 2015 between two classes of third year undergraduate pre-service EIL teachers studying collaboratively from their separate institutions. This VE, which has now become institutionalized, has taken place every fall over the last five years with different cohorts, numbering over 250 participants. The VE was designed and is facilitated by two lecturers from the respective institutions. A hybrid telecollaboration model of VE, comprising synchronous and asynchronous communication and face-to-face teaching, was adopted to give the pre-service teachers participatory experience in this type of pedagogy, as well as the skills necessary to implement such an exchange in their classrooms.

There was no marked development of ICC skills in the first two VE courses, which ran in 2015 and 2016. Despite students' attempts to foster group identity, and genuine collaboration, they avoided dealing with misunderstandings. This was confirmed by lecturers' observations of the participants' communication during the synchronic meetings. In addition, in a pre and post survey completed by students, ICC skills were ranked high in the pre survey with no significant difference in the post survey (Waldman et al., 2019), suggesting that participants perceived they already possessed ICC skills before participating in the course. As a result of these findings, from the third course onwards, the lecturers took more active roles in manipulating the course so that the participants could not avoid issues of cultural differences. Nevertheless, a safe place for communication was provided through explicit mentoring. O'Dowd and colleagues (2019) define teacher mentoring in VE "as the strategies and techniques that teachers use in their classes to support student learning" (p. 147).

The mentoring adopted emphasized intercultural communication in several ways. One way, suggested by Ware (2013) is to tutor intercultural communication strategies. The lecturers did this by sharing with the students recorded communications from previous collaborations. For example, they showed excerpts of a Zoom session, in which students did not take turns, but rather one student monopolized the microphone. Other examples included language switches to mother tongues to hide communication from international partners, and the use of hand gestures, which could be misinterpreted and may have even seemed offensive. Other examples of written communication showed lengthy responses including praise from one of the students, and a short one or two word response from an international partner. These examples, along with others, were presented to the students to engage them in discussion about what they noticed about the interaction, how they thought the participants felt about it, and how they think they would interact differently to show understanding and appreciation of their partners.

Another pedagogical mentoring strategy, used by the lecturers, suggested by Muller-Hartmann (2012,) concerned designing specific tasks to facilitate intercultural exchange. The lecturers designed sessions devoted to intercultural comparisons, thereby enabling the participants to explore the complexity of culture and identity. The members of each international team were required to find an advertisement or clip on YouTube, which they believed was a representation of the others' culture. During the video conferences, the team members viewed the content and discussed what the identities represented. This task aided in circumventing avoidance strategies like 'playing it safe' and conversing only about 'light' cultural topics, such as traditional foods or holidays.

5   Research and Data Collection

In order to discover the impact of these two types of exchange on students' intercultural competencies, we collected data through written reflections and in-depth interviews and performed qualitative content analysis. We followed the Ethical Standards of the American Educational Research Association (AERA, 2011), particularly regarding confidentiality, integrity and informed consent. All participants were reassured that participation or lack of in the study would not interfere with their assessment or grade for the course.

The data were analyzed to identify the emerging themes of ICC and identity. Each theme is illustrated by quotes selected from the students' reflections and interviews. After each quote, there is a symbol showing whether the respondent is a student in Israel (I) or in Germany (G) and if they participated in the virtual exchange (VE) or study abroad (SA). The salient themes that we found included: stereotyping, readiness to change perspective, and issues of identity.

5.1   Stereotypes and Readiness to Change

A careful analysis of the reflections from the participants in both the VE and the SA show that stereotyping was a common theme, as seen in the following:

> Israelis are waaaay more open and direct than Germans. I obviously knew this from the beginning, because I know a lot of people from the Middle East and, therefore, also know the differences in mentality. But still, it was hard at first to adapt to this. (G, SA)

In this quotation, it is evident that, for the speaker, stereotyping is not confined only to Israelis, but to all peoples from the Middle East, when the interviewee assumed that they share characteristics based on their geographical location. 'Othering,' through the use of personal pronouns, such as 'I,' and naming, such as, 'the other students,' 'Germans,' 'Israelis,' as well as generalizations, were also common to many of the reflections relating to this theme. Here are some examples. "At first, I thought the other students would be very polite and organized to the point where it might be a little cold and detached" (I, VE). "I also knew that German culture revolves around punctuality, order, discipline and excellence" (I, SA).

Initially, the students were operating from an essentialist position. They perceived their partners as different, due to their culture and ethnicity, and this resulted in initial bias. During the course of the VE, in most cases, these views disappeared and a transformation began to emerge, indicating readiness to change one's perception. "It was interesting to talk about the stereotypes each other has, but also to be able to dissolve these stereotypes. It is a mistake to assume that you know everything about someone else's culture" (G, VE). "When I listened to the other teammates, no matter how different they were from me, I was more open to learning new things about their culture and, perhaps, about myself" (G, VE). "After working with my teammates, I understood that my prejudice and stereotyping led me to think wrongly about them" (I, VE).

In the reflections relating to the theme of readiness to change perception, the students showed non-judgmental interest in their international partners. In addition, their use of words, such as 'my teammates' and 'each other' are used to show commonality, rather than distancing. For example, one student said: "I think I have acquired a new intercultural skill, I wasn't even aware I needed any" (I, VE).

One assumption is that change took place because the students had formed personal relationships. However, the SA students, in their extended stay abroad, also formed personal relationships. However, they did not seem to have adjusted their preconceived notions regarding stereotypes. As one student said, "German people are generally more reserved; at times, it was difficult for me emotionally. I didn't understand how much I love the Israeli warmness, until I lived in Germany. Germans keep their own space" (I, SA).

Although in their interviews and reflections, the SA students claimed to be open-minded, and interculturally competent, even prior to their six months abroad, their responses did not reveal this. Furthermore, their existentialist positions persisted regarding the students they met in the international dormitories. For example, one interviewee noted: "… students from Laos are more spiritual and holistic in their approach to life. Students from South Korea are stricter and have a very developed technological background – they are proud of their parental strictness and upbringing" (I, SA). This generalization was based on meeting two people from Laos and three from South Korea, showing that the student did not change her automatic prejudice about people from other cultures. We assume, therefore, that the students' perceptions in the VE changed not due to contact and interaction only, but due to the deliberate intercultural mentoring during the course, whereas in the SA program, there was no such explicit mediation.

5.2 *Identity*

The interrelationship between culture and identity emerged as a salient theme in the students' reflections. Some revealed that they felt that their identity was defined by the way others perceived their interactional behavior. Many of them, as expressed in the example below, showed that they wanted to change this perception and suggested ways to temper their identity.

> I now know that when texting on Whatsapp with someone from another culture, who does not know me well, I might sound like a blunt person. For the other person to understand my humor, I could use more emojis. That might help them to understand me. (I, VE)

The student attempted to reframe how she is perceived by others, as she did not wish to be perceived as the stereotypical 'blunt Israeli.' The following quote, from a different student, reinforces this second student's desire to change her identity by imitating the behavior of others. "This experience made me learn that in order to work well as a team, I need to bridge this cultural gap by acting like my partners" (I, VE).

In addition to students' attempts to fashion their own identity differently from the way that their national identity was perceived by others, a few students endeavored to shape the identity of 'the other' to fit a preconceived image.

> It was nice to see that I could actually help my Israeli friend see her country in a more positive light. So, what I noticed was that people see themselves in a different way from how you might see them. (G, VE)

In other instances, students expressed dismay at some of the characteristics that their international partners suggested were an aspect of their cultural identity. This was evident when team members from Germany shared a traditional Jewish song in Yiddish with their partners in Israel believing that ultra-orthodox religious music was an aspect of Israeli national identity. However, their partners, young, secular women, who did not identify with this music, felt that this characterization was an affront to the global identity that they believed they were portraying through their dress and behavior. "The song was in Yiddish and sounded very strange and depressing. We were very surprised at the song choice and it made us question if they really understand who we are" (I, VE).

This cultural misunderstanding, as well as others, were opportunities for learning to take place and allowed the VE lecturers to step in and coach the students about culturally related issues of identity. In contrast to the feeling of discomfort about identity implied in the reflections of the VE participants, one SA student expressed feeling more comfortable with her Palestinian cultural identity, as a young woman, who wears a hijab. "Being able to be 'me' and be comfortable with that is a great feeling and something that I will miss when I go back home! I never felt that I was being looked at because of how I look or what I believe in" (SA, I). As a religious Muslim female in Israel, she feels like an outsider to the mainstream Israeli culture, since her attire immediately identifies her as belonging to a religious group. This reflection, from a minority student, reveals how an international setting can strengthen a connection to one's own culture.

6 Discussion and Conclusions

In this chapter, we added to the debate concerning how internationalization experiences, both at home and abroad, can prepare pre-service EIL teachers to become interculturally effective educators. We have seen that students, who participated in the VE, developed ICC skills more readily than those who participated in an extended SA. We suggested that the reason for this was the explicit mentoring carried out during the VE course, especially in response to critical incidents due to cultural misunderstandings. The SA students, who received no mentoring, did not fare so well. It appears that some SA students' time abroad reinforced negative stereotypes about the host culture and some experienced loneliness and isolation.

Similar findings have been reported in other research on teacher education study abroad programs (Hurtado et al., 2013; Walters et al., 2009). Although student participants in our study reported their readiness to change their preconceived notions and expressed a desire to learn more about each other's culture, we cannot claim that either of the internationalization initiatives contributed to radical transformation or serious development of students' ICC skills. However, many students displayed a tendency towards openness and curiosity.

Since one-time internationalization experiences, whether they are VE or SA, do not seem to have a far-reaching impact on students' ICC skills, we suggest that such endeavors be an integral component in all teacher education programs, and that students participate in several international courses throughout their degree. By engaging in several experiences, in which they collaborate with partners from diverse cultures and receive explicit mentoring in intercultural skills, students will be able to practice and, hopefully, strengthen their ICC.

Such competencies are critical for all teachers, not only for those planning to seek work abroad, but also, for those planning to teach in their own communities. This is due to the diversity among pupils in their own classrooms. For example, in Israeli secular schools, children from families born in the former Soviet Union, France, Ethiopia and other countries, study side by side. Teachers are expected to be experts in their discipline, focus on lesson content, attend to 30–40 pupils, assess their level of engagement, behavior, and manage learning. Israeli-born teachers, who do not possess ICC, might not know how to manage the dynamics of a culturally diverse classroom. As a result, teachers, especially novice or pre-service teachers, may become frustrated and upset, which could lead to burnout and early attrition. Cultivating ICC during teacher education, however, has the potential to prepare teachers to understand better their pupils' behavior. They will be less judgmental and more likely to deal sensitively with behavior, which is different. In turn, this may lead to greater teacher resilience and teacher retention.

Since VE, with explicit mentoring, seemed to have facilitated some intercultural learning, we propose that several models be considered for internationalization programs, in order to ensure that students' experiences lead to growth and development, and do not solely remain as 'nice to have' experiences. One model could be students participating in a VE in order to prepare for their extended SA. Successful completion of the VE and their ability to show intercultural competence would be a prerequisite to their studying abroad. Another model could involve blended mobility, which is a combination of VE and SA. Students would participate in a VE prior to a short SA experience of between one and four weeks. On returning to their home institutions, they would continue with the VE. This model would capitalize on the in-depth learning of the discipline, as well as include collaboration, lecturer mentoring and a short overseas immersion in the other culture.

In these uncertain times of the COVID-19 pandemic, there has been a worldwide increase in acts of xenophobia, nationalism, racism and discrimination. Such acts are evident in national and social media, such as nations characterizing other cultures as 'dirty' (Dervin et al., 2020, p. 95). In such a climate, developing ICC has become even more vital than before. With the closing of borders and national lockdowns, SA has become precarious. Therefore, internationalization at home programs, via VE, will enable HE to keep their international partnerships alive and thriving and to continue to provide students with opportunities to practice their ICC skills.

Notes

1 Evaluate was an Erasmus funded project that ran between the years 2017–2019. Its goal was to evaluate the impact of virtual exchange on initial teacher education. Part of the initiative included preparing teacher trainers to facilitate VE. The Evaluate team then analyzed the impact of participation in the project from the position of teacher educators and student participants in the VEs that took place. The fall report may be found at http://www.evaluateproject.eu/
2 EVOLVE: Virtual Exchange as Innovative Practice across Europe Awareness and Use in Higher Education. In general, findings of this research project showed that VE was not widely known as an educational practice by key stakeholders in implementation, such as educators, educational supporters, internationalization officers and policy officers and managers. The full report is at https://evolve-erasmus.eu/wp-content/uploads/2019/03/Baseline-study-report-Final_Published_Incl_Survey.pdf

References

Allport, G. W. (1954). *The nature of prejudice*. Perseus Books.
American Educational Research Association. (2011) Code of ethics. *Educational Researcher, 40*(3), 145–156.

Barrioluengo, M. S., & Flisi, S. (2017) *Student mobility in tertiary education: Institutional factors and regional attractiveness*. Publications of the EU.

Bijnens, H., Boussemaere, M., Rajagopal, K., Op de Beeck, I., & Van Petegem, W. (2006). *Virtual mobility: A best practice manual*. Europace IV2W. https://www.eurashe.eu/library/modernising-he/mobility/virtual/WG4%20R%20Virtual%20Mobility%20Best%20Practice%20Manual.pdf

Braun, V., & Clarke, V. (2006) Using thematic analysis in psychology. *Qualitative Research in Psychology, 3*(2), 77–101.

Byram, M. (1997). *Teaching and assessing intercultural competence*. Multilingual Matters.

Byram, M., Gribkova, B., & Starkey, H. (2002). *Developing the intercultural dimension in language teaching: A practical introduction for teachers*. Language Policy Division, Directorate of School, Out-of-School and Higher Education, Council of Europe.

Council Recommendation of 28 June 2011. (2011). Youth on the move – Promoting the learning mobility of young people. *Official Journal of the European Union*. https://eur-lex.europa.eu/legal-content/EN/TXT/PDF/?uri=CELEX:32011 H0707(01)&from=EN

Dervin, F., Chen, N., Yuan, M., & Jacobsson, A. (2020). COVID-19 and interculturality: First lessons for teacher educators. *Education and Society, 38*(1), 89–106. https://doi.org/10.7459/es/38.1.06

Helm, F. (2018). *Emerging identities in virtual exchange. Research-publishing.net*. Voillans. https://doi.org/10.14705/rpnet.2018.25.9782490057191

Hurtado, I. G., Coronel, J. M., Carrasco, M. J., & Correa, R. I. (2013). Internationalization of the practice in education degree: Students' intercultural experiences in the teaching and learning process at Sahrawi refugee camps. *Journal of Education and Learning, 2*(1), 253–261.

Jager, S., Hauck, M., & Shannon S. (2019, September). *Addressing the challenges of mainstreaming Virtual Exchange in both language and non-language disciplines* [Paper presentation]. Eurocall. Louvain, Belgium.

Kern, R. (2014). Technology as pharmakon: The promise and perils of the internet for foreign language education. *Modern Language Journal, 98*, 340–357.

Knight, J. (2004). Internationalization remodeled: Definition, approaches, and rationales. *Journal of Studies in International Education, 8*(1), 5–31.

Kramsch, C. (2014). Teaching foreign languages in an era of globalization: Introduction. *The Modern Language Journal, 98*, 296–311.

Marginson, S., & van der Wende, M. (2006). *Globalisation and education*. OECD. http://www.oecd.org/edu/research/37552729.pdf

Muller-Hartman, A. (2012). The classroom based action research paradigm in telecollaboration. In M. Dooly & R. O'Dowd (Eds.), *Researching online foreign language interaction and exchange* (pp. 163–203). Peter Lang.

O'Dowd, R. (2015). Supporting in-service language educators in learning to telecollaborate. *Language Learning and Technology, 19*(1), 63–82.

O'Dowd, R., Sauro, S., & Spector-Cohen, E. (2019). The role of pedagogical mentoring in virtual exchange. *TESOL Quarterly, 54*(1), 146–172. https://doi.org/10.1002/tesq.543

Pettigrew, T. F., Tropp, L. R., Wagner, U., & Christ, O. (2011). Recent advances in intergroup contact theory. *International Journal of Intercultural Relations, 35*(3), 271–280.

Porto, M., Houghton, S. A., & Byram, M. (2017). Intercultural citizenship in the (foreign) language classroom. *Language Teaching Research, 22*(5), 484–498.

Quezada, R. L. (2010). Internationalization of teacher education: Creating global competent teachers and teacher educators for the twenty-first century. *Teaching Education, 21*(1), 1–5.

Sadler, R., & Dooly, M. (2016) Twelve years of telecollaboration: What we have learnt. *ELT Journal, 70*(4), 401–413.

Van De Mieroop, D., & Clifton, J. (2012). The interplay between professional identities and age, gender and ethnicity introduction. *Pragmatics. Quarterly Publication of the International Pragmatics Association (IPrA), 22*(2), 193–201.

Waldman, T., Harel, E., & Schwab, G. (2019). Extended Telecollaboration Practice (ETP) in teacher education: Towards pluricultural and plurilingual proficiency. *European Journal of Language Policy (Special Issue), 11*(2), 167–185.

Walters, L., Garii, B., & Walters, T. (2009) Learning globally, teaching locally: Incorporating international exchange and intercultural learning into pre-service teacher training. *Intercultural Education, 20*(sup 1), S151–S158. doi:10.1080/14675980903371050

Walther, J., Hoter, E., Ganayem, A., & Shonfeld, M., (2014). Computer mediated communication and the reduction of prejudice: A controlled longitudinal field experiment among Jews and Arabs in Israel. *Computers and Human Behavior, 53*, 5–22.

Ware, P. (2013). Teaching comments: Intercultural communication skills in the digital age. *Intercultural Education, 24*(4), 315–326.

Zimmerman, D. H. (1998). Identity, context and interaction. In C. Antaki & S. Widdicombe (Eds.), *Identities in talk* (pp. 87–106). Sage Publications.

CHAPTER 14

Developing Culturally Proficient Global Peace Education Changemaker Educators for Culturally Diverse Schools and Classrooms

Reyes L. Quezada

1   Introduction

This chapter discusses cultural proficiency as a theoretical framework to develop teachers and teacher educators to be culturally proficient global peace education changemakers. This chapter supports the focus of this book on activist pedagogy, shared life, and shared education. The goal is to prepare inclusive teachers and teacher educators to emulate the characteristics of changemaking, such as empathy, leadership, and collaboration, and to promote teambuilding for shared life and shared education. The purpose is to transform teachers and teacher educators to teach in culturally proficient, globally minded, changemaker type designated schools, classrooms, and universities, in which peace education is at the forefront and integrated into the core curriculum. A brief context on peace education in schools is provided, and the cultural proficiency model is introduced and described, as it relates to peace education and educator preparation. Social and best activist education pedagogy practices to be used by teachers and teacher educators are discussed and shared.

2   Teaching to Achieve Social Justice through Peace Education

Recent and past social upheaval, both in the United States and abroad, has given us an opportunity to witness many events. These include the end of apartheid, rapid changes in technology, biogenetics, terrorism and war that can be seen in social medial and live television, as they are unfolding. There are many changes that are yet to appear, and many more at our doorsteps: changing demographics in schools and nationally in the United States, continued research on the COVID pandemic and vaccine, management of the environment to stop climate change, floods and fires, and reflection of social values, which seems to be near impossible (Quezada & Romo, 2004).

© KONINKLIJKE BRILL NV, LEIDEN, 2022 | DOI:10.1163/9789004512740_015

The world is now experiencing the near impossible, with three main shifts: social, educational, and political. First, the coronavirus pandemic has wreaked havoc worldwide, with more than 804,266 deaths in the United States as of December 18, 2021, and over 5.3 million worldwide, resulting in harsh, global economic, social, political, and educational disruptions. The virus is not distinguishing between social classes, as world leaders have contracted the virus, including former President Donald J. Trump, his wife Melania, many members of his administration, the United Kingdom's Prime Minister Boris Johnson, and Brazilian President Jair Bolsonaro. Each initially downplayed the virus and its effects; they also did not promote the wearing of masks to protect others, a culturally blind attitude that has had negative consequences. Millions of individuals have lost jobs, businesses, and stable incomes to support their families. As a result of the killing of George Floyd, Breonna Taylor, and others, as well as the Black Lives Matter and anti-racism movements, many people from different ethnicities have joined together in support of their case, caused by a distrust in law enforcement.

Second, the closing of schools around the world and a shift to online and remote teaching and learning has tested the resilience of students, teachers, and educational systems. This caused them to rethink, reimagine, and transform educational pedagogies with minimal planning time in late Spring of 2020. In the United States, for approximately a year, many elementary, secondary and institutions were closed, as teachers continued to teach remotely, or in some form of hybrid manner (on campus and online).

Third, the global and local political landscapes have shifted, as a result of the signing of the Abraham Accord agreements. These agreements established formal ties between Israeli and two Arab states, the United Arab Emirates and Bahrain. These agreements left the Palestinian community/state to figure out where they fit in, in the complexity of the legal accord agreement, placing them on the sidelines.

In the United States, a political shift also occurred, when Joe Biden and Kamala Harris won the 2020 presidential/vice-presidential election, which ended Donald Trump's tenure. This change confounded the political complexity. The Democratic Party now has control of both the House of Congress and the Senate, after the State of Georgia elected two democratic senators, rebuking Trump's support of the Republican incumbents, who aligned with his policies. To date, former President Donald Trump has not acknowledged his loss: he continues to claim that there was massive election fraud, even after both the Congress and Senate certified the election results.

The unimaginable event that unfolded live on television channels in the US and throughout the world by many of President Trump's supporters was the storming and breeching of the Capitol of the United States, as a result of his culturally destructive speech, after learning that Vice President Mike Pence would not take his side and refuse to certify the election results. This event occurred while the certification of the Electoral College's results was taking place. It placed senators, congressional representatives, their staffs and capitol police in danger. The storming of the Capitol resulted in the killing of one police officer and four civilian deaths. Soon after, this caused a vote for the second impeachment of President Trump by the House of Representatives. The trial moved to the US Senate, but the result was that former President Trump was not found guilty.

Lastly, the Senate Republicans confirmed Amy Coney Barrett as a Supreme Court Justice, just two weeks prior to the 2020 elections. This was due to the recent death of Justice Ruth Bader Ginsburg, who had an inter-generational impact. This was former President Trump's third, consecutive appointment of conservative justices on the Supreme Court. Justice Ginsburg's legacy includes the rights of women to make their own decisions pertaining to abortion rights, and most importantly, the importance of work for peace and justice, and equal rights for both men and women.

3 Our Role as Teacher Educators

With the above in mind, peace, peace education, and social justice should be interpreted, portrayed, taught, and discussed in our K-12 schools and in institutions of higher education. What is our role as teacher educators in preparing new teachers in our teacher preparation programs? How do we go about teaching these three shifts in our schools and institutions of higher education? Our challenge is how to best prepare effective global peace education teachers and teacher educators who will be culturally proficient. It is paramount, as it will require us to transform learning in order to become changemakers and leaders of change. We should not embark on this endeavor solely, because of international, national, or state licensure mandates, but because there is a lack of trained educators who have the ability to teach from a global perspective, with a focus on peace and shared education, in which activist pedagogy practices are evident and implemented in our schools.

3.1 *Defining Peace Education as Transformational Learning*

The International Day of Peace was celebrated globally on September 21, 2020. It is a day that is devoted to strengthening the ideals of peace, both within and among all nations and people. Peace Education is also supported by UNESCO's Sustainable Development Goal 4 (SDG4), which supports the notion of ensuring inclusive and equitable quality education for all, as well as promoting lifelong learning as a key factor. Objective SDG 4.7 further supports the:

> ... sustainable development and sustainable lifestyles, human rights, gender equality, promotion of a culture of peace and nonviolence, global citizenship and appreciation of cultural diversity and of culture's contribution to sustainable development. (Mwaniki, 2017, para. 5)

What will it take to attain the SDG 4 Goal and objectives? It will take a culturally proficient, activist, pedagogy education model that can be defined as an intentional educational practice, in which participants engage in guided and transformative learning activities that help them see themselves as capable of affecting change for social and ecological justice in our schools (Niblett, 2014). As Omoregie (2007) stated:

> Issues are becoming global rather than national and they demand global rather than national attention. The belief is that a globally competent teacher is that teacher that is adequate and fit to teach globally. He not only is an effective teacher in his nation but in other nations of the world. (p. 3)

Therefore, as we discuss the future of education, it is not about the best schools in the world, but rather about the best schools for the world in which educators engage hearts, heads and hands to drive positive change. They do so by providing a peaceful future as a foundation for peacemaking and skills for constructing it. Changemaker education gives young people the knowledge, skills, values, and sense of purpose to succeed on a lifelong journey of learning that will allow them to thrive in an interconnected world and drive positive change in their communities.

According to Harris (1996), peace education is an instructional effort that can create better citizens in this world and contribute to the overall knowledge of students in our elementary and secondary schools, and in our universities. As a transformational education and learning process that is integrated philosophically, it promotes and teaches nonviolence, as a means of supporting environmental issues, and for supporting the humanity of life. Magro (2015) further describes what transformational learning entails: "Transformative education within a context of social justice involves teaching for personal, social, and global change" (p. 109). It provides different approaches by teaching about the reasons for and the causes of violence. Students are taught the knowledge that is needed to be informed global citizens and about the critical issues connected to activist pedagogy, peace education, peacekeeping, peacemaking, and peacebuilding. Furthermore, "the experience of learning through 'peaceful pedagogy' can ideally be seen as learning through human rights. Enacting learning within the classroom, throughout the school or beyond the school can be seen as learning for human rights" (McLeod, 2014, p. 1).

Therefore, when defining peace education within this context, it is:

> ... a planned program with key concepts of positive peace among individuals, groups, nations, and the global environment, including the values of social justice, nonviolence, economic well-being, ecological balance, and participation in decision-making by using the process of conflict resolution." In UNICEF, peace education is very succinctly defined as "a planned program with key concepts of positive peace among individuals, groups, nations, and the global environment, including the values of social justice, nonviolence, economic well-being, ecological balance, and participation in decision-making by using the process of conflict resolution. (Castro-Nvarro & Galace-Nario, 2008, p. VIII)

Such education integrates UNESCO's themes of inclusive education, education for sustainable development, human rights education, and education in support of intercultural dialogue.

4   Cultural Proficiency as a Framework in Support of Peace Education and Intercultural Dialogue

When we think of Intercultural dialogue (ICD), we know that it "occurs when members of different cultural groups, who hold conflicting opinions and assumptions, speak to one another in acknowledgment of those differences" (Leeds-Hurwitz, 2014, p. 1). It builds upon and supports the concept of *dialogue,* in which at least two people are holding a conversation. It also builds upon the *intercultural*, which refers to "people communicating across differences in nationality, race and ethnicity, or religion" (Leeds-Hurwitz, 2014, p. 1). Dialogue takes on multiple meanings. It can take the form of dialogue in a script, in which people are talking. However, in most cases, it refers to "a quality of communication characterized by the participants' willingness and ability simultaneously to be radically open to the other(s) and to articulate their own views. Dialogue's primary goal is understanding rather than agreement" (Stewart, 2014, p. 1).

To reach this intercultural understanding through authentic dialogue, I introduce a theoretical framework – the cultural proficiency model. Cultural proficiency is a theoretical framework that can be used in different contexts. In this chapter, it is introduced as a model to develop culturally proficient global peace education, changemaker, and activist pedagogy teachers and teacher educators. It introduces the cultural proficiency continuum as a rubric that can identify unhealthy and healthy policies and practices as a way to move individuals, educators, schools, and organizations toward cultural proficiency. The goal is to prepare these individuals and bodies to emulate changemaker characteristics of empathy, leadership, collaboration, and team-building, so they may teach in culturally proficient globally minded universities, schools and classrooms, where peace education is integrated into the core curriculum.

Peace education in schools is discussed, and a description of the cultural proficiency model, as it relates to peace education, activist pedagogy, shared life, and shared education in educator preparation, is presented. Therefore, I pose questions that have emerged when making a commitment to cultural proficiency and peace education, from the need to address violence, equity, and social justice issues in our society. The following questions are discussed: What is and what does it mean to be culturally proficient? What is peace education? What is the role of preschool to grade 12 schools and institutions of higher education in support of peace education? And, finally, what is the role of teacher educators in infusing the concepts, principles, and practices of peace education, equity, social justice, activist pedagogy, shared life, and shared education in a culturally global and multicultural curriculum? I will examine some possible answers to these questions. Thus, it is important to define the concepts, so you will be able to follow the views and ideas I share.

4.1 *The Cultural Proficiency Model*

The cultural proficiency model, developed by Terry L. Cross (1989), and adapted in education by Lindsey and colleagues (1999, 2019), provides a theoretical framework and suggestions for teaching activist pedagogical practices that can assist individuals, schools, and organizations "interact effectively in a culturally diverse environment" (Lindsey et al., 1999, p. 21).

A focus of the cultural proficiency framework is the "inside-out" approach to assessing individuals and institution's knowledge and ability to work with differences of the "other." This focuses "on those of us who are insiders to the schools, encouraging us to reflect on our own individual understandings and values" (Lindsey et al., 1999, p. 25) and to think about the school's culture, in relation to difference. By taking a self-reflective approach, the cultural proficiency model relieves those "outsiders" from "the responsibility of doing all the adapting" (Lindsey et al., 1999, p. 25).

The inside-out approach asks educators to assess where they and their institutions are positioned, with respect to how they react and support peace education, as well as individual cultural differences. The cultural proficiency model provides a unique framework to guide that reflective assessment (Quezada & Osajima, 2004). The cultural proficiency continuum defines six "unique ways of seeing and responding to difference" (Lindsey et al., 1999, p. 31). These six unique points can assist in defining how individuals, groups, schools, and organizations can develop in order to become culturally proficient 21st century global teachers, and teacher educators for their roles as peace educators, who can teach from an activist pedagogy, shared life, and shared education perspective.

4.2 The Cultural Proficiency Continuum

The six points of the cultural proficiency continuum are introduced to assist in the conceptual development of cultural proficient peace education and activist pedagogy teachers. The cultural proficiency continuum begins with the lowest three negative points: *cultural destructiveness, incapacity*, and *blindness*. These three points are on the left side of the continuum and represent *negative peace* that includes *unhealthy policies and practices* and promotes a culture of reaction. It has a focus on the "what," or the product, and not on the individual. In comparison, on the right side of the cultural proficiency continuum, are the positive indicators of *cultural pre-competence, competence*, and *cultural proficiency*. Here there is "positive peace" that includes "healthy policies and practices" and promotes a "culture of prevention," while focusing on the "who," the person.

There are also five essential elements/principles supporting cultural proficiency that are the behavioral standards for measuring and planning for growth toward cultural proficiency. They are (a) assessing cultural knowledge, (b) valuing diversity, (c) managing the dynamics of difference, (d) adapting to diversity, and (e) institutionalizing cultural knowledge. There are also barriers to reaching cultural proficiency, set by individuals, or society, as a whole. These include the presumption of entitlement, systems of oppression and suppression, the unawareness of the need to adapt, and resistance to change.

The six points on the cultural proficiency continuum help define how individuals, groups, schools, and organizations can develop toward achievement of the goals of the model. This will help them in their roles, as culturally proficient 21st century global peace and activist pedagogy teachers and teacher educators. Concepts of peace and examples are integrated in the description of each point on the continuum, to support peace education efforts within our society, as well as in education and schooling. The points further support

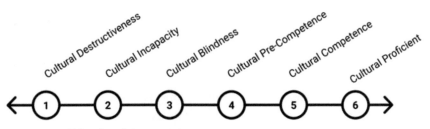

FIGURE 14.1   Cultural proficiency continuum

concepts of activist pedagogy that have been elaborated in other chapters of this book by other authors. So let us begin by introducing the *Cultural Proficiency Continuum* (see Figure 14.1).

4.2.1   The Six Points

The cultural proficiency continuum's lowest point begins with *cultural destructiveness* – see the difference and stomp it out – eliminating other people's culture (language, religion, one's being). Here it refers to attitudes, policies and practices destructive to individual or group's cultures and individuals within a culture. It is also evident in schools, where particular ethnic groups have been omitted completely from the curriculum or have been denigrated by the dominant culture in how they are portrayed.

Culturally destructive acts include the use of military/terrorist tactics to kill and maim, without exploring peace discussions or options. Genocide, death squads, and torture are used as forms of doing away with a person's/group's culture. The victims include innocent children, entire families, and citizens who, through no fault of their own, are caught in the middle of conflicts. Policies are enacted with increasing frequency and increased levels of harm. Destructiveness reverberates nationally, and at the local level. Negotiations for the attainment of peace are not an option. Other examples include:

– The storming of the United States Capitol, with the intent to kill or hurt Congressional Representatives and Senate members who opposed the electoral college certification of President Elect Joe B. Biden and Vice President Elect Kamala Harris by former President Donald Trump supporters, after verbal incitement by the former president.
– The Holocaust (Shoah): the World War II genocide of European Jews, in which Nazi Germany and its collaborators systematically murdered over 6 million Jews, or the genocide of indigenous communities in the Americas and in other parts of the world.
– The Middle East conflict in Syria; the September 11th attack in New York of the Twin Towers, in which over 3,000 died in one day; the New Zealand terror attack at Al Noor ("The Light"); the Linwood Mosques in the Christchurch

massacre, where Mr. Tarrant killed 50 innocent persons; and the Holland shooting. Most recently, there have also been instances of police brutality and the killings of George Floyd, Breonna Taylor, and other Blacks in the United States.
- In education or schooling, education is unsupported, causing illiteracy among entire populations, for generations to come.
- The repression and elimination of cultural and language programs in schools, and English-only policies, have left many communities with language and cultural losses.
- The degradation of particular ethnic communities, due to their cultural, language or religious beliefs, relating to them as if they do not exist, and/or rendering them as unworthy.
- Most recently in the United States, the elimination of federal funding from agencies that support issues of social justice and cultural diversity, under the guise that it teaches students and individuals to hate others and to hate the United States.

Next is *cultural incapacity,* which is dismissive and blames individuals as the culprits. This point describes "an organization, school systems, or individuals that demonstrate extreme bias and prejudice in many forms. They believe and perpetuate the superiority of the dominant cultural group, usually themselves and assume a paternal posture to so-called lesser groups" (Lindsey et al., 1999, p. 34).

Unhealthy practices reflect conditions and behaviors in which nations, states, organizations, school systems or individuals hold rigid stereotypes and fears, and severely limit opportunities for change to happen systemically. There are excessive economic, social and cultural inequalities among people that arouse tensions and conflicts, and endanger peace. During war and during conflict, peace negotiations are a part of the process; however, the killing continues and supports the "reminder concept," in which atrocities continue to make a point. The use of print and social media is allowed, but often these media are used more as tools for scare tactics than to let people learn about the inhumanity of the atrocities being waged against minority groups.

Negativism and intolerance are expressed against the other's culture, language, and religious beliefs, and are used in schools, as part of the education curriculum. There is disavowal of the positive influence of students' and families' cultural and language assets; as a result, minimal and remedial educational services are used to repress these groups further. Teachers are blamed for their lack of knowledge, while being poorly paid. They receive minimal training in peace education and other pedagogies, which are neither provided, nor perceived as a priority. Therefore, teachers lack the knowledge and tools to engage in capacity building and to be effective peace educators.

The next point on the continuum is *cultural blindness*: "See the difference; act like you don't." According to Lindsey and colleagues (1999, p. 35), this is: "Acting as if cultural differences do not matter or as if there are no differences amongst and between cultures. It is the belief that color and culture make no difference and that all people are the same." This is also the most vexing point on the continuum. Even well-intentioned culturally-blind educators have difficulty recognizing the persistence of the challenges linked to cultural and racial differences and injustices.

In his book, *Racism without Racists*, Eduardo Bonilla-Silva (2003) pointed out that color-blindness is an ideological position dominant among Whites. This leads them to deflect, often in a defensive manner, attention away from structural racism. Often, individuals, school staffs, and university personnel find themselves at this point on the continuum.

Unhealthy practices include practices that support peace education and teach that war and conflict are wrong. They also provide excuses that help substantiate reasons why war and conflict are occurring. Print and social media are still used to educate and misinform the general population or students, as to the reasons why war and conflict are being conducted. The UNICEF Learning for Peace Programme Report 2012–2016 reports that poverty, inequality, and development are key causes of conflict and violence. Much of the curriculum is insensitive to the context, in which conflict and disaster exist. Leaders and educational systems do not pay attention to the disparities, to inequality, to social in/justice and educational access. Therefore, this exacerbates conflict and policies that lead to less peace, violence, and social educational exclusion, at all levels.

As one moves to the right of the cultural proficiency continuum, one is able to see the difference both in language and in actions. Healthy policies and practices are evident in the action taken. The fourth point on the continuum begins with *cultural precompetence*. "See the difference; but one responds inappropriately. We begin to know what we don't know, it is becoming aware of culture. It is an awareness of the limitations in cross-cultural communication and outreach" (Lindsey et al., 1999, p. 36).

Healthy practices occur when individuals support the fair treatment of others, but are unaware of the options available in the support systems they may provide. At this point of the cultural proficiency continuum, leaders of nations, states, and organizations are open to negotiations, but remain skeptical concerning possible outcomes. Individuals agree that something needs to be done to move forward. In schools, curriculum on peace education, activist pedagogy, and shared education are evident and integrated into various content subjects.

Colleges of education, schools, and political leaders demonstrate openness to working with religious communities and sharing what they have to offer the work of peace and democracy.

The next point on the continuum is *cultural competence* – "See the difference; understand the difference that difference makes." School personnel and others "accept and respect differences, carefully attend to the dynamics of difference, continually assess their own cultural knowledge and beliefs, continuously expand their cultural knowledge and resources, and make various adaptations of their own belief systems, policies and practices" (Lindsey et al., 1999, p. 37).

Healthy practices, within the cultural dimension, "refer[s] to deeper patterns (often less conscious) related to how people within a group, a community or a nation make sense of things, understanding conflict and its appropriate response" (Catholic Relief Services, 2013, p. 12). In schools, peace education is evident in approved courses and core curricula, and specific courses in peace education, including conflict resolution, ethical decision making, and problem solving. At the elementary, middle, high school, and university levels, partnerships are formed, and the community is invited to participate in school efforts to teach aspects of peace and shared education. Teaching for peace is seen as an enriching resource and thinking about peace and how we work toward it – by identifying the root causes of conflict. Teaching is also seen as a vehicle for/as a dialogue partner for anyone dedicated to peacebuilding and democracy.

The highest point on the continuum is being *culturally proficient* – "See the difference – respond positively. Engage and adapt." Here, one looks at multiple ways of responding to difference and the "other," and includes educators and others who engage in anti-racist behaviors and inequities, by supporting culturally proficient policies and practices in all of the facets in learning environments.

Healthy practices refer to the ability of educators and leaders to navigate and demonstrate effectiveness in different cultural and educational contexts. Furthermore, when presented with new cultural groups and situations, they know how to gather research, data and resources to support their learning about the newly presented cultures (Lindsey et al., 1999, p. 37). These practices include trust-telling discussions, restorative justice, discussing the role of forgiveness, conflict resolution and reconciliation. Culturally proficient educators make cultural knowledge the norm and actively institutionalize attendant policies and practices, as part of the school program. They possess cross-cultural communication skills needed to articulate their vision to all students, parents, community members and other school personnel. They take proactive steps to involve a wide variety of people in educational decisions (Quezada & Osajima, 2005).

In schools, peace education concepts, activist pedagogy, shared education, and its principles are not just part of the regular curriculum, but are embedded, and practiced through social interaction. The curricula are not only content based, but designed to be culturally and economic relevant to the local context in schools and the community. They meet the needs of all students, English language learners, homeless people, at-risk youth, and marginalized communities. Community service-learning projects are part of the fabric of the school and support the concepts and principles of peace education. Education is active and interactive, and dialogical, and creates peace educational models that are based on problem solving and inquiry

Healthy practices are learner centered. They also move new paradigms and ideas and shared understandings into the hands of school communities. Students address global matters that include making personal commitments and social world peace projects. Peace and shared education prevention programs can be captured in the curriculum and include violence prevention, alcohol and drug prevention, conflict resolution, mediation, conflict management, cultural awareness, inclusive education, and social-emotional programs. Programs, such as Peacebuilders and Tribes, are programs that can support classroom teachers in promoting peace education efforts in their classrooms. Teaching peace offers a foundation for peacebuilding within colleges of education. Interior peace flows from the gift of one's faith or one's beliefs and positive upbringing. Peace education is fully supported and programs to support it are made a priority, so they may be part of the regular curriculum.

Educating for a culture of peace, in the context of a school, dovetails with educating for coexistence. Both deal with working on the dynamics and conditions of the relations between people, so they become harmonious, respectful and enriching, while ensuring equitable, democratic and transparent social organization. Teaching global and peaceful citizenship in schools is achieved through education in peaceful coexistence (Sampere, 2013, p. 13). Therefore, the cultural proficiency model further supports Novelli and Sayed's (2016) 4Rs framework that captures the economic, cultural, political, and social dimensions of inequality in education. The way these concepts relate to conflict and peace is by integrating the dimensions of recognition, redistribution, representation and reconciliation into teaching. These will move individuals, educators, schools, organizations and institutions of higher education from having cultural destructive policies and practices to making them culturally proficient.

5   Conclusions

In this chapter, I introduced the cultural proficiency model as a tool for educators to self-reflect or to identify where individuals, educators, schools, or organizations fall on the cultural proficiency continuum, as it relates to peace education, shared life, and activist pedagogy. The six points on the continuum move from the lowest point (i.e., culturally destructive, which perpetuates unhealthy policies and practices) to the development of healthy policies and practices, in order to achieve the highest point – being culturally proficient. The model was supported by peace education literature and offers a vision of a peaceful future. It further serves as a foundation for peacemaking and the skills needed for constructing it.

In many instances, federal and state governments in countries around the world have provided limited support for peace-focused education. Due to a lack of curricula for such instruction, teachers have the upmost responsibility for developing and creating the lessons and curricula that support their lessons about peace, and how to achieve it. Therefore, they need preparation in order to be able to design and provide peace education.

The challenge entails that teacher educators, and primary and secondary school teachers need to train and prepare our youth academically, emotionally, and socially to live and thrive in a global society. How do we know this? For the most part, students in elementary, middle, secondary schools, and teacher preparation programs in higher education in the US continue to lack cross-cultural and intercultural experiences with people, who are different from them. Therefore, many teacher candidates do not develop respect for differences or the comparative educational and social skills needed to contribute effectively to a sustainable local, state, national, and global society. This phenomenon is not unique to schools in the United States. In actuality, this statement applies to other, less diverse countries in the world, where teachers teach what they have learned in their educator preparation programs, and in their teacher staff development workshops. If diversity is important, but the materials and training are not provided, teachers will avoid making it a part of their daily instruction. Therefore, there is a need to focus our attention on preparing 21st century, culturally proficient global teachers and teacher educators for their roles as peace and changemaker educators, and activist pedagogics, who wish to make a change in this world.

6   Questions for Reflection

– Where on the cultural proficiency continuum would you locate yourself? Your peers? The school/teacher preparation program in which you work?
– What attitudes, circumstances/conditions help/hinder your movement (the movement of your peers/your school/teacher preparation program) toward cultural proficiency?

- In thinking about peace education, activist pedagogy, and shared education and the culturally/linguistic/religious diverse student population in your class/school/teacher preparation program, what curricular and teaching approaches would be most suitable to meet their needs? What support do you need to bring those approaches into your work?
- In what ways can you support and address the need for promoting peace education, activist pedagogy, and shared education? What additional information, resources, and support can help you meet those needs?
- In assessing your own college of education or teacher preparation program, and those of your peers in peace education, activist pedagogy, and shared education, what works well and what areas need improvement?

References

Catholic Relief Services. (2013). *Strategic community: Peacebuilding in practice* [Laletek project manual]. Catholic Relief Services – Timor Leste. https://www.crs.org/sites/default/files/tools-research/strategic-communitypeacebuilding-in-practice.pdf

Castro, N. L., & Galace, N. J. (2008). *Peace education: A pathway to a culture of peace.* Center for Peace Education.

Harris, I. (1996). *Peace education in a postmodern world.* Lawrence Erlbaum.

Leeds-Hurwitz, W. (2014). Intercultural dialogue. Key concepts in intercultural dialogue. *Creative Commons, 14*(1).

Lindsey, R. B., Robins, K. N., & Terrell, R. D. (2019). *Cultural proficiency – A manual for school leaders* (4th ed.). Corwin Press.

Magro, K. (2015). Teaching for social justice and peace education: Promising pathways for transformative learning. *Peace Research: The Canadian Journal of Peace and Conflict Studies, 47*(1/2), 109–141. https://www.peaceresearch.ca/pdf/47/PRJ_47_1-2_Karen_Magro_Full.pdf

McLeod, J. (2014). A peaceful pedagogy: Teaching human rights across the curriculum. *Procedia-Social and Behavioral Sciences, 152,* 1225–1232.

Mwaniki, C. G. (2017). *The role of education in promoting peace.* Global Partnership for Education. https://www.globalpartnership.org/blog/role-education-promoting-peace

Niblett, B. (2014). *Narrating activist education: Teachers' stories of affecting social and political change* [Doctoral dissertation]. Lakehead University. http://knowledgecommons.lakeheadu.ca/handle/2453/604

Niblett, B. (2017, April). Facilitating activist education. *What Works? Research into Practice, Monograph #66.* Ontario Association of Deans of Education and the Student Achievement Division. https://thelearningexchange.ca/wp-content/uploads/2017/06/facilitating-activist-education-ww-66.pdf

Novelli, M., & Sayed, Y. (2016). Teachers as agents of sustainable peace, social cohesion and development: Theory practice and evidence. *Education as Change, 20*(3), 15–37. https://doi.org/10.17159/1947-9417/2016/1486

Omoregie, N. (2007). The globally competent teacher in secondary level of education. *Education, 128*(1), 3–9.

Quezada, L. R., & Romo, J. (2004). Multiculturalism, peace education. *Multicultural Education, 11*(3), 2–11. http://eprints.covenantuniversity.edu.ng/9057/1/The%20Conceptual%20Definitions%20of%20Peace%20and%20Conflict1.pdf

Sampere, C. M. (2013). *Peace and co-existence educating in school settings: A teacher training perspective.* Evens Foundation.

Stewart, J. (2013). *U & ME: Communicating in moments that matter.* Taos Institute Publications.

United Nations Children's Fund. (2016, June). *Peacebuilding education and advocacy in conflict-affected contexts programme.* UNICEF Learning for Peace programme report 2012–2016. UNICEF. https://files.eric.ed.gov/fulltext/ED573879.pdf

Peace Education Resources

20 World Organizations that strive to establish world peace: https://listsurge.com/20-world-organizations-strive-establish-world-peace/

Teaching Peace Creating Solutions: https://peaceeducation.org/

The Conflict Education Resolution Connection: https://creducation.net/peace_education_resources/

Montessori Children's House: https://www.mchkids.com/peace-education-resources.html

PART 4

Reconciling Dialogue in the Face of Conflicting Narratives

CHAPTER 15

The Holocaust and Its Teaching in Israel in View of the Conflict

General and Pedagogical Implications and Lessons

Daniel Bar-Tal and Galiya Bar-Tal

About 50 years ago, Amos Elon diagnosed the effect of the Holocaust on Israeli society in the following way:

> The Holocaust remains a basic trauma of Israeli society. It is impossible to exaggerate its effect on the process of nation-building ... There is a latent hysteria in Israeli life that stems directly from this source ... The trauma of the Holocaust leaves an indelible mark on the national psychology, the tenor and content of public life, the conduct of foreign affairs, on politics, education, literature and the arts. (Elon, 1971, pp. 198–199)

This description holds today as well and indeed the effect of the Holocaust cannot be exaggerated, because it continues to be the chosen trauma,[1] which provides the foundations of the Jewish collective memory, the basis for the national ethos and even contributes to the demarcation of the collective identity (Liebman & Don-Yihya, 1983; Ofer, 2009; Segev, 2000; Zertal, 2005).

1   Holocaust in Israel

The position of the Holocaust in the collective psyche of Jewish-Israeli society serves an important function, with the society making an effort to maintain this space for continuous commemoration. Therefore, it is imperative, in the view of the establishment, that every Israeli, including the Arab population, learns about the Holocaust from a very early age. The Holocaust has become one of the central learning themes in the educational system, the Memorial Day has become a day of national mourning, the Holocaust has become a frequent part of the regular public discourse, and Yad Vashem[2] has become one of the principal societal, political educational and cultural institutions in the Israeli state (Bauer, 2002). In sum, the society has developed various mechanisms to impart its meaning and lessons to members of society.

In analyzing the position of the Holocaust in the State of Israel, we need to remember that the Jews in Israel are involved in an intractable conflict[3] that has lasted for over 100 years, and the Holocaust plays an important role in this conflict. It has direct and indirect effects on the nature of the conflict, its processes and continuation. We will explain this observation in a few words.

1.1 The Israeli-Arab Conflict as a Factor in Remembering Holocaust

The Jews came to Israel under the auspices of the Zionist Movement – a national movement with the central premise that the Jewish nation could only continue to exist if masses of Jews returned to their ancient homeland, establishing a national state. Although the waves of immigration, fulfilling the aspirations of the Zionism, began to arrive to Palestine at the end of the 19th century, the major stream of immigrants arrived after the end of the World War II. This was when the Holocaust survivors began to flow to Mandatory Palestine and later to the state of Israel, seeing it as the sanctuary for the Jews. However, the Arab population had already settled the ancient homeland of the Jews. This population was also developing national aspirations at more or less the same time, and they too wanted to realize those aspirations in the same territory.

The dominant feeling, on each side, was one of "sole legitimacy" – an attitude that views legitimacy as a resource that cannot be shared or divided. It was everything or nothing. The Arabs related to themselves as having the right of "precedence" over the land and, thus, viewed the Jews who had arrived as immigrants, or even more severely, as invaders and colonialists. The Jews, in contrast, related to the land as a legacy promised to them by God in the Torah, as their historical-cultural homeland. Therefore, it was perceived as a natural place of refuge, considering the dangers that the Jewish nation had faced in Europe, and were still facing.

All attempts to settle the dispute by peaceful means – and there were such attempts – failed. The minimum demands on the Palestinian side were greater than the maximum concessions that the Israeli side was willing to make (Morris, 2001; Podeh, 2015). The combination of goals considered existential, asymmetric power relations and the absence of possibilities for achieving peace, led the sides to entrench themselves in their positions and even to justify the use of violence and to "die for the homeland," if necessary. Nevertheless, because the Israeli state is surrounded by Arab states, occupies the Palestinian nation in the West Bank that was conquered in the 1967 war, and has experienced a number of wars and countless violent attacks, Jewish society in Israel can be characterized as living under constant threat. This results in chronic fear, stress, insecurity and anxiety. Moreover, there are those who maintain that Jews live in the mentality of being in siege, under constant chronic trauma (Bar-Tal & Antebi, 1992).

Of special importance in this short summary is the fact that the continuous, bloody and lasting conflict created the perception among Israeli Jewish society members that they were the sole victims in this conflict. The self-perception of Jews as victims, surrounded by a hostile environment, was based on the total opposition of the Arabs to establishment of a Jewish state during the British Mandate period, and then greatly strengthened immediately following the establishment of the state, when the armies of the Arab countries invaded Israel in an attempt to occupy it.

In 1979, Israel established peaceful relations with Egypt; in 1993, the Government of Israel and the Palestine Liberation Organization (PLO) signed an agreement of mutual recognition, and in 1994 Israel and Jordan signed a peace agreement. Nevertheless, the agreement with the Palestinians, in spite of the good beginning, did not continue toward a peaceful settlement of the conflict. In 2000, the conflict escalated, and continues to escalate until today. Both sides have used violence and, from the Israeli perspective, it only validated time after time the sense of the Jewish collective self-victimhood and Palestinian mal-intentions and intransigence (Bar-Tal & Raviv, 2021).

At this point, we need to note that these attitudes did not appear in one day; they are based on Jewish self-perception, throughout the generations, as a nation persecuted by a hostile world filled with traditional antisemitism that peaked with the Holocaust. The mass killings in cities and towns, the railroad trains carrying people to their deaths, and the millions murdered in the gas chambers have all become canonic impressions that perpetually accompany many Jews and act as a lighthouse guiding their way (Dawidowicz, 1975; Grosser & Halperin, 1979). This paramount event constitutes a trauma, which cannot be expunged and dwarfs everything else that the Jews underwent for hundreds of years, and anything experienced by other nations. The trauma of the Holocaust is recreated and reconstructed on Holocaust Remembrance and Heroism Day, and also throughout the year. It is proliferated via a wide range of channels. Jewish people in Israel (and also in other part of the world) have constructed the status of being eternal victims (Peleg, 2019).

1.2 *The Functionality of Being a Victim*
The status of being an eternal victim has many advantages for Israeli society that is involved in an intractable conflict (Bar-Tal et al., 2009).

1.2.1 Illuminating the Conflict Situation
First, the sense of self/collective victimhood serves as the epistemic function of illuminating situations and especially the context of intractable conflict. The intractable conflict is extremely threatening and accompanied by vulnerability, uncertainty and fear, and shatters previously held worldviews. The

sense of being a victim helps in coping with stress created by the conditions of intractable conflict, by making sense of and finding meaning in the stressful conditions (Antonovsky, 1987; Frankl, 1963).

1.2.2 Moral Justification

In its moral function, the sense of being a victim delegates responsibility for both the outbreak of the conflict and the subsequent violence to the opponent – the Arabs, and especially the Palestinians. In addition, it provides the moral weight to seek justice and oppose them, and thus serves to justify and legitimize the harmful acts of the Israelis towards them, including violence and destruction (Jost & Major, 2001).

1.2.3 Differentiation and Superiority

The sense of being a victim creates a sense of differentiation and superiority. It sharpens intergroup differences, because while it describes the Arabs, in general, and the Palestinians, in particular, in delegitimizing[4] terms, at the same time it perceives the groups as responsible for the unjust and immoral acts. This sense presents the Israeli Jews in glorifying images and as the sole victim of the conflict (Bar-Tal & Teichman, 2005).

1.2.4 Preparation and Immunization

The sense of being a victim also prepares Israeli society for threatening and violent acts of the enemy, as well as for difficult living conditions. It attunes the society to information that signals potential harm and continuing violent confrontations, allowing psychological preparations for the lasting conflict and immunization against negative experiences. Jewish-Israeli society is attentive and sensitive to cues about threats, so no sudden surprises can arise (e.g., Antonovsky, 1987; Lazarus & Folkman, 1984).

1.2.5 Solidarity

The sense of being a victim serves as a basis for unity and solidarity, because it implies a threat to the collective's well-being and even to its survival (Rosenberg, 2003). Those are important conditions for survival in view of the continuous harm caused by the rival. Collective victimhood may serve as "social glue," bonding members of the collective together on the basis of the present threat and past "chosen traumas" (Volkan, 2001).

1.2.6 Patriotism and Mobilization

The sense of being a victim has the function of motivating patriotism, mobilization and readiness for action (Bar-Tal & Staub, 1997). It highlights security needs as a core value and indicates a situation of emergency, which requires mobilization and sacrifice that are crucial for countering the threat. It implies the necessity to exert all the group's efforts and resources in the struggle against the perpetrator. In addition, it reminds group members of past violent acts by the rival and indicates that they could recur. This function is, therefore, essential to meet the challenge of withstanding the enemy in the conflict.

1.2.7 Gaining International Support

Victimhood in a conflict enables avoidance of criticism and expression of support from the international community. Victims are not blamed for the outbreak of the conflict and the violence that follows when they suffer from the unjustified violence of the aggressor. This is crucial in obtaining the backing of worldwide public opinion and increasing the likelihood of moral, political and material support.

Finally, three significant consequences of being a victim augment the functionality of this status. The first is called *moral disengagement* that enables the victim to reduce moral accountability and responsibility by inhibiting feelings of guilt, empathy and compassion toward the adversary, when carrying out violent behavior (Bandura, 1999). The second is called *moral entitlement*, which is defined as a conviction that society is allowed to use whatever means it decides it needs to ensure its safety, with little regard for moral norms (Schori, Klar, Roccas & McNeill, 2017). Finally, there is *moral silencing*, which denotes a belief that being a victim should prevent other nations from criticizing, condemning or denouncing the society.

In sum, all these delineated benefits of being a victim perpetuate the sense of self-collective victimhood of Jewish society in Israel. The experience of the Holocaust, with the six million murdered Jews, as well as the ongoing experience of the bloody conflict with the Palestinians, have frozen the sense of victimhood among the Jews in Israel and turned the sense of self-collective victimhood into a hegemonic societal belief.

1.3 *The View of the Holocaust in Israel*

In view of the centrality of the Holocaust experience in the Israeli consciousness, the national ethos and the public discourse have been shaped, according to five principles.

1.3.1 Expansionism

The concept of the Holocaust has been expanded to represent different circumstances and conditions. The Holocaust became a code for a very threatening situation that is used by leaders, the media, and even ordinary people. It has become part of public discourse, because the term does not need an explanation providing an unequivocal meaning that is understood by every Israeli. For example, in 2019, the Israeli Minister of Education, Rafi Peretz, compared Jewish intermarriage in the United States to a "second Holocaust."[5]

1.3.2 Timeless and Spaceless

The Holocaust has been presented as being possible in any time and in any place. According to this view, history is a chain of events that happens in different contexts and in different periods, but all have the same denominator: the wish to exterminate the Jewish people. The persecution of Jews, annihilation and destruction are part of one continuation. Different periods are defined in terms of the maltreatment of Jews, pogroms, devastation and anti-Semitism. As an example of this conception, we cite the words of the late Yitzhak Rabin, who was the Minister of Defense at the Holocaust Memorial Ceremony in 1987: "In every generation they rise up to destroy us, and we must remember that this could happen to us in the future. We must therefore, as a state, be prepared" (Ha'aretz, 1987, April 27).

1.3.3 Unification of the Enemy

Although the enemies of Jewish people who aspired to annihilate the nation were different – Egyptians, Assyrians, Persians, Greek, Romans, Germans, or Arabs – they all had the same goal. Nations of the world throughout history do not differ. All of them hate Jews and, therefore, the Jewish tradition speaks about people that shall dwell *alone* (Numbers 23, 9) and states that "The whole world is against us." As Charles Liebman noted "Jewish tradition finds anti-Semitism to be the norm, the natural response of the non-Jew ... The term 'Esau hates Jacob' symbolizes the world which Jews experience. It is deeply embedded in the Jewish folk tradition" (1978, p. 45). The unification of the enemy has a kind of magical representation of the nemesis that fuels the fear and insecurity.

1.3.4 The Holocaust as a Unique Event

The Holocaust is viewed as a unique event, incomparable to other acts of genocide. It cannot be taught with other evil events, but has to stand by itself. This view is applied in Israel to learning about the Holocaust in schools and in its commemoration (Keren, 1998).

1.3.5 Connecting the Holocaust and the Israeli-Palestinian Conflict

During the years of the long conflict with Arab and the Palestinian leaders, the mass media has made connections between Nazis and Arabs (Bar-Tal & Teichman, 2005). This connection has been made to emphasize the delegitimization of Arabs, portrayed as murderers, cruel, violent or blood thirsty, and their intentions to annihilate Jews in Israel. This connection enabled presenting the conflict as having a very real and threatening characteristic, and as having existential consequences. In 1982, before the First Lebanon War, Former Prime Minister Menachem Begin spoke against the Palestinian Liberation Organization to justify the upcoming invasion of Lebanon "Believe me, the alternative to this is Treblinka, and we have decided that there will not be another Treblinka."[6]

In sum, the present paper not only intends to show the unique place that the Holocaust, as the chosen trauma, has in the ethos of the Israeli Jewish society, but also how it is misused by the state institutions for constructing a particular consciousness that serves the political goals of the Israeli leadership through the years (Bar-Tal, 2019, 2020).

After this introduction that provides the basis for the understanding of the place of the Holocaust in Israeli society and its relationship to the present context of the intractable conflict, we can now turn to the discussion of the educational implications of the Holocaust.

2   The Holocaust and Its Educational Implications

To impart and treat the Holocaust as the chosen trauma, the Holocaust has to be continuously remembered and noted, commemorated institutionally, imparted to the new generations, and used frequently in public discourse. Indeed, the State of Israel devotes time, resources, pedagogy, contents and means to impart the history, the meaning, and the lessons of the Holocaust to the entire new generation, who will continue the transmission with its specific understanding to their children. This is the challenge that the state has undertaken (Romi & Lev, 2007). Since, in the first part of the chapter, we described the contents that are transmitted in Israel, in this section, we will focus on two major elements: the lessons and the pedagogy of the transmission, with a special focus on Israeli teenagers' journeys to Poland.

2.1   *Lessons*
The major lesson of the Holocaust that is imparted to the Jewish population, including the young generation, states "Never again" (Klar, Schori-Eyal & Klar, 2013). This lesson means that another Holocaust must be prevented –will be prevented – and will never occur for the Jewish people. This part is well-accepted by the entire nation. Then, a second part details how it can be prevented. In general, there are two different, not mutually exclusive approaches to the prevention: particularistic and universalistic approaches.

The particularistic view that is dominant in Israel focuses on the particular situation that allowed the Holocaust of Jews and elaborates the conditions that can prevent this happening again to Jews. In this view, the Holocaust took place because Jews had neither a state of their own nor a powerful army that could defend them. Therefore, Jews need their own state, with a very potent army that is highly skilled and possesses the most advanced technological capacities. The universalistic view focuses on the conditions that enabled and facilitated the genocide. It assumes that Nazi Germany built a political dictatorship based on a racist, nationalistic, and anti-democratic ideology. The ideology that was imparted to millions of Germans, in a very specific context, allowed the Nazi party to ascend to power in democratic elections (but, with violent means) and then transform Germany into an evil dictatorship with systematic indoctrination with all the means and in all the institutions. Thus, prevention of another Holocaust requires imparting to the people democratic values, principles of human rights and universal moral norms that need to be internalized and carried by the generations.

There is no doubt that both parts of the lesson can be combined. However, they lead to different curricula and emphases, contents of collective memory, ways of transmission to the people, institutions of memory, public discourse, cultural products, ways of commemoration, ways of passing on instructions to the new generation, integration into the culture, and guidance for future norms and practices.

As we noted, Israel chose the particularistic lesson and almost completely disregarded the universalistic lesson. Thus, in line with this choice, it developed educational contents, materials, pedagogy, practices, experiences and means to transmit the lesson of the Holocaust to the next generation. This choice is not accidental, in view of the way Israeli leaders perceive the position of Israel and constructed the hegemonic narrative that has been imparted to the Jewish population. The conflict-supporting narrative that provides the contents of the national collective memory[7] and the ethos of conflict[8] were hegemonic during the first 30 years of the state's existence (Bar-Tal & Raviv, 2021). Then, with the peace with Egypt and the beginning of the period of the peace process, it competed with the narratives that promoted peacemaking. However, since 2000, these narratives again began to be dominant and, at present, are hegemonic.

2.2 *The Goals of Holocaust Education*

In 2014, under the guidance of the moderate Minister of Education, Shai Piron, the ministry published a new curriculum for the study of the Holocaust, called "In the Path of Memory." The new curriculum was planned to be taught to all students, from kindergarten to high schools (Kaminka, 2016). Its rationale explained that: "The Holocaust of the Jewish people is one of the low points in the history of mankind and deserves to be taught and passed down from generation to generation," and "as the Haggada to your son, wherever one strives to educate a society of values whose acceptance, compassion, concern for others, human dignity and value are a candle." The 11 stated objectives even included five universalistic goals as "commitments to struggle against racism" or "strengthening democracy values and tolerance and cultivation of the aspiration to build paragon society."

However, the reality moved the educational system in a very different path. The Ministers of Education, who came after Shai Piron, had a very different political orientation. They were nationalists, and even racists, who abandoned altogether the universalistic goals and focused only on the particularistic ones. These pertained to the knowledge of the Holocaust in its wide spectrum, knowledge about Jewish life before the Holocaust and the commitment to the continuation of the Jewish people. However, inculcation of the conflict-supporting narratives became a central focus, with their major themes: the collective memory and the ethos of conflict. These hegemonic narratives also largely dictate the educational objectives.

In this vein, the study of the Holocaust is awarded a key place, because its themes, as selected to be presented in the framework of learning about the Shoah (the Holocaust), correspond greatly to the conflict supporting narratives. The most important theme relates to the "The Jewish victim as a human story: Their lives before and during the Holocaust and how they were able to rebuild their lives afterwards." The latter part of the sentence connects the Holocaust to the establishment of the Israeli state. In accordance with the conflict-supporting narratives, this appears to be the rationale for having a state, for identifying the enemies that threaten the existence of the state, the readiness for mobilization to defend the Jewish state, including the need to sacrifice life for the state, and the moral superiority of the Jewish nation. The major message is that the Jewish nation succeeded in surviving and moved from the Holocaust to rebirth by establishing and building the Jewish state with a powerful military force that prevents another national disaster. Thus, the young generation, from the early age, is required to take part in this holy mission of preventing another Holocaust.

2.3 *Modes of Learning about the Holocaust*
In this part of the chapter, we will present the primary educational modes used by the educational system to impart the major themes related to the Holocaust, either directly or indirectly.

2.3.1 Narratives

The primary mode contains the narratives that are told through various means about the Holocaust, the Jewish victims, Jewish life before and during the Holocaust, the systematic extermination of the Jews, Jewish resistance, the assistance of the gentiles, and then the narratives of survival, and the establishment of the strong Jewish state. The narratives of the collective memory become integrally interwoven with the narratives of the national ethos of the Israeli state. They emphasize Jewish victimhood throughout the history, on the one hand, and the bravery of those who fought for freedom, on the other hand. In these narratives, a special place is kept for the rebels and fighters in the ghettos and the forests. The rebels of the Warsaw ghetto serve as a foremost example of Jewish courage and sacrifice. The narratives are told to very young children, via lectures, stories, textbooks, books, films and so on. They appear in different subject matter, such as Hebrew, Literature, History, Social Sciences and Civics.

2.3.2 Ceremonies

Another mode of transmitting themes related to the Holocaust is through ceremonies. Ceremonies, based on the collective memories of the Jewish people, have been documented as influential events, which transmit content for the formation of national identity, as well as effective tools that the nation uses to convey its official doctrines to its members (Ben-Amos & Bet-El, 1999; Handelman & Katz, 1990). In Israel, approximately 10 yearly ceremonies take place in the educational system. One of them is the Memorial Day of the Holocaust (usually in April) that focuses on the national victimhood and the threats to security of the Jewish nation. However, other ceremonies also relate to the theme of victimhood, patriotism, threats of enemies and the justness of establishing the Jewish state. The ceremonies have an accumulative effect, remaining relatively stable in their patterns and contents (Maymon, Ben-Amos & Bar-Tal, 2016).

2.3.3 Testimonies and Museums

Two additional educational means used in teaching about the Holocaust are testimonies of the survivors and visits to memorials and museums dedicated to the preservation of the Holocaust's memory. The former brings survivors of the Holocaust to the classrooms to tell their personal stories of the struggle to survive and the rebuilding of their families. The latter consists of visits to different Holocaust memorial sites and museums, in Israel, to commemorate the Holocaust. The most well-known site is Yad Vashem in Jerusalem, but there are others, as well: The Ghetto Fighters' House – Itzhak Katzenelson Holocaust and Jewish Resistance Heritage Museum in Kibbutz Lohamei Hageta'ot and the Massuah Institute for the Study of the Holocaust in Tel Yitzhak. They have exhibition and educational centers that give lectures, seminars etc. Yad Vashem, as the state institution, presents the hegemonic narratives of the state regarding the Holocaust, its consequences, and the lesson of the Holocaust, including its implications.

2.3.4 Journeys to Poland

Of special focus in this chapter are journeys to Poland, taken by high schoolers, 16–18 years old.[9] This mode of learning about the Holocaust has become one of the major ways used for education about the genocide. The Ministry of Education defined the goals of the journeys in the following way: "to strengthen national belonging and the connection to history and heritage." Every year, tens thousands of Israeli youth travel to Poland for seven to ten days in a journey that we call the "journey of death." We use this term because most of the journeys are very similar and include visits to the death camps of Auschwitz-Birkenau, Majdanek, and Treblinka, cemeteries, past ghettos, and places of mass murder, to illustrate the horrors of the Holocaust, without visiting Germany (Feldman, 2008; Soen & Davidovitch, 2011). The journeys include visits, lectures, testimonies of Jewish witnesses to the Holocaust and ceremonies in many of the visited places. Some of the journeys include also a meeting with Polish youth.

Because the journeys to Poland constitute, in some way, a final chapter of socialization in the educational system that begins in kindergarten, and because they encompass the majority of (Jewish) students in the educational system under the control of the Ministry of Education, we propose to view this journey as the *initiation ceremony* of entering Israeli Jewish society. The Israeli adolescents, at this stage, leave the schools and the majority of them are recruited into mandatory military service. *Initiation* is defined as a rite of passage marking entrance or acceptance into a society. It can be seen as formal or informal admission to adulthood in a community. In an extended sense, it can also signify a transformation, in which the initiate is 'reborn' into a new role. An example of an initiation ceremony is the Jewish Bar or Bat Mitzvah that represents symbolic acceptance into adulthood.

The new generation of teenagers travels to Poland to experience the atrocities of the chosen Jewish trauma of the Holocaust, as a kind of initiation: preparation for entering Israeli Jewish society. In this journey, they see with their own eyes how the Jewish people were almost exterminated and they come to understand the central function of the State of Israel, with its army. The teens must comprehend the dangers and threats that were, and still remain, because, as Jews, every Passover, when reading the Haggada, they say: "In each and every generation they rise up against us to destroy us. And the Holy One, blessed be He, rescues us from their hands." The Holocaust can happen again and the young Jewish citizens of Israel, as part of their initiation, entering society, need to internalize the fear of this possibility. It is figuratively embedded in the Jewish DNA, because of their experiences throughout history, from the days of the establishment of the nation, during the Egyptian time as slaves, and then when the Hebrews entered Canaan, in order to build own kingdom.

This fate has continued throughout the centuries and continues in the present, when enemies, like Palestinians or Iranians, are looking for an opportunity to annihilate the Jewish people and their state. The aim of the journey is to help the young men and women internalize the importance of serving in the army, as part of their commitment to the existence to Israel, the Jewish state. They will undertake their mandatory service. Some will continue to serve as professional soldiers and most of the males will continue to serve in reserve duty for approximately 20 years afterward, every year for dozens of days.[10]

Since the journeys to Poland are especially powerful learning experiences, because they provide concrete, systematic and concentrated imagery of Jewish victimhood during the Holocaust, and they provide a very strong emotional experience, we will describe in detail, as a case study, one journey that the second author, who was a high school senior, took in September 2019. It will be told in her words.

3 Death Journeys to Poland: The Case Study

3.1 *Preparations*

Since the journey to Poland is quite complex (emotionally, pedagogically and logistically), students are prepared for the trip by the schools. The preparation for the journey to Poland took many months in our junior year. It was carried out through different activities, including lectures, seminars, and preparatory meetings in the school, led by our teachers and the guides from Yad Vashem.[11] In addition, we visited Yad Vashem and the International Institute of Holocaust Studies, Massuah. The preparatory lectures were not particularly thought provoking. They mainly consisted of "black and white" discussions of complex topics, such as the role of Poles in the Holocaust, or the silence that surrounded the Holocaust in Israel, which was broken only with the trial of Eichmann (in 1961). There was also a concrete preparation for the journey that centered on the issue of security. This focus further reinforced the idea that Jews are always facing threat.

The preparations also conveyed the connection between the State of Israel, the grief over the fallen soldiers and the War of Independence, by pursing a special project: each student was instructed to choose a survivor of the Holocaust, who came to Israel and died fighting in the War of Independence, with no family members left. The fallen had special meaning, because they were the last descendants of their families. We were asked to learn about them: their history in surviving the Holocaust and then the circumstances of their death in the Independence War.

3.2 *The Journey's Route*

At the beginning of the senior year (2019), there was the ultimate climax: the journey itself. The journey was led by the motif of 'death.' All the places we visited were morbid: none provided a glimpse into the life, neither before the Holocaust, nor the life after it. In addition, we did not receive a formal glimpse of the new Poland, with its culture, except a very short meeting with Polish youth at the end of the journey.

The Ministry of Education singled out Auschwitz as a mandatory site, in the journey to Poland, even though almost all, if not all, schools plan to visit almost only places of mass murder, such as death camps, or places of mass execution, concentration camps, past ghettos, monuments to commemorate the victims, Jewish cemeteries, or remains of the graveyards. Thus, our journey was very much a "Death Journey."

We began the journey with the visit to Katovic and Tarnow. We visited the Jewish quarter of Tarnow, and the slaughter pits (Tötung Grube) in the forest, close to Tarnow. Then the route of the journey brought us to Auschwitz, Auschwitz-Birkenau, the place where the ghetto of Krakow was, Treblinka, Majdanek and Plashov. We travelled to Kielce (where there was a pogrom of Jewish survivors of the Holocaust, in 1946), the streets of Ghetto Warsaw, the Warsaw Jewish Cemetery in Okopowa, and finally to the Umschlagplatz,[12] from which the Jews (including almost all the members of my family) were sent to the death camp in Treblinka from Warsaw. We only had one day, in Krakow, which was outside this framework. This was a day in the Jewish Quarter in Krakow to get to know old Jewish life, including two hours of free time in the main old market square.

A day in the journey consisted of visiting several sites, where the tragedies occurred. Each day ended with a "processing session," in which students shared their feelings and thoughts about what they had seen and experienced during the day. Most students were emotionally moved by what they saw. However, a few students were completely uninterested; they listened to music in their headphones, while walking through Auschwitz.

The journey provided a concrete, graphic image of the Holocaust – it transformed representations related to the Holocaust from abstract concepts into concrete images. Suddenly, students saw before their eyes the camps, the barracks, the ovens, executions' places, the barbed wires, and they could sense the tragedy, and experience a personal connection and feel grief. The content of the guides' and witnesses' explanations also helped the students visualize the extent of the genocide – it consisted of personal stories and tragedies, that evoked great sadness among students, and a sense of commitment to the message the journey conveyed. The journey not only graphically presented the atrocities of the Holocaust, but also transmitted the very particular lesson of "Never again." This promise was based on the existence of the strong state that protects Jews and is able to prevent a second Holocaust.

3.3 Ceremonies

In addition to the visits in the above-noted sites, an integral part of the journey were the ceremonies. All the participating 150 students and teachers joined to commemorate the pain and the death. The ceremonies had a similar structure: The Israeli flag was raised, symbolizing the connection between the State of Israel and the Holocaust, silently conveying the message that only the State of Israel can prevent another Holocaust. All the students were required to wear a white hoodie, unifying them. The songs that were selected were the "classic" Holocaust ceremony songs, that brought tears to the eyes, such as *Afar Ve Avak* (ashes and dust) and the national anthem, *Hatikva* (The hope). These songs were sung during every ceremony, reminding the students where we came from to this journey. The main message of the ceremonies consisted of the reminder that we, the third generation, must carry the Holocaust memory forward, and should not forget it. The phrase, "Never Forget," was repeated in every ceremony. In the ceremonies, the message that was conveyed was that we should celebrate the fact that the Jews managed to survive and establish a state with a strong army that would prevent the Holocaust from happening again.

The ceremonies evoked strong emotional reactions, and served as a catharsis. Students were encouraged to cry, to hug each other, and some students even felt strange that they did not experience such strong emotions. The journey evoked emotions of great pain and grief for the people who were murdered in the Holocaust, thus providing students with meaning – that a second Holocaust cannot happen again.

3.4 Thoughts after the Journey

On the societal level, I observed how the particularistic lesson of the Holocaust was imparted. It meant that the militaristic nature of Israel was glorified and related to the Holocaust in a way that justified the continuous violence of the state, in the context of the Israeli-Palestinian conflict and other ongoing conflicts with Syria, Lebanon and Iran. The Holocaust was framed in the present context of existential threat, maintaining the idea that Jews always face possible annihilation. Therefore, a "strong Israel" is the only way to ensure the security of the Jewish people, so that another Holocaust will never happen again.

The journey was sad for me – not just because of the Holocaust – but because it is immersed in a sense of victory, even though humanity has remained the same. Victory was presented in the context of how Jews, who endured unbelievable suffering and pain, being almost exterminated, managed to establish a 'safe state' with a strong army. National pride was connected to the military victories that Israel has had, because of having a very strong army. During the journey, I thought a lot about how and why it happens that no one mentioned the universalistic lesson for Israel in the present.

Standing on the Polish soil of the Holocaust, I concretely realized that Jews did not learn the universal lesson and, after establishing their state, they behave as many other nations have behaved that have violated the human rights of the others. They have forgotten that just decades ago, they were total victims of a genocide and that they should serve as examples of humanity and morality. However, instead, they repress the Israeli occupation of the Palestinians, discrimination of the Arab minority in Israel, the violation of human rights, the antidemocratic climate in Israel, and/or the nationalism and racism that dominate present-day Israel. It made me angry and sad, that the discussion on the fundamental lesson, our bloody present and bleak future, was pushed aside to make space for nationalism, in its narrow particularistic sense.

I strongly believe that the lesson of the Holocaust must be framed within a universal context of values: a context that must examine the danger of blind obedience, of toxic nationalism, of horrifying racism, or of the process of dehumanization of the other (which is a global process and serves as 'psychological license' to commit murder, in any national context). Such a framework will pass the responsibility of preserving a true democracy to the younger generation, encourage them to fight against injustices and struggle for humanity, and for the universal and equal compassion for all human beings – a principle that must serve as a pillar of the society. Such a lesson will locate the memory of those who perished in the realm of the desired values that could prevent the Holocaust.

And, as for my personal takeaway from this journey, I believe that while it is crucial to have the knowledge of the past, this knowledge must be the key to the desire to build a democratic, humanistic and moral future and not stay frozen, preserving the pains of the past. The memory of the Holocaust in museums (especially Yad Vashem), ceremonies and the journey to Poland should be used to create a base for these values and the universalistic lesson, as well. Israel needs to be saved from the authoritarian, nationalistic and racist road upon which it has embarked. The Jewish People, whose blood is soaked in the European soil, should have been vigilant about the danger of spreading hate, and should have known more than most nations about the importance of nurturing humanity and democratic values. However, recent years have shown that Israeli Jews have made a terrible and dreadful deviation from this path.

The ashes of my family are scattered in Treblinka, ashes that pave the universal path. This path continued to be paved by my grandmother, Zosia, when she was protesting against the occupation, as part of the "Women in Black" movement, which consisted mostly of older women – many of them survivors of the Holocaust.

I believe that it is important to remember that human beings can be atrocious and compassionate, in the same breath. In Treblinka lie the remains of human beings, and with them the remains of human hearts – the heart we all possess, the heart that became rotten, by many during those terrible times. It is sad that we need still to continue the struggle against the decline and even disappearance of human compassion. This struggle is crucial for the State of Israel and for future Jewish generations that need to hold up the candle of humanity.

This is what I wrote on the tomb of my grandmother's father, who died in 1933, to commemorate the murder of his wife and his seven children in Treblinka: "We carry in our hearts your memory and with it we weave the fabric of humane love – that so desperately was needed." Being in Treblinka, my father's words, spoken to me over the phone, are etched forever in my heart:

> We must fight fearlessly, without self-censorship for justice, for freedom. It is the only way to remember those who have been taken from us, the good souls who were murdered. By doing so, this is the only way to continue paving their path.

Notes

1 *Chosen trauma* is defined as shared societal mental representation of a historical event in which the group suffered a catastrophic and traumatic defeat, loss, and humiliation at the hands of its enemy. It has a determinative effect on the shared societal feeling of being a victim by society members. Of importance is the fact that the group did not heal from this experience and is unable to mourn it properly. Therefore, the event becomes something externalized, leaving indelible imprinting upon the psyche of the group, marking its memory

2 Yad Vashem is Israel's official memorial to the victims of the Holocaust.
3 Intractable conflicts are fought over goals viewed as existential. They are violent, perceived as being of a zero-sum nature and unsolvable. They preoccupy a central position in the lives of the involved societies, require immense investments of material and psychological resources and last for at least 25 years (Bar-Tal, 2013; Kriesberg, 1993).
4 Delegitimization is defined as "categorization of a group, or groups, into extremely negative social categories that exclude it, or them, from the sphere of human groups that act within the limits of acceptable norms and/or values, since these groups are viewed as violating basic human norms or values and therefore deserve maltreatment" (Bar-Tal & Hammack, 2012, p. 30).
5 Retrieved May 6, 2020, from www.timesofisrael.com
6 Yedioth Ahronoth, June 1, 1982.
7 Collective memory of conflict describes the outbreak of the conflict and its course, providing a coherent and meaningful picture of what has happened from the societal perspective (Bar-Tal, 2013; Devine-Wright, 2003; Tint, 2010).
8 *Ethos of conflict* is defined as the configuration of shared central societal beliefs that provide a particular dominant orientation to a society at present and for the future in the contexts of intractable conflict (Bar-Tal, 2013). Both narratives contain eight major themes about issues related to the conflict, the in-group, and its adversary: (1) *societal beliefs about the justness of one's own goals*, which outline the contested goals, indicate their cru*cial importance, and provide the*ir explanations and rationales; (2) *Societal beliefs about security* stress the importance of personal safety and natio*nal survival, and outline the conditions for their* achievement; (3) *Societal beliefs of positive collective self-image* concern the ethnocentric tendency to attribute *positive traits, values, and b*ehavior to one's own society; (4) *Societal beliefs of victimization* concern the se*lf-presentation of the in-group as the victim o*f the conflict; (5) *Societal beliefs of delegitimizing the opponent concern beliefs tha*t deny the adversary's humanity; (6) *Societal beliefs of patriotism* generate attachment to the country a*nd society, by propagatin*g loyalty, love, care, and sacrifice; (7) *Societal beliefs of unity* refer to the importance of ignoring internal conflicts and disagreements during intractable conflicts to unite the *society's forces in the* face of an external threat; Finally, (8) *Societal beliefs of peace* refer to peace as the ultimate desire of the society.
9 In Israel, there are two state educational systems: *The state religious system*, established mostly for orthodox students (about 18% of the Jewish pupils). The state secular-educational system is diverse and pluralistic, serving Jewish families that are not orthodox or strictly religious. There is also an independent ultra-orthodox (Haredi) educational system, in which there are a minority of students. Its institutions focus mainly/only on religious studies. The first two systems have a curriculum for Holocaust studies and travel to Poland.
10 Most young adults who do military service attended the state's two educational system.
11 The guides from Yad Vashem, who participated in the preparations, were also the one who instructed us later during the journey.
12 *Umschlagplatz* (German: *collection point or reloading point*) was the term used during the *Holocaust* to denote the holding areas adjacent to railway stations in occupied Poland, where Jews from ghettos were assembled for deportation to Nazi death camps ... The largest collection point was in Warsaw, next to the Warsaw Ghetto, from where the Jews were sent to the death camp of Treblinka.

References

Antonovsky, A. (1987). *Unraveling the mystery of health: How people manage stress and stay well.* Jossey-Bass.

Bandura, A. (1999). Moral disengagement in the perpetration of inhumanities. *Personality and Social Psychology Review, 3*(3), 193–209.

Bar-Tal, D. (2013). *Intractable conflicts: Socio-psychological foundations and dynamics.* Cambridge University Press.

Bar-Tal, D. (2019). The essence of lack of security in Israel. In I. Keynan & I. Harboun (Eds.), *Defense is not everything: The civic aspects of security* (pp. 75–99). Pardes and the Center for Academic Studies. [in Hebrew]

Bar-Tal, D. (2020). Creating insecurity and fear for political goals. *International Perspectives in Psychology: Research, Practice, Consultation, 9,* 5–17.

Bar-Tal, D., & Antebi, D. (1992). Siege mentality in Israel. *International Journal of Intercultural Relations, 16,* 251–275.

Bar-Tal, D., Chernyak-Hai, L., Schori, N., & Gundar, A. (2009). A sense of self-perceived collective victimhood in intractable conflicts. *International Red Cross Review, 91,* 229–277.

Bar-Tal, D., & Hammack, P. L. (2012). Conflict, delegitimization, and violence In L. R. Tropp (Ed.), *The Oxford handbook of intergroup conflict* (pp. 29–52). Oxford University Press.

Bar-Tal, D., & Raviv, A. (2021). *The comfort zone of a society in conflict.* Steimatzky. [in Hebrew]

Bar-Tal, D., & Staub, E. (Eds.). (1997). *Patriotism in the lives of individuals and nations.* Nelson-Hall.

Bar-Tal, D., & Teichman, Y. (2005). *Stereotypes and prejudice in conflict: Representations of Arabs in Israeli Jewish society.* Cambridge University Press.

Bauer, Y. (2002). *Rethinking the Holocaust.* Yale University Press.

Ben-Amos, A., & Bet-El, I. (1999). Holocaust Day and Memorial Day in Israeli schools: Ceremonies, education and history. *Israel Studies, 4,* 258–284.

Dawidowicz, L. S. (1975). *The war against the Jews, 1933–1945.* Rinhehart and Winston.

Devine-Wright, P. (2003). A theoretical overview of memory and conflict. In E. Cairns & M. D. Roe (Eds.), *The role of memory in ethnic conflict* (pp. 9–33). Palgrave Macmillan.

Elon, A. (1971). *The Israelis.* Weidenfeld and Nicolson.

Feldman, J. (2008). *Above the death pits, beneath the flag: Youth voyages to Poland and the performance of Israeli national identity.* Berghahn.

Frankl, V. E. (1963). *Man's search for meaning.* Washington Square Press.

Grosser, P. E., & Halperin, E. G. (1979). *Anti-semitism. The causes and effect of a prejudice.* Citadel Press.

Handelman, D., & Katz, E. (1990). State ceremonies of Israel – Remembrance Day and Independence Day. In D. Handelman (Ed.), *Models and mirrors: Towards anthropology of public events*. Cambridge University Press.

Jost, J. T., & Major, B. (Eds.). (2001). *The psychology of legitimacy: Emerging perspectives on ideology, justice, and intergroup relations*. Cambridge University Press.

Kaminka, E. (2016). Teaching about the Holocaust in Israel: A pedagogical approach adopted by the Israeli Ministry of Education. *Contemporary Review of the Middle East, 3*(3) 237–249.

Keren, N. (1998). Preserving memory in the oblivion: The struggle for Holocaust studies in Israel. *Zmanim, 64,* 56–64. [in Hebrew]

Klar, Y., Schori-Eyal, N., & Klar, Y. (2013). The 'never again' state of Israel: The emergence of the Holocaust as a core feature of Israeli identity and its four incongruent voices. *Journal of Social Issues, 69,* 125–141.

Kriesberg, L. (1993). Intractable conflict. *Peace Review, 5,* 417–421.

Lazarus, R. S., & Folkman, S. (1984). *Stress, appraisal, and coping*. Springer.

Liebman, C. (1978). Myth, tradition and values in Israeli society. *Midstream, 24,* 44–53.

Liebman, C. S., & Don-Yihya, E. (1983). *Civil religion in Israel: Traditional Judaism and political culture in the Jewish state*. University of California Press.

Maymon, M., Ben-Amos, A., & Bar-Tal, D. (2016). Stagnation or change of the conflict supporting narrative: Israeli commemorative ceremonies for the fallen soldiers, 2010. *Public Space, 11,* 63–93. [in Hebrew]

Morris, B. (2001). *Righteous victims: A history of the Zionist-Arab conflict 1881–2001*. Vintage Books.

Ofer, D. (2009). The past that does not pass: Israelis and Holocaust memory. *Israel Studies, 14,* 1–35.

Peleg, I. (Ed.). (2019). *Victimhood discourse in contemporary Israel*. Lexington Books.

Podeh, E. (2015). *Chances for peace: Missed opportunities in the Arab-Israeli conflict*. University of Texas Press.

Romi, S., & Lev, M. (2007). Experiential learning of history through youth journeys to Poland Israeli Jewish youth and the Holocaust. *Research in Education, 78,* 88–102.

Rosenberg, S. (2003). *Victimhood*. Intractable Conflict Knowledge Base Project, Conflict Research Consortium, University of Colorado. http://www.intractableconflict.org/m/victimhood.jsp

Schori-Eyal, N., Klar, Y., Roccas, S., & McNeill, A. (2017). The shadows of the past: Effects of historical group trauma on current intergroup conflicts. *Personality and Social Psychology Bulletin, 43*(4) 538–554.

Segev, T. (2000). *The seventh million: Israelis and the Holocaust*. Holt.

Soen, D., & Davidovitch, N. (2011). Israeli youth pilgrimage to Poland: Rationale and polemics. *Images, 9,* 5–27.

Tint, B. (2010). History, memory, and intractable conflict. *Conflict Resolution Quarterly, 27*(3), 239–256.

Volkan, V. D. (2001). Transgenerational transmissions and chosen traumas: An aspect of large-group identity. *Group Analysis, 34*(1), 79–97.

Zertal, I. (2005). *Israel's Holocaust and the politics of nationhood*. Cambridge University Press.

CHAPTER 16

Teaching History and Citizenship in Schools in Northern Ireland

Gavin Duffy, Tony Gallagher and Gareth Robinson

1   Introduction

Various writers (Gallagher, 2004, 2017; McCully & Waldron, 2013; Richardson & Gallagher, 2011; Smith, 2005; Terra, 2014) have previously provided detailed commentary on the development of the education system in Ireland and Northern Ireland. These commentaries have described the establishment of the Irish National school system in 1830s and the emergence of a parallel or separate system of church-run schools for Catholics and Protestants. They have also described how different education systems developed on either side of the border, after partition in the early 1920s, when Northern Ireland became part of the UK, and was separated from the rest of the island of Ireland. These writers have also considered the role that education played during the period often referred to as the Troubles, beginning in the late 1960s through until late 1990s. They reflected on the efficacy of various educational initiatives (Smith, 2005) that responded to conflict and on the wider debate, as to whether separate schools for Protestant and Catholics in Northern Ireland acted as 'incubators of conflict or as potential mechanisms for ameliorating community division' (Gallagher, 2017, p. 6).

Given this context, this chapter considers the teaching of history and citizenship education in Northern Ireland, in a divided society, emerging from conflict, made more complicated, because there is no consensus on a single narrative of the past. On the contrary, the past is contested and, indeed, there are multiple narratives, many of which are intimately tied up with notions of identity, nationality, politics and religion.

This chapter will first examine the teaching of history, focusing more on the period between the 1990s to the present, since others, cited above, have extensively dealt with earlier periods. This period saw the introduction of the Northern Ireland Curriculum (NIC) and a common and prescribed curriculum for subjects, such religious studies and history, which meant that schools for Protestants and Catholics were now teaching the same curriculum in these subject areas. Later, in 2007, the curriculum was further revised and much of the prescribed content removed, opting instead to recognize the professionalism of teachers and shift the focus of learning to a more skills-based approach. In history, students examine Irish, British, European and global events. Key elements include World Wars, Irish-British relations and the conflict in Northern Ireland. A multi-perspective approach is taken concerning historical narrative, acknowledging that there are some aspects of history, in which the interpretation or significance of events differs between the two communities.

The chapter will then turn to citizenship education, which was introduced to schools as part of the revised curriculum. Given the conflict in Northern Ireland and the divided nature of society, the very notions of citizenship and conceptions of community, along with the symbols and rituals of nationhood are contested, whereas in other societies these might form essential components to be explored in schools as part of a citizenship education program. Instead, citizenship education in Northern Ireland is sensitive about how these themes are examined in the classroom and, instead, locates them within broader human rights based themes, such as diversity and inclusion, rights and responsibilities, equality and social justice and democracy and active participation.

The chapter will then examine the linkages between the subjects. Both subjects adopt a similar pedagogical approach and are thematically complementary, particularly concerning themes, such as identity, nationality and conflict. Each subject addresses controversial and challenging themes and there are also some tensions between the subjects. We will also consider the role of shared education, which offers an alternative means by which students from different cultural backgrounds, in separate schools, can explore issues of identity, nationality and active citizenry together in each other's schools.

2 The Teaching of History Since the Introduction of the Northern Ireland Curriculum in 1991

Prior to the introduction of the NIC in 1991, Terra (2014) argued that there is little evidence of the way in which schools approached history. Where history was taught, schools themselves were largely responsible for setting the scope and sequence of instruction (Terra, 2014). During the decades from partition through the Troubles, until the introduction of the NIC, history was typically taught in the latter years of primary school and the early years of post-primary school. All or most schools studied British history, but Terra highlighted that Catholic schools were still teaching the Irish perspective. Conway (2001) asserted that a distorting myth emerged that only a few Protestant schools studied Irish history, while occupying a central position in Catholic schools.

Drawing on the work of Magee (1970, 1975), McCully and Waldron (2013) contend that Irish history was being taught, but only where it did not encroach upon or possibly contradict the history of Great Britain.

The Education Reform (NI) Order, 1989 led to the introduction of the NIC in early 1991. This largely mirrored similar curricular reforms under Thatcher's Conservative government in England and it was the first time that a common curriculum for Catholic and Protestant schools had been tried. Aside from traditional subjects, new common programs of study in subjects, such as religious education and history, were developed, which recognised the two main cultural and religious traditions in Northern Ireland (McGuiness, 2012). Smith (2005, p. 143) argued that efforts to create a common curriculum focused primarily on including Irish history as a gesture of fairness toward nationalists and that this would dispel notions that the 'other' schools were teaching negative materials about 'us.'

During this period, six units of study were prescribed for the first three years of post-primary schools (ages 11–14). Three of the units focused on the history of Ireland and Britain between the years 1100–1922. They examined the Norman conquest of Britain and Ireland, European rivalries in the 17th century and the Act of Union, from 1801 until the partition of Ireland in 1922. The fourth unit covered a topic in the 20th century, and schools typically opted for either the First World War or the Second World War. The remaining two units focused on a local study, which tended to cover a significant event, a place of interest or a turning point in history (Kitson, 2007; Terra, 2014).

2.1 *The Revised Curriculum to the Present*

The curriculum was reviewed again in the early 2000s, leading to the implementation of the Northern Ireland Revised Curriculum in 2007. Gallagher (2017) argued that, overall, the new curriculum was intended to be less prescriptive and offered teachers more autonomy over their subjects. How did this influence the teaching of history? According to Terra (2014), much of the prescribed historical content and specific unit requirements were removed. Instead, the curriculum became more skills-based. McCully and Waldron (2013) argued that history was now much more focused on examining social history, personal identity, culture and lifestyle. Barton and McCully (2010) argued that history had shifted towards promoting historical skills and concepts, such as causation, chronology, and perspective-taking.

2.2 *Teaching History in Primary Schools*

Primary schools in Northern Ireland do not teach history as a discrete subject; rather history is taught within a broader, cross-curricular area of learning, referred to as The World Around Us, which enables teachers to take a flexible approach in making connections between history, geography, science and technology (CCEA, 2017a). Teachers are not required to focus on any particular historical themes, persons or events. Instead, the Council for the Curriculum, Examinations and Assessment (CCEA) offers guidance on topics that teachers might want to address. These include personalised histories of parents and grandparents; the differences between pupils' lives and those of the past; examining local and wider historical locations and buildings; how the local community has changed over time; how transport, goods and services have changed, and the reasons for change.

2.3 Teaching History in Post-Primary Schools

2.3.1 Key Stage 3 (Age 11–14)

At this stage, history is taught as part of a wider area of learning, referred to as Environment and Society, and includes both History and Geography as subject strands. Teachers have the choice to teach these subjects together, connect learning between the subjects or teach them as separate subjects. Importantly, this is the only stage in which history is compulsory. There is a range of minimum requirements that must be taught, and most notable, given the focus of this chapter, is the partition of Ireland and how this has influenced contemporary Northern Ireland. Other topics include personal identity, culture and lifestyle, selective interpretation and the creation of stereotypes, significant events and ideas of the 20th century, critical issues in history, and individuals who have behaved ethically or unethically. Students also investigate how skills developed in history can be useful in a range of careers. Importantly, teachers at this level are required to address only one topic relating to Irish history. However, as these topics are the minimum statutory requirement, there is latitude for teachers to explore other Irish/British historical events or periods. Alongside the statutory minimum requirements, the CCEA suggests examples of topics that could be taught. For the themes of personal identity and culture, the CCEA suggests that teachers might examine topics, such as religion, nationality, language, the Reformation and the Plantation of Ireland. Similarly, for the theme of selective interpretation and the creation of stereotypical perceptions, the CCEA suggests that teachers might examine the Troubles, the Arab/Israeli conflict or even slavery or apartheid.

2.3.2 Key Stage 4 (Age 14–16)

Students at this level will undertake formal qualifications, known as General Certificates in Secondary Education (GCSE). History is still taught within the wider area of learning, referred to as Environment and Society, which includes geography and builds on the learning experiences of Key Stage 3. Schools are required to teach at least one of these subjects at this level and, as such, history is an optional subject. Students are expected to complete 120 hours of guided learning over two years.

History at this stage is comprised of two units. Unit 1 involves a modern world study with an option (A), to examine Nazi Germany from 1933–45 or life in United States of America from 1920–33, and a local study, with an option (B), to examine Northern Ireland from 1920–49 or Northern Ireland from 1965–1998. Unit 2 is an outline study of international relations from 1945–2003. Schools tend to examine the Cold War.

Gallagher (2017, p. 8) describes the arrangement of Option B as bizarre, since students are limited to an either/or choice on the history of Northern Ireland, and there is a risk that the options play directly into community narratives. There has been recent controversy about this in the UK and Irish press in which articles (Abrams, 2020; de Souza 2020), drawing on a study (Davies, 2020), claimed that the teaching of history was divided along religious lines. The study claimed that controlled schools are more likely to opt for an examination of Northern Ireland, from 1920–49, which covers the period of the partition of Ireland and Northern Ireland in wartime. Catholic schools are more likely to opt for Northern Ireland from 1965–1998, which covers the emergence of the civil rights movement, the outbreak of violence, paramilitary ceasefires and resulting peace agreements. McCully, in a BBC interview (Meredith, 2020) acknowledged elements of this assertion, but pointed to the fact that more controlled schools have been switching to the later 'Troubles' period and argued that "presenting pupils with opposing Catholic and Protestant narratives was a 'blunt and dated approach.'" Furthermore, the Chief Examiners report (CCEA, 2019a) revealed that 75% of all students in Northern Ireland chose to examine the later period on Northern Ireland history.

2.3.3   Post 16 (Age 16–18)

After GCSEs, students can opt for a range of academic and vocational post-16 qualifications. One strand, the General Certificate of Education (GCE), offers advanced level History as an option. In the first year, students undertake two units of study, offering options covering European history from 1500s to 1945. There is one option that examines Irish History between 1823 and 1867. In Year 2, there are a further two units of study offering options covering European, American, English and Irish History (CCEA, 2019b). The second year offers more options to study periods in Irish history than previous key stages.

Examining the Chief Inspectors report for history (CCEA, 2019c) reveals that, in the first year, the majority of students opted to examine Germany 1919–45 and Russia 1914–41. In the second year, most students opted to examine either the American Presidency 1901–2000 or the Clash of Ideologies 1900–2000. During this second year, most students opted to examine the Partition of Ireland 1900–25. While most schools opt to use the CCEA curriculum at this stage, some schools opt to follow English exam boards and can avoid examining Irish history altogether.

3   Adopting a Multi-Perspectival Approach

Much of the academic research has focused on trying to understand the complexities surrounding how history could be taught in a divided society, in which notions of nationality, identity and the past remain sources of conflict (Barton & McCully, 2005; Conway 2004; Smith, 2005). One approach, McCully (2012) argues, may be to try to construct a common narrative, which is acceptable to all groups. Another involves presenting multiple or contested narratives alongside one another. The former might offer a common sense of heritage and nationality and might even help in the process of post-conflict reconstruction. However, it is open to political imposition and might not be inclusive of all groups in a society. The latter contends that history is constructed from multiple narratives of the past and recognizes that a society may be comprised of various national or ethnic groups, each of which has a stake in the construction of the past. Smith (2005, p. 189) argues that this runs the risk of a type of historical relativism. The key to this type of discourse is to "accept that history can be seen from many perspectives and none of these is mutually exclusive." However, it is also important to recognize that when teaching this way, accurate observation and objectivity are vital and teaching multiple narratives might offer students the opportunity to empathize for "how others experienced history."

McCully describes how a multiperspectival approach became embedded into the way history has been taught since the early 1990s. This approach originated from the Schools' Council History Project (SCHP) in England, which was an enquiry-based approach to history provision that sought to teach about historical events using multiple primary and secondary sources and to treat historical narratives as provisional and open to question. According to McCully (2012, p. 148), students were encouraged to view history as "process orientated and to recognize that actors in the past often saw events differently and to evaluate differing (and conflicting) interpretations in the light of available evidence." Terra (2014) conducted an analysis of history textbooks over time, since the introduction of the NIC, and demonstrated how content has shifted from presenting narrative to becoming more source driven, enquiry-based and reflective of diverse perspectives. Crucially, Terra argues that later textbooks have been constructed in such a way as to avoid presenting whole, coherent narratives, but rather emphasize multiple interpretations of historical events and position students as historical investigators, who evaluate evidence.

Academic research (Barton, 2001, 2005; Barton & McCully, 2005, 2008, 2010) during this period also began to focus on how social context, beyond the school, influenced young people's understanding of history. Barton (2001a) argues that significant elements of young people's historical knowledge is socially constructed and often from 'unofficial sources,' such as family, peers, the wider community and museums. Even television and the internet acted as important sources of historical knowledge for students. Elements of this research further reinforced the idea that singular or consensual narratives in schools were problematic and that there was wide variation in terms of young people's knowledge about history. Furthermore, this research seemed to point to tensions between historical knowledge developed in school and outside of school.

4 Citizenship Education in Schools in Northern Ireland

Citizenship education is often associated with the development and maintenance of a national identity or a sense of common citizenry (Niens & McIlrath, 2010; Smith, 2003). Where countries are politically stable, citizenship education often involves a focus on symbols and rituals of nationality, including flags, anthems, institutions and political leadership (Gallagher & Duffy, 2016, p. 541). However, from the outset, citizenship is also a contested concept (McMurray & Niens, 2012; Niens & Chastenay, 2008; Osler & Starkey, 2003), made complex by the fact that many societies are not politically stable or indeed ethnically and culturally homogenous (Kiwan, 2016; Kymlicka, 2011; Leonard, 2007) and can often be defined by majority and minority relations. The very notion of nationality, Niens et al. (2013) argue, is a depreciating concept, and any design of citizenship education is likely to vary across different cultural contexts, depending on local historical and political circumstances and differing societal needs or challenges (Quaynor, 2010). One of the ways in which this complexity can be observed is in societies affected by ethnic, political or even religious conflicts, where citizenship education, is often positioned as means of ameliorating the impact of conflict or as a means of reconstruction, especially in post-conflict settings (Gallagher, 2004).

Citizenship education in Northern Ireland faces an intricate dilemma. While it cannot be constructed around the promotion of a singular national citizenry, it still needs to address local issues of identity, cultural difference and reconciliation. Smith (2003, p. 24) argued, "concepts of citizenship based on rights and responsibilities rather than national identity may offer the best potential to transcend the two nationalisms in Northern Ireland." If the idea or the potency of national identity is diminishing, Niens et al. (2013) argued that attention must turn toward a search for a set of values that might act as an alternative type of social glue.

Examples of this can be seen in the early pilot work in schools in Northern Ireland in the late 1990s, particularly that of the Social, Civic and Political Education Project (SCPE), which was supported by the Department of Education (DE) and initially established to shore up existing official educational approaches promoting mutual understanding and reconciliation in schools. Various commentators have also provided an historical timeline tracing the origins of this program and seeing how it connects with previous school and community-based initiatives designed to address peace building, conflict and promote social cohesion (Gallagher, 2004; Gallagher & Duffy, 2017; McEvoy, 2007; Smith, 2003).

SCPE sought to develop a new conceptual framework, introduce a new value base, promote a focus on human rights and democracy and develop a methodology to support the teaching of citizenship education in schools (Arlow, 2004; Watling & Arlow, 2002). Arlow (2004) argued, at the time, that citizenship education should adopt an enquiry-based approach and encourage active student participation. It should not be overly transmissional, so as to avoid accusations of indoctrination and should focus on local, European and global contexts. Because of this work, citizenship education was introduced in Northern Ireland alongside the revised curriculum in 2007.

4.1 *Personal Development and Mutual Understanding (PDMU) in Primary Schools*

Primary schools are required to encourage children's emotional, social and moral development. PDMU is an area of the curriculum, which addresses two interconnected strands. The first strand addresses personal and emotional issues, and health, wellbeing and safety matters. The second, and more relevant, strand examines personal and social relationships, and the need for tolerance and respect (CCEA, 2020b).

4.2 *Citizenship Education in Post-Primary Schools*

4.2.1 Key Stage 3 (11–14)

All students at key stage 3 are required to study Learning for Life and Work (LLW), an area of the curriculum with four subject strands: local and global citizenship, employability, personal development and home economics. Local and global citizenship is based around four core themes that emerged from the SCPE pilot in schools. (i) In *diversity and inclusion*, students explore themes, such as identity, diversity and inclusion at the local and global level. (ii) In *human rights and social responsibility*, a core theme underpinning the others, students examine rights, global value-based systems, such as the UN Convention on the Rights of the Child (UNCRC) and the Declaration of Human Rights (UDHR). (iii) In *equality and social justice,* students explore themes, such as inequality and injustice and the role of individuals, groups and society in promoting equality and justice. (iv) In *democracy and active participation,* students explore democratic institutions, mainly on how to participate in democratic processes (CCEA, 2017b).

4.2.2 Key Stage 4 (14–16)

Learning for Life and Work is a compulsory element of the curriculum at this stage. Schools must offer a minimum statutory content. This content develops three of the thematic areas from key stage 3: local and global citizenship, employability and personal development. Schools can decide on how best to approach these areas. Schools are also required to offer at least one related course from a possible range of subjects, such as business studies, hospitality, preparation for adult life, economics, government and politics, home economics, health and social care, etc. A GCSE qualification in Learning for Life and Work (LLW) is also available, which covers three units: local and global citizenship, employability and personal development, and an additional Investigation Unit, which is a controlled assessment where students undertake a research project and produce a written report on a theme from one of the three units. Perhaps, most relevant to this chapter, is the Local and Global Citizenship unit. Students examine six themes: diversity & inclusion, rights & responsibilities, government and civil society, democratic institutions, democracy and active participation and the role of non-governmental organizations. Across the six themes, students examine a range of topics, which develop and extend those from key stage 3. Topics of relevance include: cultural identity, inclusion conflict, balancing rights, social inequality, social injustice, and the role of government and democracy (CCEA, 2017b).

5 Implementing Citizenship Education

Since the pilot initiative to the present, there have been a series of issues surrounding the implementation and curricular focus of citizenship education. Niens et al. (2009), who were responsible for the evaluation of the pilot initiative, pointed to a lack of senior leadership engagement in many schools.

Consequently, the status and credibility of the subject struggled during the pilot stage. Furthermore, the authors pointed to limited cross-curricular connections between citizenship and other subjects and the fact that many schools were not recognizing how the deeper implications of the subject could impact school policies or ethos, or enable them to address issues, such as racism, homophobia, relationships and democracy in schools. Gallagher (2007), and then later Niens et al. (2013), also highlighted that the topic of racism, in the face of increasing immigration to NI, was not being adequately addressed, while themes, such as sectarianism, were being over-played.

McMurray and Niens (2012) focused on the way that schools were making connections with community organizations and NGOs, and argued that given the separate or segregated system of education, in which Protestants and Catholics are, for the most part, educated separately, schools tended to make connections and allegiances in their own communities. As a result, this limited opportunities for the development of bridging social capital across communities. Niens and Chastenay (2008) compared citizenship education programs in Quebec and Northern Ireland, and suggested that espoused student democratic and political participation might actually be tokenistic in many schools, given that schools are traditionally organized around hierarchical structures. Furthermore, they argued that themes related to national/cultural identity do not receive enough attention in classrooms and tend to be subsumed or buried in a range of wider generic social themes. Niens et al. (2013, p. 132) also argued several years later, that since citizenship education had been embedded within the curriculum, the absence of an explicit examination of a national context, in the design of the curriculum, had led to "diffuse interpretations and limited awareness and debate" of this issue among teachers.

6 The Linkages between History and Citizenship Education

Various writers have explored the linkages between history and citizenship education (Lee & Shemilt, 2017; McCully, 2017; Waldron & McCully, 2016; Wrenn, 1999). Lee and Shemilt (2007, p. 14) argued that there could be "no meaningful understanding of citizenship without an historical dimension"; the subjects should have a complementary relationship in which history is seen as "central to citizenship formation in any open and democratic society" (2007, p. 17). McCully (2017) argued that the history curriculum in Northern Ireland was well-positioned to interact positively with citizenship.

There are obvious links between the two subjects, in terms of pedagogy, in that both use an enquiry-based approach, adopt multi-perspectivity and lend themselves to the development of skills, including critical thinking, problem solving and communication. Both subjects have an important role to play in the peace process in terms of helping students from different cultural backgrounds learn together about their identities and the different narratives that contribute to our critical understanding of Northern Ireland. Both subjects also play an important role in developing citizens who have the knowledge and capacity to play an active role in maintaining a just and democratic society. Both subjects are organized around the same overarching themes of helping young people to develop as individuals, contributors to society and contributors to the economy and environment. The subjects offer students opportunities for historical and contemporary investigations of identity, nationality, politics, democracy and rights. Both explore conflict and peacebuilding themes pertaining to Northern Ireland, including key events, people, organizations, political structures, symbols and cultural practices, and both subjects adopt a local and global perspective.

However, some have pointed to possible tensions between the two subjects. Indeed, McCully (2017) posed the question as to whether history and citizenship were natural allies or uncomfortable bedfellows. Some of the literature considers that the subjects might be competing for space in the timetable, the possible colonization of history by citizenship, or even the assimilation of history into a broader humanities framework, (Lee & Shemilt, 2007). Others have raised concerns that history is at risk of no longer being taught as a discrete subject, but rather is incorporated into other subject areas, such as geography, or social or civics based subjects (Smith, 2005). Arguably, this can be seen in the primary and post-primary history curricula in Northern Ireland. McCoombe's doctoral study (2006) revealed reservations from some teachers that the introduction of Local and Global Citizenship into the curriculum might actually lead to the diminution of time allocated to subjects, such as history, given some overlap in subject matter and pedagogical approach.

McCully (2017, p. 7) argued that, to date, there is limited evidence of history and citizenship teachers working and planning together "to map and exploit the obvious knowledge conduit between" the subjects. A similar point was also raised by the Education Training Inspectorate's (ETI) (2018) evaluation of the Shared Education Signature Project, which recommended that more explicit links should be made between the subjects.

The research evidence also points to a common and enduring issue related to teaching controversial issues. Conway (2004, p. 72), reflecting on teaching history in the early 1990s while the conflict was still ongoing, argued that teachers were concerned about not "bringing the troubles of the streets into the classroom." McCall (2013) similarly argued that many teachers were uncomfortable about addressing issues of the conflict that might challenge each community's perception of the cherished past. Niens et al. (2013), in their study, reported that while most teachers were comfortable addressing difficult issues, there were differing levels of willingness, largely determined by contextual issues (Reilly & Niens, 2014) and professional capacities. The authors highlighted that subjects, such as sectarianism and the conflict, remained difficult themes to teach. Since the emergence of citizenship education, some have suggested that a culture of avoidance has developed among some teachers (McCully & Emerson, 2014; Niens & O'Connor, 2006; Richardson & Gallagher, 2011). Smith (2005) argued strongly that teaching that recognizes the perspectives of different groups is difficult to undertake and, as such, recommended as a key policy that teachers should receive more training. He further asserted that textbooks, curricula and teaching methods should be revised to enable the effective delivery of a multi-perspective approach.

Perhaps the most significant challenge facing both subjects is the way in which pupils from Catholic and Protestant backgrounds are, for the most part, educated in separate schools. The out-workings of such a system has meant that students, from different cultural backgrounds, have, in the recent past, had limited opportunities to adequately explore together complex themes, such as identity, nationality, politics, conflict and reconciliation. There has been a range of educational initiatives over the last four decades, which have attempted to do this, but the evidence points to a limited impact (see Chapter 6). The most recent initiative, Shared Education, has been much more impactful (Duffy & Gallagher, 2017; Gallagher, 2016) and encourages sustained and regular engagement between schools, where students learn together in each other's schools. Shared learning is also supported by teachers, who collaborate, plan and undergo professional development training together.

The Education Authority (EA) (2020a) reported that, during the academic year 2018/2019, there were 159 shared education partnerships, based on 371 schools involved in the Shared Education Signature Project. In the same year, just over 65,000 pupils and just over 6,000 teachers were involved. A number of formal reports have recently been produced, which examined the impact of Shared Education. Each of these has emphasized the importance of history and citizenship as subjects, which students from different schools and different communities should study together. The Education and Training Inspectorate (ETI) (2018, p. 18) conducted an evaluation of shared education across Northern Ireland and indicated that:

> When partnerships explored sensitive and controversial issues, such as aspects of history, the learning was deeper than in other situations.

Through the exploration of aspects of recent history, pupils were enabled to appreciate differing perspectives and interpretations and understand how narratives around the past have shaped attitudes and actions.

The Department of Education for Northern Ireland (DE) (2018) produced a report for the NI Assembly and similarly highlighted that subjects, such as the World Around Us, PDMU and LLW have emerged as prominent subjects for schools involved in Shared Education. Two years later, the EA (2020b) similarly reported that, for primary schools, The World Around Us, PDMU and the Arts were the most popular subjects for primary school shared education partnerships, with just over 15,000 students exploring World Around Us and just under 9000 students exploring PDMU together in shared lessons. EA (2020b) also reported that Learning for Life and Work and Environment and Society were the two most popular learning areas for post-primary school partnerships. Just over 6,800 pupils studied LLW each term together and just under 3000 pupils per term participated in shared lessons related to the area of Environment and Society.

It appears that many school partnerships consider subjects, such as history and citizenship education, as ideal for shared education. However, perhaps one important caveat to emerge from the official reports cited above is that teachers continued to find some themes controversial or challenging to teach in shared settings, and required further support and professional development training. DE (2018, p. 37) reported that some partnerships struggled with objectives associated with reconciliation and that, in some cases, young people's knowledge of the conflict and peace process was limited. The ETI (2018) report suggested that some partnerships still needed time to strengthen relationships and develop trust between schools, before they were able to tackle the more controversial themes in shared classrooms.

7 Conclusions

This chapter has provided an outline of how schools in Northern Ireland approach history and citizenship education. The literature that has been reviewed helps demonstrate clear linkages between both subjects, in terms of the way in which they both use a similar pedagogical approach, which is enquiry-based, and values multiperspectivity. Both subjects help students understand more about the contemporary society, in which they live.

The literature reviewed earlier in the chapter highlights that there are themes in each subject that may pose challenges for teachers, especially those themes that relate to conflict, nationality and reconciliation. Shared Education offers an innovative way in which citizenship and history can be taught, in that students, from different cultural backgrounds, are able to learn together in each other's classrooms. While this approach is innovative and indeed valorous, it is not without challenge. This is because schools have opted to explore themes that risk discord, and students, and even teachers, from different communities, examine themes and narratives together, over which they might disagree.

However, there also appears to be widespread recognition on the part of our schools that although there are elements of these subjects that are difficult to teach, they are, nonetheless, important as Northern Ireland emerges from conflict. Therefore, they should not be avoided. Schools have emerged as the pioneers of this approach and we are beginning to see evidence of a systemic shift in the way that we examine our past and sense of identity.

A key learning point from this chapter is that it is important that we continue to support and applaud schools that are involved in shared education. Furthermore, we should invest in teachers of history and citizenship, in terms of providing both initial and continuous professional development training. We should also continue to consult them and listen to what they need. It is important that we continue to support school partnerships going forward, as it is likely that strong partnerships will be better able to support their teachers, making it more comfortable for them to tackle challenging issues together.

References

Abrams, F. (2020). Is the curriculum dividing Northern Ireland's schools along Troubles lines? *The Guardian.* https://www.theguardian.com/education/2020/jul/14/is-the-curriculum-dividing-northern-irelands-schools-along-troubles-lines

Arlow, M. (2004). Citizenship education in a divided society: The case of Northern Ireland. In S. Tawil & A. Harley (Eds.), *Education, conflict and social cohesion* (pp. 255–313). International Bureau of Education.

Barton, K. C. (2001). "You'd be wanting to know about the past": Social contexts of children's historical understanding in Northern Ireland and the USA. *Comparative Education*, 37(1), 89–106.

Barton, K. C. (2005). "Best not to forget them": Secondary students' judgments of historical significance in Northern Ireland. *Theory & Research in Social Education*, 33(1), 9–44.

Barton, K. C., & McCully, A. W. (2005). History, identity, and the school curriculum in Northern Ireland: An empirical study of secondary students' ideas and perspectives. *Journal of Curriculum Studies*, 37(1), 85–116.

Barton, K. C., & McCully, A. W. (2007). Teaching controversial issues ... where controversial issues really matter. *Teaching History, 127*, 13–19.

Barton, K. C., & McCully, A. W. (2010). "You can form your own point of view": Internally persuasive discourse in Northern Ireland students' encounters with history. *Teachers College Record, 112*(1), 142–181.

Conway, M. M. K. (2010). *An exploration of sensitive issues in history teaching at secondary school level in England and Northern Ireland, 1991–2001* [Unpublished doctoral dissertation]. Institute of Education, University of London.

Council for the Curriculum, Examinations and Assessment (CCEA). (2017a). *GCSE history specifications*. https://ccea.org.uk/downloads/docs/Specifications/GCSE/GCSE%20History%20%282017%29/GCSE%20History%20%282017%29-specification-Standard.pdf

Council for the Curriculum, Examinations and Assessment (CCEA). (2017b). *CCEA GCSE specification in learning for life and work*. https://ccea.org.uk/downloads/docs/Specifications/GCSE/GCSE%20Learning%20for%20Life%20and%20Work%20%282017%29/GCSE%20Learning%20for%20Life%20and%20Work%20%282017%29-specification-Standard.pdf

Council for the Curriculum, Examinations and Assessment (CCEA). (2019a). *GCSE history Chief Examiner's report*. https://ccea.org.uk/downloads/docs/ExamMod-Reports/GCSE/GCSE%20History%20%282017%29/2019/GCSE%20History%20%282017%29-Summer2019-Report.pdf

Council for the Curriculum, Examinations and Assessment (CCEA). (2019b). *GCE history specification*. https://ccea.org.uk/downloads/docs/Specifications/GCE/GCE%20History%20%282019%29/GCE%20History%20%282019%29-specification-Standard.pdf

Council for the Curriculum, Examinations and Assessment (CCEA). (2019c). *GCE history Chief Examiner's report*. https://ccea.org.uk/downloads/docs/ExamMod-Reports/GCE/GCE%20History%20%282019%29/2019/GCE%20History%20%282019%29-Summer2019-Report.pdf

Council for the Curriculum, Examinations and Assessment (CCEA). (2020). *Environment and society: History key stage 3*. https://ccea.org.uk/key-stage-3/curriculum/environment-society/history

Department of Education (DE). (2018). *Advancing shared education: Report to the Northern Ireland Assembly*.

De Souza, E. (2020). Three different versions of our shared history being taught on the island. *The Irish Times*. https://www.irishtimes.com/opinion/three-different-versions-of-our-shared-history-being-taught-on-the-island-1.4426815

Duffy, G., & Gallagher, T. (2017). Shared Education in contested spaces: How collaborative networks improve communities and schools. *Journal of Educational Change, 18*(1), 107–134.

Education and Training Inspectorate. (2018). *The shared education signature project evaluation report.*

Education Authority (EA). (2020a). *DSC: Shared education signature project.* OBA report card: Section 1(June 2020).

Education Authority (EA). (2020b). *DSC: Shared education signature project.* OBA report card: Section 2 and 3 (June 2020).

Gallagher, A. (2017). Addressing conflict and tolerance through the curriculum. In M. Bellino & J. Williams (Eds.), *(Re)constructing memory: School textbooks, identity, and the pedagogies and politics of imagining community* (Vol. III, pp. 191–208). Sense Publishers.

Gallagher, E. (2007). Racism and citizenship education in Northern Ireland. *Irish Educational Studies, 26*(3), 253–269.

Gallagher, T. (2004). *Education in divided societies.* Palgrave/MacMillan.

Gallagher, T. (2016). Shared education in Northern Ireland: School collaboration in divided societies. *Oxford Review of Education, 42*(3), 362–375.

Gallagher, T., & Duffy, G. (2016). Recognising difference while promoting cohesion: The role of collaborative networks in education. In I. Honohan & N. Rougier (Eds.), *Tolerance and diversity in Ireland, North and South.* Manchester University Press.

Kitson, A. (2007). History education and reconciliation in Northern Ireland. In E. A. Cole (Ed.), *Teaching the violent past: History education and reconciliation.* Rowman and Littlefield.

Kymlicka, W. (2011). Multicultural citizenship within multination states. *Ethnicities, 11*(3), 281–302.

Lee, P., & Shemilt, D. (2007). New alchemy or fatal attraction? History and citizenship. *Teaching History, 129,* 14.

Leonard, M. (2007). Children's citizenship education in politically sensitive societies. *Childhood, 14*(4), 487–503.

Magee, J. (1970). The teaching of Irish history in Irish Schools. *The Northern Teacher, 10*(1), 15–21.

McCombe, J. A. (2006). *School history and the introduction of local and global citizenship into the Northern Ireland curriculum: The views of history teachers* [Unpublished doctoral dissertation]. University of Ulster.

McCully, A. (2007). *Recent research on teaching history in Northern Ireland: Informing curriculum change.* UNESCO Centre, Ulster University.

McCully, A. (2012). History teaching, conflict and the legacy of the past. *Education, Citizenship and Social Justice, 7*(2), 145–159.

McCully, A. (2017). Teaching history and educating for citizenship: Allies or 'uneasy bedfellows' in a post-conflict context? In T. Epstein & C. Peck (Eds.), *Teaching and learning difficult histories in international contexts: A critical sociocultural approach* (pp. 160–174). Routledge.

McCully, A., & Emerson, L. (2014). Teaching controversial issues in Northern Ireland. In T. T. Misco & J. de Groof (Eds.), *Cross-cultural case studies of teaching controversial issues: Pathways and challenges to democratic citizenship education*. Wolf Legal Publishers.

McCully, A., & Waldron, F. (2013). A question of identity? Purpose, policy and practice in the teaching of history in Northern Ireland and the Republic of Ireland. *History Education Research Journal, 11*(2), 145–158.

McEvoy, L. (2007). Beneath the rhetoric: Policy approximation and citizenship education in Northern Ireland. *Education, Citizenship and Social Justice, 2*(2), 135–157.

McGuinness, S. J. (2012). Education policy in Northern Ireland: A review. *Italian Journal of Sociology of Education, 4*(1).

McMurray, A., & Niens, U. (2012). Building bridging social capital in a divided society: The role of participatory citizenship education. *Education, Citizenship and Social Justice, 7*(2), 207–221.

Meredith, R. (2020). *GCSE history: NI teachers reject criticism of lessons*. BBC. https://www.bbc.co.uk/news/uk-northern-ireland-53436275

Niens, U., & Chastenay, M. H. (2008). Educating for peace? Citizenship education in Quebec and Northern Ireland. *Comparative Education Review, 52*(4), 519–540.

Niens, U., & McIlrath, L. (2010). Understandings of citizenship education in Northern Ireland and the Republic of Ireland: Public discourses among stakeholders in the public and private sectors. *Education, Citizenship and Social Justice, 5*(1), 73–87.

Niens, U., & O'Connor, U. (2006). *Local and global citizenship at key stage 3: Preliminary evaluation findings*. CCEA.

Niens, U., O'Connor, U., & Smith, A. (2009). *Evaluation of the pilot introduction of education for local and global citizenship into the revised Northern Ireland curriculum*. University of Ulster.

Niens, U., O'Connor, U., & Smith, A. (2013). Citizenship education in divided societies: Teachers' perspectives in Northern Ireland. *Citizenship Studies, 17*(1), 128–141.

Osler, A., & Starkey, H. (2003). Learning for cosmopolitan citizenship: Theoretical debates and young people's experiences. *Educational Review, 55*(3), 243–254.

Quaynor, L. J. (2012). Citizenship education in post-conflict contexts: A review of the literature. *Education, Citizenship and Social Justice, 7*(1), 33–57.

Reilly, J., & Niens, U. (2014). Global citizenship as education for peacebuilding in a divided society: Structural and contextual constraints on the development of critical dialogic discourse in schools. *Compare: A Journal of Comparative and International Education, 44*(1), 53–76.

Richardson, N. (2011). *Education for diversity and mutual understanding: The experience of Northern Ireland* (Vol. 1). Peter Lang.

Smith, A. (2003). Citizenship education in Northern Ireland: Beyond national identity? *Cambridge Journal of education, 33*(1), 15–32.

Smith, M. E. (2005). *Reckoning with the past: Teaching history in Northern Ireland*. Lexington Books.

Terra, L. (2014). New histories for a new state: A study of history textbook content in Northern Ireland. *Journal of Curriculum Studies*, 46(2), 225–248.

The Belfast Agreement. (1998, April). HMSO.

The Education Reform (Northern Ireland) Order. (1989). http://www.legislation.gov.uk/nisi/1989/2406

Waldron, F., & McCully, A. (2016). Republic of Ireland and Northern Ireland: Eroded certainties and new possibilities. In R. Guyver (Ed.), *Teaching history and the changing nation state: Transnational and international perspectives* (pp. 53–73). Bloomsbury Academic.

Wrenn, A. (1999). Build it in, don't bolt it on: History's opportunity to support critical citizenship. *Teaching History, 96*, 6.

CHAPTER 17

Successful Failure: A Dual Narrative Approach to History Education

An Israeli Palestinian Project

Eyal Naveh

1   Introduction

History education aims to disseminate information about the past in order to create historical knowledge and, by doing so, construct historical literacy and historical consciousness in a given society. By a deliberate selection of past events, government officials in modern nation-states create and distribute to the public an approved and agreed upon narrative. This narrative appears in various circles, such as the official school system, non-formal education, youth movements, museums, films, websites, memorials sites, etc. It seems that history education operates as an essential tool of identity building through constructing collective memory in various public spheres, even more than by studying the discipline of academic history (Apple, 2003; Carretero, Berger & Grever, 2017; Stearns, Seixas & Wineburg, 2000).

2   The Challenge of Post-Conflict History Education

Since the 19th century, while becoming an academic discipline, the study of history served as an ideological cornerstone of the construction of nation-state identity (Berger & Conrad, 2015). In most modern nation-states, history became an essential part of the school curriculum, thereby forming the historical narrative of a given country. Such a historical narrative aimed to provide an inspiring common denominator between the members of a given nation through discovering (or inventing) a generational chain. This served as a way to connect the national past, the national present and, eventually, the national future. Based on the official school curriculum, history textbooks, in most countries, provided one single narrative, which aimed to inculcate a national, glorious heritage in the future generation, and by doing so, imbue them with pride, as well as loyalty and legitimacy toward their country (Carretero, Asensio & RodríguezMoneo, 2013; Wilschut, 2010).

In conflict zones, the rival sectors usually create a narrative, which nurtures and fuels the conflict. They develop a "double V" paradigm, portraying the in-group as Victorious Victims and the out-group as Vanquished Villains. Sometimes, the narrative emphasizes events of a painful past that ultimately culminated in the victorious present. In other cases, it stresses an ongoing struggle, full of suffering and sacrifice that eventually will turn the dark present into a bright future, while depicting present-day victims as the heralders of forthcoming victory (Ahonen, 2014; Foster & Crawford, 2006).

In the immediate aftermath of the First World War, many historians and educators criticized and condemned the national patriotic narratives, which contributed to the war spirit. The League of Nations even invited historians from rival countries to reform their history textbooks, an attempt that ended without results (Elmersjö, 2014; Wilschut, 2010). Only after the end of the Second World War, and particularly after the end of the Cold War, when many conflicts subsided and ended, historians and educators in various countries engaged in numerous attempts to revise and reform national history education. Looking at the new post-conflict environment as desirable, and yet still fragile, history educators tried to develop a mode of history education that would eventually disarm the previous "double V" paradigm, thus turning the enemy of yesterday into a partner of today and tomorrow. They strove to re-construct the historical narrative of the contested past, which ultimately would strengthen and stabilize the post-conflict new reality of the present. This would, then, be able to pave the way for an enduring and peaceful, reconciled future (Epstein & Peck, 2017; Korostelina & Lässig, 2013; Pingel, 2010). In order to accomplish such a reform, most experts advocated and supported a multi-perspective approach. Thus, taking a multi-dimensional perspective and engaging in critical thinking became the principle guidelines for many projects in the field of history education in Europe and beyond (Elmersjö, Clark & Vinterek, 2017; Epstein & Peck, 2017).

The most successful model was the French-German joint project, which, in 2006–2007, produced joint history textbooks designed for high school pupils in both countries. Although the distribution of this textbook is still very limited, the very presence of these textbooks appeared as a great achievement (Defrance & Pfeil, 2013). Other attempts, such as the German-Polish history reform project, is still a work in progress (Lässig & Strobel, 2013). Similar projects took place during the early 2000s in East Asia between China, Japan, and South Korea; in the former Yugoslav Balkan states; in the Baltic States; in Northern Ireland; in South Africa; and in Cyprus and other conflict or post-conflict zones (Korostelina & Lässig, 2013; Stojanovi, 2008; Terra, 2013; Wang, 2009).

This essay will discuss a specific project of re-writing a history textbook by Israeli and Palestinian teachers and academics that took place during the first decade of the 21st century. The initiative, which followed the Oslo Accords of 1993, emerged within the abovementioned context of reviewing and re-writing history textbooks in regions that were attempting to move from violent conflicts to post-conflict co-existence.

3   Israel and Palestine: From the Illusion of Post-Conflict to the Reality of Intractable Conflict

History education appeared as an obstacle to attempts for attaining a culture of peace building in the Israeli-Palestinian enduring conflict. Israeli government officials have often argued that Palestinian history textbooks serve as instruments of incitement by de-legitimating the very existence of Israel as a sovereign state for the Jews (Vorgan, 2010). On the other hand, some independent researchers, in and outside Israel, raised criticism concerning Israeli textbooks, which view Arabs and Palestinians as a problem, ignoring their claims for self-determination and statehood (Peled-Elhanan, 2013; Pingel, 2003; Podeh, 2002; Raz-Krakotzkin, 2001). As a result, following the Oslo Accords, there was a need to work on a project of reforming textbooks on both sides.

Experts in the region, and beyond, discussed and initiated the ideas of such a project in the hopeful days of the Oslo Accords, when people anticipated that the two societies were going to establish a new future, based on mutual recognition and peaceful coexistence. PRIME – The Peace Research Institute in the Middle East, a non-governmental organization (NGO), based in Bet-Jala, received funds from the "Wye River" agreement of 1998, that supported projects that aimed to enhance activities that would contribute to peace. The institute, co-chaired by two professors – one Palestinian and one Israeli – decided to face the difficult task of history education and to write a new history textbook on the Arab-Israeli conflict.

When Johan Rauch, the President of Germany visited the area, he met with PRIME officials and promised European support, while introducing the successful German-French project as a guideline and model for such a project. In early 2000, a steering committee was formed and decided to carry out the task, hoping to write a unique history textbook for both sides that would incorporate both narratives into one and all-inclusive narrative, free of incitement and de-legitimation of the other.

Unfortunately, those hopes were premature. Peacebuilding initiatives that followed the Oslo Accords ran into difficulties from the beginning. During the late 1990s, they deteriorated while resumption of violent hostilities between the sides increased. Hence, from the beginning, the initiative of writing a joint textbook took place in an unreceptive, conflict environment, rather than in a post-conflict reality.

Nevertheless, despite the hostile atmosphere, two teams of history teachers were formed, one Israeli and one Palestinian. Each team included six high school teachers and was headed by a history professor. When the first meeting took place in early 2001, the Oslo Accords had totally collapsed and the atmosphere between the two nations deteriorated into violence and aggression. The dual narrative approach that the group finally developed, emerged as a default – a partial solution that enabled continuing the project and ultimately to complete the textbook.

4   The Process

Being the historian who mentored the Israeli teachers in this project, I will briefly discuss and explore the various stages of the process and reflect upon its outcome. I view the process as a "successful failure" and as a first step, however controversial, of paving the way toward acknowledgement of the other in an intractable, enduring conflict situation.

Most meetings took place in East Jerusalem and Beth Jala, in Palestinian territory under Israeli sovereignty. Therefore, the very act of meeting was difficult because of control of and access to territory. Each of the meetings required logistic operations and some of them were cancelled at the last moment. The meetings that took place convened frequently without the full participation of all members of the teams.

The participants started with a pilot project of dealing with three historical contested events: The Balfour Declaration, the War of 1948, and the first Intifada. Two teachers from each nationality were assigned to write the history of the events, according to the way they taught it in their schools, with the help of a professional historian. First, each national group worked separately and created its narrative in its own language. Upon completion, the group translated its draft to the language of the other and the teachers assembled, according to the topics. For example, two Israeli and two Palestinians, who wrote about 1948, worked together as a binational, 1948 working group.

After the mutual exchange of the drafts, these binational groups, following the initial shocks of reading the other's narrative, started a dialogue and debate about their topic. During that delicate antagonistic encounter with the narrative of the other, the group developed certain rules for engaging in discussions that would lead to the final version. The essential rule, which, in principle, all participants agreed to follow, forbade each group from imposing its version on the other group. The members could argue, make suggestions for change, voice their resentment and reservations, try to convince the other to change focus, revise the tone, alter the interpretation and use different terminology, more acceptable to the other. However, neither group could force the other group to change its narrative.

The second rule, defined as "no incitement," was difficult to implement. Often one side perceived as incitement something that the other side insisted on emphasizing. The boundaries between legitimate critical description or interpretation of the other, and incitement that insults and delegitimizes the other, were very hard to draw. Therefore, this entire stage of moving from the first draft to the final one took a long time. Overall, the bi-national discussions, which occasionally included observers from other countries, who also served as mediators, affected the final draft by tempering the hostile tone, and largely reducing the assaults.

When both groups finally finished their mutual reviews, each of them revised its narrative and sent the final version for translation and printing. The three topics appeared as chapters in booklets, printed in Hebrew, Arabic and English. Each page in the booklet presented the Israeli narrative on one side and the Palestinian narrative on the other. A blank space in the middle of each page visually separated the two narratives, thus indicating symbolically that the narratives remained parallel narratives, unable to merge into one integrative, multidimensional piece. From a pedagogical perspective, the empty space invited creative teachers and curious students to fill it with comments, questions and learning devices, thus, stimulating critical thinking and scholarly reflection as part of a meaningful learning experience of both narratives.

5 Success and International Praise

Distributing the English version of the booklet worldwide among students, history educators, academic historians, officials in the ministries of education, journalists, experts on public history and many other interested parties instantly received widespread applause and approval. The book was translated into French, Spanish, and Italian. Other languages followed, and so the book was disseminated to larger audiences. The initiators of the project were awarded six international peace prizes. Numerous academic, educational and political institutions invited project members to international conferences, as panelists, keynote speakers and workshop leaders, to share their experience with others. The entire venture received extensive global media attention, not only in the US and Europe, but in countries like Morocco, South Africa, Qatar,

Taiwan, Macedonia, Georgia, Cyprus and other conflict or post-conflict zones, as well. Consequently, the startling success of the booklet enabled PRIME to apply and ultimately to receive a generous grant from the European Union. This grant was used to expand the pilot into a full, two-narrative, history textbook. Upon completion of the book, the grant required implementation of the material in the classes of the teachers who participated in the project, in both Israel and Palestine.

The EU grant allowed for the expansion of the teams. Both sides incorporated more teachers and experts in the project. The group decided to turn the pilot into a complete textbook that would describe the history of Israel and Palestine from the rise of Zionism at the end of the 19th century until the end of the 20th century when peace attempts between both sides turned into renewed violence.

For a few years, the group continued to work, trying to overcome many obstacles that resulted from the enduring conflict and lack of peace initiatives in the area. Since the situation outside the program hindered the progress of the endeavor, with the help of international NGOs, most of the work took place outside the area. The team spent summer workshops abroad, once in Istanbul, Turkey and participated in three consecutive summer seminars, at the George Eckert Institute for textbook research in Braunschweig, Germany.

In this unstable context, difficulties in the process emerged frequently. Above all, the disparity and asymmetry between the Israeli and Palestinian members of the team surfaced on various levels when working together. One notable gap related to academic knowledge of the discipline of history. The level of critical historical research and professional knowledge in Israeli universities, teachers' colleges and other academic institutions is much more advanced than it is in Palestine. This difference was reflected in the content, tone and structure of the teachers' narratives, as well. While the Israelis integrated reflection and self-criticism in their narratives, the Palestinians were not accustomed to doing so. Therefore, they adhered to a one-sided ideological narrative, in which they were the ultimate victim and the Israelis were the ultimate villain.

In the political realm, the asymmetry was even more apparent. Israel is a sovereign state that controls most of the Palestinian territories and Palestine has the status of an Authority, operating under Israeli occupation. Unlike France and Germany, which are two sovereign states living in peace under the umbrella of the European Union, who looked back in order to understand their contested past, Israel and Palestine are still in the middle of a violent conflict which touches everyone's life in both countries. The past conflict is far from ending and rather has been increasing, with no signs of waning in the future.

On the one hand, the Palestinians suffer under Israeli occupation that controls their lives and denies them national self-determination and basic human needs. On the other hand, Israel, which is not under occupation, is suffering (to a lesser degree) from violent attacks against its population. This kind of political relationship between the Israeli group – who represented (even unintentionally) a sovereign state, and the Palestinian group – who represented people under Israeli occupation – affected the process and the outcome of the textbook.

Despite their inherent disparity, which sometimes made the positive encounter between the groups difficult, both sides continued to work. With the help of many international mediators, they completed the project. In November 2009, the Hebrew and Arabic versions of the textbook were published by PRIME, under the title, *Learning the Historical Narratives of the Other*. In 2012, New Press published the English version with a different title: *Side-by-Side*. The English version also omitted the empty space between the two narratives. This decision overlooked the pedagogical and symbolic meaning of the empty space. The German version, which appeared in 2015, kept the empty space and the original title of the book. Some colleges in the US, England and Canada have used the English version in courses about the Arab Israeli conflict. Many institutions of history education familiarized themselves with the English and German version of the book. The project ended successfully, because it received funds and benefitted from international support and professional endorsement. However, the goal of writing the two narratives, according to the same professional standards, ran into difficulties and failed to materialize, most of the time.

6 Text Samples of Standards' Asymmetry

The nine chapters of the book focused on the same subjects and organized them according to a chronological structure. However, the visual display, the use of terminology, the tone of the discourse, as well as a few concrete contested issues, varied significantly between the two narratives. The following examples are among the most noticeable ones.

Visually, most of the Palestinian pictures in the textbook expressed sorrow and suffering, while most of the Israeli pictures highlighted progress and achievements. The different choice of pictures caused unbalanced outcomes that sometimes required reconsidering the group's selection. For example, asking to choose the most significant picture for the back cover of the book, the Israelis picked a crowd of jubilant Jews reacting to the UN resolution to establish a Jewish state with smiles, while dancing in the streets and waving flags. The Palestinians put a painful picture of a refugee convoy leaving their homes. Placing the pictures side by side created the impression that grief and misery of the Palestinian people caused joy for the Jewish people. Therefore, in order to reduce the insult, as much as possible, the Israeli team decided to replace their picture with the photograph showing David Ben-Gurion announcing the Declaration of Independence.

Another case of visual representation that ended with revision dealt with the Israeli and Palestinian flags. Originally, the team decided to put an Israeli flag at the top of the Israeli narrative, on the left side of each page, and a Palestinian flag at the top of the Palestinian narrative, on the right side of each page. When the Palestinians saw the first draft, which had the flag they see in their daily lives at checkpoints, military bases, prisons, settlements and other occupation sites, they expressed anger and resentment. Conversely, the Israelis, perhaps because they perceived themselves as the stronger side, did not mind seeing the flag of their defeated enemy on each page. This imbalanced reaction to the flags ended with the decision to delete both flags from the top of each narrative and to replace them with headers: "Israeli Text" on one side and "Palestinian Text" on the other.

Terminology appeared to be one of the most complicated elements to overcome, and the discussions between the groups only partly help to bridge the differences. The Israelis, for example, used the term, "The Arabs of the Land of Israel," when they referred to the non-Jewish population that inhabited the land prior to the creation of the State of Israel. Palestinians were offended by this term and after several meetings, the Israelis changed the term to "Palestinians," when defining the non-Jewish residents of the land. Another dispute emerged when the Palestinians characterized the entire territory as Palestine, and when they mentioned Israel, they used terms such as "the Zionist Entity" or "so-called Israel." The Israelis expressed reservations about such definitions and persuaded the Palestinians to change them, claiming that both sides should acknowledge in their vocabulary the very existence of the other.

Sometimes the request of one side to the other to change its language or tone of the narrative was denied. For example, when summarizing the significance of the Balfour Declaration, the Palestinians insisted using a phrase that the Israeli team did not accept:

> This unholy relationship between British colonialism and colonialist Zionist movement ... whereby Britain granted a land it did not possess (Palestine) to a group who did not own it (the Zionists) at the expense of those who possessed and had the right to it. (Adwan et al., 2012, p. 11)

While the Israelis tried to convince the Palestinians to tone down this summary, they failed.

There were cases when only one side complied with the request of the other, while the other side refused. For example, when dealing with the events of 1948, each side portrayed the military forces of its enemy in similar, negative terms. Palestinians called the Israeli fighters for independence "the Jewish gangs" and the Israelis termed the Palestinian fighters, "the Arab gangs." One of the international mediators asked both sides whether they could avoid altogether the term "gangs." Nevertheless, only the Israelis complied and replaced "gangs" with "military forces" in the final version. The Palestinians refused the suggestion; therefore, in their version, the Israeli forces appeared as gangs (Adwan et al., 2012, p. 115). This different reaction demonstrated the disparity between the two teams. The stronger side, while describing a historical victory, was generous enough to call the defeated enemy in non-offensive terms, while the vanquished side needed the offensive term to label the enemy as an evil criminal that inflicted suffering on innocent victims.

When writing about recent historical events, such as the violence of the 1990s that followed the breakdown of the Oslo Accords, both sides felt that they were the innocent victims. Consequently, they each described the other's activity as "an act of terror" (Adwan et al., 2012, pp. 314, 315). When the same mediator suggested omitting the term "terror" and to describe the violent acts in concrete/descriptive terms – Palestinian suicide bombers that killed civilians in Israel, or Israeli air force attacks that killed civilians in Palestine – both parties rejected the suggestion. It seems that in cases in which there were no clear-cut results of victory and defeat, both sides were reluctant to utilize neutral or conciliatory terminology to depict tragic historical events.

Specific issues, such as the nature of Zionism, the Holocaust, the Palestinian refugees, or massacres that one side inflicted on the other, were portrayed differently, of course. The Israeli group portrayed the Zionist movement as an authentic Jewish national movement that emerged out of a need to end Jewish suffering in the Diaspora. The Palestinians, however, described Zionism as a form of European colonialism. Neither side could convince the other side to incorporate both aspects of the Zionist movement into the texts. Both sides argued that when students would read these two different narratives, they would have to face the difficulties of dealing with opposing definitions. The participants hoped, nevertheless, that with the help of the teachers, the students would realize the difference and acknowledge the difficulties reaching reconciliation on this particular issue.

The Israeli narrative portrayed the Holocaust as a catastrophe that validated, to a certain extent, the Zionist position that Jews needed their own homeland to secure their collective existence. Palestinians, on the other hand, completely ignored the topic in their early draft. When asked by the Israelis and the European mediators to relate to this tragedy in their final version, they agreed. Finally, the Palestinian narrative briefly mentioned the Holocaust and expressed deep sorrow for the Jewish fate in the Holocaust. Nevertheless, they asserted that they – the Palestinians – had not committed this crime against the Jews. In their narrative, the Palestinians argued that they had been the people who paid the price for this genocide. Both sides dealt with the issue in a sensitive way. In contrast to politicians, who often utilize this topic to denounce the other, the teachers refrained from using the term "racist" when describing the other, and avoided comparison with Holocaust victims when they emphasized their own troubles.

The Palestinian refugee problem appeared in the Israeli narrative as a tragic, but unavoidable outcome of the war that resulted from the refusal of Palestinian leaders to accept the partition plan, which would have divided the country into two states. It was derived from the voluntary evacuation of Arab population, as well as from the forced expulsion of the Palestinians, in specific localities. In the Palestinian narrative, the refugee problem resulted directly from an Israeli intentional and pre-planned transfer policy, which aimed to clear the land of its indigenous population. The Palestinian teachers insisted that the Israeli forces carried out this policy during the war and even afterwards. They refused to look critically at the role of their leaders in this tragedy. The Israelis acknowledged that their forces indeed expelled many people when they won a battle in a war of defense, having to choose between "fight or flight."

The Israelis told stories of massacre of Jews in place, such as Hebron and Jerusalem, and the Palestinians emphasized many massacres, such as massacres that took place in Dir Yassin and Kfar Kassem. In the discussion, the groups agreed to mitigate the tone and to avoid, as much as possible, graphic descriptions of horrors. Nevertheless, neither side fully kept to this decision.

Overall, each side presented itself in the historical events as an innocent victim. However, the tone of victimization is more noticeable in the Palestinian narrative for the obvious reason: they are still the losing side, without a state and living under occupation. In the text, the Israeli tone is much less victim-oriented because they are strong and secure enough to look at their past from other angles than sheer victimization. In many cases, the Israeli narrative introduced some critical interpretation of its own historical narrative, based on the findings of a new generation of historians that have looked critically at various past events. The Palestinian side has not developed in this way, and its narrative is rarely self-critical. The different tone of victimization in the text clearly reflects the imbalance in the asymmetrical power relations between the sides.

7   Failure and Local Rejection

Despite the worldwide distribution, the book failed to be adopted by the Israeli and Palestinian school systems. In the initial stages of the project, the Israeli teachers used the chapter that they had written in their classroom. They received unofficial permission from their principals to use the material in extracurricular activities. Overall, the results were encouraging: in general, students liked the two-narrative approach and many of them appreciated the fact that, for the first time, they read the story of the other side. Some of them mentioned that they became more empathic and tolerant toward the Palestinians. Others argued that they understood better the other's point of view, but did not change their basic opinions. Some were unhappy with the imbalanced historical approach, stressing that while the Israeli side is informative, analytical and open to the complexity of historical events, the Palestinian side is emotional, one-sided and overemphasizes victimization.

In Israel, the project had no official approval and, in fact, contradicted the perspective of the Ministry of Education. Therefore, in order to avoid objections from the authorities, the implementation process kept a 'low profile.' However, an independent journalist heard about the textbook and published a favorable article in a local journal. Consequently, the officials at the Ministry of Education reacted, and forbade use of the material in any class. They even published a written warning to the teachers and their principals that their jobs would be at risk if they continued to use the book. The history education supervisor invited the teachers, who had participated in the project, to his office and told them not to use any chapter from the booklet at school. He clarified that in order to use any text in classroom, the teachers needed to receive official approval, which the ministry never granted (Naveh, 2017).

Following this official Israeli ban, the project continued without the ability to examine its impact. The ministry denied all further requests to use the book, with a bureaucratic answer that the material in the textbook contradicted the official history curriculum. Some professionals in the ministry argued that both narratives portrayed a pro-Palestinian and anti-Israeli historical picture. Others claimed that exposing Israeli adolescents to the hostile narrative of their enemy, by simultaneously learning both narratives, would lessen the students' patriotic feeling and weaken their commitment to fight for their country. A few experts of education stated that such a project was more appropriate for the university level, but was very dangerous for the development of high school students, who had not yet formed their identity, and knew nothing about their own national history.

Following the publication of the book, one school decided, after receiving full consent of the pupils and their parents, to introduce some of the chapters to a group of 15 students that had already finished their formal study of history, in an extra-curricular activity. Even in that case, the ministry reacted by calling the principal to an official hearing and ordered him to stop the experiment. In the public debate that followed, the Minister of Education, while presenting the book publicly before the Knesset, declared that he would never allow such an abomination to enter Israeli classrooms (Naveh, 2017).

On the Palestinian side, most teachers could not use the material in their schools because the principals refused to allow them to do so. Two teachers took a group of students to their homes and taught them the material on a voluntary basis. The results were mixed: some students questioned whether they should learn the narrative of the enemy and occupier. Others were curious to participate in the experiment. They expressed hostile feelings toward symbols and images more than toward the content of the material. There were no further attempts to implement the narratives in any other Palestinian institution. The Palestinian head of the project received threatening letters that warned him to stop the collaboration with Israelis and accused him of "normalization" with the Israelis. Therefore, the Palestinian participants of the project preferred not to publicize their activities at all.

The hostile reaction appeared on both sides, but differed in content, style and mode of justification. In Israel, the official rejection opened a public debate and finally tended to apply legal and bureaucratic excuses to justify the ban. In Palestine, threats, unofficial pressure and silencing led to self-censorship of the participants, who continued to work secretly. Therefore, despite the official prohibition, many Israeli NGOs expressed high interest in the project and welcomed the approach. Institutions of higher education, teachers' training colleges, and research centers throughout the country familiarized themselves with the book and implemented the two-narrative approach in curious audiences. Nothing similar happened in the Palestinian Authority. Due to the inability to implement the project, no solid research could explore its impact on students in both societies. Consequently, the European Union rejected any further financial support for the project, because it did not meet the condition of implementation.

8   Conclusions

Real reconciliation between former enemies requires a three-stage mechanism of mutual acknowledgment: acquaintance, recognition, and dialogue. In the field of history education, *acquaintance* means that each side views its own narrative as truth and the narrative of the other as false, with the overall aim to know the other narrative, but never to accept it. In the case described here, each side approached its past as the correct reality, while looking at the past of the other as an erroneous myth. *Recognition* means that each side starts to perceive some elements of truth in the narrative of the other. Recognizing truthful past events in both narratives, each side slowly admits that the historical narrative of the other side can provide a basis for mutual discussion, and even empathy. *Dialogue* usually develops when the issue of historical true decreases in its importance for both sides. The sides become secure enough to acknowledge that their own historical narrative is a human construction of truths and fallacies, facts and myths, research-proved evidence and imagined storytelling. Such an attitude provides both sides with the ability to critically reflect upon their past, rather than being a captive of their past. This critical attitude toward the past builds the bridge for reconciliation and re-humanization of the other (Bar-Tal & Rosen, 2009; Psaltis, Carretero & Čehajić-Clancy, 2017).

The project described in this chapter achieved only the first stage. Acquaintance seems to be the first necessary step of future reconciliation between past and present enemies. As seen in the content of the textbook, presenting both narratives side by side served the purpose of initial acquaintance, but nothing further than that. However, in the context of the Israeli-Palestinian conflict, such achievement is, in and of itself, a significant success, which received wide professional and international approval. However, within the political context of a violent, ongoing conflict, even acquaintance seems dangerous for officials and leaders who prefer to maintain the conflict, over looking for ways of reconciliation.

Ten years after its publication, the book has had a significant impact in professional circles and the media. Nevertheless, the declared goal to use it as a history textbook in the classroom failed. In the midst of an intractable conflict, both sides rejected any attempt to challenge the historical consciousness of their younger generation by encouraging re-humanization of the enemy. Therefore, the role of NGOs to promote reconciliation in an ongoing conflict was shown to be necessary and crucial.

References

Adwan, S., Bar-On, D., & Naveh, E. (2012). *Side-by-side – Parallel histories of Israel-Palestine*. New Press.

Ahonen, S. (2014). History education in post-conflict societies. *Historical Encounters: A Journal of Historical Consciousness, Historical Cultures, and History Education*, *1*(1), 75–87.

Apple, W. (2003). *The state and the politics of knowledge*. Taylor & Francis.
Bar-Tal, D., & Rosen, Y. (2009). Peace education in societies involved in intractable conflicts: Direct and indirect models. *Review of Educational Research, 79*(2), 557–575.
Basingstoke.Carretero, M., Asensio, M., & RodríguezMoneo, M. (Eds.). (2013). *History education and the construction of national identities*. Information Age Publications.
Berger, S., & Conrad, C. (2015). *The past as history: National identity and historical consciousness in modern Europe*. Palgrave Macmillan UK.
Carretero, M., Berger, S., & Grever, M. (Eds.). (2017). *Palgrave handbook of research in historical culture and education*. Palgrave Macmillan.
Defrance, C., & Pfeil, U. (2013). Symbol or reality? The background, implementation and development of the Franco-German history textbook. In K. Korostelina & S. Lässig (Eds.), *History education and post-conflict reconciliation* (pp. 52–68). Routledge.
Elmersjö, H. A. (2014). History beyond borders: Peace education, history textbook revision, and the internationalization of history teaching in the twentieth century. *Historical Encounters: A Journal of Historical Consciousness, Historical Cultures, and History Education, 1*(1), 62–74.
Elmersjö, H. Å., Clark, A., & Vinterek, M. (2017). *International perspectives on teaching rival histories: Pedagogical responses to contested narratives and the history wars*. Palgrave Macmillan.
Epstein, T., & Peck, C. L. (Eds.). (2017). *Teaching and learning difficult histories in international contexts: A critical sociocultural approach*. Routledge.
Foster, S. J., & Crawford, K. A. (Eds.). (2006). *What shall we tell the children? International perspectives on school history textbooks*. IAP.
Korostelina, K. V., & Lässig, S. (Eds.). (2013). *History education and post-conflict reconciliation: Reconsidering joint textbook projects*. Routledge.
Lässig, S., & Strobel, T. (2013). Towards a joint German-Polish history textbook – Historical roots, structures and challenges. In K. Korostelina & S. Lässig (Eds.), *History education and post-conflict reconciliation* (pp. 90–119). Routledge.
Naveh, E. (2010). Public uproar over history curriculum and textbooks in Israel. In I. Barca & I. Nakou (Eds.), *Contemporary public debates over history education* (pp. 133–151). IAP.
Naveh, E. (2017). *The past in turmoil – Debates over historical issues in Israel*. Mofet and Hakibbutz Hameuchad. [in Hebrew]
Peled Elhanan, N. (2012). *Palestine in Israeli school books: Ideology and propaganda in education*. I.B. Tauris.
Pingel, F. (Ed.). (2003). *Contested past, disputed present: Curricula and teaching in Israeli and Palestinian schools*. Verlag Hahnsche Buchhandlung.
Pingel, F. (2010). *UNESCO guidebook on textbook research and textbook revision*. UNESCO.
Podeh, E. (2002). *The Arab-Israeli conflict in Israeli history textbooks, 1948–2000*. Bergin & Garvey.

Psaltis, C., Carretero, M., & Čehajić-Clancy, S. (2017). *History education and conflict transformation: Social psychological theories, history teaching and reconciliation.* Springer Nature.

Raz-Krakotzkin, A. (2001). History textbooks and the limits of Israeli consciousness. *Journal of Israeli History, 20*(2–3), 155–172.

Stearns, P. N., Seixas, P. C., & Wineburg, S. (Eds.). (2000). *Knowing, teaching, and learning history: National and international perspectives.* New York University Press.

Stojanovic, D. (2008). Balkan history workbooks – Consequences and experiences. *European Studies, 7,* 157–162.

Terra, L. (2014). New histories for a new state: Astudy of history textbook content in Northern Ireland. *Journal of Curriculum Studies, 46*(2), 225–248.

Vorgan, Y. (2010). *Palestinian textbooks: Attitude toward the Jews, Israel, and peace.* Knesset Center of Research and Information. http://din-online.info/pdf/kn39.pdf [in Hebrew]

Wang, Z. (2009). Old wounds, new narratives: Joint history textbook writing and peace-building in East Asia. *History & Memory, 21*(1), 101–126.

Wilschut, A. (2010). History at the mercy of politicians and ideologies: Germany, England, and the Netherlands in the 19th and 20th centuries. *Journal of Curriculum Studies, 42*(5), 693–723.

CHAPTER 18

The Narrative Approach to Shared Education
Insights from Jerusalem

Myriam Darmoni-Charbit and Noa Shapira

1   Introduction

> I grew up in the Triangle. We had good relationships with the Jewish villages close by ... I was an Israeli Arab. This was my identity until October 2000, when the police killed fourteen young Arabs. One of them was from Jat (an Arab village in Israel), and like a brother to me. Things started to change inside. At the Hebrew University, I came across right wing students that were cursing us for no reason, only because we were Arabs. Was I really Israeli? How could this have happened? How should I define myself? Palestinian? Israeli? October 2000 events changed my life. I decided to stay in Jerusalem, became an educator because I wanted to have an impact. To this day, my identity is in movement, evolving.

This testimony by Hassan,[1] a school principal in East Jerusalem, is an example of the narrative approach that the Center of Educational Technology (CET) has used since 2015. The aim of the approach is to build good and robust relationships between Jewish and Arab educators in Jerusalem in order to establish regular joint lessons on various topics for pupils from West and East Jerusalem, studying in different schools.

The Shared Education initiative is based on the Northern Ireland Shared Education approach. This educational program was developed at Queens University in Belfast (Duffy & Gallagher, 2016; Payes, 2017) and adapted to the Israeli-Palestinian context by the Center of Educational Technology (CET) in Tel Aviv.

The Israeli context of the ongoing conflict between Jews and Arabs began with the rise of the Zionist movement at the end of the nineteenth century. Following the establishment of the independent Jewish state in 1948, the Palestinian population spread into separate communities – Arab citizens of Israel, Palestinian inhabitants of the West Bank and the Gaza Strip, and refugee camps in neighboring Arab countries (Kriesburg, 2005). Consequently, the internal Jewish-Arab conflict inside the 1967 borders is related to the wider Israeli-Palestinian conflict (Maoz, 2011; Steinberg & Bar-On, 2002).

The intractable nature of the conflict in our region creates a very different context for the original Shared Education model. In Northern Ireland, educators could build on the Good Friday peace agreement to engage their communities in reconciliation through joint learning. In Israel, while Jews and Arabs are citizens, they speak different languages, embrace different faiths, study in different schools, and mostly live in different cities and villages. In Jerusalem, the political, geographical and linguistic divides are deeper. Jerusalem is a "contested" space, par excellence: although it is the capital of the State of Israel, 40% of the population of Jerusalem is Palestinian with resident status, but no citizenship. These Palestinians benefit from social rights and freedom of movement in Israel, but cannot vote in national elections.

This chapter is based on analyses of protocols of encounters between principals and teachers from East and West Jerusalem between 2015 and 2020 in the "Learning together in Jerusalem" program. This was a professional development program for principals and teachers, based on a partnership between The Department of Education of the Jerusalem municipality, the Civic Education team at the Center for Educational Technology, the Ministry of Education of Israel and the Shared Education Center at the University of Queens in Belfast.[2] Since 2015, five groups of principals (N = 120) and 20 groups of teachers (N = 430) took part in training courses. In this on-going program, approximately, 3000 pupils studied together yearly.

This chapter demonstrates to what extent the sharing of personal stories, if presented openly and honestly, contributes to the development of positive feelings of empathy and openness that are crucial for building the necessary trust to engage in regular and sustainable educational cooperation between schools from East and West Jerusalem. We briefly present the main findings that encouraged us to design the program, according to Contact theory (Allport, 1954) and the Narrative approach (Bar-On, 2010; Shenhav, 2015). We then present analyses of quotes from protocols of the encounters, from the various phases of the program. Finally, we present suggestions for addressing challenges described in the literature on encounters of groups in conflict.

2 In-Group, Outgroup, and Intergroup Contact

Extensive research in social psychology has focused on the relationships between groups. A meaningful part of the lives of most people derives from their belonging to different groups, and from the fact that one's individual life is inextricably interwoven, in a way, within collective structures, events, and processes. Societal members construct the societal beliefs that constitute a shared view of the perceived reality of that society. Some of these beliefs turn into the collective narrative of the society.

Social psychology theorists consider individuals as members of groups, rather than as self-contained entities (Tajfel, 1982). People also differentiate the groups to which they belong (in-groups) from groups to which they do not belong (outgroups) (Tajfel & Turner, 1979; Turner, Hogg, Oakes, Reicher & Wetherell, 1987). Most research on intergroup relations, prejudice, and discrimination appears to accept the idea that in-group favoritism and outgroup negativity are reciprocally related (Brewer, 1991).

The program, "Learning together in Jerusalem," was designed and implemented according to both *Intergroup Contact Theory* (Allport, 1954) and the *Narrative approach* (Bar-on, 2010). It implied that intergroup contact, under the appropriate conditions of *equal group status, common goals, intergroup cooperation,* and *institutional support*, may increase positive inter-group emotions and enhance empathy, as well as reduce negative emotions, such as anxiety (Allport, 1954; Pettigrew & Tropp, 2006, 2008; Tam et al., 2008).

These optimal conditions were difficult to achieve in Jerusalem, a city characterized by a context of conflict, geographical separation between groups, and strong negative emotions. The CET team that designed the program invested the necessary efforts for these four conditions to be fulfilled, if not fully, at least, partly.

Equal status of groups   all participants were either principals or teachers (with the same academic background and professional status). All encounters were co-facilitated by an Israeli and a Palestinian and, simultaneously, translated, into Arabic and Hebrew, to enable smooth communication. The groups were equal, in terms of the participants' national and gender identity. Encounters took place in both East and West Jerusalem although this was very challenging for the participants of both groups who tend to feel threatened when they exit their own neighborhoods.

Common goals – all participants agreed to work together in order to enable a better future for all the children of Jerusalem.

Intergroup cooperation – all participants were aware that the dialogue encounters were intended to build trust and enable regular and sustainable educational cooperation between the schools and joint lessons for the students.

Institutional support – the support of the Education Department of Jerusalem and the Ministry of Education was a pre-condition to launch the program. Thus, no formal Palestinian institution provided its support for the program, because of the Israeli authorities' interdiction of Palestinian representation in East Jerusalem and because of the anti-normalization issue.[3]

This chapter is based on the assumption that intergroup contact, under optimal conditions, can form the necessary basis to implement efficiently the narrative approach and generate dialogical moments between groups in conflict. Below we present the rationale and reasons for choosing the narrative approach.

3 Societal Collective Narratives

Collective narratives offer individuals a role in their community, a sense of shared and social identity, a meaning to and justification for their experiences (Bruner, 1990; Shenhav, 2015; Tajfel & Turner, 1979). Narrative, as a psychological concept, offers individuals an integrative prism through which to interpret lives in their social and political complexity (Hammack, 2011). The collective narrative of a society provides a basis for common understanding, good communication, interdependence and the coordination of social activities, which are necessary for the functioning of the social systems (Bar-On, 2010; Bar-Tal & Salomon, 2006). However, collective narratives do not emerge from nowhere. Their most important source is the groups' history: the group constructs and interprets its past. Thus, collective narrative and collective historical memories are inseparable (Salomon, 2004). Collective historical memories not only provide the roots for a group's collective narrative, but also are reciprocally colored by the narrative: historical events are "made to fit" the narrative, and are added or excluded from the narrative according to the needs of the group (Sezgin, 2001).

3.1 *Collective Narratives in Times of Conflict*

Societies involved in an intergroup conflict construct conflict-supporting narratives that provide justification for and explanation of the entire conflict. These narratives play an important role in satisfying basic socio-psychological needs of the individuals and collectives involved. To fulfill this role, the narratives tend to be selective, biased, and simplistic. Social groups, therefore, strive to maintain the hegemony of their own dominant narratives among in-group members. These efforts are especially prevalent during intractable conflicts that last for very long periods (Oren, Nets-Zehngut & Bar-Tal, 2015).

The collective narratives are shared by the group members and are treated by many of them as truthful accounts of the past and the present. The narratives include societal beliefs about one's own victimization, delegitimization of the opponent, extreme patriotism, etc. The narratives intend to tell the past in a manner that is instrumental for the group's present existence and daily functioning (Ben Hagai, 2016). Thus, being a Jew or a Palestinian in Israel determines many of the personal experiences that individuals face in their lives (Bar-Tal & Salomon, 2006). As a result, the relations between the Jews and Palestinian in Israel are often characterized by mutual negative attitudes, prejudice and stereotypes, de-legitimization of the other and dehumanization (Bar-On, 2008; Bar-Tal, 2000, 2001; Bar-Tal & Teichman, 2005).

To generate change, group members, in times of intractable conflict, need to change their societal mindset and begin a process of reconciliation (Bar-Tal, 2013). Studies conducted around the world and in Israel address the appropriate strategies for intergroup contact that may increase positive intergroup emotions, enhance empathy, and reduce negative emotions, such as hatred, fear, and anxiety (Pettigrew & Tropp, 2006, 2008; Shapira et al., 2016; Tam et al., 2008). Among them is the narrative approach.

4 Stories Matter: The Narrative Approach

Social narratives are course of events that are communicated by persons and societies within various channels and provide to all the ability to live in the present, while feeling a strong connection to the past. As such, the narratives extend the temporal boundaries. Narratives are disseminated among the members of any society through a process of repetition and variation, called Multiplicity (Shenhav, 2015). In the context of dialogue encounters, the narrative approach enables participants to address controversial issues and difficult emotions in a personal manner, through storytelling. The narrative approach acts like a vaccination: when the conflict is raised within a safe space and a structured setting, it creates "dialogue moments" that are loaded emotionally with both painful and positive feelings. These moments are rare and highly valuable; they create emotional turmoil that enables the participants to stick to the positive relationship, even when the dissonance of the reality challenges it strongly.

When an individual tells her/his life story, s/he constructs it carefully and intentionally, choosing which parts of the story and identity to present to the specific audience (Bar-On, 2010). This strategy of choosing which specific events to share with the others is at the heart of the work of shared education in Israel/Palestine. The effect of the narrative approach on conflict mitigation can also lead to conflict reduction between groups.

Contact theory was instrumental for building the program's framework, according to the four necessary conditions for effective contact, as defined by

Allport (1954). This framework, which was translated into concrete practice, was the structure that enabled the implementation of the narrative approach under the best possible circumstances.

5 Description of the Program's Stages

"Learning together in Jerusalem" started with one year of intensive encounters for principals and teachers, and ran from October to June. These crucial stages enabled the principals and the teachers to build robust inter-personal relationships through co-facilitated dialogue. It is important to note: (1) the context: CET staff interviewed the candidates during the very violent context of the "Knife Intifada," a period characterized by violence and fear on the streets of Jerusalem. Between October 2015 and March 2016, there were more than 200 stabbings and 42 car-rammings of Israelis by young Palestinians: 30 Israelis and two Americans were killed. Israeli security forces killed over 200 Palestinians. (2) In Israel, most Jewish participants (the majority group) could neither speak nor understand Arabic. Among the Arab participants, those who are citizens of Israel understood and spoke Hebrew but East Jerusalem residents did not. Since we were aware of this challenge, we implemented simultaneous translation in the program, thus, enabling equal status. The yearlong training process had three components: (1) learning about each other; (2) uni-national encounters; and (3) deepening the narrative dialogue.

5.1 *Learning about Each Other*
The first goal was to achieve acquaintance between the participants at a superficial level and, thus, reduce the anxiety inherent to personal contact between participants involved in an intractable conflict. In other words, the participants needed to gradually feel more comfortable together. The technique used to achieve this goal was sharing personal information (sharing a story about their name, professional choices) through dialogue in pairs and small groups. The first meeting was also directed toward the reasons for their professional choice to work in the field of education, their cultural and religious background and their interests.

However, during the first meeting of the first group, while the facilitators were planning for a soft introductory encounter, Rakefet, a West Jerusalem principal, opened with the statement: "I know it may not be politically correct, but I must ask: Why are you educating your children to hate us?" Reem, an East Jerusalem principal, answered immediately: "I have a question back to you: Why are you killing our children?" This exchange demonstrated that, in difficult times, some participants are willing to stress a positive element of the social identity of their own group and a negative element of the out-group. However, other voices were also heard during that encounter. Ibtisam, an East Jerusalem principal, said:

> Because of the 'situation,' we see each other as a threat. We stop thinking rationally; feelings are leading us. In all of my life, I never felt immediate danger like today. Our role as educators is to change this horrible situation in which all of us are threatened.

"Learning together in Jerusalem" did not intend to blur the distinction between the in-group and the out-group. All participants were encouraged to be authentic and not to hide behind generalizations, such as "We are all humans." On the other hand, they were asked not to act as "representatives" of their national groups, but rather to explain the complex effects of the collective narratives on each group and on themselves, as individuals, who see themselves as belonging to a national group.

We observed a strong need of the Palestinian participants to have their suffering acknowledged by the Israelis. When the Palestinians received expressions of compassion, they were very grateful and appreciative, and it had a positive impact on their commitment to the program. Hiba is a principal from East Jerusalem (she is not an Israeli citizen). She undertook her graduate studies at a university in the West Bank, and is heading a school in an extremely poor neighborhood, across the Israeli-West Bank barrier. Before the program, she had only met Israelis in formal professional venues. She had mixed feelings about the program; she complained that she could not arrive in time to the encounters because of the checkpoint she had to cross daily to reach her school.

In the middle of the program, Hiba was attacked by a group of ultra-orthodox young men, who cursed her and damaged her car, with a metal bar. When the program staff learned about what happened, they shared it with the Israeli participants. Many decided to call Hiba, expressed their anger toward the assailants, and gave her their blessings for a prompt recovery. It completely changed her attitude toward the Jewish participants. From then on, she arrived on time and was more committed and engaged in the dialogue.

In the principals' groups, the goal of reaching basic acquaintance was mostly achieved. The participants were happy to meet and mostly committed to attending the workshops. However, for many participants from both groups, it was challenging to remember the names of the outgroup members.

Another aspect of learning about each other took place during the study tours. The goal here was to provide basic knowledge about the demographic and economic situation in the highly divided city of Jerusalem. Our technique to achieve this goal was to invite expert lecturers (Jewish and Arabs, because of the need for equal status) and to use valid data from the Jerusalem Institute for Policy research, a non-partisan think tank. The plan was that after learning the facts from lectures and reports, the participants would break into small groups and share how the data resonated in their lives. This stage was very challenging for the groups. For the Jewish participants, it created a very strong cognitive dissonance and, for the Palestinians, it was emotionally loaded to acknowledge the high level of poverty of the East Jerusalem population. This stage generated anger and anxiety and often made it necessary for the group to break into uni-national sessions at the next meeting.

The Palestinians focused on the lack of infrastructures (schools located in inadequate buildings, narrow streets, lack of street lighting, sidewalks and sewage, housing shortage) and security challenges, such as checkpoints for pupils arriving from homes across the Separation Wall. The Jewish participants were uninterested in raising demographic or economic crucial issues. They mostly focused on Israeli national monuments: Herzl Mount and Yad Vashem. It seems that after realizing and experiencing the depth of the gaps between the sides of the city, they were in need of reaching symmetry by sharing the Israeli narrative, as they knew it from their own socialization. This included the Shoah, Zionism, and bereavement.

Yael, a teacher from West Jerusalem, reflected on the visit to a school in the Palestinian neighborhood of Shuafat and the Shuafat refugee camp checkpoint:

> The classroom was so small, the staircase narrow and the building old. The lack of parental cooperation described by the principal was despairing, like a survival situation for our fellow teachers ... It was hard to stand at the checkpoint and see children and adults walking in the rain ... When you open your eyes, you can't ignore the reality.

Noor, an East Jerusalem teacher, reflected on her feelings, after the visit in West Jerusalem:

> It is very special for me to meet Jewish teachers that are genuinely interested to hear about my life, especially because of the police entering Essawia (her neighborhood) all the time. When we visited K. school today, I spoke with you, Boaz (an art teacher) and you were so proud to show me your pupils' work ... Most of all, I loved that you, Rachel, invited us to your house. It is the first time that I am in a Jewish house ... Despite the differences ... there are other things that unite us ... Intolerance and

fanaticism are not here. We came to exchange ideas, respectfully. We look at the things around us deeply and honestly.

The Jewish participants were very willing to hear about Noor's daily life. She spoke in the dialogue circle about her two-year-old daughter having difficulty falling asleep at night and being anxious, because of the presence of military jeeps and armed soldiers in the streets. Noor had tears in her eyes and all the participants were also moved to tears.

These dialogue moments that are emotionally loaded enabled the Palestinian participants to stick to the positive relationship along the road. Even when they experienced difficult situations, they were capable of making the distinction between the "perpetrators" and their colleagues, who cared about them. For the Jewish participants, the program aimed to have them experience empathy, but not to feel guilty. The goal was to motivate all participants to act together in the educational realm, in order to bring about an improved situation for all.

Ronit, a West Jerusalem teacher said:

> During the study tour in West Jerusalem, we were together, Israelis and Palestinians, at the military cemetery at Mount Herzl. It was very powerful to stand there together ... we were capable of talking frankly about hurtful topics, to raise arguments, not from a victimized point of view, but in an authentic and sincere manner.

Leah, a West Jerusalem religious teacher, who teaches in a secular school, had mixed feelings about the program. She was very afraid of Arabs. She decided not to attend the tour in East Jerusalem. In the debriefing circle after the study tour in West Jerusalem, she shared her breakthrough with the group:

> Today, when we visited together the synagogue at the H. religious school, it was amazing. We were there together, standing next to the Holy Torah scrolls. You (the Arab teachers) were moved, curious and grateful. I felt for the first time that it may be possible to do good together.

Bar-Tal (2000, 2001) refers to the conflict-supportive narratives that emphasize dangers inherent to the conflict situation as threats to the physical existence of the in-group, and to its cherished values. When Leah felt that the Palestinian teachers respected the Holy Bible, it enabled her to re-think her social belief that all Arabs are only interested in harming her.

Study tours are very powerful tools for deepening mutual understanding and for nurturing empathy. Standing next to the Separation Wall or facing the lesser infrastructure of East Jerusalem, creates cognitive dissonance among the Jewish participants and motivates them to act in order to reduce the gaps and hostility. For Palestinian participants, the visits to the Jewish schools that are usually better off than their schools, or to Herzl Mount, devoted to the construction of the Israeli national narrative, were hurtful experiences. However, the fact that the Palestinian educators visited these places, together with their Jewish colleagues, who hosted and explained what they were seeing, made the tours instructional and meaningful.

The lack of symmetry was very prominent. Palestinian participants focused on the economic gaps and their hope for equality, while the Jewish participants wanted to present the Israeli/Zionist narrative to their colleagues. However, both groups listened carefully and we have extensive data showing that, in many cases, these encounters brought about transformation in their views of the out-group.

5.2 Uni-National Encounters

The goal of the uni-national sessions was to encourage multiple voices to be heard. This setting enabled all participants – even those who chose to be "representatives" and whose stories lacked the personal angle – to gain in authenticity. The technique was to create space in the agenda for uni-national sessions at the beginning and at the end of the program. Each time, the facilitators saw a need for such meetings.

It was especially complex for the Palestinian participants, who felt they ought to present a united front, although their differences were very profound. The divide between participants, who were citizens of Israel and those who are residents of Jerusalem, was very clear, since Israeli citizenship provides a range of civic rights that residents do not have such as a passport and the right to vote in the Parliament elections.

Among the West Jerusalem participants, it was important to voice the differences within the Jewish group. Menashe, a Jewish principal of Mizrahi descent, brought up the social hierarchy that exists within the Jewish group (his in-group) and between Israelis and Palestinians:

> I have an academic background, but my six brothers that were born in Morocco did not study at all .... Why do most Sephardi have low status jobs? Why are all the janitors in the schools of Jerusalem Arabs? ... This is not my private story; it is about lack of equal opportunities.

Meaningful dialogue facilitates lifting the veil over the "others' feelings." Asher, a religious Jewish teacher, said:

> When I discussed with Rasha the issue of her Muslim head covering, she told me of the incident that occurred two years ago and has traumatized her. She was chased and attacked in a Jewish ultra-orthodox neighborhood. I myself remember the overwhelming fear I experienced in 2000 during the terrorist attacks. By sharing her memory with me, Rasha enabled me to become aware of the complex reality of the city of Jerusalem. I realized that we are not the only ones that experience fear, Palestinians are also afraid ... Rasha enabled me to come close and to express empathy.

Palestinian participants used the meetings to voice differences that they were not too keen to display with the Israelis in the room. Often, they would choose this setting to express various expectations from the program or painful insights. Here are some examples:

> I didn't join this program to change the political situation, but to bring some benefits to my pupils.

> The other side has a memory and things to be proud of. We also have suffered. All of us are marked by the history.

> I would like to live in an ordinary state, like any other state. I don't care who rules and who is ruled. We live on the same land.

> It is hard to be the losing side in this conflict, again and again, to this day. I want justice for the Palestinian people.

In some cases, the uni-national meetings were an opportunity to reflect on in-group stories. Eilin, an East Jerusalem principal who grew up in a village not far from the city of Akko, told a story at the Narrative Seminar that was related to, in a uni-national meeting:

> When I was a girl, we would go every week to the market in Akko. And each week, my grandmother would cry when she saw an olive grove on the way. She would say: 'These were my father's trees and weep. We would then arrive at the market and she would say, 'You see this shop? It was my father's shop' and weep again. It was annoying to me. I didn't understand.

> My parents never told me about the Nakba, I learned about it later on, when I was a student at the Hebrew University. I realized then that I was an internal refugee and this is why my family had no land.

In the uni-national debriefing meeting, Samer, an East Jerusalem principal, reacted to Eilin's narrative: "This is the first time, I realize that you, the Arab citizens, also suffered. Because we suffer so much to this day, I never thought of your pain, only of your privileges. Thank you for telling us." Uni-national dialogue encounters were opportunities to discuss and reflect on controversial issues within the in-group. The ventilation of internal disputes, along with the reinforcement of in-group shared values, had a beneficial impact on the inter-group dialogues.

5.3 Deepening the Narrative Dialogue at the Ein Gedi Residential Seminar

The goal of the seminar was to create an emotional breakthrough and to nurture the empathy of the participants toward the other national group. The methodology was explained to the participants prior to the seminar: they received a short letter with very clear instructions about the setting and the preparations.

> Think of a personal story that is connected to the collective history. The rules are that every story is a good story. One should not interfere, ask, erupt or respond, while another person is telling her story – this is an opportunity to practice active listening. There will be time for clarifications and reactions. Last, but not least, privacy must be carefully maintained. What is said in a circle, remains in a circle.

War is a recurrent theme in most personal narratives (but, so is peace). Elham, a principal from East Jerusalem, who is an Israeli citizen, told her story:

> My family is from a Christian village in the Galilee. My mother was three years old in 1948. My grandparents heard that the Jews were killing small children; therefore, they decided to escape to Lebanon. I was told they nearly left behind my baby mother, because she was crying. After some time, they could return because there was an arrangement between Israel and the Church ... at least, I am bringing peace into my own circle and hope it helps peace come.

Arnon, a West Jerusalem principal in the same group, shared his story, right after Elham:

> I was born in November 1973. My father served on the Sinai front in Egypt, during the Yom Kippur War in October that year. His brother was killed in the Six-Day War in 1967. When I was in high school, Hezbollah in Lebanon killed my beloved brother, Oren of blessed memory, during his military service ... There is not a day that I don't think about Oren. Life taught me that nothing is more important than pursuing peace. I decided to learn Arabic because knowing the language is crucial to understanding each other.

In Elham and Arnon's stories, the theme of war appears as central in both narratives; but, peace, or the hope for peace, is an irrepressible urge, despite the pain. This may be the reason they chose to become partners and are leading a beautiful partnership in which elementary pupils study together Hebrew and Arabic, via the arts.

Arnon's story shows the inter-generational character of the conflict. Arnon and his father both lost a brother. Such tragic narratives shocked many participants. A recurrent sentence was, "You suffered so much, how can you even sit here with us?" Stories were experienced repeatedly as heart openers – they were inspirational and motivational. Many participants said at the debriefing that these kinds of narratives encouraged them to lead the change, take action and build robust educational partnerships.

Adnan, a principal in East Jerusalem, who is a resident of the city, told the group his personal story:

> In 1948, my grandfather lost the hotel he owned in Jaffa and our family house in Bakaa (West Jerusalem). He moved to Sheikh Jarakh (East Jerusalem) neighborhood and became a clothes dealer. In 1993, I got married .... My wife was from Hebron (West Bank), so I had to submit a request for family reunification for us to live together in Jerusalem. For 10 years, we were living apart. I was working as a teacher in Jerusalem; we reunited on the weekends in Hebron. After 10 years, I went to court and we finally received a one-year permit. First thing, we went to Jaffa. My boys had never seen the sea and that was their wish. Both our children drowned in the sea that day. I wanted to die myself, but I am a believer. Our third son was born in 2006 and his sister in 2007.

The participants could hardly breathe after listening to Adnan's tragedy, especially the Jewish participants, who felt that this was a story with which they "cannot compete." One person asked: "Do we need to compete? ... or is it about mutual understanding and responsibility for reconciliation, because all of us have already suffered too much?"

Members of the dominant group may also feel that the other group's collective narrative undermines the legitimacy of their own collective stories. This can result in feelings of insecurity, or lead to withdrawal. Alon, a principal from West Jerusalem, said:

> I listened to Hiba's story, growing up in Jabel Mukaber (East Jerusalem) ... the poverty, the violence, the occupation and the urge to study and to make her way up against all odds. How can we grow together from here without ... apologizing all the time?

Luckily enough, it was not often the case. Ronen, a principal in West Jerusalem, reflected on the two-day seminar: "I feel more hopeful today. I am closer to you all, thanks to your personal stories that connected me to you all." Suheir, a principal in East Jerusalem, told Jacob, a principal from West Jerusalem, who shared with the group that his father was killed by a young Palestinian in October 2015: "Dear Jacob, your story moved me to tears. I am not sure how I would have reacted myself to such a terrible tragedy ... I will educate against revenge and for non-violence by telling your story to my teachers and pupils." This is an example of a personal story resulting in the deconstruction of the dominant story lines and the motivation to take the path of reconciliation.

In order for intergroup dialogue to result in some social healing, both sides must "work through" their unresolved pain, trauma and anger regarding the past (Bar-On, 2010). Suheir said:

> In 1967, I was a little girl. When the war started, we moved to Bet Hanina. I remember watching the planes throwing the bombs. ... they were Israeli soldiers, they told us to come out. I remember myself with my parents against a wall with our arms up. Now, I have a responsibility, as a principal .... Each time, I see soldiers chasing a child, it reminds me of myself. We have a responsibility to bring about the change. This is why I encouraged six of my teachers to participate in the training course.

"Working through" in the context of intergroup conflict is about openly and verbally coping with the painful past, without silencing it (Bar-On, 2010).

In sum, the principals shared their personal stories gradually in the various stages of the program. Below are some lessons learned and concluding remarks, which stemmed from this process:

a. Reflectivity is crucial for the intergroup dialogue to result in a breakthrough. In this program, we used questions, such as "When and how did I discover that the conflict has had a strong impact in my life?" "Can I talk

with both the perpetrator and the victim in me, and can these two parts of my identity relate to each other?" "Am I ready to listen carefully (not to hear in order to react) with a genuine intention to understand the others' stories and points of view?"
b. Although there is no symmetry between the groups (social gaps, civil rights, access to housing, top-down vs bottom-up narratives, etc.), reciprocity is necessary to enable the establishment of good relationships between the educators. Creative thinking is crucial for locating areas of reciprocity, such as common needs or diverse areas of expertise, which are instrumental to the building of robust partnerships.
c. While there is an imbalance of power, outside of the discussion room, the presence of both facilitators working together and modelling trust, across the national divide, enables all participants to enjoy the benefits of equal treatment and to believe that transformation is possible.
d. The facilitators of intergroup dialogue should see stories not as either true or false accounts of an objective reality. As suggested by Winslade & Monk (2000): "It is therefore more useful to concentrate on viewing stories as constructing the world rather than viewing the world as independently known and then described through stories." Stories can contribute to the development of a shared understanding of the conflict and its solutions.
e. The group should develop together its own 'good enough' stories that create empathy and facilitate intergroup dialog moments, instead of 'bad enough' stories that merely replicate the distance and discordant aspects of intergroup relations (Maoz, 2004).
f. The dialogue must be undertaken in a progressive manner: from meeting to meeting, the participants need to have enough time to process what they heard and make room in their hearts. It is important to move gradually from the accessible stories about names, career, cultural and religious festivals, toward the stories that hold the core of the conflict such as wars, loss or inequality.

6   Conclusions

In addition to the chapter's practical contribution, it also has a theoretical contribution to the field of intergroup relations (Pettigrew & Tropp, 2006, 2008; Tam et al., 2008). It is possible to improve intergroup relations, even in the context of an intractable conflict, by nurturing optimal contact conditions (Allport, 1954) that enable the implementation of the narrative approach and transformation, thanks to meaningful dialogue moments (Bar On, 2010). Each of the stages of the program is necessary to enable and sustain the partnership between schools, both at the principals' and teachers' levels.

The process of gradually getting to know each other is valid, both during the training year and later, while implementing Shared Education with the students. Establishing good relationships between the educators is the robust basis to Shared Education in Israel, as it is in Northern Ireland (Duffy & Gallagher, 2016). However, in Jerusalem, the conflict is ever present in both groups' everyday lives. The fact that principals usually chose their partners for Shared Education according to the interpersonal bond nurtured within the circle of dialogue enabled them to cope successfully with political events and spurges of violence. Thanks to the good relationships, the principals were more capable of leading honest, though complex, conversations and finding practical solutions on the ground. These two variables (personal connection and successful experience in addressing complex and emotionally loaded issues) seem to have enabled the school partnerships to flourish, regardless of the challenges of the dissonant reality (Rosen & Perkins, 2013).

In this chapter, we demonstrated that it is possible to achieve the improvement of inter-group relationships crucial to implementing Shared Education, in the context of an intractable conflict (Bar-Tal, 2013).

Learning about the issues, with which the out-group deals, encourages the participants to be aware of multiple points of view. When the dialogue process is successful, the participants gradually develop empathy toward members of the out-group (Pettigrew & Tropp, 2006, 2008; Tam et al., 2008).

Uni-national conversations during the training year were subsequently held by educators – who implemented Shared Education – with their students, as a debriefing routine. These meetings enabled multiple voices to be heard and respected. Moreover, the meetings enabled the participants to share concerns or fears that could be addressed later, while planning the next joint session with colleagues from the other group (Bar-On & Kassem, 2004).

Dialogue moments, resulting in emotional breakthroughs, can be reached during group encounters, study tours and residential seminars. They have very strong transformational power. They enable participants to internalize the complexity of their lives in an intractable conflict in a manner they never experienced before, simply by listening to the "enemy's" story. As Ganz (2009) put it, moving from the "Story of Self" to the "Story of Us," and finally to the "Story of Now" is highly instrumental. It helps build robust partnerships between educators, enables collaborative work, and resists the inevitable setbacks and bumps on the road.

Thanks to the efforts of the outstanding educators that bravely engaged in the path of dialogue, more than 3000 pupils from East and West Jerusalem studied together in 2019–2020 in the "Learning together in Jerusalem" program. The last sentence belongs to Maysoon, a teacher from East Jerusalem: "We must nurture our humanity, develop good relationships and take responsibility to improve the lives of our students."

Acknowledgments

"Learning Together in Jerusalem" could never have happened without the determination of its first allies: Moshe (Kinli) Tur Paz, Yoav (Zimi) Zimran, Tony Gallagher, Gavin Duffy, Mazen Faraj, Dana Friedman, Gila Ben Har and Batya Kallus.

The authors wish to acknowledge the team that developed and/or implemented the program with competence and grace: Michal Levin, Mazen Faraj, Dr. Shula Mola, Mira Munayer, Gameel Sharkia, Inssaf Shuhana, Dr. Shany Payes, Dima Kanaan, Saed Tali, Ayelet Ha-Shahar Levi, and Dikla Tomer Kayan.

Last, but not least, we would like to thank all the bold and brave principals and teachers, who shared their personal narratives and chose to listen to their colleagues. Day after day, they are leading a lifesaving educational endeavor, united by a common hope for dignity and equity for all Jerusalemites.

Notes

1 All names were changed to protect the participants' privacy.
2 The Shared Education initiative is implemented across Israel in the Sharon/Triangle area, Ramle, the north region and in Jerusalem. In this chapter, we focus only on the Jerusalem program.
3 The anti-normalization movement demands that any dialogue or project between Israelis and Palestinians must include a clear focus on "resistance," meaning the project must focus on ending the occupation.

References

Allport, G. W. (1954). *The nature of prejudice.* Addison-Wesley.

Bar-On, D. (2008). *The others within us: Constructing Jewish-Israeli identity.* Cambridge University Press.

Bar-On, D. (2010). Storytelling and multiple narratives in conflict situations: From the TRT group in the German-Jewish context to the dual-narrative approach of PRIME. In G. Salomon & E. Cairns (Eds.), *Handbook on peace education* (pp. 199–212). Psychology Press.

Bar-On, D., & Kassem, F. (2004). Storytelling as a way to work through intractable conflicts: The German-Jewish experience and its relevance to the Palestinian-Israeli context. *Journal of Social Issues, 60*(2), 289–306.

Bar-Tal, D. (2000). From intractable conflict through conflict resolution to reconciliation: Psychological analysis. *Political Psychology, 21*(2), 351–365.

Bar-Tal, D. (2001). Why does fear override hope in societies engulfed by intractable conflict, as it does in the Israeli society? *Political Psychology, 22*(3), 601–627.

Bar-Tal, D. (2013). *Intractable conflicts: Socio-psychological foundations and dynamics.* Cambridge University Press.

Bar-Tal, D., & Salomon, G. (2006). Israeli-Jewish narratives of the Israeli-Palestinian conflict: Evolvement, contents, functions and consequences. In R. I. Rotberg (Ed.), *Israeli and Palestinian narratives of conflict: History's double helix.* Indiana University Press.

Bar-Tal, D., & Teichman, Y. (2005). *Stereotypes and prejudice in conflict: Representations of Arabs in Israeli Jewish society.* Cambridge University Press.

Brewer, M. B. (1991). The social self: On being the same and different at the same time, *Personality and Social Psychology Bulletin, 17,* 475–482.

Duffy, G., & Gallagher, T. (2017). Shared education in contested spaces: How collaborative networks improve communities and schools. *Journal of Educational Change, 18,* 107–134.

Ganz, M. (2009). Why stories matter – The art and craft of social change. *Sojourners,* 16–21.

Hammack, P. L. (2011). Narrative and the politics of meaning. *Narrative Inquiry, 21*(2), 311–318.

Kriesburg, L. (2005). Nature, dynamics, and phases of intractability. In C. Crocker, F. Osler Hampson, & P. Aall (Eds.), *Grasping the nettle: Analyzing cases of intractable conflict* (pp. 65–99). Springer.

Litvak-Hirsch, T. (2006). The use of stories as a tool for intervention and research in the arena of peace education in conflict areas: The Israeli–Palestinian story. *Journal of Peace Education, 3*(2), 251–271.

Oren, N., & Bar-Tal, D. (2007). The detrimental dynamics of delegitimization in intractable conflicts: The Israeli-Palestinian case. *International Journal of Intercultural Relations, 31,* 111–126.

Oren, N., Nets-Zehngut, R., & Bar-Tal, D. (2015). Construction of the Israeli-Jewish conflict-supportive narrative and the struggle over its dominance. *Political Psychology, 36*(2), 215–230.

Payes, S. (2017). Education across the divide: Shared learning of separate Jewish and Arab schools in a mixed city in Israel. *Education, Citizenship and Social Justice,* 1–17.

Pettigrew, T. F., & Tropp, L. R. (2006). A meta-analytic test of intergroup contact theory. *Journal of Personality and Social Psychology, 90*(5), 751–783. https://doi.org/10.1037/0022-3514.90.5.751

Pettigrew, T. F., & Tropp, L. R. (2008). How does intergroup contact reduce prejudice? Meta-analytic tests of three mediators. *European Journal of Social Psychology, 38*(6), 922–934. https://doi.org/10.1002/ejsp.504

Rosen, Y., & Perkins, D. (2013). Shallow roots require constant watering: The challenge of sustained impact in educational programs. *International Journal of Higher Education, 2*(4), 91–100.

Sa'di, A. H. (2002). Catastrophe, Memory and Identity: Al-Nakbah as a Component of Palestinian Identity. *Israel Studies, 7*(2), 175–198. https://www.jstor.org/stable/30245590

Salomon, G. (2004). A narrative-based view of coexistence education. *Journal of Social Issues, 60*(2), 273–287.

Shapira, N., Kupermintz, H., & Kali, Y. (2016). Design principles for promoting intergroup empathy in online environments. *Interdisciplinary Journal of e-Skills and Lifelong Learning, 12*, 225–246. http://www.informingscience.org/Publications/3605

Shenhav, S. R. (2015). *Analyzing social narratives*. Routledge.

Tajfel, H. (1982). Social psychology of intergroup relations. *Annual Review of Psychology, 33*(1), 1–39.

Tajfel, H., Billig, M. G., Bundy, R. P., & Flament, C. (1971). Social categorization and intergroup behaviour. *European Journal of Social Psychology, 1*(2), 149–178.

Tajfel, H., & Turner, J. C. (1979). An integrative theory of intergroup conflict. *The Social Psychology of Intergroup Relations, 33*(47), 33–47.

Winslade, J., & Monk, G. D. (2000). *Narrative mediation: A new approach to conflict resolution*. Jossey-Bass.

CHAPTER 19

Imagined Communities

Staging Shared Society in Israel

Lee Perlman and Sinai Peter

1   Introduction

The term 'shared society,' adopted in recent years to signal support for principles, such as greater equality, partnership and active citizenship, in the context of the Jewish and Palestinian relationship in Israel, generally refers to Jewish-Arab relations and to efforts undertaken in civil society and the wider context of Israel's multicultural and diverse society (Eytan, Marshood & Strichtman, 2019; Hai, 2014).

A range of theatrical forms have been utilized to date, since the 1970s, which express, embody and promote shared society between and among Jewish and Palestinian citizens in Israel. These theatrical undertakings occur in theatres and other public settings, ranging from established repertory and fringe theatres, alternative performance spaces, theatre festivals, community centers, universities and public protests (Nasrallah & Perlman, 2011). Theatre practitioners have not often been an active or intentional 'player' in Israel's shared society ecosystem of public, private and non-profit sector groups and individuals, which include educators, grassroots activists and leaders, researchers, policy makers, business people and entrepreneurs and philanthropists. While not conceived like shared society educational, professional cooperation, economic development or advocacy paradigms, many of the productions' rehearsal processes have been conducted like dialogue/structured group interactions between Israelis and Palestinians. Some of these endeavors have resembled the contact model. Others have resembled the confrontation model, most notably the five stages of the Neve Shalom School for Peace paradigm, in which the Jewish-Israeli and Palestinian theatre artists share a stage and essentially wage the national conflicts between them, in a non-violent manner (Perlman, 2017). These artistic endeavors often constitute Palestinian/Jewish precarious artistic mobilization, expressing non-violent resistance to the state, its policies and powerful socio-political and socio-cultural forces (Perlman, 2016). They involve Jewish Israeli and Palestinian Arab citizens of Israel in the myriad of performance and production roles. They span 'artist-based' professional performances to community-based performances, to traditional rituals, each with its own distinct aesthetic assumptions and values, which require its own specific kinds of expertise and knowledge (Cohen, Varea & Walker, 2011).

This chapter will explore specific dimensions and the broader socio-political significance of four 'artist-based' shared Jewish-Palestinian productions performed between the years 1982 and 2019, and reassessed by Jewish Israeli theatre director/activist, Sinai Peter. Peter reflects upon his experiences in each of the productions. These are: *Them: Imagining the Other*, by Joseph Chaikin, Neve Zedek Theatre (1982), in which Peter acted and co-devised; *Return to Haifa*, by Boaz Gaon, based on a novella by Ghassan Kanafani, *Cameri* Theatre (2008), which Peter directed; *The Peacock of Silwan*, by Alma Ganihar, Akko Festival of Alternative Theatre (2012), which Peter co-directed with Jewish-Israeli theatre director and activist, Chen Alon; and *The Admission* by Moti Lerner, The Jaffa Theatre: Stage for Arab Hebrew Culture (2016), which Peter directed.

Peter's reflections, in dialogue with Perlman from 2016–2020, are interwoven with descriptions of the loci of initiation, themes and plot lines of each production. They are situated in the broader context of Peter's extensive experience with Jewish-Palestinian artistic collaborations, which, in over a dozen shared productions, has spanned roles, theatre milieu and geography. He has been a stage director, artistic director of a public repertory theatre, the Haifa Municipal Theatre from 2000–2005, an actor, and a writer, in mainstream and fringe theatres.

Peter's reflections underscore multiple dimensions of the roles of Jewish-Israeli theatre directors, as artistic leaders, and their role in amplifying and negotiating power relations between Jewish and Palestinian theatre artists. Similar to intentional shared society programs, these productions serve the varied ideological and organizational interests of their individual and institutional initiators and leaders, while expressing and promoting shared society. They furthermore attempt to amplify the non-hegemonic voices of Palestinian citizens, challenging inequality and disenfranchisement.

Like the vast majority of the over 300 Jewish-Palestinian theatre shared productions produced in Israel from 1982–2016, these four productions were performed primarily for Jewish audiences, usually in Jewish-Israeli theatre settings. They were produced, to varying degrees, by Jewish Israeli and Palestinian teams of actors, musicians, directors, designers and technical crews. These four productions created shared spaces and what Peter coins "imagined communities." Jewish Israeli and Palestinian artists and production crews are compelled to pay profound attention to what's happening in the present moment in their society, and are probed to give attention to and express issues to their audiences, that are often suppressed, while also embodying and performing, for the audiences, a palpable sense of community and shared society.

L.P.: Sinai, you have been involved in an extensive number of Jewish-Palestinian shared productions in Israel, spanning over three decades. What has drawn you to them?

S.P.: My biography has clearly informed my attraction to these productions. I grew up in a relatively unique communist home in South Tel Aviv, where Arab friends were part of our home and my experiences as a child. This, without a doubt, enabled me to experience the notion of a shared community of Jews and Arabs as a given, which was indeed unique. This was a community of friends. Furthermore, it was an oppositional community that chose to act together. During the period of Israel's Military Administration, from 1949–1966 when Arab citizens had to get home by curfew time, this necessitated that our Arab friends sometimes sleep over at our home. By the time I was 14, my parents left the communist movement – I joined them while they were among the founders of the New Israeli Left – this was a new experience – more uni-national, separate Jewish and Arab political activism.

L.P.: What was your first experience in such a production?

S.P.: When I grew up and became an actor, my first opportunity was in 1982 with the fringe Neve Tzedek Theater in Tel Aviv in *Them: Imagining the Other*.

2 Them: Imagining the Other

Joseph Chaikin, an American Jewish theatre director was one of the most influential figures in American avant-garde theatre in the 1960's and 1970's. After directing a production in Hebrew at the *Habima* National Theatre in Tel Aviv, of the *Dybbuk*, the famed Yiddish Theatre classic, Chaikin sought to return to Israel to create a theatre piece that "engaged the issues of the Palestinian and the Jews" (Chaikin, as cited in Ben Zvi, 1996, p. 415). Early on, in Chaikin's over three-year dialogue with Oded Kotler, when Kotler served as director of the Haifa Municipal Theatre, and subsequently after Kotler left the Haifa Theatre to launch the fringe Neve Zedek Theatre in a southern neighborhood of Tel Aviv, Chaikin said to Kotler.

> I want to create a piece that would be with Arabs and with Jews – that's the first thing, that the Palestinians and Jews are confronting each other ... it was very important to me that at no point would it appear to anybody

that there was something up somebody's sleeve. It was not some propaganda thing, so that everything should be very, very flagrant. There were to be the same number of Palestinians as Jews: actors, writers, directors and musicians. (Chaikin, as cited in Ben Zvi, 1996, p. 415)

Them: Imagining the Other was developed as a "devised performance." This is a type of collaborative creation process, in which, without a pre-existing script, theatre artists create the performance. They begin with the initial conception of the piece, move through the processes of research, discussion, improvisation, writing and rehearsal, and continue up until the completed performance (Hartnoll & Found, 1996; Heddon & Milling, 2006, Oddey, 1994; Perlman, 2016). As part of the devising and research process, the Jewish and Palestinian actors and playwrights, along with Chaikin, visited the West Bank to meet with Palestinians and Jewish settlers. Originally, seeking to explore the mythological roots of the Israeli-Arab conflict, *Them: Imagining the Other*, was a semi-documentary musical collage of vignettes of socio-political drama, satire and black humor. It contained scenes, like "Competitive Suffering," in which a referee gave and subtracted points to Jews, on one side, and Arabs, on the other, contingent on how persuasive they were in conveying their group's historical suffering, whether it be regarding the Holocaust or the Palestinian *Al-Naqba*. Another comic scene, called "Slogans," devised in an ironic, rock dance form, was based on commonly heard slogans, for example "The only way to look at an Arab is down the barrel of a gun" or "Throw the Jews into the sea" (Chaikin, as cited in Ben Zvi, 1996, p. 419).

S.P.: This process was built almost architecturally – a big effort was made for it to be symmetrical – something we hadn't seen before and never experienced since. Everything was symmetrical – actors, designers, writers. Joe Chaikin was the supervisor, mediator, director. The initiator was the Jewish-Israeli playwright, Danny Horowitz. The Arab actors were Salwa Nakkara, Mohammed Bakri and Ghassan Abbas. Sandra Johnson, Hava Ortman and I were the Jewish actors. This model was seminal – it could have only taken place in the fringe. There were other Jewish-Palestinian productions at that time, as well, like in the Haifa Theater, where Nola Chilton, the American born theatre director, was a pioneer.

On 5 June 1982, the day before the First Lebanon War began, was also the first day of rehearsals. Israeli battle planes en route to bomb Lebanon flew above our rehearsal space. Some of the Arab actors seriously considered that day abandoning rehearsals and returning to their villages. I deliberated about whether to come to the rehearsal or go to the demonstration against the impending war. On that same first day, I was called up as a reservist. I also had to mobilize my fellow tank soldiers – playing by the rules of the army, but feeling and being a part of the opposition to the war. I was able to come to the rehearsal and say goodbye. I knew that fellow actor Ghassan Abbas' brother was a Palestinian Liberation Organization (PLO) fighter in Lebanon who had left Israel a few years earlier to join the PLO. I got to my unit that night and wasn't sent to Lebanon – I was mentally prepared to refuse to serve in Lebanon– I don't know if I had the courage – but I was sent in the end to the Golan Heights.

Back at *Imagining the Other*, almost every day a different actor would replace me – but then he would be called up for the war. So, the focus of the play became this reality – rehearsals were conducted with the noise of battle planes in the skies.

I came back after 10 days. I had shared with Hava Ortman what I was going through. She initially played a character based on my experiences. She worked on it with Miriam Kainy and Riad Marsawi, the playwrights. Joe Chaikin took my stream of consciousness and expressed it as a soldier trying to get dressed, who gets tangled in his uniform, like a straitjacket. After three weeks in the reserves, I was released and able to go back to rehearsals and perform the monologue.

We eventually performed *Imagining the Other* for six months, throughout the First Lebanon War in Neve Zedek and all over Israel with talkbacks with the audience. It was a collage of satire, entertainment and Brechtian elements. It was an oppositional theatre event. Of all my experiences with Jewish-Palestinian shared productions, this was the production that maintained the semblance of symmetry.

3   Return to Haifa

In spring 2008, the *Cameri* Theatre, Tel Aviv's Municipal Theatre, produced a Hebrew language stage adaption of *Return to Haifa*, Palestinian writer's Ghasan Kanafani well-known novella, written in 1969. The production remained in repertory until 2013, including performances in Washington D.C. at Theatre J. Kanafani was also the spokesman of the Popular Front for the Liberation of Palestine and killed in 1972 in Beirut, supposedly by the Mossad (Israel's Secret Service). *The Return to Haifa* deals with a meeting in 1967 between a couple of Palestinian refugees coming back to look for their deserted son, who had been abandoned in their old house during the 1948 War and adopted and raised by a Jewish couple, childless Holocaust survivors, who had recently immigrated to Israel.

The question at its center is: who are a child's "real" parents? Those who have raised him, or those who conceived and gave birth to him? Or, in the political rendering of this question in Kanafani's work: to whom does this country belong? To those who have lived here for generations, or to those who returned to it at a time of adversity to building their home. (*Cameri* program, 2008, p. 34)

The *Cameri* Theatre approached the Kanafani's family, asking for and receiving permission to adapt the novella into a Hebrew-speaking play.

FIGURE 19.1   *Return to Haifa*, the Cameri Theatre, 2008. Dov "the soldier" with his biological parents from Ramallah. From left to right: Norman Issa, Erez Kahana and Mira Awad (photo by Moshe Shai)

S.P.:   In 2006, I was involved in a model of a mainstream-shared production, as the director of *Return to Haifa*. The *Cameri* Theatre in Tel Aviv, the biggest theater in Israel, produced the most canonical Palestinian story, adapted by Boaz Gaon. As a publically funded repertory theatre, part of the mainstream, the *Cameri* was attacked during the rehearsal period by journalists and right-wing activists, who protested that the theatre was producing a work by Ghasan Kanafani, an alleged terrorist. This surprised us, but didn't deter or weaken us. I think this was because each national group in the cast felt a responsibility that their characterizations represent each national narrative and ethos and yet there was a lot of warmth among the ensemble and staff. Despite the tensions between the Jewish and Arab characters, the fight over a shared child as allegory, rendered it very human, along with the story of an adopted child.

L.P.: How did these tensions express themselves?

S.P.: After the production went into rehearsals, we created a shared dramaturgical space of me as facilitator along with the playwright. Mira Awad, the actress, who originated the Palestinian mother role of Safiyya, insisted that we had to write for her character some responses to Miriam, the Jewish mother character, that Safiyya needed to say something and not be passive. Similar things happened in our rehearsal process of *The Peacock of Silwan*. Being in an incubator helped us build and sharpen the characters.

Return to Haifa had a successful tour in Washington DC at Theatre J, led by artistic director, Ari Roth. It received good reviews but it started to create cracks in Theater J that developed years later – the play, both in Israel and in DC, had talkbacks that evoked controversy and raised particularly difficult questions for DC Jews. *Return to Haifa* was initially performed in Hebrew, and then for the DC trip, Arabic was included and then, upon return to Israel, we included the Arabic in production. The adaptation by Boaz Gaon, a Jew, directed by me, a Jew, was criticized by some Palestinians; but the Kanafani family – his widow, granted her permission.

L.P.: Did your production depart significantly from the story line of Kanafani's novella?

S.P.: The novella ends with a declaration of war by the Arab father – and we chose not to end it that way – we chose an ending where the son lets his biological Arab parents stay over one more night and we left the ending open. Both sets of Palestinian and Jewish parents bend over him – cooperating or not – waiting for him to get up. But, that's not the way it was written in the original novella which had a conclusive ending in which the Palestinian father leaves empty-handed, saying "We will fight."

4 The Peacock of Silwan

The Peacock of Silwan was performed by an ensemble of Jewish and Palestinian actors under the leadership of Peter and Jewish Israeli theatre director and activist, Chen Alon. It premiered in 2012 at Israel's Acco Festival of Alternative Theatre, a well-established cultural and municipal institution, founded in 1980. *The Peacock of Silwan* won the 2012 Akko Festival Best Directing and Acting awards (for best actress, played by the Arab actress, Samira Saraya) and the 2015 Israel Fringe Theatre Prize for Best Play. This production performed until 2019 in the Jaffa Theatre and performed in Ulm, Karlsruhe and Recklinghausen, Germany.

The Peacock of Silwan is about the accidental death of a young Arab man. It centers on how all the characters are clarifying for themselves, and the audience, the reasons for his death and the impossibility of the situation between the residents of the Palestinian village of Silwan, located in the heart of East Jerusalem – and the Jewish settlers of the City of David, the new Israeli settlement. (The "City of David" is also an archeological site, which has been declared an Israeli national park, under government control. It is managed and developed in collaboration with the City of David Foundation.) The play is set in an old residential building in Silwan. Just meters from the sensitive area of the Al Aqsa mosque/Temple Mount, lives a Palestinian family, Jamil and his two daughters, Jasmine and Iman, who manage a beauty salon called "The Peacock of Silwan." Shosh, an Israeli settler who has taken over a side room of their home, hopes that one day the whole house will be hers. In a small apartment on the ground floor, lives a deaf youth with his mother, Amal. Underneath the building, a prominent archaeologist, Dr. Efrat Sela, is conducting a dig that she believes will uncover the ancient Kingdom of David. The security guard of the dig, Michael, serves as the narrator of the play.

Jasmine wishes to enroll in music studies in Paris, but her sister, Iman, sees this as an escape from her responsibilities and the abandonment of the struggle. Their father also strongly objects to this plan, and takes the money that Jasmine had saved for her trip. The deaf youth comes to Jasmine's aid and complicates the situation when he breaks into the car of Na'ama, a young Tel Aviv woman, who comes to Silwan, on a trip to photograph the house where her grandmother lived before 1948. Jamil, the girls' father and a community leader, applies for an injunction against the association managing the excavation and succeeds in obtaining a suspension of the dig. Yoram, the chair of the association, does not intend to accept the court decision, and attempts to have the decision overturned. A confrontation escalates between Yoram and Michael, and the Palestinian family, which culminates with the young deaf Arab man being shot dead by mistake. From this point on, each of the characters attempts to persuade the audience that they were not responsible for the death.

L.P.: In the *Peacock of Silwan*, you had two Jewish directors?

S.P.: Yes, Chen Alon and myself, and a Jewish playwright, Alma Ganihar. But, the Jewish-Arab ensemble of seven young actors and the journey was a shared one, which was very significant. The idea to create a play about this subject came from Judith Roth, from New York City, an activist psychologist, who shared with us the terrible emotional situation of the Silwan mothers. During rehearsals, we conducted visits to Silwan over a number of months. There were intense dynamics in the rehearsal rooms in Tel Aviv until we received access to a 300-year-old Palestinian home in Akko's Old City.

L.P.: Did you face challenges in launching such a politically charged shared production?

S.P.: When we were accepted to the Akko Festival for Alternative Theatre, and we knew we would do a site-specific production – the home came to life. We started to visit it a few months beforehand in order to design the spaces to make it a simulation of the Silwan story. Then, our relations with the Arab residents became fraught with tensions as they related to us as invaders, as a settlement of sorts, because they are experiencing gentrification. Their house was, in fact, bought by American Jews, like what is happening in Silwan. We were invited by the Akko Theatre Center to use the space and our encounter with the two Palestinian families was part of the experience, and they were part of the production.

L.P.: This seems quite ironic, in light of what the production was trying to express.

S.P.: In essence, we "settled" as a theatre ensemble in Palestinian Akko, similar to the Jewish settlement in Palestinian East Jerusalem. A meta-theatrical tension was created, because we did the show in an Arab home amid a growing Jewish settlement in Akko.

5 The Admission

The Admission by Motti Lerner did not premiere in Israel, rather at the Theatre J in Washington DC in the spring of 2014, in English. After successive, but unsuccessful attempts to perform the play in Israel's repertory theatres – which opted not to produce a play with such controversial content – the Jaffa Theatre agreed to host and produce the original Hebrew language version. The show premiered in September 2014.

The plot of *The Admission* takes place in the northern coastal town of Haifa in 1988, in the midst of the First Intifada, that was happening in the West Bank. It focuses on a young Jewish Israeli academic at the University of Haifa, who was seriously injured in the First Lebanon War of 1982. He is confronted with accusations of a Palestinian family, with whom he and his family have close ties, about his father: they claim that he was involved in the killing of their relatives during the conquest of their village, Tantur, and the expulsion of its inhabitants in 1948. The son rejects the accusations and tries to convince his father to expose his version of the event. The father, a wealthy building contractor, avoids discussing the affair, but as new testimonies are brought up, the father admits to his son that his regiment was caught in a difficult situation during battle and, in an act of self-defense, some Palestinian civilians were killed. However, the father refuses to discuss the event publicly, and is supported by his wife, who also served in the regiment. The Palestinian family, too, chooses to ignore the traumatic event in its past.

The Arab village of Tantur is the barely disguised name of the actual village, Tantura, on the coast of Israel, south of Haifa, where the alleged war crimes took place. Both families discover and experience the depth of the traumas of the battle and conquest of the village in 1948. The Jewish family has also lost their other son, who fought and died in the 1973 Yom Kippur War. The plot thickens with two additional sub-plots: the father is building a new neighborhood in memory of his soldier son, on part of the remnants of the Palestinian village. There is also a romantic sub-plot between the young Jewish Israeli professor and the young doctoral student from the Palestinian family.

L.P.: As opposed to your other shared productions, this one premiered in the United States. Was the cast composed of Jewish and Arab actors?

S.P.: When I directed *The Admission* at Theater J, American white cast members played the Jewish characters, including an actor who is half-Jewish, and all the Palestinian characters were played by Arab actors. This production was fraught with public controversy, especially within the DC Jewish community and the Israeli Embassy in D.C. The charged themes of the play were considered by many community leaders to be too contested, crossing what they felt was a 'red line.' Theatre J, under pressure from philanthropists and others, were asked to reduce, to whatever extent possible, the production elements of the performance and to publicize the performances as "open rehearsals." This understanding was codified in a memorandum of understanding by the hosting Jewish Community Center, which housed Theatre J. These performances were, therefore, staged as "rehearsals open to the public," but received significant public attention and critical acclaim. Later in 2014, Ari Roth, the longtime Artistic Director of Theatre J, was fired in the wake of the controversy the production sparked.

L.P.: And at the Jaffa Theatre?

S.P.: There, with the help of a Headstart campaign, we were able to bankroll a shared production of Jewish and Arab actors. The production attracted audiences to confront these issues on stage and in talkbacks with the Jewish and Arab actors after each performance.

L.P.: Did *The Admission* only perform for Tel Aviv and Jaffa theatregoers?

S.P.: While it was performed dozens of times in Jaffa, an especially memorable experience for me was a performance in Nazareth, for around 200 local Arab residents and other Jewish neighbors. The post-performance discussion about the effect of the Naqba in the ongoing collective experience of Israel's Palestinian citizens was particularly probing, and painful. Even if for only an evening, the show created a platform for a shared and rare discussion between citizens of both peoples.

L.P.: Were there frank and open discussions about the Palestinian narratives during the creative processes of these shared productions? Did the creative teams critically re-examine the Palestinian narratives similarly to the way the Zionist-Israeli narratives seemed to be re-examined?

S.P.: I will try to address this through some concrete examples. In *Return to Haifa*, as I noted, Boaz Gaon, an Israeli born playwright, adapted the canonical novella by the Palestinian writer Ghassan Kanafani. While the original novella only allowed a glimpse into the Zionist narrative, via the story of Miriam, who "inherited" the Palestinian couple's home after they fled Haifa, Gaon's version renders Miriam's story front and center, equal to the Palestinians' story. It would be accurate to say that in the context of the Israeli mainstream, just the mere presence of the Palestinian narrative on the stage of a major repertory theatre was quite significant. This also evoked various forms of opposition, which I mentioned earlier, among Israeli right-wing activists, some quite vitriolic.

During the creative process itself, the Palestinian actors asserted themselves and took the prerogative to alter, in dialogue with me, some of their characters' lines, so as to strengthen their characters' claims.

In both Kanafani's novella and Gaon's play, it is impossible to avoid Palestinian self-criticism towards their fleeing in 1948 and their abandonment of the homeland to the Zionists. Therefore, there's some self-irony in this production at the *Cameri* Theatre. Is the play also criticizing Palestinian aggression toward the Jews in 1948 and subsequently? Said's character expresses, or certainly hints at, Palestinian aggression as an option to returning the stolen lands in 1948.

For the *Peacock of Silwan*, in the adaptation and dramatization of the stories of Silwan, some real and some imagined, we very much considered the internal Palestinian discourse. There was a palpable confrontation between the Palestinian daughter, who seeks to abandon the never-ending violent conflict with the Jewish settlers, and the rest of her family members, who are battling to continue living in their homes. These are central thrusts of the play's plot. The ever-present suspicions among Palestinians' regarding their fellow Palestinians' collaboration with the Jewish authorities permeates the discourse among the characters.

L.P.: Is there Palestinian criticism towards Palestinian aggression depicted in this play?

S.P.: The only aggression displayed by the Palestinian characters is non-violent resistance, which reflects Silwan's Palestinians' resistance over the last decades.

L.P.: Was there a reckoning of Palestinian narratives in the play and the process of creating *The Admission*?

S.P.: Moti Lerner's play addresses the fates of two families, one Jewish and one Palestinian. The trauma of the 1948 War is the common denominator for the families, each from its perspective. The question of the nature and extent of the Tantur village Palestinian residents' resistance in 1948 resonated during the writing of *The Admission* and our rehearsals – their violent resistance which essentially served as a pretext for the IDF's violent conquest of the village. So, yes, there was agreement that such resistance did actually take place. Was the acknowledging of this fact reflecting criticism and an attempt to defy the accepted Palestinian narrative? I don't think so. In our production, we related to the resistance as an act of self-defense. On the other hand, Lerner's Jewish ex-veteran characters mention more than once the bloody attacks by the Arab forces against Jewish civilians during this war.

L.P.: There's an additional probing discussion of the Palestinian narrative in *The Admission*.

S.P.: Yes ... the Palestinian family, who has remained in Haifa is torn apart from within surrounding the question of whether to fight to memorialize the Nakba and demand justice from its perpetrators or alternatively cast the memory aside and concentrate on building a shared life and society between the Israeli citizens of both peoples. In *The Admission*, like in the other examples I've noted, beyond the internal cast discussions that took place, the Palestinian actors were naturally suspicious about the productions themselves. Each production was initiated and led by Jewish theatre artists, as part of Jewish-Israeli theatres. There's no real symmetry in this kind of partnership, where both sides are sitting and neutrally discussing the failings of each of the narratives. The opposite is the case. The occupation and the settlements are becoming even more entrenched and the possibilities for peace seem more elusive than ever.

6   Final Reflections

L.P.: As a Jewish citizen, often the initiator of these productions, how have you come to see the Jewish/Palestinian and other power relations playing themselves out – in rehearsals, performance, within the theaters in which you've worked on these shows?

S.P.: Primarily, that I'm the director and they're the actors. The extent of power rests upon the director – I am a facilitative director – I give the actors a dramaturgical say on what will be in the play. In my case, the variable of my role in the theatre's hierarchy is significant. There is a difference between when I am the head of the theatre or whether I am answerable to a theatre with, for example, an Arab Palestinian board. The ultimate source of authority in the given theatre producing the joint production has a major impact on the power relations.

I learned from *Imagining the Other* and my family background to aspire that the production and the process will create a play that will reflect agendas common to both the Jews and the Arabs involved in the production, and not at the expense of one or the other. I hope I succeeded in most of the cases.

L.P.: But do you think, beyond the dimension of power relations, that these multiple and conflicting narratives from both sides can be contained within artistic processes and productions being created and performed within what is thought to be such a stable, protracted conflict like in Israel-Palestine?

S.P.: While, of course, there are various differences between both situations, the South African Apartheid is rivetingly analogous to our situation. There, only after the dissolution of the Apartheid, did both sides begin to come to grips with the narratives of oppression, on the one hand, and the terror that was employed, on the other. Perhaps, in the current post-"Troubles" situation in Northern Ireland, it is conceivable that open and shared critical re-examination of the conflicting narratives is feasible among Protestant and Catholic theater artists who are working and creating together.

L.P.: What is the broader social and political significance of these joint productions?

S.P.: It depends on context – the element of separation and exclusion between the two peoples seems to consistently be reaching new peaks – alongside the growing respective inner unity of Jews in Israel and the Palestinians – and the asymmetry between the peoples. I live in a country that more and more says "it's either them or us" and there is a growing intentional isolation among Palestinians in Israel, mostly young people; not all, of course. In this context, it's important for me to create these communities – even for appearance's sake, as they are a proof that we can create, work together, argue together, that this existence is possible. In Haifa we live next to each other and there's no place you can go to without hearing Arabic, but that's not the case in the rest of Israel. I want theater to blur these differences – but not to deny the separation. Through working in practical, real ways, I don't separate, I coordinate. This praxis is very efficient – just imagine, you finish the show, *The Peacock of Silwan*, and people gather to talk to the actors and see Jewish and Arab actors talking about the process, their dreams and thoughts. You create an imagined community.

L.P.: What is their personal significance for you?

S.P.: Quantitatively, these shared productions constitute between a quarter to a third of my professional theater work, including at the Kibbutz College of Education. But, in terms of personal significance, they're close to half – like the monologue in *Imagining the Other or Return to Haifa*, which created tremor waves. These were seminal productions in my life, not just 'another production.' They're all part of my desire to create alternative discourses within Israel society. All these "imagined communities," where on stage, each gesture, characterization represents something more than just the concrete – they are proof that this shared existence is possible.

References

Ben Zvi, L. (1996). *Theater in Israel*. University of Michigan Press.

Cameri Theatre. (2008). *Return to Haifa* [Program].

Cohen, C., Varea, R., & Walker, P. (Eds.). (2011). *Acting together on the world stage: Performance and the creative transformation of conflict* (Vol. I). New Village Press.

Eytan, D., Marshood, F., & Strichtman, N. (2019). *Guide for shared society organizations in Israel*. Alliance for Middle East Peace, Shutafut, GLOCAL.

Hai, A. (2014). *Shared society between Jewish and Arab citizens of Israel. Visions, realities and practices*. Inter-Agency Task Force on Israel Arab Issues.

Hartnoll, P., & Found, P. (Eds.). (1996). *The concise Oxford companion to theatre*. Oxford University Press.

Heddon, D., & Milling, J. (2006). *Devising performance: A critical history*. Palgrave MacMillan.

Nasrallah, A., & Perlman, L. (2011). Weaving dialogues and confronting harsh realities: Engendering social change in Israel through performance. In C. Cohen, R. Varea, & P. Walker (Eds.), *Acting together on the world stage: Performance and the creative transformation of conflict* (Vol. I, pp. 122–144). New Village Press.

Oddey, A. (1994). *Devising theatre: A practical and theoretical handbook*. Routledge.

Perlman, L. (2016). בושה *Shame* خجل: *Precarious Palestinian/Jewish collaborative artistic mobilization in Israel* [Presentation]. Troubled contemporary art practices in the Middle East: Post-colonial conflicts, Pedagogies of art history, and precarious artistic mobilization Conference. University of Nicosia/Birkbeck University of London.

Perlman, L. (2017). *"But Abu Ibrahim, We're family!"* The Tami Steinmetz Center for Peace Research, Tel Aviv University.

CHAPTER 20

Arts as a Sphere for the Study of History

Philipp Schmidt-Rhaesa, Jürgen Scheffler and Lilach Naishtat-Bornstein

1   Introduction

This chapter examines how the arts can serve the study of complicated history. The unique case study discussed here is a theatrical project, based on the biography of the Holocaust survivor, Karla Raveh (1927–2017). After 40 years of silence in Israel, Raveh became an admired witness in Lemgo, her pre-war hometown in Germany, and, for 30 years, she spent every summer bearing testimony about her experiences, before thousands of Germans.

The Frenkel-House memorial site, the Karla-Raveh-Gesamtschule (comprehensive school), and the Marianne-Weber-Gymnasium, with the collaboration of Karla Raveh and her family, the Maccabim-Reut High School and the Kibbutzim College of Education joined together for a four-part theatre project. The projects were: *Rück-Sicht* (2010–2011); *Shalom Israel* (2011–2012); *Der Baum im Hof* (2013–2014); and *Shmuel Raveh* (2020–2021) (Karla-Raveh-Gesamtschule & Marianne-Weber-Gymnasium, 2011, 2012, 2014, 2021).

This chapter describes the third part of this project, "The Tree in the Yard: Lemon Tree and Apple Tree" (2013–2014). In this international collaboration, German and Israeli pupils, educators, artists, historians, and scholars combined dance, theatre, music, visual art, video, and archival and academic research. This educational experience is described by a musician-pedagogue, a memorial site director, and a literary scholar, who are part of the production team.

2   Historical Background

Karla (Frenkel) Raveh was born in 1927 to a Jewish family in Lemgo, a small town in the northwest of Germany (Pohlmann, 2016; Raveh, 1987; Raveh & Rosenberg, 1986). Her great-grandparents came to Lemgo in the middle of the nineteenth century and made their home there. In 1933, 67 Jews lived in Lemgo, most of them elderly (Meier, 1981; Pohlmann, 1999, 2011; Scheffler, 1989). By then, Raveh and her three siblings were the only Jewish children in town. The Frenkel family was deported on July 28, 1942, and sent to Theresienstadt. Raveh's parents and siblings were transferred to Auschwitz in October 1944. By the time she arrived there, several days later, they had already been murdered (Bondi, 2009). Raveh was a prisoner in Auschwitz for several months, after which she was sent to Bergen Belsen, and then to Salzwedel in Germany. She was liberated by the American forces on April 14, 1945. From the Frenkel family, only Raveh and her grandmother survived the Holocaust.

Several months after her liberation, Raveh returned to Lemgo, and reclaimed custody of the family house, which had been occupied by local German families. She collected the furniture that had been stored or sold during the war and went back to live there for several months. In Lemgo, she met her future husband, Shmuel Rubin, a survivor from Poland who had been hospitalized in the town. The two married in Lemgo and immigrated to Israel in 1949. In Israel, they built their home in Tivon, a small town near the coastal city of Haifa. The couple had two sons and hebraized their name to "Raveh." Raveh visited Lemgo several times in the 1950s and 1960s; she visited the few remaining friends she had there and took care of the house.

In 1985, after almost 40 years of living a quiet life in Israel, Raveh received a letter from Hanne Pohlmann, a teacher in Lemgo. Pohlmann (1939–2011) had been teaching the history of the Third Reich to a junior high school class in Lemgo, when one of her pupils asked her: "What happened here, in Lemgo, during the Nazi regime?" The question led Pohlmann to realize that this period in the town's history was shrouded in darkness. She decided to research this untold history and wrote to several former Jewish inhabitants of Lemgo. Most of them did not respond and those who did, declared they did not wish to give any details. Raveh was the only one who offered to share her biography with Pohlmann (Kauer et al., 1980; Pohlmann, 1988).

Driven by the letter and her husband's encouragement, Raveh delved into her past and wrote a hundred-page memoir in German, which she promptly sent to Pohlmann. She also sent a journal from her late grandmother, Helene Rosenberg, which she had kept since the two had been reunited in Basel. A local group of intellectual activists, led by Hanne Pohlmann, advocated for the publication of the manuscript. Raveh's memoir was published by the Lemgo Municipality Archive in 1986, under the title, *Survival: The Ordeal of the Jewish Frenkel Family from Lemgo* (Raveh & Rosenberg, 1986).

Raveh's book was an instant best seller in Lemgo. The memoir of the only locally born Auschwitz survivor was distributed in bookstores and museums throughout the town and its surroundings. Within two weeks, the entire edition was sold, a total of 500 copies. As a result, Raveh was invited to the town to meet with her readers in 1986. Her gift as an oral storyteller was evident from the start, when she read from her book at a public event and talked avidly with the audience. Soon afterwards, in 1987, Shmuel Raveh passed away.

In 1988, Raveh's childhood home was bought by the municipal authorities and was converted into a unique memorial site, the Frenkel House (Scheffler, 2017). On the ground floor, a small exhibition shows the history of the Jewish community in the region, while the first floor was turned into a private residence, designed for Raveh's needs. In 1997, a new comprehensive school in Lemgo was called the "Karla-Raveh-Gesamtschule," in recognition of Raveh's work as a contemporary witness.

3   Between Israel and Germany

Over the following 30 years, Raveh spent several months each summer living in the Frenkel House, where she gave testimony to thousands of people in the German language and participated in a myriad of testimonial events. Together with the Frenkel House, the Karla-Raveh-Gesamtschule became a highly visible platform for Raveh's activities and reestablished her persona as an acknowledged storyteller and the solemn carrier of Holocaust memory. In Lemgo, and due to Raveh's testimony, there have been dozens of ceremonies, internet sites, books, recordings, films, exhibitions, academic essays, and school projects. However, in Israel she remained anonymous and kept her distance from the public witnessing sphere. Even her family and close friends in Israel only acknowledged her "other life" in the vaguest of terms, and had deep reservations about her ties with Lemgo.

The story of Raveh was revealed in Israeli sphere following the distribution of Naishtat-Bornstein's film (Naishtat-Bornstein & Lubke, 2012) and publication of her book (Naishtat-Bornstein, 2017). Naishtat-Bornstein's research critically examines the different meanings imposed upon Raveh's testimony and persona by German and Israeli spheres (Naishtat-Bornstein, 2016a, 2016b, 2020; Naishtat-Bornstein & Naveh, 2018). A comparison between the German and the Israeli interpretations of Raveh's persona and testimony reveals the different ways in which societies select and employ Holocaust testimonies in the creation of a unifying historical narrative. Analyzing these disparities allows us to shed light on the distinct incentives of these societies for commemorating the past; the personal needs of witnesses and the mechanisms they employ to deal with trauma; and the multi-layered relationship between bearing witness and cultural reception.

Karla Raveh's testimony gained phenomenal reception in Germany, where it served to purge the local community from blame for its criminal past by emphasizing forgiveness, repentance in universal and personal dimensions. Raveh kept silent in Israel, where her testimony does not fit into the accepted norms that focus on suffering and sustaining the Zionist narrative and where testimonies are exposed to intense scrutiny and criticism.

The film and the book gave Israeli audiences access to Karla's story. Meanwhile, in 2011, a student exchange program, between the Maccabim-Reut Mor High School and the Karla-Raveh-Gesamtschule in Lemgo, began. Raveh was interviewed for various Israeli radio channels and several articles about her were published in newspapers and magazines in Germany, Israel and the United States (for example, The storyteller, 2011; The catharsis of storytelling, 2011; Filmmaker to speak about home, 2011; Between Germany and Israel, 2013; Garaev, 2017; Gon-Gross, 2017; Jeffay, 2017). Raveh went on to present her testimony at a number of academic conferences and public occasions. The highlight of these was a public event in Tivon. In April 2017, during the annual Holocaust Memorial Day, Raveh laid bare her story and her connections with the German community before an audience of hundreds of acquaintances and neighbors at Tivon's Commemorative Center. On May 27, 2017, a few days after a grand ceremony for her ninetieth birthday in Lemgo, Karla Raveh passed away.

4 The Tree in the Yard

"The Tree in the Yard: Lemon Tree and Apple tree" is an educational theatre project, which deals with the complex meaning found in the biography of Raveh. Its title expresses the differences between the two worlds, in which Karla Raveh lived, as well as what connects them: the lemon tree in the courtyard of Raveh's home in Tivon, and the apple tree in the courtyard of her home in Lemgo – the Frenkel House.

The concept of "home," in its multiple dimensions, crosses between a longing for the absent family and an engagement with the present for Holocaust survivors' consciousness and practice (DeKoven Ezrahi, 2000, p. 17); home as family, community and regional identities (Bourdieu, 1996); and in the "sense of dwelling" (Heidegger, 1971), as in the German word, "Heimat" (Blickle, 2002, pp. 2–5). The impossibility of returning home becomes concrete through different kinds of replacements, substitutes and memorials: "A home is something you lose" (Langer, 1995, p. 21).

In Raveh's case, "home" combines sweet childhood memoirs, destruction and loss. Observations at both her homes, the Israeli and the German homes, provides an opportunity to reveal stories, people, meanings, changes, surroundings and neighborhoods; the relation between the homes, communities and nations; and the role of the museum and its visitors in shaping these stories. How is home possible, after the Holocaust? How does Raveh manage to live in two homes? The project aimed to address these, and other questions, with artistic means. The backyard of the Frenkel House was chosen as a focal point of this project.

The Frenkel House in Lemgo is a small memorial site. What distinguishes it from other memorials relating to the Nazi period is that it is a "home museum" (Dekel & Vinitzky-Seroussi, 2017; Vinitzky-Seroussi & Dekel, 2019). In 1988, the Frenkel House was established. Due to renovations, traces of the time when the Frenkel family owned the house were not preserved. However, through the memories of Karla Raveh, the Frenkel House became the Holocaust memorial of the city of Lemgo.

Like many buildings in Lemgo, the house is a complex: there is the front building on the main street, the rear building, which was built on the site of an earlier barn, after the renovations, and the inner courtyard, which connects the front and rear buildings (see Figure 20.1).

Karla Raveh testified that the rear building, originally a barn, served as a warehouse for her father's small business for old and waste products. It was also used by the Frenkel family as a space for celebrations. According to Raveh, there was a small annex, where her father had set up his office. The truck that her father owned was parked in the passage. These trips were a sign of the close friendship that existed before 1933 between her parents and most of the neighbors, a close friendship that continued with some neighbors during the Nazi years (Scheffler & Wurm, 2012).

When the Frenkel House memorial was built in 1988, the rear building was converted into a studio. This served as an artists' residence, funded by the Young Art Scholarship ("Stipendium Junge Kunst").

A large wooden gate in the front building leads through a passage to the courtyard, which connects the two houses. In the middle of the courtyard

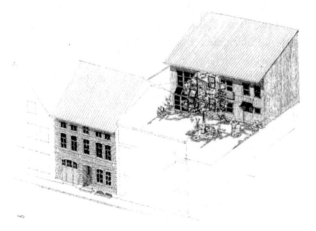

FIGURE 20.1
The Frenkel House memorial

stands an apple tree that was planted in 1988. The passage and the inner courtyard served primarily as a multifunctional area. Bicycles are parked in the passage and the garbage cans stand behind a small wooden wall. The residents hang up their laundry to dry there, and the area serves as a parking lot. From time to time, the resident artists invite an audience to the open studio, and the courtyard is a place for encounters and discussions. In the summer months, groups meet there to discuss the exhibition, before or after visiting the memorial. Regular use has developed over the years as part of the November 9 Holocaust Memorial event. The audience gathers in the yard for a ceremony, and they walk through the city center to the local synagogue memorial.

In 2012, the exhibition in the Frenkel House was fundamentally redesigned. The exhibition not only presents Raveh's biography, but also focuses on telling stories about one's autobiography. The changes in biographical narration can be explored, based on texts and film sequences from over 25 years. Working with the texts, photos and media from the exhibition in autumn 2013, created the concept for the scenes in the project.

The exhibition stimulated the pupils for their work on the play. The visits in the museum were a platform for development of scenes, choreographies, and music that deal with home, separation, displacement, reconciliation, and return. Using a concrete biographical example, a topic is dealt with that plays a major role in the lives of refugees and survivors.

The work on the first part of the project ("Shalom Israel") began in autumn 2013. Rehearsals took place in winter-spring 2013/2014. The performance in the courtyard of the Frenkel House took place in June 2014. The development and the performances were documented by video (Karla-Raveh-Gesamtschule & Marianne-Weber-Gymnasium, 2014). This film, shown in the memorial site, formed a basis for joint work between German and Israeli students from the Karla-Raveh-Gesamtschule, the Grabbe Gymnasium Detmold, and the Maccabim-Reut High School. In autumn 2014, Israeli students came to Lemgo, as part of the school exchange. The Israeli and German students had the opportunity to study the results of the dance, theatre, and museum projects documented by video and combine this with a visit to the Frenkel House. The participants from both schools had the opportunity to obtain certification of competence in culture.[1]

The idea of performing the play, "The Tree in the Back Yard," in the courtyard of the Frenkel House, was a continuation of the 2012 project. However, the museum team faced numerous challenges with this decision. The inner courtyard had to be transformed into a location for the performances. The electronical equipment and the catering were placed in the passage. The tiny room served as a restroom and storage room, and did not have space for the equipment. The artists' studio accommodated the equipment for the performances, the stage elements, the chairs for the audience, the lighting and the audio equipment. Two stages were created in the inner courtyard: one for the actors, and one for the musicians. Forty stools were borrowed for the interior space, where the audience sat. The audience could turn around in all directions and watch what was going on in the courtyard. There was no roof. When it rained during one of the four evenings, the performance had to be stopped early. However, outdoor performances were possible on three evenings.

The play was performed in the inner courtyard. We had an intense discussion about what the term "authentic place" could mean: the home of the Jewish family, from which they were deported; the home to which Karla Raveh returned for a short time after her liberation; her second home, since 1988; and the place, which served as a starting point for her witnessing work. Months of preparations came to its peak in four nights of performance. During this time, the courtyard was filled with new images, impressions and feelings, of the artistic and technological staff, the museum team, the teachers, the pupils and audience.

5 The Process of Creating the Production

Drama and dance are sometimes combined in Holocaust memorial ceremonies in German schools. Schoolteachers and theatre pedagogues take great responsibility upon themselves, when they look for an alternative way to represent torn biographies, suffering, deprivation and genocide, on stage. An enormous part of the process are the discussions held among staff and pupils about how to represent dark chapters in history.

Doris Eulenstein is a drama teacher at the Karla-Raveh-Gesamtschule, who initiated this dramatic project. Schmidt-Rhaesa is a teacher at the Marianne-Weber-Gymnasium. Together, in 2013, the teachers planned the third part of the project. The school administration was instantly interested, and five pupils from the Marianne-Weber-Gymnasium became part of the project. The production team included Eulenstein, as the school's project manager. She offered the students a chance to obtain a certificate for their cultural competence acquired in the project. Jürgen Scheffler (one of the authors) was also part of the project. He was the head of the local museum and memorial, who had previously designed the new exhibition about the Jewish families in Lemgo in the Frenkel House. It was his idea to perform the third play in its courtyard. Karin Wedeking was the director, Patricia Struffolino was the choreographer, Anna-Maria Schneider was the media producer, and Lilach Naishtat-Bornstein was the project's academic advisor. Her joint documentary with Lubke (Naishtat-Bornstein & Lubke, 2012) inspired the project. Through this documentary, the participants learned about Raveh's feelings of being torn between her present home in Israel and her former home in Lemgo.

The title, "The Tree in the Courtyard: Lemon Tree and Apple Tree," represents Raveh's commute between her home and homeland. The apple tree in the courtyard in Lemgo was planted in 1988, when the memorial site was established. The production team felt a special "genius loci," which provided a strong feeling of care. There was little space on stage and the actors surrounded the audience. The film and text sequences were projected onto the walls of the surrounding houses. The space shaped the play (see Figure 20.2).

We worked in divided groups at first, coming together approximately once a month. Wedeking and Eulenstein collected students' memories, poems, journal entries and dramatic improvisations. Struffolino collected visual images from Raveh's archive. She encouraged the students to talk with their bodies and express their feelings and thoughts. The group created intense images. For example, Raveh's recollections from deportation were shown in a very slow dance of all the actors on a single spot, holding each other and grabbing one another (see Figure 20.3). Two girls embracing one another, in order to play together on a single violin, reflected Karla's sole and unique situation after her liberation and immigration to Israel (see Figure 20.4).

Schmidt-Rhaesa directed/conducted the music of the play. Together with the pupils, he combined recorded music with live performance, improvisation, and music that had been specially composed for the production. For example, Raveh's life in Lemgo was represented by a small hand-cranked music box that

FIGURE 20.2   "The Tree in the Back Yard" 1 (photo by Anna Maria Schneider during the first rehearsal in the courtyard in September 2013, and during the performance in May 2014)

FIGURE 20.3   "The Tree in the Back Yard" 2 (photo by Anna Maria Schneider during the first rehearsal in the courtyard in September 2013, and during the performance in May 2014)

FIGURE 20.4   "The Tree in the Back Yard" 3 (photo by Anna Maria Schneider during the first rehearsal in the courtyard in September 2013, and during the performance in May 2014)

was put into a green suitcase. The melody evoked memories of childhood and dream, and had an almost hypnotic effect. In other parts of the play, the music was improvised to the dance, by using sharp and spherical sounds of metal percussion instruments. Following the performance, Schneider created a documentary about the process (see Figure 20.5).

The walls of the neighboring houses were used as projection surfaces for texts and photos. A small ladder, standing in front of the apple tree, was used as an elevated seat for Svea, a 17-year-old pupil. She recited impressions from her diary of the joint visit of the German and Israeli pupils from Maccabim-Reut school to the Wannsee Conference memorial in Berlin.

ARTS AS A SPHERE FOR THE STUDY OF HISTORY

FIGURE 20.5   "The Tree in the Back Yard" 4 (photo by Anna Maria Schneider during the first rehearsal in the courtyard in September 2013, and during the performance in May 2014)

Villa Wannsee, Berlin […] Again and again we had been confronted with the indigestible truth, didn't talk, avoided glances. […] In silence we sat in the room of the conference […]. You are my friends, I love to laugh with you. You are like us. But suddenly in this room our history is separating us. We talk about this experience. The Israeli are so interested in our opinion and suddenly, they start singing again […]. We want to sit together and do what we, as a generation of friends, can do best: laughing together.

6   Aftermath

In December 2018, the production team and the pupils met to talk about the project's long-term effects. All of them reported that the production left a great personal impact on them. Some said the project was "the best thing in their whole school time." Others reported a deep change in their conception of history, racism and solidarity. Some of them aimed for a career in the arts; others changed their career aspirations to pedagogical professions. The meaningful experience and the warm feedback encouraged the team to continue with the project.

The production team insights were divided into eight main aspects:

a. *Working with a multi-professional, multi-artistic and international team.* Teachers often feel lonely and isolated in their work. Frequent communication with other colleagues helps to sort out difficult questions. The collaboration between artists, pedagogues, museum staff and scholars enabled a fruitful process and made it possible for individual points of view of the group members to be pursued in depth. The integrated connection between Germans and Israelis, and with Karla Raveh and her family, charged the project with extra value and contributed unique novelty experiences to the daily routine.

b. *Cooperation between institutions.* Collaboration between schools, institutions of higher learning, museums, memorials and archives creates new forms of knowledge. When teachers and pupils gain access to historical materials and theoretical issues, this is a precious contribution. Collaboration between different specialists and professionals is profitable for all the partners.

c. *Public funding.* Schools cannot work with professional artists and scholars without paying them properly. There are many ways to receive public funding in Germany. We took part in the federal state program, "Culture and School," that makes it possible to hire artists for an entire year for school projects. In addition, we received resources from different ministries, institutions and memorials. The "Frenkel House" provided a great amount of the funding.

d. *Time.* Our projects run for an entire school year, usually from August to June. This gives enough room and time for a meaningful process.

e. *Structure.* We chose not to follow the story in chronological line, but to compose a collage from the ideas of the different participants. This decision led to a continuously developing dramaturgy and provided space for different views and individual positions. The experiences of the participants can easily be mixed with the tales of eyewitnesses, personal reflections of the pupils, poems, songs and visual material.

f. *Art as a language for the unspeakable.* The pupils' artistic tendencies were suited to express complicated issues. Working with video, music and a dance pedagogue enhances the repertoire of expressions, especially when dealing with appalling and tragic contents.

g. *Genius loci.* The location of the project in a historical site – the courtyard of the Frenkel House – was of crucial importance. The original location designed the whole play. In the 2020–2021 project, the local museum was scheduled to host the performance and create a special exhibition on the subject of the play. The audience would be able to enter into the "field of tension," between the artistic and the scientific perspective.

h. *Not being stuck in melancholy.* A crucial point in our work on the project was Naishtat-Bornstein's visit in Lemgo. In November 2013, she was invited to the workshop "Karla Raveh –Biography of a Holocaust Survivor in Germany and Israel," to give a lecture. She talked with the pupils about productive ways to deal with their sadness concerning Karla's experiences on stage. Naishtat-Bornstein suggested not to be sad all the time and not to try to tell everything about the Holocaust. She asked the students to talk about what it has to do with their own lives today. One student summarized what Naishtat-Bornstein said: "First, there may be sadness, but then there is more."

Only a very few Holocaust survivors are still alive. They will be replaced by their descendants, educators, historians, scholars and artists, to keep the memories alive. Karla Raveh's son, Michael, edited parts of her legacy, in order to share the biography of his father, Shmuel Raveh. Michael Raveh's book was released in summer 2020 (Raveh, 2020). A fourth theatre project began at the Karla-Raveh-Gesamtschule with the original production team that began in 2010. We hope that other educators, historians, artists, and scholars will follow this concept.

Note

1 A "Certificate of Cultural Competence" ("Kompetenznachweis Kultur") is an educational certificate given to young people who actively participate in artistic, cultural, or educational projects. The pupils reflect upon their work process, with a trained teacher as their partner. Cultural and educational institutions in Germany honor this certificate when the pupils apply for studies or jobs.

References

Between Germany and Israel. (2013, April 5). *Kol Herzliya*. [in Hebrew]
Blickle, P. (2002). *Heimat: A critical theory of the German idea of homeland*. Camden House.
Bondi, R. (2009). Therezin. In G. Miron & S. Shulhani (Eds.), *The Yad Vashem encyclopedia of the ghettos during the Holocaust*. Yad Vashem. [in Hebrew]
https://www.yadvashem.org/yv/he/research/ghettos_encyclopedia/ghetto_details.asp?cid=452

Bourdieu, P. (1996). On the family as a realized category. *Theory, Culture & Society, 13*(3), 19–26.

Dekel, I., & Vinitzky-Seroussi, V. (2017). A living place: On the sociology of atmosphere in home museums. *European Journal of Cultural and Political Sociology, 4*(3), 336–362.

Dekoven-Ezrahi, S. (2000). *Booking passage: On exile and homecoming in the modern Jewish imagination*. University of California Press.

Filmmaker to speak about home, identity, and conflict. (2011, February 14). *Republican*. https://www.masslive.com/living/2011/02/home_identity_and_conflict_subject_of_talk.html

Garaev, P. (2017, May 17). Holocaust survivor returns to German hometown to mark 90th birthday. *I24news*. https://www.i24news.tv/en/news/international/145450-170517-holocaust-survivor-returns-to-german-hometown-to-mark-90th-birthday

Gon-Gross, Z. (2017, January 27). *Radio interview on International Holocaust Memorial Day*. Galei Zahal. [in Hebrew] https://glz.co.il/NewsArticle.aspx?newsid=33282

Heidegger, M. (1971). *Building, dwelling, thinking poetry, language, thought* (A. Hofstadter, Trans.). Harper Colophon Books.

Jeffay, N. (2017, April 1). Survivor who returns each year to the city that sent her to Hell. *Jewish Chronicle*. https://www.thejc.com/news/world/survivor-who-returns-each-year-to-the-city-that-sent-her-to-hell-1.435433

Karla-Raveh-Gesamtschule, & Marianne-Weber-Gymnasium (Producers). (2012). *Rück-Sicht* [Performance & video]. [in Hebrew]

Karla-Raveh-Gesamtschule, & Marianne-Weber-Gymnasium (Producers). (2014). *Shalom Israel* [Performance & video].

Karla-Raveh-Gesamtschule, & Marianne-Weber-Gymnasium (Producers). (2016). *Der Baum im Hof* [Performance & video]. [in German]

Karla-Raveh-Gesamtschule, & Marianne-Weber-Gymnasium (Producers). (2021). *Shmuel Raveh* [Performance & video].

Kauer, M., Kopsieker, K., Luchterhandt, M., Pohlmann, H., Remmert, C., & Riewe, B. (1980). *Von der Weimarer Republik in das Dritte Reich. Lemgo 1930–1933*. VHS Lemgo.

Langer, L. (1995). *Admitting the Holocaust: Collected essays*. Oxford University Press.

Levi, D. (2017, January 9). The rejected child from World War II became the Germans darling. *La-Ishah Magazine*. [in Hebrew] https://www.thejc.com/news/world/survivor-who-returns-each-year-to-the-city-that-sent-her-to-hell-1.435433

Meier, K. (1981). *Geschichte der Stadt Lemgo*. FL Wagener.

Naishtat-Bornstein, L. (2016a). *Their Jew: Right and wrong in Holocaust testimonies*. Hebrew University and MOFET Institute. [in Hebrew]

Naishtat-Bornstein, L. (2016b). "The listener I chose to be, shed new light on the testimony": Questioning the memory of the Holocaust through autoethnographic methodology. *Gilui Daat, 9*, 15–44. [in Hebrew]

Naishtat-Bornstein, L. (2020). "I am their Jew": Karla Raveh's testimony in Germany and in Israel. *History and Memory, 32*(2), 110–145.

Naishtat-Bornstein, L., & Lubke, H. P. (Directors & Producers). (2012). *Between home and homeland: The story of Karla Raveh* [Video]. Lupro Films and Your Story Group.

Naishtat-Bornstein, L., & Naveh, E. (2018). From empathy to critical reflection: The use of testimonies in the training of Holocaust educators. *Journal of International Social Studies, 8*(1), 4–36.

Pohlmann, H. (1988). Echternstraße 70: Vom Wohn- und Geschäftshaus der Familie Frenkel zum Judenhaus. In J. Scheffler & H. Stöwer (Eds.), *Juden in Lemgo und Lippe. Kleinstadtleben zwischen Emanzipation und Deportation* (pp. 259–270). Verlag für Regionalgeschichte.

Pohlmann, K. (1999). *Juden in Lippe in Mittelalter und früher Neuzeit: Zwischen Pogrom und Vertreibung, 1350–1614*. Gesellschaft für Christlich-Jüdische Zusammenarbeit in Lippe. (in German)

Pohlmann, H. (2011). *Judenverfolgung und NS-Alltag in Lemgo: Fallstudien zur Stadtgeschichte*. Verlag für Regionalgeschichte. [in German]

Pohlmann, K. (2016). Das städtische Zunfthandwerk und die Juden. Der Konflikt um die Zuwanderung und Niederlassung der Familie Frenkel in Lemgo und die historischen Hintergründe. In J. Scheffler (Ed.), *Das Frenkel-Haus Lemgo: Wohnhaus, Erinnerungsort, Gedenkstätte* (pp. 49–109). Verlag für Regionalgeschichte. [in German]

Raveh, K. (1988). Jüdisches Kleinstadtleben in Deutschland und Polen: Ein Erinnerungsbericht über Lemgo und Demblin. In J. Scheffler & H. Stöwer (Eds.), *Juden in Lemgo und Lippe: Kleinstadtleben zwischen Emanzipation und Deportation* (pp. 154–158). Verlag für Regionalgeschichte. [in German]

Raveh, K., & Rosenberg, H. (1986). *Überleben: Der Leidensweg der jüdischen Familie Frenkel aus Lemgo*. Stadt Lemgo. [in German]

Raveh, M. (2020). *Shmuel Raveh (1925–1986): Die Geschichte meines Vaters*. Verlag für Regionalgeschichte.

Scheffler, J. (1989). Frenkel-Haus Museum: Dokumentations- und Begegnungsstätte in Lemgo. *Aus westfälischen Museen, 5*(1), 16–20. [in German]

Scheffler, J. (Ed.). (2016). *Das Frenkel-Haus Lemgo: Wohnhaus, Erinnerungsort, Gedenkstätte*. Verlag für Regionalgeschichte. [in German]

Scheffler, J., & Veith, U. (Directors & Producers). (1986). *Karla Raveh: Lebensstationen einer Lemgoer Jüdin* [Video]. [in German]

Scheffler, J., & Wurm, H. (2012). *Interview with Karla Raveh*. Museen der Stadt Lemgo, Frenkel Haus Audio files.

The catharsis of storytelling: Home and identity in a Holocaust survivor's reality. (2011, February 24). *Mount Holyoke News*. http://themhnews.org/2011/02/features/the-catharsis-of-storytelling-home-and-identity-in-a-holocaust-survivor%E2%80%99s-reality

The storyteller: Filmvorführung mit Lilach Naishtat-Bornstein. (2011, September 7). *Salzekurier*. [in German]

Vinitzky-Seroussi, V., & Dekel, I. (2019). Moving gender: Home museums and the construction of their inhabitants. *European Journal of Women's Studies, 26*(3), 274–292.

Concluding Notes: Towards an Activist Pedagogy

Tony Gallagher, Nimrod Aloni, Dafna Yitzhaki and Zehavit Gross

We would like to open these concluding notes with a look at the larger context in which we are working and within which this book was written. From our vantage point, activist pedagogy and shared education in divided societies is a topic that cannot stand meaningfully alone outside a concrete social context and historical moment. Any serious discussion let alone program suggested in this sphere of discourse must be attentive to what John Dewey wrote in *Democracy and Education*: "thinking what the known demands of us" (1966, p. 326). In our case, engaged with the predicaments and challenges of humanity in the third decade of the 21st century, it means addressing the larger cultural context. It must attend to cultural trends that are inextricably bound together, including the risks to the young embedded in the destruction of the natural environment, the growing populism in our political democracies and the colonization of the mind by digital technology and the new media.

For we have seen the escalation of significant global risks and countervailing actions which have underscored prevailing systems of power. The 2008 financial crash was a crisis of neoliberalism and in its wake has been the growing dehumanizing phenomena of homelessness, poverty, ignorance, and marginalization. Neoliberalism is based on the notion that competition between autonomous individuals will work to the benefit of all, whereas by commodifying relationships and value, it exacerbates inequalities. These processes are toxic in any society, but can become even more so in contexts where community divisions are manifest. The response of populist politicians is to seek, through essentialist appeals to communitarian interests, to shift responsibilities onto the 'other,' particularly minorities, whether defined in numerical or power terms. An activist pedagogy then has to focus on different layers of affect, by promoting a sense of agency among students, legitimizing community identities while promoting intercultural engagement, and doing so within a framework based on justice, equality and human rights.

The crash in fact accelerated the rise of populist politics and produced a period of unusual political instability. The 'headline' imagery of ultra-right-wing parties, often employed little more than thuggery as their core strategy, may have helped disguise the consolidation of power by extreme right-wing parties in some countries. That they achieved this through democratic processes which they then tried to subvert only served to underline their lack of commitment to democratic norms. Their dehumanizing discourses have also sparked a blizzard of attacks on refugees, asylum-seekers, and migrants. That the refugee crisis is itself a consequence of proxy and internationalized wars simply adds to the bitter taste engendered. The rise of populism almost achieved a shocking apogee with the attack on the US Capitol by members of the 'white supremacy,' but perhaps still will as we witness the barely believable sight of elected politicians denying the fact of an insurgency to which many of them were direct witnesses.

On top of this is the climate crisis and the already-present threat to the natural environment. As Greta Thunberg claimed in her speech at the Glasgow climate convention (November 5, 2021), we cannot and should not think of the climate crisis as a separate evil (or hardship, crisis, or predicament) but rather as a continuation of a manifold thoughtless and immoral forms of:

> exploitation of people and nature and destruction of present and future living. ... The climate and ecological crisis doesn't exist in a vacuum, it is directly tied to other crises and injustices that date back to colonialism and beyond. Crises based on the idea that some people are worth more than others and therefor have the right to steal others, to exploit others... and it is very naïve of us to think that we could solve this crisis without addressing the root cause of it.

Within education we can see the effects of this worldview through a narrowing of purpose towards a largely economic agenda and the neglect of the cultivation of cognitive and affective competencies required for repairing the world and peaceful shared life such as critical thinking, autonomous deliberation, empathetic imagination, and democratic sensibilities. As with the wider context, an activist pedagogy committed to bridging between alienated and hostile communities, often involved in violent conflicts, does not exist in a vacuum. It involves, as John Dewey (1966) defined it, the "fundamental dispositions intellectual and emotional, towards nature and fellow men" (p. 328). It calls not for scientific, economic or technical solutions but mainly for an ethical shift from an egotistic, competitive, and self-serving mentality to a thoughtful, empathetic, communal, and responsible outlook; from continuously struggling with others towards victory and domination, to the pursuit of peaceful, caring, and just living with others.

It is on that basis that we have explored a two-track strategy of activist pedagogy for shared education in divided societies in this volume. The first of these is the pedagogical-institutional track of humanizing education in schools and other education settings that empowers human agency and the ethical dispositions required for peaceful, just and shared living in diverse societies, based on the principles of reconciliation, intercultural dialogue and democratic culture. The second involves the social-political that consists in transforming the lived reality and the social-political settings so they would be instrumental in enhancing shared life by providing contexts for intercultural dialogue and engagement.

Finally, we can also address the two general issues raised in the Introduction on the role of the international perspective, and the question of what counts as success. We had considered the three comparative contexts identified by Salomon (2002) set alongside the specificities of national or regional contexts, but in retrospect perhaps it was Dewey's notion of 'breaking walls,' highlighted by Aloni in our opening chapter, which best captures the role of the international perspective. Dewey talked about breaking the walls between the child and the curriculum, school and society, democracy and education to produce new conceptualisations, knowledge and practice. Perhaps this is the key to the international perspective in that it allows us to break down the walls of parochialism and taken-for-granted assumptions, and challenges us to think anew. This sense of challenge and renewal may also be key to our understanding of success.

Throughout the examples we have considered in this volume there are examples of progressive change, but many more examples of constraints. This is hardly surprising – the hegemonic crises of the 21st century have underpinned the role of self-serving elites globally and served to reinforce ideologies of acquisition. If anything the coronavirus global pandemic has reinforced inequality and an ethic of self-interest, but as our chapters have emphasized and re-emphasized, the need for an alternative ethic based on humanistic values and democratic principles has never been more important, and the examples of progressive change show that a better alternative is possible and achievable, but it can only be attained through conscious effort and will or, as Gramsci so memorably put it, "pessimism of the intellect, optimism of the will."

References

Dewey, J. (1966). *Democracy and education*. Macmillan Co.
Salomon, G. (2002). The nature of peace education: Not all programs are created equal. In G. Salomon & B. Nevo (Eds.), *Peace education: The concept, principles, and practices around the world* (pp. 2–14). Lawrence Erlbaum Associates.